D1518230

European Manuscript Sources of
the American Revolution

European Manuscript Sources of the American Revolution

W.J. KOENIG
&
S.L. MAYER

BOWKER
LONDON & NEW YORK

CD
1002
K63

CONTENTS

vi CONTENTS

NORTHERN IRELAND

REPUBLIC OF IRELAND

PART II
THE NETHERLANDS, FRANCE, SPAIN

THE NETHERLANDS

FRANCE

PART III
AUSTRIA, GERMANY, ITALY
RUSSIA, SWEDEN

AUSTRIA

SWEDEN

GENERAL INTRODUCTION

It has long been accepted that the American Revolution could not have been brought to a successful military conclusion by the armies commanded by George Washington without substantial aid from abroad. This aid took various forms: supply of arms and munitions, military advisers, diplomatic support, naval support for American military operations, diversionary naval operations outside British North America, partial blockades, and an 'Armed Neutrality'. What began as a rebellion of colony against metropolis became a revolution which called into question the whole principle of mercantilism and the viability of a colonial empire in the long term. There was also the threat that the ideas for which many Americans were fighting might spread to the British Isles and encourage the forces behind liberal electoral, economic and social reform. The American Revolution cannot therefore be studied within a strictly American context but must be viewed more broadly as a problem involving the whole of the British Empire as well as the home islands themselves. Originally a local event, the American Revolution came to shake the European capitals so that, toward the end of the war, Britain was involved in no less than a world-wide conflict fought in Africa and Asia as well as Europe and the West Indies, with most of the powers of Europe either overtly or covertly hostile. The Treaty of Paris of 1783 was not only a concession of political independence to the United States but an international territorial settlement which altered the formerly pre-eminent position held by Britain in the colonial world.

Historians of the American Revolution have thus been obliged to examine European as well as American documentary material on any number of questions. Indispensable to this examination has been the series of guides to material in Europe covering American history, published by the Carnegie Institution of Washington earlier in this century, most of which have now been reprinted. More recently, scholars have had the benefit of B. R. Crick and M. Alman, *A Guide to Manuscripts Relating to America in Great Britain and Ireland*, and the Deutsche Gesellschaft für Amerikastudien's *Americana in Deutschen Sammlungen*, published in 1961 and 1967 respectively. The available guides vary in both treatment and age and tend to be weak on aspects other than the diplomatic and military history of the Revolution. There has also been no general guide to European documentary sources specifically for the American Revolution. Hence we thought it would be useful to students to prepare the present volume. It is not our intention to provide a comprehensive guide to the documentary material in Europe, but rather to offer the scholar, particularly the graduate student, an introduction to the source material in Europe so that research can be more effectively planned. This volume is really a *point d'appui* and time saver, a tool which the scholar can use to identify repositories, with summaries of their contents and notices of relevant bibliography.

The approach has generally been to draw on the existing guides to material relating to America and to update and expand these by drawing on archival guides, inventories, reports and other printed works. Throughout we have cited our printed sources so that the reader can refer to these as he needs. The entries given are usually summaries based on more extensive descriptions in a catalogue, inventory or other compilation. The main topics of a document, volume/bundle or series are usually listed, but if a given subject is not mentioned the reader should not necessarily assume that it is absent from the material. It is also the case that sometimes catalogue entries are uninformative or highly selective concerning the nature of the material. Thus the relevance of some material may not be apparent without an examination of the documents themselves.

The exceptions to this approach are the British Museum and the Netherlands. Many volumes of manuscripts were examined in the British Museum to expand and update the earlier surveys by Andrews and Davenport and by Crick and Alman. A listing was also made of the contents of the Burney Newspaper Collection for which no printed catalogue exists. In the case of the Netherlands, there was no previous guide to Dutch material for American history. Nevertheless, the States-General was one of the belligerents in the War of American Independence, while Dutch bankers played an important role in financing the United States during the war. A special survey of Dutch material was thus undertaken in the hope of bringing these rich and voluminous sources to the attention of scholars so that they may be explored more extensively than heretofore.

The British sources for the American Revolution are by far the most extensive and most important so these have been presented first. The material involves not only Britain's foreign relations and military responses but also the political upheavals going on in Britain which were in some measure precipitated by the American Revolution. France, Spain and the Netherlands follow, as these powers were the other belligerents and allies of the United States. Material of a diplomatic, military, naval and economic nature has been included, since the war against Britain was fought on all these levels. Material in Germany, Sweden, the USSR, Austria and Italy has been included for the broader diplomatic background and the 'Armed Neutrality'. The amount and detail of coverage of the various countries has been dictated primarily by their importance for the study of the Revolution and secondarily by the availability of reference material. Spain, for example, deserves more coverage than it has received, but the catalogues and guides available did not permit it. Similarly, we did not feel equipped to deal adequately with Poland

and Portugal and we thought it best to omit these countries.

We wish to acknowledge the advice and courtesies of Professor J.W. Schulte-Nordholt of the Historisch Instituut in Leiden during the work in the Netherlands. Mr Denis Mahaffey in Paris supplied answers to our questions about French libraries and archives together with much helpful information. The staffs of the Western Manuscripts and General Reading Rooms of the British Museum and of the Institute of Historical Research in London were also helpful with our requests and questions.

It is our hope that this volume will be a useful introduction for students preparing for research in Europe concerning the American Revolution and that it will perhaps encourage more students to take advantage of the riches available here.

London   W.J. KOENIG
15 November 1973   S.L. MAYER

PART I
THE BRITISH ISLES

THE BRITISH ISLES

INTRODUCTION

The Treaty of Paris of 1763 which ended the Seven Years War left Britain in control of the seas and the colonial world. France and Spain, whose territories in North America had once seemed to be overwhelming, had been eclipsed by British sea and land power. Although France still maintained the most powerful army in Europe, there was no question about who was the stronger in the world outside Europe. The monopoly which Britain now enjoyed east of the Mississippi encouraged George III and his ministers to tighten the loose framework of the Navigation Acts and enforce regulations which for a century had largely been winked at. In addition, Britain hoped to confine their English-speaking colonials to the territories east of the Appalachians, despite the fact that westward expansion was considered, by many townsmen and frontiersmen alike, to be the new Americans' inherent right. Indeed, many frontiersmen had already crossed that barrier into Kentucky and Ohio during the years of the French and Indian War, as the Seven Years War was called in North America. Therefore, in the years after 1763 problems of territorial expansion, economic rivalry between the American colonies and Britain as well as Britain's restrictions on the Americans' freedom of trade (or freedom to smuggle) accentuated and deepened. As the divergence of interests widened, Britain was drifting towards what could be described as a civil war in her colonies which was going to have serious repercussions within Britain's domestic political milieu.

The Anglo-American conflict came to affect almost all aspects of British society. Apart from its military manifestation, the conflict had its economic consequences which became translated into opposition to government policy on the home front. It became the focus of parliamentary politics and brought to an end the attempt of George III at none too benevolent despotism. Above the level of pragmatic politics, issues were raised which many Britons saw as having profound implications for their status as British subjects, so that a large and articulate opposition formed as early as the mid-1760s to oppose government policy on legal and ideological grounds. The American Revolution was an early manifestation of issues in British society which were later expressed in the Reform Bill of 1832. The conflict had its international repercussions as well, providing Britain's enemies with the opportunity to gain temporarily the upper hand by making common cause with the rebels. What began as a tedious provincial rebellion in 1775 metamorphosed into a worldwide maritime war and ended with Britain facing the combined forces of

France, Spain, Holland and the United States.

Since the American Revolution did touch so many aspects of British society, it is difficult to draw a line between what is and is not relevant. The inclination has been to be inclusive rather than be exclusive, since the Revolution was an internal conflict of the British body politic. The range of material reported on has therefore tended to be broad, especially in the cases of trade and the internal British politics of the period. The following survey covers a wide spectrum of official records and personal papers, the bulk of which are in the Public Record Office and the British Museum in London. A significant portion also lies outside London and an attempt has been made to cover this as well as possible under the circumstances.

Part I has relied heavily on the labours of several earlier compilers of Americana in Britain. The pioneering effort of Charles M. Andrews and Frances G. Davenport, *Guide to Manuscript Materials for the History of the United States to 1783, in the British Museum, in Minor London Archives, and in the Libraries of Oxford and Cambridge* (Washington, DC., Carnegie Institution, 1908), has been searched for relevant material, corrected in places and updated, especially for the British Museum entry. B. R. Crick and M. Alman, *A Guide to Manuscripts Relating to America in Great Britain and Ireland* (London, Oxford University Press, 1961), is the standard and indispensable reference supplementing and expanding the work of Andrews and Davenport for London and surveying for the first time material in the remainder of Great Britain and Ireland. The coverage of Crick and Alman is continued in B. R. Crick, 'First List of Addenda to A Guide to Manuscripts Relating to America in Great Britain and Ireland', *Bulletin of the British Association for American Studies*, New Series, 5 (December 1962), and two further lists of addenda in the same publication, New Series, 7 (December 1963) and New Series, 12/13 (1966), cited as 'Addenda 1962, 1963, 1966', respectively. David M. Matteson, *List of Manuscripts concerning American History preserved in European Libraries and noted in their Published Catalogues and similar Printed Lists* (Washington, D.C., Carnegie Institution, 1925), surveys the catalogues of a number of British libraries and contains an occasional item not found in other compilations. Charles O. Paullin and Frederic L. Paxson, *Guide to the Materials in London Archives for the History of the United States since 1783* (Washington, D.C., Carnegie Institution, 1914), occasionally supplements or corrects Andrews and Davenport. Although the present survey covers the American colonies for much of the same period more comprehensively, the student may still find it useful to consult Lawrence H. Gipson, *A Guide to Manuscripts Relating to the History of the British Empire 1748–1776* (New York, Alfred Knopf, 1970), for its wider scope. Other bibliography pertaining to specific archives and collections is given where appropriate in the text.

More than 200 reports on manuscript collections in Britain have been published since 1869 by the Historical Manuscripts Commission, Quality

House, Quality Court, Chancery Lane, London WC2. These reports are here cited as 'HMC'. See also *Reports of the Royal Commission on Historical Manuscripts, Revised to 31 August 1956* (London, HMSO, 1956).

Founded in 1945 as a branch of the Historical Manuscripts Commission, the National Register of Archives (at the same address) compiles reports on privately owned manuscript collections and maintains indexes of names, places, subjects, and owners. The NRA issued an annual 'List of Accessions to Repositories' until 1967, but from 1968 this publication has been issued by the HMC. The NRA 'Bulletin' was published from 1948 to 1967, but thereafter was superceded by the annual 'HMC Report of the Secretary to the Commissioners'. All entries in this text ending with 'NRA' are drawn from NRA reports. In cases where the documents reported on are in private hands, application to examine these must always be made to the NRA and never direct to the private owner.

The National Register of Archives (Scotland) began to locate and survey manuscripts in private hands in 1946. It produces reports on collections. Until 1965 it published biennial reports, which are guides to the individual surveys; from 1966 the reports are annual. Enquiries concerning access to documents surveyed by the NRA (Scotland) should be sent to the National Register of Archives (Scotland), P.O. Box 36, H.M. General Register House, Edinburgh, and never direct to the listed owner, except when the desired material is held by a library or university, in which case the enquiry can be made direct.

Much of the material surveyed below has been microfilmed by American institutions. The Virginia Colonial Records Project and the Office of Archives and History of North Carolina, for example, have in recent years inventoried and microfilmed many thousands of documents pertaining to the colonial history of these states. The Library of Congress, to name yet another, has been microfilming since the 1920s. Since relatively few British archives and libraries maintain a readily available list of which of their holdings have been reproduced and for whom, it has been beyond the resources of this survey to indicate when documents have been filmed unless such information turned up as routine. There are three guides to which the researcher can turn, although it must be noted that such information can never be up-to-date since filming by a variety of educational and commercial concerns goes on apace. See Grace Gardner Griffin, *Guide to Manuscripts Relating to American History in British Depositories Reproduced for the Division of Manuscripts of the Library of Congress* (Washington, D.C., Library of Congress, 1946); Lester K. Born, *British Manuscripts Project: a Checklist of the Microfilms Prepared in England and Wales for the American Council of Learned Societies, 1941–1945* (Washington, D.C., Library of Congress Photoduplication Service, 1955); Richard W. Hale, *Guide to Photographed Historical Material in Canada and the United States* (Ithaca, N.Y., Cornell University Press, 1961).

Although there is normally no question about access to publicly owned papers, papers in private possession are private property which researchers have no inherent right to use. It is therefore important that the researcher explains to the owner why the papers are relevant, seeks permission to quote from them in print, and informs the owner of such published work as results. It is also advisable always to write well in advance to local record offices where archivists will often search out and prepare papers if given prior notice.

The Institute of Historical Research, Senate House, Malet Street, London WC1, is a useful place for the visiting scholar in London, in that it has a helpful and knowledgeable staff and many of the catalogues and other reference works necessary for the scholar on open shelf in contrast to its neighbour, the British Museum.

ENGLAND

BEDFORDSHIRE

Bedfordshire Record Office, Shire Hall
Bedford

LUCAS MANUSCRIPTS

Papers of Thomas Robinson, 2nd Lord Grantham (1738–86), Commissioner for Trade and Plantations, 1766, Ambassador to Spain, 1771–9, Foreign Secretary, 1782–3. The papers include:

Notes on conversations with Lord Germain, 1776, and Maj. Balfour, 1777, on the American situation.

Letters to Lord Polworth from Sir Francis Carr Clerke, 1776–9, including 1 from camp at Saratoga and some from North Balfour, 1777–9, all on the war.

29 letters, 1778–86, from William Horner and his supporters concerning his confiscated property in Maryland and Virginia to Grantham's brother, Frederick Robinson, M.P.

(Addenda 1963, 56)

LUCAS PAPERS

3 documents, 1773–86, relating to the disposal of property at Carlton, Beds., by Thomas Palmer who emigrated and became a merchant in Philadelphia. (Crick and Alman, 3)

STUART PAPERS

The Stuarts are descended from the Earls of Bute and are connected by marriage with the descendants of William Penn. Included in the *c.* 200 documents, 2 volumes, and 2 maps:

Papers pertaining to boundary disputes with Maryland, 1732–80, unlawful settlement in Pennsylvania by men from Connecticut, 1754–74, and interference in trade by Virginians, 1774. (Crick and Alman, 3)

Duke of Bedford, Woburn Abbey
Woburn

BEDFORD PAPERS

List of papers, 1764–5, relating to the affairs of the North American colonies, in the handwriting of John Russell, 4th Duke of Bedford (1710–74). (Crick and Alman, 5)

BERKSHIRE

Berkshire Record Office, Shire Hall
Reading

DOWNSHIRE PAPERS

'Present State of the British Colonies in America, 1773', a large volume containing reports from the governors of some of the colonies, dealing with Indians, trade, smuggling, militia, forts, etc., in response to questions put by Lord Dartmouth, Secretary of State for Colonies. (Crick and Alman, 5)

HARTLEY-RUSSELL PAPERS

Papers of David Hartley (1732–1813), M.P., which contain drafts of peace propositions, letters, speeches, and pamphlets, all concerning the Revolution. (Crick and Alman, 7)

A. Godsal Esq., Estate Office, Haines Hill
Twyford

CHARLES GARTH (c. 1734–84)

M.P., agent for South Carolina in Great Britain, 1762–75, and also briefly for Georgia and Maryland.

Letter books (copies), 1762–74. (For a description of these letter books and Garth's career: Lewis Namier, 'Charles Garth and his connexions' and 'Charles Garth, Agent for South Carolina', *English Historical Review* LIV, 1939, 443–70, 632–52. Crick and Alman, 5)

The Royal Archives, Round Tower, Windsor Castle
Windsor

The Royal Archives contain the personal papers of the Royal Family and are not open for inspection. The chief papers concerning the Revolution have been published or used in the following works: S. M. Pargellis, ed., *Military Affairs in North America, 1748–1765. Selected Documents from the Cumberland Papers in Windsor Castle*, London and New York, 1936; Sir John Fortescue, ed., *The Correspondence of King George the Third from 1760 to December 1783*, London 1927–8, 6 vols.; Sir Lewis Namier, *Additions and Corrections to Sir John Fortescue's Edition . . .*, Manchester, 1937; M. S. Guttmacher, *America's Last King: An Interpretation of the Madness of George III*, New York, 1941.

BUCKINGHAMSHIRE
Dr J. Spencer Bernard, Nether Winchendon
Aylesbury

BERNARD FAMILY PAPERS

This collection of family papers, at present unsorted, is thought to contain some correspondence of Sir Francis Bernard, Governor of New Jersey 1758–60 and of Massachusetts 1760–71. (The bulk of Bernard's papers are in the Harvard University Library. NRA 7343)

Buckinghamshire Record Office, County Hall
Aylesbury

HOBART PAPERS

'Sketch of the case of Capt. Benjamin Roberts'. Roberts was superintendent of Indian affairs among the Six Nations just before the war broke out. (Crick and Alman, 11)

HOWARD-VYSE DEPOSIT

Letters and reports, 1775 and 1777, from Richard Reeve of Boston to Sir George Howard, M.P., mostly describing the opening months of the war.

5 letters and accompanying reports, 14 May to 1 December 1775, describing in detail the events of that period.

Manuscript entitled 'Establishment and disposition of His Majesty's land forces at the close of the year 1777, also general state of the army in America to the same period'.

3 printed items:
'A circumstantial account of an attack that happened on the 19th April 1775, on His Majesty's troops by a number of the people of the Province of Massachusetts Bay';
copy of a letter, 28 April 1775, from Jonathan Trumbull to General Gage, with Gage's reply, 3 May 1775;
Massachusetts Gazette and the *Boston Weekly News-Letter*, 30 November 1775.

(Crick and Alman, 10–11)

SHARDELOES PAPERS (Amersham)

1 letter, 24 February 1779, from Robert Bourne to William Drake of Shardeloes, relating the situation in the Mississippi Valley. (Crick and Alman, 12)

CAMBRIDGESHIRE
University Library
Cambridge

H.M. FORCES

Volume of Returns, 1782. (Add. 4376)

Details the commands of Carleton and Haldimand with an abstract of the total forces.

(Crick and Alman, 17)

CHESHIRE
Trustees of the late 2nd Duke of Westminster
Eaton Estate Office (Muniment Room)
Eccleston

WESTMINSTER PAPERS

Original grant, 1769, by George III of 12,000 acres of land in East Florida to the Rt. Hon. Richard Lord Grosvenor. (Crick and Alman, 23)

CORNWALL
G. C. Fortescue Esq., Boconnoc
Lostwithiel

GRENVILLE PAPERS

Correspondence of William Wyndham Grenville, Baron Grenville (1759–1834).

Various letters, January–March 1783, from Earl Temple, Lord-Lieutenant of Ireland, mentioning the evacuation of Charleston, S.C., flight of Loyalists from America, trade and emigration to America. (Crick and Alman, 24)

Earl of St Germans, Port Eliot
St Germans

ELIOT PAPERS

1 letter, 31 May 1775, from Edward Gibbon to his patron Edward Eliot, 1st Baron Eliot (1727–1804), on the rebellion. (Printed in J. E. Norton, ed., *The Letters of Edward Gibbon*, II, London, 1956, 72–3. Crick and Alman, 28)

Cornwall Record Office, County Hall
Truro

1 letter, 1776, from Thomas Davey in Pensacola to his aunt with minor reference to the war. (Addenda 1963, 56)

CUMBERLAND
Rev. P. B. Lyon, St Mary's Kells
Whitehaven

GEORGE MARTIN (London solicitor)

1 volume, 1779–1800. of claims and dealings concerning property confiscated and sold by the Virginia Assembly in 1779. (Microfilm held at Colonial Williamsburg. Crick and Alman, 32)

Public Library, Catherine Street
Whitehaven

JOHN BRAGG

1 volume of diary and letters, 1774–90. Most of the diary entries between 1774–83 relate to the Revolution. (Microfilm of the letters held by the Library of Congress. Crick and Alman, 32)

DERBYSHIRE

Marquess of Lothian, Melbourne Hall
Derby

BUCKINGHAMSHIRE PAPERS

Letters, minutes, extracts, 1770–82, in the correspondence of John Hobart, 2nd Earl of Buckinghamshire (1723–93), Viceroy of Ireland, 1777–80.

Includes some papers concerning the Stamp Act crisis, the disorders in Massachusetts Bay, 1770, and a manuscript in Hobart's handwriting, 'Commencement of the American Rebellion'. (HMC 62, 260–1, 289, 291–2)

Godfrey Meynell Esq., Meynell Langley
Derby

JOHN ANDRÉ (1751–80)

Poem, 1781, 'Monody on Major André' by Anna Seward.

1 letter, 31 October 1781, from André to George Washington requesting to be shot rather than hanged.

(NRA 4101)

DEVONSHIRE

Mrs C. Drummond, Oak Lodge
Budleigh Salterton

JOHN PRATT

14 letters, 1779–1805, concerning military operations and orders of the 4th (American) Pioneer Regiment. (NRA 5972)

Devon Record Office, County Hall
Exeter

SIMCOE PAPERS, 1776–c. 1800 (Deposit 1038)

Included are the papers of Sir John Graves Simcoe (1752–1806). In 1775 Simcoe went with his regiment to America where he was wounded at Brandywine and twice captured and exchanged. In 1777 he founded the Queens Rangers, a unit of Loyalists renowned for its efficiency. Invalided to England in 1781, he became Lt. Governor of Upper Canada in 1791. (Addenda 1963, 57)

Earl Cathcart, Sandridge Park
Stoke Gabriel

CATHCART PAPERS

Letters and papers, 1763–81, including letters from Col. Robert Clerk to Lord Shelburne on American matters; from Sir Henry Clinton, 1780–1; from Andrew Eliot, Lt.-Governor of New York, on political and military affairs; Lord Chatham's plan, 1775, for settling American affairs. (NRA 3946)

DORSET
Viscount Hinchingbrooke, Mapperton
Beaminster

SANDWICH PAPERS

Volume of treaties and letters, 1739–78, of John Montagu, 4th Earl of Sandwich (1718–92). (Some of these have been published in E. R. Barnes and J. H. Owen, eds., *The Private Papers of John, Earl of Sandwich, First Lord of the Admiralty 1771–82*, London, 1932–8, 4 vols. NRA 5472)

Dorset Record Office, County Hall
Dorchester

WHITAKER FAMILY

Papers relating to legacies, etc., in Maryland, 1771–3, of various members of the Whitaker family. (Addenda 1966, 61)

DURHAM

University of Durham
(Department of Palaeography and Diplomatic)
The Prior's Kitchen, The College
Durham

GREY OF HOWICK PAPERS

This very large collection includes the papers of Charles Grey, 1st Earl Grey (1729–1807), which contain copies of dispatches and letters of Sir Guy Carleton during the war. (Crick and Alman, 46)

ESSEX

Essex Record Office, County Hall
Chelmsford

AUDLEY END PAPERS

Letter, 12 April 1779, from Lord Rockingham to Sir John Griffin Griffin, stating that many Americans are in favour of returning to their allegiance. (Crick and Alman, 49)

ROBERT GREENWOOD (d. *c*. 1814), Quaker of Chelmsford

Commonplace book, *c*. 1710–93, containing a few references to North American affairs in 1774 and 1780. (Addenda 1963, 57)

RIGBY PAPERS

Papers relating to the clearing of the public accounts of Richard Rigby, Paymaster-General to H.M. Forces, 1768–82. (Crick and Alman, 49)

ROUND PAPERS

7 letters, 1765–76, from Thomas Falconer to Charles Gray on the state of the colonies and the causes of unrest. (Crick and Alman, 49)

RUSSELL PAPERS

2 Journals of Risks, 1759–74, of insurance underwriters of William and Samuel Brand, merchants of London. (Crick and Alman, 49)

SMYTH PAPERS

2 letters, 1781, to Sir Robert Smyth, M.P. for Colchester, on the Franco
–American alliance from two local rectors. (Crick and Alman, 49)

W. Weston Underwood Esq., The Maltings, Aldham
Colchester

WESTON PAPERS

Copy of Sir William Johnston's preliminary peace treaty with the Seneca
Indians, 13 April 1764.

Copy of a portion of Gen. Gage's letter, 21 September 1764, concerning a
conference of Indian tribes at Niagara.

9 letters, 1765–70, from Edward Sedgwick to Edward Weston concerning the
growing disaffection in America.

1 letter, 12 August 1768, from Sir James Porter to Edward Weston with the
former's views on the American disorders.

(HMC 10(1), 217–422 *passim*)

GLOUCESTERSHIRE
Bristol Record Office, Council House
Bristol 1

JOHN COGHLAN

Articles of Agreement, 1781. Authorization for Coghlan, a Bristol merchant,
to privateer against enemy vessels. (Crick and Alman, 56)

Moravian Church, Maudlin Street
Bristol 1

RECORDS OF PIONEER MISSIONARY WORK IN NORTH AMERICA, 1751–77

There are only 3 references to American material in the revolutionary period:

Diary of the New York Moravian Church, 1777.

Extracts of a diary concerning Indian congregations, 1777.

Part letter on settlement on the Beaver River in Ohio, 1770.

16   ENGLAND

(These records have been calendared by F. M. Blandford, 'Catalogue of the
Archives of the Bristol Moravian Church', Part III, Diploma in Librarian-
ship, University of London, 1950; available in microform from Micro-
methods Ltd)

Public Libraries, College Green
Bristol 1

BRISTOL PRESENTMENT WORKS

Weekly or bi-weekly listings of imports and exports at Bristol. Imports
covered: 1770, 1775–80. Exports covered: 1773–80. Drawn from the Custom
House Records by Samuel Worrell but not official Custom House Papers.
(Crick and Alman, 58)

MERCHANDISE IMPORTED INTO BRISTOL, 1774–88

Account book listing vessels entering Bristol and commodities carried. (Crick
and Alman, 58)

SOUTHWELL PAPERS

10 bound volumes of letters and other documents of the Southwell family,
merchants of Bristol. The volumes covering 1745–76 have some reference to
the tobacco trade with Virginia and Maryland, the duty on American tobacco, and smuggling. (Crick and Alman, 58)

Society of Merchant Venturers,
Merchants' Hall, Clifton Downs
Bristol 8

The records of the Society throw much light on trade with America in the 18th
century. The study by John Latimer, *The History of the Society of Merchant
Venturers of the City of Bristol*, Bristol, 1903, gives an idea of the nature of the
records.

W. E. Salt Esq., Director, Department of Adult Education
University of Bristol, 20A Berkeley Square
Bristol 8

HENRY CANER (?1700–92), Anglican clergyman and Loyalist.

Letter book, 1728–78, contains many letters on ecclesiastical affairs, family affairs, financial matters, and some to Governor John Wentworth of New Hampshire. (Crick and Alman, 60)

Earl Bathurst, Cirencester Park
Cirencester

BATHURST PAPERS

Letters, 9 December 1777, from Bathurst to Lord . . . , criticizing the handling of the rebellion and advocating peace. (Crick and Alman, 62)

HAMPSHIRE
Southampton Record Office, Civic Centre
Southampton

PETTY CUSTOMS BOOKS

The volumes for 1763–83 contain occasional references to exports, mainly salt, to America, giving name of ship, home port, name of master, date of sailing, name of consigner, and type and quantity of goods. (Crick and Alman, 74)

HERTFORDSHIRE
Earl of Verulam, Gorhambury
St Albans

VERULAM PAPERS

Journal of a tour through the Midlands in 1768, probably by the 3rd Viscount Grimston, containing some passing references to trade with America.

2 letters, 1776 and 1781, from J. Merwin Nooth to Viscountess Grimston concerning the war and American dislike of the French.

(Crick and Alman, 77)

HUNTINGDONSHIRE

Huntingdonshire Record Office, County Buildings
Huntingdon

MANCHESTER COLLECTION

Memorial, 1784, of Lord Charles Montagu, sometime Governor of South
Carolina, to the Commissioners for American claims, requesting compensation for loss of lands in Carolina and a request for proportionable lands in
Nova Scotia. (Crick and Alman, 80)

KENT

Kent Archives Office, County Hall
Maidstone

WYKEHAM-MARTIN PAPERS

Correspondence of the Culpeper, Fairfax, and Martin families, referring particularly to the family estates in Virginia, the difficulties of owning American
property after the Revolution, and compensation claims. Many letters from
Bryan Martin (1731–98) who settled permanently in America. (Crick and
Alman, 81)

TWISDEN FAMILY PAPERS

1 notebook, 1776–84, with references to Sir William Twisden going to
America with James Gambier 1777.

1 notebook by an unidentified writer which includes four pages on the war, *c.*
1780.

(Crick and Alman, 82)

Marquess of Abergavenny, Eridge Castle
Tunbridge Wells

ABERGAVENNY PAPERS

23 letters, 1774–84, most to Lord North from John Robinson and William
Eden.

1 letter, 1778, from Lord Amherst on the need for 30,000 more troops in America.

Several letters from the American Peace Commissioners in 1778.

1 letter, 1777, from General Howe to John Robinson on why the war will not end with the current campaign. Several letters, 1777, from Burgoyne to North concerning reinforcements and conciliation with the colonists.

(Crick and Alman, 431–2)

LANCASHIRE

Athenaeum Library, Church Alley
Liverpool 1

PAMPHLET COLLECTION

Includes at least 16 pamphlets, 1769–83, concerning the political or military relationships between Britain and America. (Crick and Alman, 83)

Public Libraries, William Brown Street
Liverpool 3

JAMES CURRIE (1756–1805)

'Journal of a Voyage from Nixonton, N.C. to the Island of St. Martin's', 1775–6.

(For assessment of his five year stay in America: W. W. Currie, ed., *Memoir of the Life, Writings, and Correspondence of James Currie*, London, 1831?, 2 vols. Crick and Alman, 88)

HOLT AND GREGSON PAPERS

19 volumes of MS. and printed material collected for a history of Liverpool by John Holt and Matthew Gregson.

Vol. 19 contains a list of all ships taken by Liverpool privateers, 1778–9. There may be other relevant material as well.

(Crick and Alman, 88)

LIVERPOOL TOWN BOOKS

These records contain occasional references to the Revolution, such as September 1779 concerning defence measures to be taken against possible attack by John Paul Jones. (In process of being published as *Liverpool Town Books 1550–1862*. Crick and Alman, 86)

PARKER FAMILY PAPERS

Much of this collection relates to the career of James Parker (1729–1815) as a Norfolk merchant and captain in the British Army during the Revolution. Includes:

Parker's diary of the war in letter form and papers relating to prize money accounts.

Letters on the Boston and York River Tea Parties and a letter on the Arnold–André treason case.

(J. M. Hemphill, 'Virginia and the Parker Family Papers', *Liverpool Libraries, Museums and Arts Committee Bulletin* VI, 1956, 25–7. Microfilms held at Colonial Williamsburg and the Virginia Colonial Records Project. Crick and Alman, 87)

DAVID SAMWELL (1751–98), Surgeon in London and on ships
56 letters, a few containing comment on Anglo–American relations, 1774–5. (H. A. Taylor, 'David Samwell', *Liverpool Libraries, Museums and Arts Committee Bulletin* VI, 1956, 32–46. Crick and Alman, 88)

SPARLING AND BOLDEN

Letter book, 1788–99, of John Sparling and William Bolden, Liverpool merchants. Much correspondence with Virginia merchants about commerce and attempts to settle debts contracted before the war. (Crick and Alman, 88)

TARLETON PAPERS

Letters, deeds, and business accounts, 1754–80, of John Tarleton (1719–73), Liverpool merchant. These contain some references to American trade and include two letters, 1780, from his son Sir Banastre Tarleton (1754–1833), a well-known and controversial officer serving in America. (W. R. Serjeant, 'The Tarleton Papers: a Merchant's Accounts', *Liverpool Libraries, Museums and Arts Committee Bulletin* VI, 1956, 28–31, which includes a reproduction of one of the letters from his son. Crick and Alman, 87)

John Rylands Library
Manchester 3

SLAVE TRADE DOCUMENT

1 folio, 1756–73. Contains a list of ships engaged in the slave trade during the years 1749–87, showing where slaved, where sold, numbers died, and net sales. Some cargoes are noted as being sold in America. (Crick and Alman, 100)

MORAVIAN CHURCH

There is also an extensive collection of Moravian Church diaries, letters, etc., concerned with American missionary activities which may contain some references to the revolutionary period.

McLachlan Library, Unitarian College, Daisy Bank Road
Manchester 14

HENRY HULTON (c. 1731–91)

16 copy letters, 1769–76, from Hulton to Robert Nicholson, Liverpool merchant; 15 of which are from the Boston vicinity where Hulton was Revenue Commissioner, giving eye-witness accounts of the beginning of the war and the perils faced by revenue officials from the colonists. (Copies of these letters are also included in the *Shepherd Manuscripts*, Vol. 18, held by *Manchester College Library, Oxford*, OXFORDSHIRE. Crick and Alman, 106)

Public Libraries, St Peter's Square
Manchester 2

THOMAS JEFFERSON

Notes on the State of Virginia. Jefferson had 200 copies of this book privately printed in 1782 for his friends. In addition to a British and a French edition, there were many subsequent American editions. There is a 1784 copy autographed by the author in the British Museum. (Crick and Alman, 103)

Lancashire Record Office, Sessions House, Lancaster Road
Preston

CROMBLEHOLME ACCUMULATION

11 letters, 1760–6, from William and Henry Rigby of Philadelphia to their Lancashire relatives on the international situation and Indian affairs. (Addenda 1962, 50)

GRUNDY FAMILY PAPERS

1 letter, 14 December 1782, from Parson and Prior of New York to Cooke, Relph, and Barnardeston of London concerning a large textile order, transport conditions and the need for convoys. (Addenda 1962, 50)

Public Library, Peel Park
Salford 5

AMERICAN LETTERS, 1702–1818

Collection of 10 letters whose correspondents include John Adams, Richard Henry Lee, James Monroe and the Marquis de Lafayette. (Crick and Alman, 112)

Public Library, Rodney Street
Wigan

EDWARD HALL MS. DIARY COLLECTION

Diary of George Folliott, general merchant of New York, of a visit to England, 1765–6, spent mainly in London. Much comment on trade matters and record of a discussion of American affairs, especially the question of a molasses tax, with Lord Rockingham. (Crick and Alman, 113)

LINCOLNSHIRE
Duke of Rutland, Belvoir Castle
Grantham

RUTLAND PAPERS

Large group of letters, 1763–80, to the Marquess of Granby, including:

General Gage from New York, 20 December 1766, on the transport of troops.

Samuel Martin, 16 January 1768, recommending his brother for the position of Quartermaster-General in North America.

4 letters from Edmund Stevens, June–December 1776, describing the fighting on Long Island and the capture of General Lee.

Several letters from various correspondents concerning the Saratoga disaster.

Many letters, 1777–80, from Lord Robert Manners concerning the French Fleet and Cornwallis' campaigns and situation at Yorktown.

(Crick and Alman, 114)

Lincolnshire Archives Office, Exchequer Gate
Lincoln

ASWARBY MUNIMENTS (Whichcote Family Papers)

Letters, 1742–84, from A. Johnston and George Appleby, with some reference to Indian problems. (Crick and Alman, 118)

AMCOTTS DEPOSIT

Deed of partnership, 1779, between Robert Weston Cracroft and his brother Francis and Robert Bourne, planter of Katesbourne, West Florida, to share the profits of planting and the buying and selling of negroes. (Crick and Alman, 118)

LONDON
Allen & Hanburys Ltd, Bethnal Green
London EC2

BUSINESS RECORDS, 1777–1855

This firm of manufacturing chemists and makers of surgical instruments had considerable trade with America before, during and after the Revolution.

11 letter books, the earlier of which contain a number of letters to New York customers about orders and shipping problems.

10 ledgers, 1777–1866, including the accounts of American customers.

Order books, 1 containing orders for 1777; 'waste' books with some information for 1773 and 1776–8.

(Crick and Alman, 119)

British Library of Political and Economic Science
London School of Economics, Houghton Street
London WC2

LETTERS OF EMIGRANTS TO AMERICA, 1745–1911

Deposited by the British Association for American Studies. Contains:

1 letter, 5 June 1775, from James Aitken, Wilmington, N.C., to his father John Aitken in Glasgow, noting that the locals are drilling regularly.

JEVONS COLLECTION

134 bound volumes of 18th- and 19th-century pamphlets. Probably contains some from the revolutionary period.

British Museum, Bloomsbury
London WC1

Next to the Public Record Office, the Department of Western Manuscripts of the British Museum contains the largest collection of source material in Britain for the study of the American Revolution. As an introduction to the tools for using the collections of the Department, intending researchers should consult T. C. Skeat, *The Catalogues of Manuscript Collections in the British Museum* (London, 1962, rev. ed.).

The present survey covers the *Additional, Egerton, Hargrave, King's, Lansdowne*, and *Stowe Manuscripts*, as well as the *Burney Newspaper Collection*. It incorporates the work of Andrews and Davenport, pp. 1–169; the additions to their work by Paullin and Paxson, pp. 494–555; and the more recent survey by Crick and Alman, pp. 126–82. In the case of the Additional and Egerton Manuscripts, the years 1926–56 covered by Crick and Alman have been resurveyed as printed catalogues and more indexing are now available for most of this period, and the survey extended to Additional 57845 (May

1973) and Egerton 3786 (1971). Although many volumes have been examined, it has not been possible to make an exhaustive survey because of the magnitude of the task, especially for the post-1948 period for which catalogues are as yet unpublished. The hundreds of as yet uncatalogued volumes of Holland House Papers, for example, surely contain more material than the supplementary papers of Charles James Fox herein noted. Researchers should always make full use of the indexes available in the Department. It should also be noted that the Additional and Egerton Manuscripts receive additions periodically; hence no survey will ever be up-to-date.

ADDITIONAL MANUSCRIPTS

5842. *f. 332.* Jenyns Verses on the American Madness, 1775.

5847. *f. 192b.* Copy of a letter from General Burgoyne with a description of the Battle of Bunker Hill, including his proclamation from his camp at Putnam Creek, 29 June 1777.

5851. *f. 143.* American Colonists Rebellion, Address of English Roman Catholics, 1778.

6134. *f. 8b.* Account of a conversation with Benjamin Franklin subsequent to the peace in 1783.

8133B. *f. 2.* Observations of the 'American Drawback' Act of 4 George III date after 1783).

f. 7. Account of total amount of old subsidy retained upon foreign goods exported from England to North America, 1773–4.

f. 141. Account of the amount of bounties paid on hemp, flax, and wood imported from America, 1771–5.

ff 160–5. Indigo statistics, 1771–5.

ff. 177–9. Naval stores statistics, 1771–5.

ff. 194–5. Plantation rum statistics, 1770–9.

ff. 283–302. Sugar statistics, 1770–9.

f. 309 ff. Tea statistics.

f. 350 ff. Tobacco statistics.

8133C. *ff. 1–4.* Small printed book containing lists of the commissions of the customs and successors of the commissioners' from 1672 to 1785, with dates of letters of patent, numbers of commissioners and their salaries, names of new commissioners, etc. Many subsequent papers relating to the consolidation of customs duties in 1777.

f. 85. Report, 16 September 1763, concerning prevention of frauds by colonial commissioners of customs.

ff. 89–94. Agreement, 10 March 1766, of West Indian and North American merchants regarding opening the island of Dominica and proposals for indemnifying purchases at Dominica.

f. 97. Present state, products, and commercial advantages of St Lucia and Dominica, by J. G. Felton.

f. 131. List of customs officers at the port of London discontinued, 1771–82, includes 'Assistant plantation clerk in the secretary's office, £80' and 'Assistant to the husband of the Four and a half per cent duty, £20'.

f. 140. Annual amount of salaries paid to officers in the plantations from customs revenues, 1766–78.

f. 149. 'The underwritten articles are entitled to bounty on importations from the British plantations in America,' 6 November 1781.

ff. 163–8. Accounts of bounties paid at London and the outposts include figures for 'American raw silk', 1770–5.

f. 179. Account of the value of exports from England to North American colonies, 1763–9, distinguishing each colony.

f. 202. 'Plan for the better examining and passing the accounts of the several plantation collectors, whereby their respective debts to the Crown may be the more speedily recovered', by Felton.

ff. 204–17. Memorial of merchants and planters interested in and trading to Barbados and the Leeward Islands, to Lords of the Treasury, with objections and observations upon it.

f. 218. Account of the gross and net produce for such part of the Four and a half per cent as has passed through the hands of the husband and comptroller of that duty, 1770–7 (also *ff. 219–32*).

f. 233. Account of enumerated and new duties received in the ports on the continent of America since 29 September, 1764, so far as the accounts have been received, and also of the remittances made on account of said duties, distinguishing ports.

f. 234. Annual amount of the enumerated duties, 1761–5.

8949. Journal of the Travels of Jonathan Carver in 1766–7, including a survey journal from Detroit to Michilimackinac, a different version of this journal with comments on the country and various maps and drawings.

8950. Fair copy of Carver's survey and journal, with engraved map and coloured drawings, 1 May 1767, evidently intended for publication.

9344. Letters to George Jackson from Pitt, 1774, for information on sailings of Admiralty ships to New York or Quebec; Adm. Jervis on naval matters; Adm. Rodney on preventing the junction of Washington and the French, 1789; Lord Sandwich on naval affairs.

9828. *f. 122.* Governor Pownall on 'whether lands granted in America can be resumed and regranted upon bare suggestion that the Conditions have not been complied with and without any legal inquest', 22 July 1773.

f. 169. Letter, 2 February 1774, from Benjamin Franklin to his son William on his dismissal from the post office.

ff. 170–4. Letters from same to same on family matters, the British dispute, etc., 1774–5.

f. 178. Letter, 25 July 1777, from Washington to William Franklin concerning the latter's request for release from confinement.

ff. 179–81. Correspondence, 1783–6, between Washington and Mrs M. Bristow concerning loss of property occasioned by the war.

11287. Map of Cantonment of Forces in North America, 11 October 1765, showing regiments, companies, half companies, detachments, capital towns and forts.

11288. 'Cantonment of His Majesty's Forces in North America, according to the dispositions now made and to be compleated as soon as practicable, taken from the general Distribution, dated at New York, 26 November 1766, by Dan. Patterson, As't Q'r. M'r. Gen'l.'

12099. *f. 22*. Letter from Franklin to Governor Bernard, 11 January 1764, regarding a son of Bernard.

12440. Duplicate correspondence of Governor Moore of New York with Ministers, 1766.

13974. *f. 474*. Report on payment of tithes by Jesuits in America, 1765.

f. 502. Tables of exports and imports with America, 1748–1815.

13976. *f. 154*. Commerce between Barcelona and America, 1778.

14034. Papers of the Board of Trade containing abstracts of Acts concerning taxes, duties, imports, etc., passed in America and the West Indies, 1683–1774.

14038–9. Papers regarding the conduct of V.-Adm. Graves during the period he commanded the North American Station, 1774–6.

15317. Copy of proceedings in the general court of Virginia between John Hite *et al.*, plaintiffs, and Thomas, Lord Fairfax, defendant, relative to certain lands there, and other papers relating to the suit, 1771.

15484. Ports, districts, and towns of America (the colonial seaboard), *c.* 1770.

15485. Account of shipping, imports, exports, their value and character of articles carried, 1768–9.

15488. *f. 162*. 'A list of the Gentlemen of the Council of Massachusetts Bay who have been turned out of the Council since the repeal of the Stamp Act,' n.d., with dates and a brief account of each.

ff. 163–4. Extracts of letters from Governor Bernard of Massachusetts.

ff. 165–74. Extracts of letters from Lord Shelburne and others to Bernard.

f. 175. Extracts of the Journals of the House of Assembly, Massachusetts, 1761–4.

15489. *ff. 33–43*. Papers concerning the case of John Freebody *v.* Jahleel Brenton before the committee of the Privy Council, 1766–9.

f. 59. Petition from Peter Wihoff and Joseph Reed to the King, 6 September 1772, New Jersey.

ff 84–109. Letters, 1771–9, mostly to, but a few from, Governor Horatio Sharpe of Maryland.

ff. 146, 148, 150 ff. Correspondence, 1771, of Secretary George Clarke of New York.

15491. Papers relating to Montreal, Quebec, and Newfoundland, dated 1771.

15535. Various plans of military operations in America, including Boston and Yorktown, and Bowles's engraved map of the US, 1783, with a continuation of the boundary in MS.

16367. *a–n*. Various maps and plans: New York, Brooklyn, and part of Long Island, 1781; battle of white Plains, 26 October 1776; Falmouth Harbour, 1777; West Florida, St Augustine.

18738. *f. 196*. 'Remarks on the conduct of the war from Canada', by George III.

20237. Letters of Gen. Frederick Haldimand with Sir John Johnson, Superintendent of Indian Affairs.

20733. *f. 111*. Comment by Thomas Pownall, former Governor of Massachusetts, on the retirement of Lord Germain and the abolition of his office, November 1781.

f. 145. Letter, 11 December 1781 from Philadelphia, from Dr Hugh Williamson, author of *History of North Carolina*, to John Almon.

20926. *ff. 108, 238, 340*. Diaries in Spanish of the naval campaign of Spain against England in 1779, with map of fleet movements and various naval reports for 1780.

20986. 'Noticias Militares de America', 1596–1783 (in Spanish), includes the Pensacola expedition of 1781.

21506. *ff. 161–6*. Letters, 1784, from Franklin to John Paul Jones concerning charges arising aboard the *Serapis* and *Countess of Scarborough*.

21661–892. *Papers of Sir Frederick Haldimand* (1718–91), who served in America from 1756–66 in New York and Canada, commanded Pensacola 1766, and was Governor of Canada from 1778. The papers cover the years 1758–85 and consist of correspondence with Amherst, Gage, Stanwix,

Robertson, Taylor, Abercrombie, Murray, Sir Ralph Burton, Sir William Johnson, various governors and subordinate officials in America and Canada, and officials in England. Also included are many reports on conditions in Canada; papers relating to Indian affairs; many letters from and papers relating to Loyalists; general orders and instructions from Amherst, Gage, Maitland, Carleton, and others; government instructions, military rules, directives, journals, diaries, commissions, warrants, etc. Later volumes contain intelligence papers, documents relating to suspected persons, packets, valuations, memorials, trade statistics, etc. (A copy of the Haldimand papers is in the Canadian Archives, B1–B232, and are calendared in Brymner's *Canadian Archives*, 1884–9)

See **20237**. Haldimand's correspondence with Sir John Johnson, Superintendent of Indian Affairs; **24320**. The report to Haldimand on the surrender of Fort Sackville (Vincennes) in 1779; **29237**. Other letters of Haldimand.

22129. Register of Civil Offices in the Royal Colonies, from Quebec to Dominica, giving name of the office, name of the incumbent, how appointed, salary, how paid, 1776?.

22130. *f. 16.* Letter, 9 May 1781, Washington to Col. Menenville, ADC to Rochambeau, concerning the supply of artillery for the defence of Rhode Island.

22679. *Correspondence of Governor Henry Moore of New York*, 1763–8. Among the general business and personal correspondence are a few letters and petitions concerning Indian Affairs and the following letters concerning the Stamp Act—*f. 8:*

3 January 1766, from Jasper Ingersoll in New Haven requesting Governor Moore to receive into the fort of New York the stamp papers consigned to him.

23 February 1766, from Bernard concerning the Stamp Act rioting at New London.

17 April 1766, from Lt. Colville in Halifax promising aid if needed.

29 May 1766, from Bernard about the Stamp Act *furor* and Governor Colden's letter about Bernard communicated to the newspapers.

14 July 1766, from Ingersoll asking that Moore see the stamps safely aboard ship for England.

Address of the General Assembly of New York to Moore, 15 December 1766, in reply to his message of 17 November 1766.

23206. *f. 77.* Letter, 14 April 1782, from Franklin in Paris to David Hartley in London on the general treaty of peace.

23651. *Rainsford Papers*, 1776–8, relating to the Hanau and Anspach troops. Rainsford was commissary to George III to receive the German troops and transport them to America. In addition to much correspondence, the volume contains commissions, instructions, memoranda, remarks, lists, oaths of loyalty, summaries of costs, and accounts.

24131–8. 'Abstracts of English State Papers in the collection formed by William, Earl of Shelburne, 1st Marquis of Lansdowne, and now preserved at Lansdowne House', concerning the peace of 1763, the American war, the general pacification in 1783, navy, trade, customs, etc. (The actual Shelburne Papers are in the William L. Clements Library, Ann Arbor, Michigan. C. W. Alvord, 'The Shelburne Manuscripts in America', *Institute of Historical Research Bulletin*, i, 1923)

24157–79. *Correspondence of Thomas Robinson*, 2nd Lord Grantham (1738–86), as Ambassador to Spain, 1771–9.
24157–66. Original letters from, with a few draft letters to, members of the British ministry, chiefly Rochford, Stormont, and Weymouth, and various ministers at the European courts. Also included are the instructions and other papers delivered to Grantham.
24167–73. Original letters from, and drafts of letters to, the British consuls in Spain and the Canary Islands.
24174–6. Copies of letters to Rochford, Weymouth, Grimaldi, Floridablanca and Musquiz.
24177. Copies of letters to ambassadors and foreign ministers at Madrid and to British ambassadors at various courts..
24178. Copies of letters to British consuls and merchants in Spain.
24179. Copies of letters from Frederick Robinson, brother of Grantham and Secretary of the Embassy at Madrid, to Rochford and Weymouth, 1772–8.
(For other papers of Grantham: Bedfordshire Record Office, Lucas Manuscripts.)

24320. Papers relating to the surrender of Fort Sackville (Vincennes) by Lt.-Governor Henry Hamilton to George Rogers Clark, February 1779, including Hamilton's diary, much correspondence, and his report to Gen. Frederick Haldimand. (This last published in *Michigan Pioneer Collections, IX*)

24321. Letters in cipher (deciphered) relating to American affairs, mostly 1771, but also David Hartley to Franklin on the peace moves of 1777; Vergennes to Gérard, 1778; Victor Amdaeus II of Sardinia to Marquis de Cordon, Turin 1778, and others.

24332. Miscellaneous letters, etc., relating to American affairs, 1718–96. Much correspondence between 1775 and 1783, including Germain to Clinton, Percy to Gage, Rodney to the Admiralty, etc., and some material on Loyalists in Canada, 1784–5.

24323. Letters, 1770–80, from Sir William Johnson, Sir John Johnson, and Col. Guy Johnson to John Blackburn, London merchant, mostly relating to Canada.

25490. *f. 31.* Observations upon the attack made by Commodore Sir Peter Parker upon Fort Sullivan, S.C., 28 June 1776.

25699. Chronicles of the Indians of North America, by S. G: Drake, Boston, 1836.

25893–5. 'Extracts for a fair and impartial history of Paul Jones', 10 copy books, lettered A–K, partly printed, MS. autograph, by Dr Richard Filkin.

27578. Correspondence of Rev. W. Butler, vol. II, 1763–71, containing 3 letters, 1768, from Thomas John Claggett of Maryland.

27891. Sailing directions for different parts of the eastern coast of the North American seaboard, 1772–8.

27916. *ff. 5–11.* 'A Short Hint to both sides of the Atlantic,' written before the Declaration of Independence by Francis Godolphin Osborne, Secretary of State.

27918. Many memoranda on the career of Francis Osborne, Secretary of State, in Parliament, with occasional references to American matters.

28103. *f. 117.* Letter, 30 June 1781, Barbados, H.M.S. *Sandwich*, from Rodney concerning the French in the West Indies.

28605. Journal of John Lees of Quebec from London in 1768: London to Boston, Rhode Island, New York, Albany, Mohawk River, Fort Stanwix, Fort Orange, Fort Oswego, Fort Niagara, Lake Erie, Detroit and Montreal.

28727. *ff. 118–23.* Letters, 1768–77, from John Bartram to Peter Collinson.

28851. Narrative of Secret Negotiations with Spain, 1780–1. Written by R. Cumberland and addressed to Lord Shelburne, dated 20 May 1782, and describing efforts made by the British to break up the Franco-Spanish alliance and prevent the Spanish from joining the French in aiding the American cause.

29198. *f. 19.* Extract from Capt. Morris' Journal 'Account of an expedition to the American Indians', August–September 1764.

29237. Letters and papers, 1774–83, of the Johnson family of Johnson Hall, New York, mainly concerning transactions with the Indians and the Revolution.

29256A–9L. 'Returns of his Majesty's forces at home and abroad,' monthly tables from November 1768 to September 1775, imperfect series.

29263. 'An enlarged and improved survey of the British Customs; containing the rates of merchandise as established by the Acts of 12th Car. 2 dus. and 11th Geo. I. cap. 7, and other statutes, with particular states of all the branches of duties, drawbacks, bounties, etc., payable thereon under all circumstances of importation and exportation; the whole continued to the end of the session 23d Geo. 3d.'

29475. *Auckland Papers.* Miscellaneous letters of William Eden, Baron Auckland.

    f. 9. 30 July 1777, Lord Stormont from Paris to Eden on Howe's manoeuvres in 1777.

    f. 11. 3 August 1777, Henry Dundas to Eden on the progress of the war.

    ff. 13–14. 23 January 1778, Stormont from Paris to Eden on the probability of a Franco-American alliance and its probable terms.

    f. 15. 1778?, 'N' to Eden on the Franco-American pact.

2960. Papers relating to America, 1725–96, chiefly concerning the Principio iron works in Maryland. 12 letters and documents, plus earlier papers concerning the company.

29973. 'A Short Description of the Province of South Carolina, by Surgeon General George Milligan Johnston, M.D. 1763', printed work with notes and corrections by the author.

30262. *f. 52.* Letter, 18 September 1780, Benedict Arnold to Col. Beverly Robinson.

    f. 54. Robinson's reply, 19 September 1780.

30868–75. Correspondence of John Wilkes, containing letters from John Almon, 1764–9; John Adams, 1768–9; B. Church, 1769; Samuel Adams, 1770; Joseph Warren, 1769–70.

32303. Deciphers of diplomatic papers, *Vol. 51*, America 1780–1841.

32413. 'Some Account of the American War between Great Britain and her colonies, in the form of a diary by Lt. William Digby, 53d Regiment serving under General Guy Carleton in the campaign from 8 April to 16 November 1776, and under General Burgoyne in the campaign from 6 May to the surrender at Saratoga, 17 October 1777.'

32627. Journal of Alexander Chesney, endorsed 'Memo by my Father on some of the events of his life. F.R.C.'.

32686–3057. *Newcastle Papers.* Official correspondence of Thomas Pelham Holles, Duke of Newcastle (1697–1768), containing much correspondence and many documents concerning America, all but a few pre-dating 1763. The volumes are fully indexed so that post-1763 material can be easily located.

32969. *f. 380.* Circular letter, 1765, of Charles Lowndes of the Treasury to the governors in America and the West Indies.

32971. Various papers on trade, bullion and smuggling, regarding the colonies, especially *ff. 193–228.*, letters from the British Government to the colonial governors regarding suppression of the Stamp Act tumult with other documents relating to the Stamp Act unrest.

32973. *ff. 246, 332.* Resolutions as to affairs in America, 1766.

32975. *f. 250.* Resolution of the House of Commons respecting imports to America, 1766.

f. 477. Vote of thanks to the Duke of Newcastle from the House of Representatives of Massachusetts Bay, 1766.

32980. *f. 116.* Protest of the House of Representatatives of Massachusetts Bay against the Stamp Act, 1767.

32981. *ff. 48, 51.* Extracts from the Journals of the Upper House of Assembly of Georgia, 1767.

32982. *ff. 16, 21, 29, 75, 225.* Papers relating to the province of Quebec, 1764, 1767.

ff. 62, 64, 66, 68, 71, 73, 97, 121, 134, 198. Papers relating to Massachusetts Bay, 1767.

33028–30. *Newcastle Papers.* 'Papers relating to America and the West Indies', 1701–1802.

33029. *f. 50.* Copy of a letter from Grey Cooper to Governor Bernard concerning the attitude of the Lords of Treasury toward the Stamp trouble in Boston, October–November 1765.

33030. Many documents on trade in general, the Stamp and Molasses Acts, customs duties and smuggling.

33046. *f. 240.* An account of Capt. Henry Clinton's service in the army (his early career, 1745–8, in America and Canada).

33056. *ff. 54, 202.* Appointment of William Tryon as governor of North Carolina and warrant for salary, 1765, 1766.

f. 56. Appointment of Henry Moore as governor of New York, 1765.

33057. *f. 93.* Memorial of Geo. Clarke, Lt.-Governor of New York, to the Duke of Newcastle, concerning his losses from the rebels.

33231. *N.N. 1.* Sketch of action between the British forces and the American provincials, 17 June 1776.

N.N. 8. Rough sketch plan of the Delaware River and islands from Chester to point above Philadelphia showing some particular operations there on the part of a fleet, 15 November 1777.

33741. *Grenville Papers.* An account of the sums granted by Parliament for all naval services, 1775–1809.

33977. *f. 141.* Letters, 1782, of John Adams to Sir J. Banks.

34187. Letters addressed to George Jackson, Second Secretary of the Admiralty and Judge-Advocate. The first series relate chiefly to the Revolution, the second to suits arising from the capture of property on St Eutatius in 1781.

34312–471. *Auckland Papers.* Political and private papers of William Eden, 1st Baron Auckland (1744–1814), Under-Secretary of State in the Northern Department, 1772–8; Member of the Board of Trade, 1776–82; Joint Peace Commissioner to the American colonies, 1778–9. The papers from 1772–9 deal largely with the rebellion and the activities of American spies and agents in France and Britain. An important collection, especially concerning the work of the Peace Commission.

34412–18. Cover the period to 1783, after which there are the following scattered items:

34419. *f. 103.* Letter, 1783, George Johnstone to Eden; *f. 201.* Letter, 1782, Thomas de Grey to Eden; *f. 276.* William Knox to Eden.

34420. *ff. 280, 351.* Same to same 1777–86.

34428. *f. 162.* Losses sustained by British settlers in Honduras from the Spanish, 1779.

34444. *f. 374.* Letter from Clinton to Eden, n.d.

34461. *ff. 302–28.* 'General Reflexions and Remarks on the State and Disposition of the country and people of New England, and particular descriptions of Worcester in the province of Massachusetts Bay, and other parts of the four provinces, tending to furnish ideas and hints toward a plan for its speedy reduction to the legal authority of Parliament,' author and date unknown.

f. 331. Pen and ink map, folio, of part of Pennsylvania, all of Maryland, and part of Virginia, 1778?.

f. 332. Memorandum of goods shipped to North America from Great Britain, with marginal note regarding the manufactures of France, *c.* 1778.

f. 334. Notes of what appear to have been a speech on the subject of the troubles in America, n.d.

f. 336. 'State of facts to prove against popular and received opinions,' colonial history from British viewpoint.

f. 428. Notes concerning the life and family of George Washington, 18th century.

Other Auckland Papers are **29475, 45728–30, 46490–1, 46519**.

(The papers as a whole were used by G. Hogge, ed. *The Journal and Correspondence of William, Lord Auckland*, London, 1861–2, 4 vols.)

34813. *f. 88.* Letter, 25 August 1775, York Town, Va., from Matthew Pope to

John Jacob, stating the view that independence is not desired in the colonies.

34990. *f. 32.* Plan of operations by General Dalling, Governor of Jamaica, for an attack on Grenada on Lake Nicaragua.

f. 156. Address to Prince William, Duke of Clarence, from the Virgin Islands, West Indies, 1783.

35155. *ff. 13–20.* Various papers relating to the West Indies, Grenada, Dominica, St Vincent, 1764–84.

35192. *ff. 1–18.* 49 letters from William Pitt to Adm. Hood, 1773–7.

35349–6278. *Hardwicke Papers.* Correspondence and collections of the first four Earls of Hardwicke and other members of the Yorke family.

35349–813. Correspondence; **35814–6278.** Other papers.

Material pertaining to the Revolution is:

35350. *f. 60.* Letter, 26 August 1776, from William Robertson to Philip Yorke, describing plans for his *History of America*.

35372. *f. 323.* Letter, 30 September 1782, from Sir Joseph Yorke to Philip Yorke, mentioning the mystery surrounding the Paris negotiations; *f. 327.* Same to same, concerning the peace treaty.

35374–5. Letters, 1747–87, from Joseph Yorke to Lord Hardwicke containing some American references.

35381. *ff. 34, 42, 49, 50, 52.* Various letters commenting on the peace treaty.

35427. Letters to Philip Yorke, 2nd Earl of Hardwicke, from Thomas Hutchinson, former Governor of Massachusetts which supplement the letters from Hardwicke to Hutchinson in *Egerton* **2659–75.**

The correspondence of Philip Yorke with William Henry Cavendish Cavendish-Bentinck, 3rd Duke of Portland, 1783–4, and other members of the Yorke family, 1764–1830, is in **45030.**

35433 *ff. 174–8,* 184–9. Notes from the British Government to the United Provinces concerning Dutch neutrality and supply of munitions to the Americans, 1775–8.

ff. 180, 182. Resolution of the States of Holand on the request by George III for the loan of the Scottish brigade serving in the Netherlands, with a protest by Baron Johan Dirk van der Capellen, 1776.

35504. *f. 111.* Letter, 1782, from Sir Basil Keith, Governor of Jamaica, to his brother, Sir R. M. Keith.

35506. *f. 141.* Same to same.

35509. *f. 203.* Letters from Sholto Douglas of Jamaica to Sir R. M. Keith (see also **35510,** *ff. 107, 199;* **35512.** *f. 159;* **35514.** *f. 125;* **35523.** *ff.* **342;** **35525.** *f. 141:* letters dated 1775–82).

35511. *ff. 208, 232, 234, 236, 243, 256.* Copies transmitted to Sir R. M. Keith of correspondence of George Cressener, British Resident at Liège and

Minister to Cologne, with Count Metternich and others, regarding the stoppage of the Hessians at Coblenz, 1777.

35512. *ff. 198, 221, 269.* Letters, 1777–8, from his wife to Sir Basil Keith, Governor of Jamaica (see also *ff. 153, 188;* **35514.** *f. 119*).

35513. *f. 180.* Copy of 'L'ambassadeur sousigne de la Majesté très Chretienne a reçu l'ordre expres de remettre à la cour de Londres la declaration suivante'. Then follows in French a declaration of France concerning a treaty with America, signed by de Noailles, London, 13 March 1778.

35525. *ff. 94, 99.* Letters, 1782, describing Rodney's victory over de Grasse in the West Indies.

35609. *f. 36b.* Letter, 1771, from Thomas Yorke of Philadelphia to Philip Yorke.

35613. *f. 277;* **35614.** *ff. 7, 11, 15, 30, 32, 36, 38, 58;* **36520.** *ff. 135, 160, 180–5;* **35621.** *ff. 38, 61, 63.* Letters, 1777–82, from Robert Auchmuty, former Judge of Admiralty in Massachusetts, to Philip Yorke.

35616. *f. 9.* Intelligence from Governor Hay of Barbados regarding movements of the fleet in the West Indies, 1779.

35621. *f. 364.* 'Extract of a letter from an American at New York', n.d., no name but mentions the non-departure of Col. Tarleton as good news.

35916. Hardwicke Papers relating to the West Indies, 1734–1803.

36133. Volume containing warrants to the Attorney-General for patents of public officials, with accompanying papers, including:

f. 61. James Grant, Governor of East Florida, 1763; *f. 71.* George Johnstone, Governor of West Florida, 1763; *f. 151.* Lord Charles Grenville Montague, Governor of South Carolina, 1766; *f. 291.* John Wentworth, Governor of New Hampshire, 1766.

36219–20. Printed statements of cases on appeal from the plantations to the Privy Council, many with marginal notes by Yorke as Attorney-General. Considerable information on trade and some references to smuggling in the 1760s.

36226. *f. 353.* 'Mr. Curuy's [Thomas Augustus Cruwys?] scheme for an American stamp bill, presented to the Commissioners of Stamps', 30 September 1763 (see also **33028.** *f. 376;* **35910.** *f. 137;* **33030.** *f. 334*):

f. 357, 'Draft of conference with Mr. M'Culloch, 12th October, 1763. Copy for the Board [of Stamps].'

36593–6. Papers of Caleb Whitefoord, Secretary to the British Peace Commissioners, 1782–3.

36806. Letters, 1783, to Viscount Montstuart, British Ambassador to Spain, concerning Spanish participation in the American war and possible British military actions against Spanish colonies.

37021. *f. 27.* Letter, 30 April 1764, from Franklin to Peter Collinson.

37653. 'Signals and Instructions in Addition to the General Printed Sailing and Fighting Instructions,' printed, with many manuscript alterations and additions, signed by G. B. Rodney, and dated 'on board H.M.S. Sandwich at Spithead, 18 December 1779' (on his appointment to command the fleet for the West Indies), and addressed to Capt. John Douglas of H.M.S. *Terrible* . . . , 22 pp.

37772. *f. 9.* Letter, 1779, Alexander Hamilton to Brig. Woodford, with rumours of reinforcements for the Comte d'Estaing's fleet.

37835-83. Correspondence of George III with John Robinson, Secretary of the Treasury, 1770-82. The correspondence covers the period 2 August 1772 to 1 November 1784; it is rich in material concerning the Revolution as Robinson was the King's confidential agent in both private and political affairs and served as the channel of communication between the King and his ministers.

38161. Notes of speeches and debates in Parliament taken by Philip Yorke, 1st Earl of Hardwicke, Philip Yorke, 2nd Earl of Hardwicke, and others.

38202. *f. 342* Refusal by the Assembly of Massachusetts of the offered alternative to the stamp duty, 1764.

38335. *ff. 1, 14-36, 68-77.* Reflections on the settlement and government of British North America, 1763.

ff. 81, 95b-8, 240. Accounts of the Virginia tobacco duty, 1763.

ff. 103, 144, 154, 327-31. Reports, Treasury Minutes, etc., on the customs revenues of North America, 1763.

f. 233. Report to the Lords of Trade on the colonization of Florida, 1763.

f. 243. Estimates of tea, sugar, and molasses illegally imported into North America, 1764?

38336. *f. 155.* Account of Spanish Florida by Dr Campbell, *c.* 1763.

38337. *f. 1.* Abstract of a Bill for encouraging the trade of British North America, 1763?

f. 60. Quit-rents of the several provinces, Virginia, the Carolinas, Georgia and New York, 1764.

ff. 162-173b. Extracts from a report on whale fishing, fur trade, and bounty on hemp in the American colonies, 1764.

f. 234. Note on the trade of North America, especially imports of Carolinian rice, 1764.

f. 245. Report of seizures of unaccustomed and prohibited goods at Philadelphia, Boston, Quebec and Virginia, 1763-4.

f. 314. Auditor-General's report on the Quit-Rent Act of New York, 1764.

38338. *f. 39.* Address, 1764, from the Assembly of New York to Lt.-Governor

Cadwallader Colden concerning consent in taxation and the 'many mischiefs' arising from the Sugar Act.

38339. *ff. 131, 182–9, 306*. Notes on the right to tax the colonies, *c.* 1765.

f. 180. Change of military establishment in American colonies, 1750, 1765.

f. 235. Agreement of West Indian and North American merchants, 1766.

f. 302. Decrease of British exports to North America since the repeal of the Stamp Act, 1766.

38340. *ff. 163–5*. Estimates of military expenses in British North America, 1767.

f. 192. Petition, *c.* 1767, of London merchants trading with North America on the serious effect of the Townshend duties on trade and asking for relief by Parliament.

ff. 201–378b. Papers relating to the collection of customs in British North America, 1767–71, including the legal opinion of Jonathan Sewall, Attorney-General of Massachusetts, 1768.

38341. *ff. 29, 69, 163, 329*. Papers relating to the collection of customs in British North America, 1767–1771.

ff. 104–35. Proposals for amending the taxation of the North American colonies, *c.* 1769.

f. 125. Ships entered outwards from London for British North America, 1765–70.

f. 324. Quantities of wheat exported from British North America, 1768–72.

38342. *f. 32*. Protest of Massachusetts against claims of Parliament to authority over the colony, 1773.

f. 34. Paper on the state of unrest in Massachusetts, *c.* 1773.

f. 39. Paper on the Virginia tobacco trade (after 1773), with a brief history of the trade in the 18th century.

f. 82. Note on the rate of exchange in New England, 1774?.

f. 153. Paper on grants of land in North America, *c.* 1775–6.

f. 157. Paper, n.d. but probably late 1760s, proposing creation of a special fund for the American colonies to set up an orderly system of government and prevent intractability from developing.

ff. 161–221, 281. Letters and papers on the rebellion, 1774–7, including declarations and petitions of the colonists, proposals for parliamentary bills, etc.

38343. *ff. 1–22b* (also **38342.** *f. 302*). Account of what the Treasury has done in freighting provision ships for America, lists of ships, etc., 1775–7.

ff. 117–219b. Papers relating to the Revolution, 1777–8.

38344. *ff. 103–24*. Plans for a permanent union between Great Britain and her American colonies, 1779, sent by Joseph Galloway, an American Loyalist of Philadelphia, to Charles Jenkinson.

38345.*59*. Articles 4–6 of the treaty of peace between Great Britain and America, 1783.

38374.*f. 107*. Reflections on the rebellious state of New York, 1775.

38375.*f. 136*. Memorial of Duncan Campbell, Chairman of the Committee of Merchants of London, Bristol, Liverpool, Whitehaven and Glasgow, trading with America, complaining to the Foreign Secretary of their inability to recover debts in America.

38387.*f. 53*. 'Account of all foreign goods exported to the British colonies in America, particularly wines and calicoes,' 1762–4, by John Tankyns, Assistant Inspector-General of Customs, 12 June 1765.

38465.*f. 210*. 'Account of the number of seamen employed in the merchants' service at the several ports in America, 1763–1772.'

38577.*f. 1*. Grievances of the several provinces of North America, 1769.

38650. *ff. 1–34*. Letters relating to North America, 1775, 1780, including Governor Tryon to Lord Dartmouth and Thomas Jefferson.

39168. *f. 128*. Letter, 1 February 1774, from William Fraser, Secretary of State, to the Earl of Holderness on the Massachusetts petition asking the King to remove Governor Hutchinson and Lt.-Governor Oliver.

39190. *Mackenzie Papers, Vol. 4, ff. 204–11*. 3 letters, 1774–5, from Boston from Maj. John Pitcairn of the Royal Marines to Lt.-Col. John Mackenzie of the Marines on the former's difficulties in America.

39869. Miscellaneous Papers on Naval Matters. 'Abstract of the general printed Sailing and Fighting Instructions and Vice-Admiral Arbuthnot's Additional Signals, 1779 . . . for the North American Station.'

40122. *ff. 47, 50*. 2 notes, 10 March 1778 and 27 May 1779, possibly draft letters to George III, on Spain's attitude to the American conflict, by Spanish diplomats.

40177. *Papers of George Nugent-Temple-Grenville*, 1st Marquis of Buckingham (1753–1813), Lord-Lieutenant of Ireland. 2 letters, 1783, to Lord North on Irish trade with America.

40690. *f. 21*. Letter, 5 April 1779, Washington to George Clinton, Governor of New York, concerning the movement of troops from Minisnick, New York. (Published in John C. Fitzpatrick, ed., *Writings of George Washington*, Washington, D.C., 1936, XIV, 337–8)

    f. 23. Letter, 10 October 1779, same to same, concerning preparations for an expedition against New York. (Fitzpatrick, op. cit., XVI, 452–3) *f. 27*. Letter, 10 January 1781, from Baron von Steuben to Maj. Benjamin Walker offering an appointment as ADC.

41346–51. *Papers of Col. Samuel Martin* of Antigua, mainly business correspondence with his son Samuel Martin, Jr. (1714–88), M.P. and Joint Secretary of the Treasury, 1756–62.

41348. Correspondence for 1768–77 containing some references to American affairs.

41353. *f. 95*. Letter, 12 December 1780, from Josiah Martin, Gov. of North Carolina, mentioning British successess and the likelihood of an early peace.

f. 132–3. Letter, 13 August 1780, from Samuel Martin, Jr., to his nephew with passing comment on the international situation.

41355. *ff. 206–10*. Account of a meeting and conversation, 12 February 1766, between Lord Bute on one side, and Duke of Bedford and Mr Grenville on the other, written by Samuel Martin. Reference to the political crisis, the need to repeal the Stamp Act, and the displeasure of the King at the opposition.

f. 238. Various notes on parliamentary proceedings concerning North America, 1768 and n.d.

41357. Papers and letters relating to the supposed negotiations for the formation of a ministry between Lord Bute and Lord Chatham, including letters from Sir James Wright and Dr Anthony Addington, with accounts of the negotiations by Addington.

41361. Correspondence, 21 December 1752 to 19 November 1785, of Josiah Martin, mainly with his brother Samuel Martin, Jr. Josiah was Governor of North Carolina 1771–6. There are about 35 letters covering the period 1771–80 which touch on various matters such as the defection of New York from the other colonies, the sale of patents in New York, the riots in North Carolina under his predecessor Tryon, revenues of the various colonies, his flight from North Carolina in 1775, and the Clinton expedition of 1780 to South Carolina which Martin accompanied.

42074. *ff. 61–109*. 'Memoir relative to the Island of Jamaica. Shewing the nature and strength of the Country; the situation of the Retreats and Military Posts; together with The Disposition and General Plan of Defence, Established in 1782 by Major-General Archibald Campbell Governor and Commander in Chief.' (Original copy in *King's Manuscripts* **214.** *ff. 16–109*)

42083–8. *Grenville Papers*. Correspondence and papers of George Grenville (1712–70), politician, and his brother Richard Grenville-Temple, 2nd Earl Temple (1711–99). (The bulk of the papers relate to the years 1761–8, and have been printed, though not entirely, in William J. Smith, ed., *The Grenville Papers*, London 1852–3, 4 vols.) There are many references to the American question in letters predominantly on other topics.

42083. Political diary of George Grenville, 3 October 1761 to 6 December 1768, in his wife's hand but with some autograph corrections; Mrs Grenville's own 'Narrative of Events, November 1763–January 1764'. (Both printed in Smith, op. cit., and include references to parliamentary debates on American affairs.)

42084–7. Correspondence of George Grenville with his brother Richard, 15 January 1766 to 17 October 1777, containing many letters partly or wholly relating to various aspects of the American problem from different correspondents but especially Thomas Whately.

42088. Miscellaneous papers, including letters of Thomas Whately to various statemen including Lord George Sackville, July 1767.

42129. 'Lord George Gordon's Narrative'. An apparently unpublished account of the movements and actions of Lord George Gordon during the Gordon riots of 29 May to 9 June 1780. In several hands but apparently not that of the author. May have been intended as part of the pamphlet *Innocence Vindicated.*

42257–496. *The Stevens Transcripts.* Transcripts of letters and papers relating to the history of the American colonies, 1664?–1784 but mainly 1776–84, collected by Benjamin Franklin Stevens (1833–1902), bookseller and antiquarian. Stevens made a number of collections of transcripts, the principal of which are:

(1) 'French Alliance Transcripts', relating to the alliance between France and America, 1778–84, consisting of about 820 documents in 4680 folios (now in the Library of Congress).

(2) 'Peace Transcripts', relating to the peace negotiations between Britain and America, 1782–4, consisting of some 1100 documents in 10,928 pages (now in the library of Congress).

(3) 'Catalogue Index' of manuscripts in European archives relating to America, 1763–83, in 180 volumes containing tiles and abstracts of 161,000 documents (now in the Library of Congress).

(4) 'Stevens Facsimiles', a printed work of 24 volumes of facsimiles of 2107 documents in European archives relating to America, 1773–83 (privately printed by Stevens, 1889–98, for subscribers).

The series of transcripts in the British Museum appear to be some of the original material on the which the 'Catalogue Index' was based. A few of the transcripts are printed or typescript, but the bulk are the work of professional copyists hired by Stevens. The transcripts are divided into five series, A–E:

A. General Series, **42257–427.** Chronological series of all documents except B. and C. below.

B. Dutch Transcripts, **42428–37**:

42428. 'Lyst van stukken, brieven, resolutien, enz. betreffende de verbouding van de Republiek der Vereenigde Nederlanden tot Noor-Amerika,

England, Frankrijk en de Noordsche Mogendheden, gedurende de jaren 1775 tot 1783, en berustende in het Ryksarchief te 's Gravenhagen. 's Hage, Sept. 1857', followed by an English translation.

42429–34. Transcripts of the *Secrete Resolutien* of the States General, 4 January 1782 to 18 December 1783.

42435–7. Transcripts of dispatches from the Dutch envoys to France, Matthjis Lestevenon van Berkenrode and Gerard Brantsen.

C. American Loyalist Transcripts, 10 September 1774 to 30 November 1783, n.d., **42438–46.** Transcripts of memorials, etc., of American Loyalist refugees, copied from the American papers formerly in the Royal Institution but now in the Public Record Office.

D. Miscellaneous, **42447–50.** Intelligence documents collected by Colonel Beverly Robinson, July–November 1778, and various order books of regiments, 1780–1.

E. Index, **42451–96.**

42525–54. *Piggott Papers.* Historical collections relating to the international law of blockade, as compiled by Sir Francis Taylor Piggott (d. 1925) for a series of legal and historical works by himself.

42529. 'First Armed Neutrality: commentary'.

42530. 'First Armed Neutrality: documents and authorities' (The documents are not those published in Piggott's *Documentary History of the Armed Neutralities, 1780 and 1800*, London, 1919)

42551. Collections illustrating French policy on questions of international maritime law before 1789.

42552–3. Collections illustrating the policy of the United States on questions of international maritime law, mostly during the period 1778–1821.

42554. Miscellaneous papers, including collections illustrating Dutch policy on questions of international maritime law, principally during the 18th century.

43771. *Chatham Papers.* Correspondence of John Calcraft, Sr., M.P. for Colne 1766–8 and for Rochester 1768–72, with William Pitt, 1st Earl of Chatham, and his wife Hester.

The correspondence consists of 30 letters from Chatham to Calcraft, and 16 letters to Calcraft from Lady Chatham, mostly written on her husband's behalf during his attacks of gout, and 24 drafts or copies of memos to Chatham from Calcraft. Concentrated in the years 1768–72, the correspondence deals mainly with parliamentary and political affairs. A main theme is the split between the Government and the City of London, while a lesser theme is the growing disaffection within England itself.

There are some specific references to the American problem: *f. 26*. 6 January 1770, report to Pitt on a speech in Parliament concerning the Government's failure to restrain the 'licentiousness of the Americans'; *f. 52*. 14 July

1770. Report stating '. . . the Ministers have declared war against Boston, and Instructions are preparing to Land and Sea Commanders accordingly'.

45124. Journal of H.M.S. *St Albans*, Charles Inglis, Captain, kept by Midshipman James Francis Grant. The journal, covering 4 December 1780 to 28 July 1783, includes convoy duty to the West Indies, 1781; the relief of St Kitts, 1782; the Battle of the Saintes, 12 April 1782; and a visit to New York, 1782.

45128. Notebook of Capitaine de vaisseau Louis Eugène Maissin, naval historian, containing *inter alia* 'Mémoire du Comte de Grasse sur le Combat naval du 12 Avril 1782' (i.e. Battle of the Saintes), a copy of the printed work of the same name by Comte François Joseph Paul de Grasse, Marquis de Tilly.

45728–30. *Auckland Papers.* Papers of William Eden, 1st Baron Auckland, supplementary to **34412–71.** Other Auckland papers: **46490–1, 46519.**

46490. *Auckland Papers.* Papers of William Eden, 1st Baron Auckland.

f. 5. 'A list of Goods Prohibited to be imported or exported from Great Britain,' (January 1775 (printed).

f. 6. Letter, 13 September 1775, from Eden on politics and the military arrangements for the American campaign.

ff. 8-11. Letter, 18 September 1775, from North to Eden with favourable comment on Governor Tryon and General Gage and reaction to Gage's recall.

f. 12. Letter, n.d., from William Fraser? to Eden, summarizing news from America.

f. 13. Letter, 1775, questioning the need for additional troops in America on the basis of reports by Gage and others.

ff. 18–19. 'Minutes on Wm. W.'s private letters and ms. No. 516', mentioning American negotiations with France, spying activities, etc., 2 January 1777.

f. 21. Report of a conversation with Mr Carmichael (an intimate of Franklin and Deane) by Thomas Jeans concerning the Franco-American negotiations, Paris, 27 March 1777.

ff. 23-9. Account of British espionage and double agents in Paris, followed by a long discussion of Franklin, Deane, and their associates, French supply of arms to America, French privateering, and American activities at the Court of Madrid, dated 9 February 1777.

ff. 37–40. 'Secret American Papers received by Lord Suffolk from Wm. Elliot . . . and given to me to be kept with the other secret papers . . .', 20 September 1777.

f. 41. ff. Many letters from William Elliot in Berlin transmitting information and documents pertaining to American diplomatic activities, inter-

44 ENGLAND

cepted letters of Franklin and Deane, and a list of documents obtained by British agents in Paris, mostly dated 1777.

46491. A continuation of **46490,** this volume contains various papers and documents, almost all of which, up to *f. 91*, pertain to the Revolution and its politics in England, including a number of letters from Eden in New York in 1778.

46519. *ff. 1–15.* 3 letters from William Elliot, transmitting documents and comments on the attempts of other powers to form an alliance against England; 2 letters from Lord North to Eden, 1777 and 1778, concerning Percy's news of Burgoyne, and the latter about the war generally.

46840. Diary of the siege of Quebec by an American force, written by J. Danford, a member of the garrison, 10 November 1775 to 6 May 1776, and entitled 'J. Danford's Book of Memorandums . . .'

47559–601. *Papers of, and relating to, Charles James Fox* (1749–1806).
  47559. Correspondence with George III.
  47561. Correspondence with Lords North, Portland, and other Prime Ministers.
  47562–3. Foreign Office correspondence.
  47561–3. Scattered references to the peace negotiations with the Americans in Paris, 1782–3, contained mainly in letters to Fox from the Duke of Manchester and concerning primarily the French and Spanish aspects of the negotiations.
  47562. *ff. 1–34.* In particular, letters to Fox from Thomas Grenville which illustrate the British wish to detach America from France in the negotiations.
  47568–9. General correspondence.
  47584–90. Collections made by Lord Holland for his 'Life' of C. J. Fox, including:
    47584. Notes of events, 1760–6;
    47585. George III Correspondence;
    47586. Eden Papers;
    47587. Shelburne Papers; etc.
  47592–601. Drafts and papers of various biographies of Fox by Lord Holland, Dr John Allen and Lord John Russell.

49086 ff. *Papers of Col. George Napier* (1751–1804), who served on Clinton's staff, 1778–81. These papers were not available for examination as they were in the process of description by the Museum, but:
  49086–8 contain Napier's general correspondence, 1767–1804; **49102** is his journal for 1779.

49510. *Papers of Gen. Sir James Willoughby Gordon* contain 'Disposition of Land Forces and Establishments, 1741–1783'.

50006–12. *Papers of George Townshend,* 4th Viscount and 1st Marquess Townshend (1724–1807).

50006–9. Papers and reports pertaining to his tenure as Master-General of Ordnance, 1772–95.

50006. *ff. 49–53.* Draft of a speech to Parliament commenting on a speech by the King on the American situation; *f. 54.* 'Plan of the French Attacks upon the Island of Grenada . . . July 1779', printed London, 21 September 1779; *ff. 56–7.* Extract of a letter from Antwerp, transmitted 25 February 1782 by John Drummond to Townshend, concerning Dutch naval strategy to divide the British fleet, privateering, and raids on the northern coasts of England and Scotland.

50008A. *ff. 34–5.* Letter, 3 December 1777, from Adj.-Gen. Paterson to Townshend on the impending move across the Delaware River, Washington's likely reaction, and Gen. Howe's ordnance problems; *ff. 54–62.* 'Report on the Defences of Halifax', 1 September 1778.

The remaining volumes contained no pertinent papers.

51457–51519. *Holland House Papers.* Supplementary papers of Charles James Fox.

51467. Family correspondence, 1755–1806.

51468–71. General correspondence, 1765–1806. **51518A & B.** Correspondence (copies made in 1832), 1768–72, with George III and Lord North.

51519. Collections for the 'Life' of C. J. Fox, 1772–82.

EGERTON MANUSCRIPTS

2134. *f. 34.* 'Address of the merchants and other loyal Inhabitants of the city of New York to the Hon. John Vaughan, Esq., Major General of H.M. Forces in North America, on his leaving the country, 20 August 1779.'

2135. *f. 5.* Letter, 2 May 1775, from 'A Real Churchman' to 'Dear Vardell' on the situation in New York and the country generally.

f. 7. Journal of the operations of the American army under Gen. Sir William Howe, from the evacuation of Boston to the end of the campaign of 1776, covering 7 March to 26 December 1776.

ff. 9–18. 2 papers, both n.d., 'Distribution of the Part of the Army not moving with the main body', written by someone in Cornwallis's army, and 'A Plan of Operations in North America'.

f. 19. Letter, 22 August 1776, from George Jackson at the Admiralty.

f. 30. Journal of an officer of the 31st regiment serving on the expedition up the North River, 4–9 October 1777.

f. 41. Paper by Andrew Durnford 'General Ideas for taking possession of the Highlands and intercepting the Rebels in the construction of their new fort at West Point and other work near New Windsor', 1778.

f. 73. Letter, 1779, from H. Sheridan in Savannah.

f. 193. Account of the battle of Long Island.

2136. *f. 176.* Letter, 29 April 1781, from P. Campbell to Lt. Sanxay on board the *Sandwich*, Barbados.

f. 183. Letter, 18 May 1781, from George Jackson, commenting on the loss of St Eustatius.

f. 193. Letter, 17 May 1781, from Gen. St Leger to Gen. Vaughan.

ff. 195–204b. Letters, 8, 11, 23, July 1782, from George Jackson on politics.

2423. 'Journal by a Lady (of Quality)' of a voyage from Scotland to the West Indies and North Carolina, with an account of personal experiences in America during the year 1775 and a visit to Lisbon on her return, 25 October 1774 to December 1775.

2612. *f.* Letter, 1782, from William Atkinson of Dominica to G. Lowdon.

2659–75. *Hutchinson Papers*, including the letter book, diary, memoranda, and general correspondence of Thomas Hutchinson, Governor of Massachusetts, 1769–74, in **2659**.

Most of the pre-1783 correspondence is in **2659**, including letters, diaries, and other papers of Chief Justice Peter Oliver, of Gage, Clarke and others.

2669. Diary of Elisha Hutchinson, 1774, 1775, 1777–8.

2670. Letters of Andrew Oliver, Lt.-Governor of Massachusetts, 1767–74.

2671. Contains the 'Origin and Progress of the rebellion in America, to 1776, by Peter Oliver', written in 1781; **2672–3** contain his journals.

3662. 6 letters, 1767–81, from the Rev. John Newton (1725–1807), Divine, to his close friend William Cowper, the poet.

ff. 3–4. 10 June 1780, almost wholly concerning the Gordon riots. *ff. 5–6.* 21 October 1780, fears that 'the late advantage we have gained in Carolina' will only draw Britain deeper into an 'impossible' endeavour, despite impoverishment, exhaustion, and division at home and the menace of France.

ff. 9–10. 3 February 1781, commenting on the lack of public concern with the consequences of extending the war and fearing attack by the combined fleets of France, Spain, Denmark and Russia.

3711. Journal of Debates in the House of Commons by Sir Henry Cavendish, entitled 'Debates from January the 9th to the 31st, 1770' (rough copy). There are a number of comments and references to the American issue but no direct debate on the question (*ff. 5, 11, 23–4, 31, 32, 37, 39, 43ff., 47ff., 65*).

HARGRAVE MANUSCRIPTS

293. *f. 257.* 'State of the different Laws and Modes respecting the Barring of Entails in the several American colonies, 1773?' (based on letters from the colonies and replies of James Booth, Lincoln's Inn, 2 May 1743, to queries put to him).

KING'S MANUSCRIPTS

201. 'Original letters from Dr. Franklin to the Rev. Dr. Cooper, written in the years 1769, 1770, 1771, 1772, 1773, and 1774, on American Politics.' (Printed in Bigelow, *Franklin's Works*)

202. 'Original letters from Governor Pownall to the Rev. Dr. Cooper, written in the years 1769, 1770, 1771, 1772, 1773, and 1774, on American politics'. (Transcripts in the Bancroft Papers, New York Public Library)

203. 'Original letters from the Rev. Dr. Cooper to Dr. Franklin, written in the years 1769–1775, on American politics'. (A few printed in Bigelow, *op. cit.*)
'Original letters to Governor Pownall, 1769–1774'. (Printed in *American Historical Review*, 8, 1902–3, 301–30)

204. A selection of the above correspondence, all of which is to be found in **201, 202, 203**.

205. 'Report on the State of the American Colonies.' Copies of letters from governors and others in America, probably obtained from Board of Trade papers.

206. 'State of Manufactures, Mode of Granting Land, Fees of Office, etc., in America.' Copies of circulars sent and replies received, 1766–7.

208. 'A General Description of the Province of Nova Scotia, by Lt.-Colonel Morse, Chief Engineer in America', 1783–4.

209. Maps and plans to accompany **208**, chiefly of Nova Scotia but also a chart of the coast of New Jersey and Delaware.

210, 211. 'Report of the General Survey in the Southern District of North America. Delivered to the Board of Trade and Plantations in three separate Returns and Sections entering with the History of South Carolina and Georgia, then proceeding to the History of East Florida; and Surveys, containing in general of said Provinces, the Climates, Beginnings, Boundaries, Figures, Contents, Cultures, Soils, Natural Products, Improvements, Navigable streams, Rivers, Cities, Towns, Villages, Vapours, . . . Ports, Bars, Number of Inhabitants and Negroes, Exportations, Riches, Number of Trading Vessels, . . . Governments, forces, Fortifications, . . . Indians . . . compiled from the surveys . . . of William Gerard de Brahm, His Majesty's Surveyor General for the Southern District of North America.'

213. 'Journal of an Officer who travelled over a part of the West Indies and of North America in the course of 1764 and 1765.' Journey from Pensacola, through Savannah, Montreal, Albany, Hartford, Boston, and New York.

2144 Memoir upon the island of Jamaica, with 7 coloured plans, by Maj. Gen. Archibald Campbell, Governor, 1782.

LANSDOWNE MANUSCRIPTS

1219. *f. 17.* 'Account of such captures of the Americans as the London merchants have had notice of', 14 February, 10 March, 6 June 1777.

ff. 18–31. Correct list of ships taken, etc., since the trouble with America, 27 January 1777, including masters' names, ports, destinations, tonnages.

f. 32. Standing interrogatories to be administered in behalf of our sovereign [George III]. 'To all Commanders, masters, officers, mariners, and other persons found on board any ship or vessel which hath been taken'.

f. 61. Petition of 5 American prisoners confined in Mill Prison at Plymouth, 1 September 1782.

f. 63. Regarding Irish troops to be sent to America, n.d.

f. 65. Minute of proceedings in Parliament regarding the non-intercourse bill with amendments and divisions.

f. 69. Memorandum of a motion for prohibiting trade and intercourse with certain colonies in America at the breaking out of the American war.

f. 72. West Indian imports for 1776 into Liverpool and Lancaster.

STOWE MANUSCRIPTS

119. *f. 164.* Names of the Committee appointed in 1777 to consider establishment of Episcopacy in America.

142. *f. 125.* Specimen of stamps designed for use in America.

261. *f. 123.* Letter, 11 February 1768, from J. C. Roberts, appointed by the King Secretary to the province of East Florida, regarding his salary.

264–5. 2 volumes of transcripts and printed papers relating to the Stamp Act and its consequences in America.

752. *ff. 227b, 230.* Notes on the American dispute, 1776.

781. *ff. 119–33.* Will of General Charles Lee, *c.* 1782.

BURNEY NEWSPAPER COLLECTION

The Burney Newspaper Collection contains the rich holdings of the Museum in 18th-century newspapers. All newspapers earlier than 1801 are entered in the General Catalogue under the heading of Periodical Publications. There is also a Manuscript Catalogue of the Burney Collection, available from the inquiries desk in the Reading Room, which must be consulted to find the location and press mark of the material. The newspapers are bound not in separate files but as a chronological series so that all issues for any given week are found together.

This listing covers the period 1763–83 and does not indicate the location of material within the Collection (for which consult the Manuscript Catalogue) but only the existence of a serial and the extent of its holding. In comparing the Manuscript Catalogue with the entries in the General Catalogue, a few pertinent materials were found which are not part of the Burney Collection, hence these have also been included with their press marks.

Adam's Weekly Courant (London). 10 April 1770; 8 September, 10 November 1772; 11 January, 1 February 1774; January, February, May, November, December 1775; January, August, November, December 1776; 4 February, 26 August to 30 December 1777; 1778 imperfect; 1779; 1780; 22 January 1782.

The Auditor (London). Nos. 1–38, 1762–3, P.P. 3611.1.(1.).

The Aurora and Universal Advertiser (London). 12 February to 3 March 1781.

Ayre's Sunday London Gazette and Weekly Monitor (London). 27 April to 4 May 1783.

Baldwin's London Weekly Journal (London). 1769–73 imperfect; 29 January to 29 February, 19 March 1774. See also *London Journal*.

Bath Journal (Bath). 19 August 1776.

Bingley's Journal; or, the Universal Gazette (London). 9 June to 29 December 1770; 1771–2; 22–9 January 1774; 11, 18 February 1775.

Bonner and Middleton's Bristol Journal (Bristol). 30 August 1783.

The Bristol and Bath Magazine; or Weekly Miscellany (Bristol). 1782–3, P.P. 537.d.

The Bristol Gazette and Public Advertiser (Bristol). No. 176, 1770.

Bristol Journal (Bristol). 8 April 1776; 1782–3.

British Chronicle; or, Pugh's Hereford Journal (Hereford). 1773–9, very incomplete.

British Gazette and Sunday Monitor (London). 24 June, 11, 18 November 1781; 19, 26 May, 28 July 1782; 9 February 1783.

British Mercury and Evening Advertiser (London). 16 November to 16 December 1780.

The Briton (London). Nos. 1–31, 38, 1762–3.

Chester Chronicle (Chester). May–December 1775; January–July, 9, 16 August, 15 October 1776; 11, 18 April 1777; 1778–80, odd issues only.

50 ENGLAND

Constitutional Chronicle (Bristol). 7 December 1780 to 4 April 1782 imperfect.

Constitutional Guardian (London). 17 November 1770.

The Craftsman; or Gray's Inn Journal (The Craftsman; or, Say's Weekly Journal) (London). 17 September 1768; 5 January 1771 to 7 December 1782, lacking most of 1777, 1778, 1781 and 1782, and some issues in other years; 1 February 1783.

The Crisis (London). Nos. 1–91, 1775–6.

Daily Advertiser (London). 5 June to 21 July 1766; 21 April 1768; 22 April, 28 November 1769; 30 January, 13 June 1771; 4 January 1772 to 31 December 1778; 12 February 1779; 28 November to 10 May 1783.

English Chronicle; or, Universal Evening Post (London). 18 March 1780; 29 March, 19, 21 July 1781; 1782–3 imperfect.

The Englishman (London). 13 March to 2 June 1779.

Farley's Bristol Journal (Bristol). 27 April, 3–10 August 1782.

The Freeholder's Magazine; or, Monthly Chronicle of Liberty (London). Vols. 1 and 2, 1769–70.

The Freeman's Journal; or, North-American Intelligencer (Philadelphia) 25 April 1781 to 16 April 1783.

Gazetteer and London Daily Advertiser (London). 1763; December 1764; 1765–72; 1773–5 imperfect; 1776–80; 1781–3 imperfect.

General Advertiser (See General Catalogue entry).

General Advertiser and Morning Intelligencer (London). 4 August 1777 to 6 May 1782, imperfect and lacking 1781. Continued as *Parker's General Advertiser* from 7 May 1782.

General Evening Post (London). 1763 imperfect; 11 November 1766; 15, 17 December 1768; 1770 imperfect; 1771–5; 1776–8 imperfect; 1779–80; 1782 imperfect; 1783.

Gloucester Journal (Gloucester). 12, 19 August 1776; 6, 19 August 1779.

Jackson's Oxford Journal (Oxford). 14 June 1766; 24 June 1769.

Independent Chronicle; or, the Freeholders Evening Post (London). 1767–70 imperfect.

Limerick Chronicle (Limerick). 23 November 1775.

Literary Fly (London). 18 January to 8 May 1779.

Liverpool General Advertiser (Liverpool). 18 April, 3 October 1777; 10, 17, 24 July; 27 November 1778; 6, 13 August 1779; 14, 21 September 1780.

Lloyds's Evening Post and British Chronicle (London). 1763–7; June 1768 to June 1769; 1770–7; 1778–82 imperfect.

London Chronicle (London). 1763–9 imperfect; 1771–80 imperfect; 1780–3.

London Courant and Westminster Chronicle (London). 25 November 1779 to 10 May 1783 imperfect.

London Evening Post (London). 1763–7; 19–21 April 1768; 1770–1 imperfect; 1772–3; 1774 imperfect; 1775–80; 1781–3 imperfect.

London Gazette (London). 1763 to 23 May 1765; July 1772–83 imperfect.

London Herald (London). January–April 1783.

London Journal (London). 30 July to 13 December 1768. Continued as *Baldwin's London Weekly Journal*.

London Packet; or, New Evening Post (London). 5 April, 3, 26 July 1771; 3, 8, 15 April 1772; 10 October 1774; 14 July, 27 April, 15 December 1775; 23–6 February, 28 October, November 1776; 14, 25 April, 9 July, 17, 20 October, 5, 7, 19 March 1777; 1 June, 13 July, 24 August, 23, 25 September 1778; 1780 imperfect; 7 March 1781; 1782–3 imperfect.

London Recorder and Sunday Gazette (Reformer) (London). 27 July 1783.

Lying Intelligencer (London). Nos. 1–4, 1763.

Manchester Mercury (Manchester). 16 November 1779.

Middlesex Journal; or, Chronicle of Liberty (London). 4 April 1769 to 14 September 1776.

Miller's London Mercury (London). 23–30 November 1771.

Mirror (Edinburgh). 23 January to 21 August, 7 December 1779; 27 May 1780.

The Moderator (London). 19 November 1763.

The Monitor, or British Freeholder (London). 1 January 1763 to 30 March 1765 (See General Catalogue entry).

The Monitor, or, Green-room laid open (London). 1767. Continued as *The Theatrical Monitor*, 24 October 1767 to 16 April 1768.

The Monthly Review; or, Literary Journal (London). A periodical work giving an account, with proper abstracts of, and extracts from, the new books, pamphlets, etc., as they came out, 1749–89 (See General Catalogue entry).

The Morning Chronicle and London Advertiser (London). 29 December 1770 to 31 December 1783, lacking most of 1771.

Morning Herald and Daily Advertiser (London). 1 November 1780 to 31 December 1783 imperfect.

Morning Post (London). 17 November 1772 to 31 December 1783, lacking most of 1772–4.

New Morning Post; or, General Advertiser (London). 13 November to 16 December 1776.

New York Gazette (New York). 27 December 1765; 13 November 1775.

New York Gazetteer (New York). 12 May 1774, 27 April, 9, 13 November 1775.

Newcastle Journal (Newcastle-upon-Tyne). 16–23 November 1771; 10 February 1776.

Noon Gazette and Daily Spy (London). 10, 26 December 1781.

North Briton (London). January–November 1763; 21 January 1764; 10 May 1768 to 11 May 1771 (See General Catalogue entry).

Occasional Respondent (Cambridge). 12 April 1764.

Occasionalist (London). Nos. 1–14, 1768.

Owen's Weekly Chronicle (London). 1 January to 26 February 1763; 14–21 July 1764; 1765 imperfect; 11–18 January, 8–15 March 1766; 3–10 January 1767; 29 April to 6 May 1769; 23–30 June 1770.

Oxford Gazette (Oxford). 12 December 1777.

Oxford Magazine; or, University Museum (London). 1768–76, P.P. 6115.

Parliamentary Spy (London). 21 November 1769 to 25 May 1770.

Pennsylvania Chronicle (Philadelphia). 16–23 March 1767; 17 September 1770 (See General Catalogue entry).

Pennsylvania Evening Post (Philadelphia). 1777, C.42.1.1.(8.).

The Pennsylvania Journal; and the Weekly Advertiser (Philadelphia) 9, 15, 22 December 1773; 4 May, 29 June, 13 July, 3, 19 August, 26 October 1774.

The Pennsylvania Ledger; or the Virginia, Maryland, Pennsylvania and New Jersey Weekly Advertiser (Philadelphia). No. 84, 1776, C.42.1.1.(9).

The Pennsylvania Magazine, or American Monthly Museum (Philadelphia). 1775, P.P. 6239.

Pennsylvania Packet (Philadelphia). 20 June, 4, 11, 18 July 1774.

Public Advertiser (London). 1763 imperfect; 1764–6; 1767–8 imperfect; 1769–83.

Public Ledger (London). 1765 imperfect; 9 September to 31 December 1770; 1771 imperfect; 1773–9 all very imperfect.

Pugh's Hereford Journal. See *British Chronicle.*

Reading Mercury; or, Weekly Entertainer (Reading). 22 December 1777; 5 January, 29 July 1778.

The Royal Gazette (Charleston, S.C.). 13 July 1782, C.42.1.1.(1.).

Scotchman (London). 21 January to 23 May 1772.

Scourge (London). No. 1, 23 January 1771.

Scourge (London). Nos. 1–19, 1780, C.121.d.6.

Scrutator (London). Nos. 1–4, 6–8, 11–18, 1764.

South Carolina Gazette and County Journal (Charleston). 9 May 1775.

South Carolina Gazette; and General Advertiser (Charleston). No. 29, 1783.

Spendthrift (London). 29 March to 9 August 1766.

St. James Chronicle, or, the British Evening Post (London). 1763–7; 1768 imperfect; 1769; 1770–2 imperfect; 1773–81; 1782–3 imperfect.

Theatrical Monitor. See *The Monitor.*

Terrae Filius (London). 15–29 March 1764.

Terrae Filius (London). 16 March to 6 April 1764. This is a different publication from the preceding.

Traiteur (London). 18 November 1780 to 13 March 1781.

Westminster Gazette; or, Constitutional Evening Post (London), 12–14 August, 30 August to 2 September 1777.

Westminster Journal; or, New Weekly Miscellany (London). 1763–72 imperfect; 1774–8 imperfect.

The Whisperer (London). 2 February 1770 to 14 September 1771; 4, 11 January 1772.

Whitehall Evening Post; or, London Intelligencer (London). 12–14 January, 29–31 March, 31 May to 2 June 1764; 5–7 June, 24–6 July 1766; 1769–78 imperfect; 1780–3.

Yorkshire Freeholder (York). 20 January to 25 May 1780.

Congregational Library, Memorial Hall, 15 Farringdon Street
London EC 4

PAPERS OF DR WILLIAM BELL SPRAGUE (1795–1876)

This collection contains about 190 autographs and letters from America, of which the following pertain to the Revolution:

Susanna Anthony to Rev. Samuel Hopkins, dated 'Nd', 9 August 1775, referring to confusion in the town following the sudden appearance of ten sail.

J. Dana to Rev. Mr Macclure, Boston, 22 July 1776, mentioning the arrival of a 'fine prize boat' and two others taken into Salem.

George Washington to Capt. Bolden, Fishkill, West Point, 5 September 1779, ordering him to join the Minister, then journeying in the company of Baron Steuben from Boston to Philadelphia.

Jesse Root to Oliver Ellsworth, Philadelphia, 1 November 1779, concerning the Connecticut delegation to Congress, reported action between the French –Spanish fleets and the British fleet, monthly requistions of taxes from the states, and urging 'noble exertions to save the Republic'.

(Andrews and Davenport, 347–9)

Corporation of London Records Office, Guildhall
London EC 2

JOURNAL OF THE COMMON COUNCIL

Contains 22 assorted letters, petitions, addresses, etc., 1774–83, to and from the Mayor and Corporation, most to the King or Parliament opposing actions being taken against the colonies. (Andrews and Davenport, 280–1)

COMMON HALL BOOKS

Contain 4 addresses to the King, 1775, opposing the war and 1 address to same, 1781, urging him to end the war. (Andrews and Davenport, 282)

Coutts and Co., 59 Strand
London WC2

RUSSELL PAPERS

About 200 letters, 1767–1806, but mainly 1773–5, of James Russell, merchant, with agents in Virginia and Maryland concerning trade in tobacco and other commodities, and the collection of debts, with some comment on the political situation. Correspondents include Richard Henry Lee, Thomas Pownall, Thomas Sim Lee, and George Plater, as well as the Fendell, Galloway, Jenifer, Johns and Warfield families of Maryland and the Washington family of Virginia.

Also 4 bonds, 1775–6, of the Rev. Charles Inglis, a well-known Loyalist of New York City.
(NRA 5612. Microfilm by the Virginia Colonia Records Project)

Customs and Excise

The administration of trade was a central issue leading up to the American Revolution, hence the extensive customs and excise records constitute a valuable source. The records are in three general categories: in the Library of H.M. Customs and Excise in London; in the Public Record Office in London; and in many outports of England and Scotland. (The best treatment of these records as sources for American history is in Crick and Alman, 188–207, which supercedes the discussion in Andrews, II)

THE LIBRARY, H.M. CUSTOMS AND EXCISE
(King's Beam House, Mark Lane, London EC3)

Access may be obtained by application to the librarian. The following are the main series of interest for the revolutionary period.

Board's Minutes and Letter Books, 1696–1869

This is the only complete chronological record of the Board's administration in this period.

Inspector-General's Ledgers of Imports and Exports, 1682–1776

These contain tables showing the quantities and values of commodities imported and exported through London and the outports to and from overseas ports, including the American colonies.

Opinions of Counsel

England, 1701–1841, and Scotland 1760–83. Some discussions of the application and interpretation of the laws of trade, nationality of ships built in America 1776–83, nationality of specific ships and seamen after 1783, etc.

Plantation Records

760. Customs yields and balances in American districts, 1767–75; **767.** List of American customs establishment, 1767; **768.** Same, 1767–71; **766,** Same, 1771–6.

PUBLIC RECORD OFFICE
(Chancery Lane, London WC2)

C.E. 3. *Inspector-General's Accounts, 1697–1780*

Ledgers showing exports and imports of British and foreign goods through London and the outports.

C.E. 16. *America, 1768–1773* (1 vol. only)

Analytical accounts of the American trade based on reports of the American Board of Customs at Boston.

C.E. 18. *Establishments, Series I, 1675–1813*

Quarterly salary books of the English customs establishment.

Classes in other groups pertaining to customs and excise matters are **C.O. 390; E. 190; T. 11, T. 38, T. 64**. (These are discussed under the appropriate groups in the *Public Record Office* main entry below)

OUTPORTS

The outports in England and Scotland also have customs and excise records, a full list of which can be found in the Customs and Excise Library in London, together with transcripts of some of the records. Access is only obtainable through application to the librarian.

The records of the outports contain, in general, material on the colonial and plantation trade and shipping. Some have references to the contraband tobacco trade with the Channel Islands and the administration of the Navigation and Stamp Acts before the outbreak of hostilities. Within the war period, there is some material on naval matters, privateers, the supply of British troops in America, the activities of John Paul Jones, and related matters.

Guildhall Library, Basinghall Street
London EC2

This Library contains the non-official papers relating to the City of London.

The following have some value for the study of the Revolution.

RECORDS OF THE NEW ENGLAND COMPANY

Originally the 'Society for the Propagation of the Gospel in New England', and after 1662 chartered as the 'Company for Propagation of the Gospel in New England and the parts adjacent in America'. The Company functioned in America continuously until the Revolution and then shifted its location to Canada. The records contain:

Treasurer's ledger, 1764–1801; Treasurer's journal, 1764–1801; General court and committee minute books, 1770–1816; loose court minutes with some committee minutes, 1655–1816; general correspondence, 1668–1818; 1 letter book, 1762–72; official copy of the minutes of the Commissioners of Indian Affairs at Boston, 1699–1784. (William Kellaway, 'The Archives of the New England Company', *Archives* II, 1954, 175–82)

RECORDS OF THE CITY COMPANIES

These include the records of most of the guilds, many of which showed a strong sympathy for the cause of the American colonies. (Philip E. Jones and Raymond Smith, *A Guide to the Records in the Corporation of London Record Office and the Guildhall Library Muniment Room,* London, 1951)

General Post Office, St Martin's le Grand
London EC1

TREASURY LETTER BOOKS

Vol. 8 (1760–71). 10 letters, memoranda, etc., mostly concerning the development of the packet service to North America and the internal development of the American postal system.

Vol. 9 (1771–8). 6 letters reflecting the effects of the war, arming of packet boats, capture by American privateers, loss of office and hardships of postmasters in America.

Vol. 10 (1778–83). 1 letter, 1779, on the general disarrangement of the postal service with and within America.

COMMISSION BOOK, 1759–1854

Entry book containing copies of correspondence and memoranda of the commissions appointing postmasters, commanders of packet boats, etc.

AMERICAN LETTER BOOK, 1773–83

Containing much of interest for the revolutionary period, including 1 letter, 31 January 1774, dismissing Franklin as Deputy Postmaster-General, and a request that postmasters send by every ship a complete file of newspapers and pamphlets such 'as may serve to show the temper and spirit of the times for the Information of the Board'.

There is other material relating to America in the revolutionary period but this appears to be largely of administrative interest.

(Andrews and Davenport, 274–6)

C. Hoare & Co., 37 Fleet Street
London EC4

MISCELLANEOUS HOLDINGS

Included are:

2 papers: one by Governor Thomas Gage certifying that Peter Oliver is Chief Justice of Massachusetts; the other a power-of-attorney given to Hoare's by William Burch, a member of the Massachusetts Commissioners of Customs.

3 letters, 1776–7, from 'suffering clergy', William Serjeant and William Clark of Boston and John Tyler of Norwich, reporting to Hoare's the drawing of money from a fund to aid colonial clergy for which Hoare's acted as agent.

(Crick and Alman, 225)

House of Commons. See House of Lords Record Office

House of Lords Record Office, Westminster
London SW1

The House of Lords Record Office is the general archive of Parliament. Practically all original Parliamentary papers from 1497 that have been officially preserved have been given over to this library and archive. Housed in the Palace of Westminster, the Record Office contains the records of both Houses of Parliament, all documents presented to or purchased by either

House, and the papers accumulated in the various parliamentary and non-parliamentary offices of the Palace. The House of Lords Record Office Search Room makes nearly all these materials available to researchers. All researchers should, however, first write concerning the specific nature of their research and if possible the particular documents which they wish to consult. All correspondence should be addressed to Clerk of the Records, Record Office, House of Lords, London, SW1.

The library of the House of Commons is private and intended solely for the use of Members of Parliament. The library contains two series of records: unprinted papers and deposited papers. Neither of these series has any reference to the second half of the 18th century.

Researchers should first consult Maurice F. Bond, *Guide to the Records of Parliament* (London, HMSO, 1971) which describes the classes of records, their development and their use.

The record classes in the House of Lords which contain material for the American Revolution are *Records of Proceedings in the House of Lords*; *Records of Proceedings in Committees of the House of Lords*; *Records of Proceedings in Joint Committees of both Houses*; *Records of Proceedings in Conferences between the Houses*; *Records of Bills, Acts and Measures*; *Sessional Papers*.

The Sessional Papers are particularly rich sources and include Command Papers, Act Papers, and Papers laid pursuant to Subsidiary Legislation. For the American Revolution, the most relevant subject classifications are *Army*, with many papers on military aspects of the war; *Colonies*, especially rich in American papers; *Customs and Trade*, also rich in American material; *Navy*, a number of specific items on the American war; and *Treaties*, covering diplomatic relations with European powers as well as with the colonies.

The House of Commons records tend to parallel those of the House of Lords in structure. The bulk of the manuscript journals of the various series of proceedings were destroyed by fire in 1834, but printed journals generally survive from 1762. The Sessional Papers survive in manuscript form only from 1850, but many earlier papers are available in printed form. Hansard published bound sets of pre-1800 Sessional Papers in 1807, of which three are known to exist and are now in the House of Lords Record Office, the British Museum and University College Library, London. Individual parliamentary papers also survive in the British Museum. It may be noted that Hansard's *Parliamentary Papers* as a series dates only from 1801.

The House of Lords Record Office also has a section of *Historical Collections*, which contains miscellaneous manuscript material, often unrelated to parliamentary matters. The only papers which might contain some relevant material are *American Papers* (*Russell, Edwards, etc.*), which are records of transactions and partnerships between British and American merchants, 1732–1836.

Hudson's Bay Company, Beaver House, Great Trinity Lane
London EC4

Chartered in 1670, the Company's archives are extensive, but vary in completeness from year to year and area to area. The records consist of:

Post records—journals, correspondence, books, accounts, dispatches, etc.

Ships' records—mainly logs.

Miscellaneous records—journals and diaries of employees.

London records—minute books, correspondence, ledgers, employee lists, etc.

Records of companies associated with or subsidiary to Hudson's Bay Company, including those of the North-West Company founded in 1776.

(These records were used extensively by E. E. Rich, *The History of the Hudson's Bay Company, 1670–1870*, London, 1958–9, 2 vols., and reflect how the Revolution affected the company in various ways, from the disorientation of trade resulting from the outbreak of hostilities and American expeditions against Canada in 1775 to the French attacks of 1782–3 on the Hudson Bay region and French interest in exploiting the war to re-establish French trade in Canada.)

Lambeth Palace
London SE1

The library contains two collections of manuscripts, the Lambeth MSS., pertaining to the office of the Archbishop of Canterbury, and the Fulham MSS., pertaining to the office of the Bishop of London.

LAMBETH MSS.

No correspondence later than December 1763, except for *1124*:

3 volumes of MS. Journals of the Society for the Propagation of the Gospel, 1758–66, which have full abstracts of letters from the Society's missionaries in America.

The Registers, 1279–1828, listing consecrations of archbishops and bishops, institutions to livings, etc., contain no American references before 1787.

The Act Book, 1663–1828, has occasional references to consecrations to American sees and ordinations to American livings.

(Andrews and Davenport, 286–301)

FULHAM MSS.

From the late 17th century to the Revolution, the colonial church was thought to be under the jurisdiction of the Bishop of London, which accounts for the existence of the Fulham MSS. The 40 folios making up this collection give an extensive picture of the colonial church and are one of the two basic collections for its history, the other being the archives of the Society for the Propagation of the Gospel in Foreign Parts. Although the orientation is primarily ecclesiastical, there is much concerning colonial society, politics, economics, and other religious bodies. The material is divided as follows:

ff. 1–20. General correspondence, containing many letters for the revolutionary period commenting on the issues of the day, the relation of the clergy to the revolutionary crisis, and the difficulties of Loyalist ministers with the rebels

ff. 21–32. Ordination Papers, dating from 1748.

ff. 33–6. Missionary bonds or bonds posted by clergymen receiving the King's bounty for emigrating to the colonies.

ff. 37–9. Lists of parishes and incumbents and of ordinands and licensees.

f. 40. Written and printed pamphlets containing no reference to the Revolution.

(A full guide to the Fulham MSS., containing detailed summaries of all the correspondence, is William W. Manross, *The Fulham Papers in the Lambeth Palace Library. American Colonial Section Calendar and Indexes*, London, 1965. 18 folio volumes of transcripts of the Lambeth and Fulham MSS. are located at the Church Historical Society, Theological Seminary of the Southwest, Austin, Texas, and at the New York Historical Society, New York City. Many documents have also been published in: Francis L. Hawks and W. S. Perry, eds., *Documentary History of the Protestant Episcopal Church in the United States of America . . . ,* New York, 1863–4, 2 vols.; W. S. Perry, ed., *Historical Collections relating to the American Colonial Church*, Hartford, Conn., 1870–8, 5 vols.)

London Library, 14 St James's Square
London SW1

AUGUSTINE PREVOST (1723–86)

Journal, 50 leaves, 1774. Maj. Gen. Prevost was apparently acting Governor

of Pennsylvania in 1774. The journal gives details of travel through Pennsylvania, Maryland and Virginia, and of negotiations with George Croghan,
Indian agent and trader, with the Shawnee Indians. (Crick and Alman, 241–2)

Middlesex County Record Office. See MIDDLESEX

Ministry of Defence, Whitehall
London SW1

Andrews and Davenport, 188, describe 4 small folio entry books of the British
Army in America, 1773–83, as being in this (formerly War Office) library.
They were transferred to the Public Record Office in 1927 and are now **W.O.
36.**

Moravian Church in Great Britain and Ireland
5 Muswell Hill
London N10

The Church was active in missionary work in America from 1735. There are
bound volumes of minutes, miscellaneous collections of material concerning
bishops, etc. Much of the material is in German, and should contain references to the revolutionary period. (The main archives of the Moravian
Church are located in Bethlehem, Pa. Crick and Alman, 246)

National Maritime Museum, Romney Road, Greenwich
London SE10

The museum contains 12,000 volumes of manuscripts, 200 collections of personal papers, and 1200 boxes of Lloyd's reports, as well as many loose papers.
The period covered is mainly mid-17th to the 19th century. (No published
catalogue is yet available, but a general introduction is K. F. Lindsay-
MacDougall, *A Guide to the Manuscripts at the National Maritime Museum*,
London, 1960. Also Crick and Alman, 248–54.) The material for the Revolution consists of both records and personal papers.

ADMIRALTY RECORDS, duplicated at the PRO

Orders from the Admiralty to the Navy Board, 1688–1815, and Navy Board
Replies, 1738–1841, 1492 vols., containing some material concerning the

acquisition of naval stores from America, undesirability of building ships there, and timber imports.

2 volumes of correspondence between the Admiralty and the Sick and Hurt Commissioners concerning American prisoners, including reports and correspondence of David Hartley, M.P., and Benjamin Franklin, the principal agents appointed for the exchange of prisoners.

1 volume of Treasury transport letters, 1783–9, concerning the emigration of American Loyalists, 1783–5.

Plans of American-built ships purchased or captured by the R.N., and R.N. ships captured by the Americans.

PERSONAL PAPERS
Include those of:

Adm. Sir George Collier (1738–95), journal and papers, 1776–9.

Adm. Sir William Cornwallis (1744–1819), letters and orders, 1770–9, including those while on the North American Station, 1777.

Adm. Thomas Graves, 1st Baron Graves (1725–1802), log book, loose papers, drafts of letters to the Admiralty, 1764–82.

Adm. Samuel Hood (1724–1816), log books, letter and order books, and letters received, 1760–1815.

Lt. John Starke 'The case of Lieutenant John Starke of H.M. Navy' and a sketch of the Canadian operations in which he participated, 1775–7, 34 pp.

Parliament. See *House of Lords Record Office*

Public Record Office, Chancery Lane
London WC2

As the official depository of the separate archives of the various departments of the British government and central courts of law, the Public Record Office contains the largest and most important collections of material in Britain for the study of the American Revolution. Considerable time can be saved at the PRO initially if the researcher is already somewhat familiar with the nature of the records and the system for their use. The following is thus a short introduction to the bibliography of the PRO and a summary of the main material bearing on the American Revolution.

To gain access to the PRO, a student must complete the application form for a reader's ticket and return it to the Secretary. British subjects must have the recommendation on p. 2 of the form made and signed by a person of recognized position. Applicants not of British nationality can either submit the form with a Council of Europe Cultural Identity Card, if they possess this, or request their embassy or legation to apply to the Foreign Office with a letter of introduction on their behalf. The Cultural Attaché at the American Embassy usually writes on behalf of American citizens.

For the student of American history, the best introduction to the PRO is the Virginia Colonial Records Project's *The British Public Record Office: History, Description, Record Groups, Finding Aids, and Materials for American History* . . . (Richmond, Va., The Virginia State Library, 1960). From this extremely useful discussion, the student can go on to the official *Guide to the Contents of the Public Record Office* (London, HMSO, 1963–8, 3 vols.). Other general works on the PRO are Hilary Jenkinson, *Guide to the Public Records —Introductory* (London, 1949), and V. H. Galbraith, *An Introduction to the Use of the Public Records* (London, 1952).

The standard work on the American material in the PRO is Charles M. Andrews, *Guide to the Materials for American History, to 1783, in the Public Record Office of Great Britain* (Washington, D.C., 1912–14, 2 vols.), which lists most of the record groups containing American material and usually gives some description of classes and pieces within these groups. Some additional material can be found in Andrews and Davenport, and Paullin and Paxson. Andrews, Paullin and Paxson, and the PRO *Guide* all include notes on the administrative history of the various departments—essential for intelligent use of the records.

The records in the PRO are divided into major divisions called 'groups' which usually but not always correspond to the administrative departments from which the records emanated. Groups are designated by an abbreviation, such as **Adm.** for *Admiralty*, **C.O.** for *Colonial Office*, etc. Within each record group are 'classes' of material, such as in-letters, out-letters, entry books, etc., which are designated by a number. Thus **Adm. 50** represents the class *Admirals' Journals* in the record group Admiralty. The next division after classes is 'pieces', which normally represent a given volume, bundle, or box. The piece number is set off from the group and class designations by an oblique stroke, e.g. **Adm. 50/47**. This system and its permutations is most lucidly described in the Virginia Colonial Records publication mentioned above. It should also be noted that the present system of references began to be introduced in 1923, so that users of earlier works will sometimes need to relate these references to the present system by using the keys available at the PRO.

There are nearly eighty record groups at present, but most do not contain material for the Revolutionary period. The remainder of this section surveys the following groups: *Admiralty* (Adm.), *High Court of Admiralty* (H.C.A.), *Chancery* (C.), *Colonial Office* (C.O.), *Customs and Excise* (C.E.), *High Court of Delegates* (Del.), *Exchequer* (E.), *Exchequer and Audit* (A.O.), *Foreign Office* (F.O.), *Home Office* (H.O.), *King's (or Queen's) Bench Court* (K.B.), *Paymaster-General's Office* (P.M.G.), *Privy Council* (P.C.), *Privy Seal Office* (P.S.O.), *Public Record Office* (P.R.O.), *Signet Office* (S.O.), *State Paper Office* (S.P.), *Board of Trade* (B.T.), *Treasury* (T.), *Treasury Solicitor* (T.S.), and *War Office* (W.O.).

The PRO publishes a series of finding aids, called *Lists and Indexes*, which give listings of the classes within groups and are most useful. When one of this series exists for a record group, it is so indicated at the beginning of the summary.

ADMIRALTY

(*Lists and Indexes* XVIII, 1904)

Adm. 1. *Secretary's Department In-Letters.* Admirals' dispatches arranged by station; Admirals's letters, under ports; Captains' letters, alphabetically; letters relating to the colonies; letters relating to the Solicitor's Department, 1767–83; letters from Governors of Plantations, 1763–90; letters from British Consuls, 1767–77; letters from the Custom House, 1757–80; letters of Intelligence, series I, 1697–1785, and series II, 1738–1800; letters from the Ordnance Office; letters from the Secretaries of State, 1763–83; letters from the Treasury, 1771–82; etc.

Adm. 2. *Secretary's Department Out-Letters.* Entry books showing the other side of the **Adm. 1** in-correspondence.

Adm. 3. *Admiralty Board Minutes*, 1773–83. Some information on American affairs, for example, the activities of John Paul Jones.

Adm. 6. *Registers, Various.* Contain Commission and Warrant Books, Lieutenants' Passing Certificates, Masters' Certificates, etc.

Adm. 7. *Miscellanea.* Register of Passes; Register of Foreign Passes; naval instructions; law officers' opinions; Register of Letters of Marque, America, 1777–83; lists of transports licenced to go to America, 1776–80; statements of exports and imports from colonial ports, 1768–9; etc.

Adm. 8. *List Books.* Monthly entry books showing the disposition of ships, the names of officers, etc.

Adm. 16. *Treasurer's Accounts*, 1681–1783. Volumes of bills paid, tabulated accounts, etc.

Adm. 20. *Treasurer's Ledgers.* Naval and victualling ledgers, 1763–83, including naval expenses at Boston, New York, etc., 1776–81, and accounts of admirals' contingency funds on the North American Station.

Adm. 30. *Registers Various*, 1779–82. Pay lists for ships engaged in America.

Adm. 31–5. *Ships' Pay Books*

Adm. 36–9. *Ships' Musters*

Adm. 49. *Miscellanea, Various*. Transports and tenders employed in America, 1775–82; Muster Books of Transports, 1776–82; Letters of the Keeper of Naval Stores, New York, 1776–84; papers concerning transport for Loyalists, 1783–6; prices of naval stores; returns of stores; Register of Hired Transports, 1763–83.

Adm. 50. *Admirals' Journals*

Adm. 51. *Captains' Logs*

Adm. 52. *Masters' Logs*

Adm. 65–80. *Greenwich Hospital Records*. Include the correspondence books, 1768–83, of Henry Hulton, Deputy Receiver of the Greenwich Hospital Duty in America; also the names of ships and amounts paid for six-pences, 1763–84. This last consists of itemized statements of payment by every vessel that came to London, which is in effect a detailed record of all colonial vessels entering or clearing the port.

Adm. 96. *Marine Pay Office Records*. Out-letters, 1778–84 contain some references to marines serving in America. Also the Muster Rolls and Returns of the Marine Grenadier Company which served in Philadelphia and New York, 1772–80.

Adm. 97–105. *Medical Department*. In-letters from surgeons, agents and commanding officers in America, 1766–79; out-letters relating to American prisoners-of-war, 1775–81; General Minutes of the Board of Commissioners for Sick and Wounded Prisoners and Exchange of Prisoners, 1775–81 (this last is very meagre).

Adm. 106. *Navy Board Records*. Letters and entry books concerning victualling, transports, officers at foreign stations, appointments, armaments, etc.

Adm. 107. *Lieutenants' Passing Certificates*, 1691–1848. Original certificates of lieutenants' services usually with baptismal certificates attached.

Adm. 110. *Victualling Department*. Letter books of out-letters, 1763–83, mainly to the Admiralty, contractors, etc.

Adm. 111. *Victualling Department*. Minutes of Board and Committees, 1763–83.

Adm. 112. *Victualling Department Accounts.* Accounts of agents at yards and stations in North America, 1776–83.

Adm. 113. *Victualling Department Registers.* Pay lists, North America, 1779–83 (for coopers, brewers, bakers, etc., at New York and Savannah).

HIGH COURT OF ADMIRALTY

H.C.A. 3. *Prize Act Books*, 1643–1786.

H.C.A. 5. *Assignation Books*, Series I, 1746–67.

H.C.A. 6. *Assignation Books*, Series II, 1767–89.

H.C.A. 8. *Assignation Books. Vols. 190–5*, 1776–89. Contain proceedings against American ships seized under the Act prohibiting trade with the colonies.

H.C.A. 13. *Examinations*, 1605–1770. Depositions of witnesses and answers to libels.

H.C.A. 15. *Instance Papers*, Series Early, 1624–1778.

H.C.A. 16. *Instance Papers*, Series I, 1772–1806.

H.C.A. 24. *Libels, Allegations, Decrees, Sentences*, etc., 1607–1782.

H.C.A. 25. *Letters of Marque, Bonds. Vols. 56–75.* American Bails, 1777–83.

H.C.A. 26. *Letters of Marque, Declarations.* Vols. 33–44. Declarations against France, 1778–83; *45–52*, against Spain, 1779–83; *53–9*, against Holland, 1780–3; *60–70*, against America, 1777–83.

H.C.A. 28. *Court Minute Books (Prize)*, 1776–83. Rough notes on the proceedings of the court with the sentences against American, French and Dutch ships.

H.C.A. 30. *Miscellanea.* Various papers regarding the origin and practice of the High Court of Admiralty, privateering, disposition of prizes; many ships' books and papers, 1773–82; intercepted mails and papers, 1763–83.

H.C.A. 31. *Monitions (Prize)*, 1763–83.

H.C.A. 32. *Prize Papers.* These relate to the trial and condemnation of ships captured in war. *Bundles 260–493.* Papers relating to the American war, 1776–86, including many packets of letters taken from captured ships and letters from Washington, Franklin, Silas Deane, Benedict Arnold, etc.

H.C.A. 34. *Sentences (Prize). Vols. 43–4* Sentences in American Prize Causes, 1776–88.

H.C.A. 39. *Warrant Books*, 1605–1772. Files of warrants, decrees, summonses, etc.

H.C.A. 41. *Prize Appeal Acts*, 1689–1787.

H.C.A. 42. *Prize Appeal, Appeals Papers. Vols. 110–65.* Pertain to the American war, 1776–83.

H.C.A. 43. *Prize Appeal, Assignation Books. Vols. 36–8.* Assignment Books, American Prizes, 1779–96.

H.C.A. 45. *Prize Appeal, Case Books*, 1763–83.

H.C.A. 47. *Prize Appeal, Miscellanea.* Draft instruments, 1689–1786; minutes, 1780–4; account books of fees, 1690–1783.

H.C.A. 48. *Prize Appeal, Sentences.* 1772 is the last year.

H.C.A. 49. *Vice Admiralty Courts.* Papers from the Court of Vice Admiralty, New York, 1775–83.

CHANCERY

C. 12. *Proceedings*, 1758–1800.

C. 21–4. *Depositions.* Various series.

C. 31. *Affidavits*

C. 33. *Entry Books of Decrees and Orders*, 1607–1783.

C. 38. *Reports and Certificates*, 1603–1783.

C. 39. *Reports, etc., Supplementary*, 1703–93.

C. 54. *Close Rolls*, 1603–1783. These are mainly concerned with the enrolment of private deeds, but also have some entries of specifications of patents.

C. 65. *Parliament Rolls*, 1603–1783. Enrolment of all public and private Acts of Parliament.

C. 66. *Patent Rolls*, 1606–1783. The Patent Rolls are the most important Chancery records for American history. They contain the enrolment of letters patent under the Great Seal, including charters of colonies and trading companies, the incorporation of colonies, the appointments of chief colonial officials, instructions to governors, etc.

C. 78. *Decree Rolls*, 1603–1783.

C. 83. *Warrants for the Great Seal*, Series II, 1714–83.

C. 103–14. *Masters' Exhibits.* These are evidences and other private documents offered by contending parties. For example:

C. 105/44. Grants of Land in East Florida, 1765–83; **C. 107/169.** Estate Records, New Jersey, and wills of persons in Philadelphia, 1775.

C. 210. *Specification and Surrender Rolls,* 1709–83. These contain specifications of certain patents.

IND. 4209–19. *Crown Office Docquet Books,* 1603–1787. These contain commissions which did not get enroled in the Patent Rolls. See also the Signet Office, Privy Seal Office, and Entry Books of Warrants in some Colonial Office classes.

COLONIAL OFFICE

The Secretary of State for the Southern Department was responsible for colonial affairs until 1768 when a third Secretary of State was appointed for this purpose. The latter became President of the Board of Trade in 1769. In 1782 both the Board of Trade and the Secretary of State for Colonial Affairs were abolished and the new Home Secretary became responsible for colonial affairs. In the mid-19th century a Secretary for Colonies was again appointed and the Colonial Office established. The pertinent colonial records of earlier times and other departments were assembled and form the present Colonial Office record group, which is one of the most significant for the study of the Revolution.

Most of the Colonial Office papers are arranged by colony with classes within each colony for in-letters, out-letters, acts, sessional papers, etc. Andrews I, 78–112, gives an introduction to the kinds of records found in this record group. Another useful introduction is Ralph B. Pugh, *The Records of the Colonial and Dominion Offices* (London, HMSO, 1964). The PRO printed list is *Lists and Indexes* XXXVI (London, 1911, Kraus reprint 1963). There are also new typed lists of material alphabetically by colony. The PRO *Calendar of Colonial State Papers relating to America and West Indies* is in course of publication, but to date extends only to 1738. Mention must also be made of a new series in course of publication. K. G. Davies in *Documents of the American Revolution 1770–1783* is providing a calendar and description of the Colonial Office records for this period, with accompanying volumes of transcripts of important documents. Only Volume I, *Calendar 1770–1771* (Shannon, Ireland, Irish University Press, 1972) has thus far been issued, but when completed this series will be the standard reference on the records of the American Revolution in the Colonial Office.

The C.O. classes pertaining to the Caribbean have been catologued in more detail than can be found in Andrews by Herbert C. Bell, David W. Parker, *et al., Guide to British West Indian Materials, in London and in the Islands, for the History of the United States* (Washington, Carnegie Institution, 1926).

A new system of references began to be introduced in this group in 1907. Andrews I, appendix B, contains a key for relating the old reference numbers to the new.

C.O. 5. *America and West Indies, Original Correspondence,* etc., 1606–1807. This class is the largest and most important in the C.O. group for colonial American history. It consists of the original correspondence and entry books of the old Board of Trade and Plantations and the Secretary of State, together with the acts, sessional papers, and miscellaneous records arranged by colony. The following is a brief survey based primarily on Andrews I, 113–85, and secondarily on *Lists and Indexes* XXXVI. The material breaks down into four natural groups: *Correspondence and Papers; Entry Books; Miscellaneous; Individual Colonies.* The numbers introducing each entry below are piece numbers.

Correspondence and Papers

7. 1755–85. Papers relating to the Boston Tea Party, provincial troops, secret instructions to Clinton, American violations of the Treaty of Paris, etc.

8. 1760–83. Many papers regarding peace negotiations, Loyalists, instructions to commanders in America, etc.

23–37. Orders in Council, sent to Board of Trade. Various instructions for governors, occasional petitions and passes, and a body of notes and minutes from the Privy Council, 1760–92.

38–9. Correspondence of Henry Pelham of Boston to many correspondents, 1759–82, and some intercepted letters largely of a mercantile character.

40. Intercepted letters, 1774–5.

43. Miscellaneous papers, 1743–83, including a narrative of Deane's mission to France, 1776; many papers on American relations with Holland, 1776; papers on the peace treaty.

65–82. Plantations general, 1760–82. Many papers on Indian affairs, letters from British officials in the colonies, etc.

83–111. Military correspondence, 1763–84. Letters and enclosures principally from Gage, Haldimand, Howe, Clinton, and Carleton.

112–13. Estimates of expenses of colonial establishments, 1767–8.

114–17. Petitions 1768–81. Includes a large number from British military personnel and civilian officials in America. (Andrews I, 127–9, gives an almost complete list)

118. Includes letters of Benjamin Franklin, Joseph Paice, Arthur Lee, Stephen Sayre and the Earl of Buchan, 1768–75.

119–32. Entry books of letters from the Secretary of State for the Colonies to the Admiralty, and original letters from the Admiralty, 1771–81. These pieces deal solely with American affairs.

133. Council Office, East India Company, and miscellaneous, 1771–4. Material on the price of tea with many letters from America.

134–7. Correspondence of the Secretaries of State for the Colonies and the Postmasters-General, 1771–80.

138–44. Correspondence of the Secretary of State for the Colonies with other Secretaries, 1771–81.

145–53. Correspondence of the Secretary of State for the Colonies with the Treasury and Custom House, 1771–81.

154–8. A valuable series of dispatches from Hillsborough, Dartmouth and Germain, and letters and memorials from sundry persons, 1771–81.

159–60. Correspondence of the Secretaries of State for the Colonies with the Solicitor General, 1772–81. Contains some interesting papers concerning the Boston Tea Party, Ethan Allen, the peace mission of 1778, etc.

161–6. Correspondence of the Secretary of State for the Colonies with the Ordnance Office, 1772–81.

167–73. Correspondence of the Secretary of State for the Colonies with the Secretary at War, 1772–81.

174. Correspondence of the Secretary of State for the Colonies with the Commander-in-Chief, 1772–82. This is the Germain–Amherst correspondence and other related papers.

175–6. General correspondence of the Secretary of State with Civil Officers of the revolting colonies, 1774–83.

177. Records of the First Peace Commission, 1776–8. This was the mission of Richard and William Howe.

178. Records of the First Peace Commission, 1779–82. This was the mission of Gen. Clinton and Adm. Arbuthnot.

179. Correspondence of Lt.-Gen. John Burgoyne and Maj.-Gen. William Heath at Boston concerning the treatment of the Saratoga prisoners, 8 November 1777 to 23 May 1778.

180–1. Records of the Peace Commission of 1778. This was the mission of the Earl of Carlisle, William Eden and George Johnstone.

182–4. Military correspondence from officers of lesser rank, 1779–84.

185. Miscellaneous in-letters, 1779–94. Contains a few letters of Franklin to William Hodgson, 1781–2.

186. Naval Dispatches: Admiral Digby, commander in North American waters.

Entry Books

188–203. Plantation entry books, 1702–71.

204. Patents, 1770–9.

205–8. Plantation entry books, 1771–84.

216. Instructions, reports, etc., 1761–9. Various papers covering revenue, Board of Trade, American agents, etc.

217. Précis of correspondence with Governors, North, 1765–6.

218. Précis of correspondence with Governors, South, 1765–7.

219. Précis of correspondence with the Commander-in-Chief, North America, 1765–7 (i.e. General Gage).

220. Dispatches to the Commander-in-Chief, 1776–8 (Shelburne to Gens. Burton and Gage).

221–7. Various entry books of correspondence, 1766–71, including two volumes devoted to Indian affairs.

228–31. In-letters to the Secretary of State, 1770–82.

232. Précis, I, 1768–75. Various papers dealing with taxation, fortifications, disorders in Massachusetts, and the 1775 expedition to the southern colonies.

233–40. Military entry books, 1768–82. Entries of letters received with enclosures from the Commander-in-Chief in America.

241–2. Dispatches to Governors, 1768–90.

243–5. Dispatches to commanding officers, 1770–83.

246. Private letters received and despatched, 1771–7. From Hillsborough, Dartmouth and Germain to various correspondents; to same from Hutchinson, Oliver, various governors, etc.

247–9. In-letters to the Secretary of State for the Colonies, 1771–82, with copies of some letters enclosed.

250–2. Out-letters of the Secretary of State for the Colonies, 1776–82.

253. Précis II, 1774–7. Mostly devoted to military operations, especially the campaigns of 1777–8.

254–62. Departmental correspondence of the Secretary of State for the Colonies, 1775–82, with the Admiralty, War Office, Ordnance Board and Treasury.

263. Secret Despatches (Out), 1778–82. Chiefly from Germain but a few from Shelburne and Welbore Ellis.

264. Minute Book: First Peace Commission, 1779–83. (Supplementary to **178** above)

265. Pardon Blanks, 1781. Printed blanks of pardon for use of the first peace commissioners with about 20 actually filled in.

266. President of the Privy Council, out-letters, 1784–8. Some material concerning Loyalists.

Miscellaneous

279–81. 'Acts of Assembly passed in the Plantations and transmitted to the Board of Trade.' This is an index of dates rather than of titles, with most of the colonies covered from 1760 to 1776.

Individual Colonies

CAROLINA, NORTH

293–304. Original papers, letters, etc., from the Governors, 1730–75.

305. Drafts of letters sent, 1765–75.

306–7. Miscellaneous papers, 1702–83.

310–18. Letters from the Governors . . . with enclosures, 1761–7.

319. Patents of land, 1707–68.

320. Grants of land, 1765–75.

321–2. Grants of land, 1774–5.

323–6. Entry books, 1730–75.

328–31. Entry books, 1766–82.

332. Secretary of State's entry book of out-letters, 1768–82.

336–41. Acts, 1755–74.

342–57. Minutes of Council, Assembly, and Council in Assembly, 1731–74.

358–80. Original papers, letters, etc., from the Governors, 1720–75.

381. Drafts of letters, 1722–74.

386. Miscellaneous, 1754–76. Mainly correspondence.

390–7. Original papers, letters from the Governors, 1762–84.

398. Abstract of records of land grants in the colony, 1674–1765.

399. Abstract of records of land grants in the colony, 1768–73.

400–5. Entry books, 1720–75.

407. Secretary of State Shelburne's entry book of correspondence, 1766–7.

408. Secretary of State's entry book of out-letters, 1768–82.

409–10. Secretary of State's entry book of in-letters, 1767–81.

412–24. Acts, 1721–70.

425–507. Minutes of Council, Assembly, and Council in Assembly, 1721–74.

508–11. Shipping returns, 1716–65.

513–18. Entry books of the Board of Police, 1777–82.

519–26. Entry books of the Board of Police, 1780–2. These are miscellaneous journals of the proceedings of the Board.

527–34. Oaths of Allegiance, 1780–1.

535. Demands against sequestered estates, 1781.

CONNECTICUT

There is no material pertinent to the revolutionary period listed for Connecticut.

EAST FLORIDA

540–7. Original papers, letters, etc., of the Governors, 1702–83, but most 1763–83.

548–61. Letters from the Governors, 1746–83.

562. Reports of the Commissioners on East Florida Claims, 1787–9.

563–4. Entry books of the Board of Trade, 1763–82.

565. Secretary of State Shelburne's entry book of correspondence, 1766–7.

566. Secretary of State's entry book of out-letters, 1768–83.

567–9. Secretary of State's entry book of in-letters, 1766–81.

570–2. Minutes of Council and Assembly, 1764–81.

573. Shipping returns, 1765–69.

WEST FLORIDA

574–81. Original papers, letters, etc., from the Governors, 1763–82.

582–98. Letters from the Governors . . . with enclosures, to the Secretary of State, 1763–81.

599–600. Entry books of the Board of Trade, 1763–82.

610–17. Entry books, 1764–80. Varied subjects, such as land grants, indentures, bonds, proclamations, etc.

618. Secretary of State Shelburne's entry book of correspondence, 1766–67.

619. Secretary of State's entry book of out-letters, 1768–81.

620–2. Secretary of State's entry books of in-letters, 1766–81.

623–4. Acts, 1766–83.

625–31. Minutes of Council and Assembly, 1764–78.

632–5. Entry books of Minutes of Council, 1764–80.

GEORGIA

644–52. Original papers, letters, etc., of the Governors, 1752–82.

657. Miscellaneous, 1733–83. Petitions, claims, ordnance papers, etc.

658–65. Letters from Governor James Wright, with enclosures, 1761–80.

675. Abstracts of grants of land, registered between 1760–68.

676. Secretary of State Shelburne's entry book of correspondence, 1766–7.

677. Secretary of State's entry book of out-letters, 1768–82.

678–80. Secretary of State's entry book of in-letters, 1767–81.

682–5. Acts, 1755–81.

692–708. Minutes of Council, Assembly, and Council in Assembly, 1741–80.

709–10. Shipping returns, 1752–65.

MARYLAND

721. Miscellaneous. Contains a small packet of papers for 1779–80.

722. Letters and enclosures from Governor Eden, 1777.

730. Acts, 1767–71.

749–50. Shipping returns, 1754–65.

MASSACHUSETTS

754. Miscellaneous. Various printed official papers, 1766–76; some petitions, 1780–1; draft of a paper on the Massachusetts disorders, 1770.

755–63. Letters and enclosures from the Governors to the Secretary of State, 1761–74.

764. Secretary of State Shelburne's entry book of correspondence, 1766–7.

765. Secretary of State's entry book of out-letters, 1768–75.

766–9. Secretary of State's entry books of in-letters, 1766–76.

778–84. Acts, 1760–74.

791–833. Minutes of Council, Assembly, and Council in Assembly, 1709–74.

834–47. Printed Journal and Votes of Assembly, 1721–74.

850–1. Naval Office lists, 1752–65.

854. Account of the Treasurer and Receiver-General of His Majesty's Revenues within the Province of Massachusetts Bay, 1760–9.

NEW ENGLAND

883–95. Original papers, letters, etc., from the Governors, Jonathan Belcher to Thomas Hutchinson, to the Board of Trade, 1741–78.

896. Drafts of letters, 1687–1774.

897. Drafts of letters, 1731–74.

918–21. Entry books of the Board of Trade, 1741–74.

NEW HAMPSHIRE

925–8, 930. Original papers, letters, etc., of the Governors . . ., 1741–78.

931–3. Miscellaneous, 1692–1794. Letters concerning naval stores, printed acts, sessional papers, etc.

934–9. Letters and enclosures from Governor John Wentworth to the Secretary of State, 1762–75.

941–3. Entry books of the Board of Trade, 1741–75.

944. Abstract of letters, 1705–75.

945–6. Secretary of State's entry books of in-letters, 1767–77.

947. Secretary of State's entry book of out-letters, 1768–77.

950–9. Acts, 1702–74.

960–6. Minutes of Council, Assembly, and Council in Assembly, 1710–74.

969. Shipping returns, 1761–9.

NEW JERSEY

970–9. Original papers, letters, etc., from the Governors, to the Board of Trade, 1702–76.

987–93. Letters from the Governors . . . to the Secretary of State, 1762–79.

994–9. Entry books of the Board of Trade, 1702–74.

1001–2. Secretary of State's entry books of in-letters, 1766–81.

1003. Secretary of State's entry book of out-letters, 1768–82.

1004–18. Acts, 1703–74.

1019–34. Minutes of Council, Assembly, and Council in Assembly, 1703–74.

1036. Shipping returns, 1743–64.

NEW YORK

1037–78. Original papers, letters, etc., from the Governors . . . to the Board of Trade, 1691–1779.

1080. Drafts of out-letters, 1738–79.

1088–90. Miscellaneous. Mostly Board of Trade papers, but also 2 letters from La Luzerne to Vergennes, 1782, and duplicate letters and enclosures from Clinton and Carleton, 1754–82.

1097–110. Letters to the Secretary of State from the Governors . . . and Maj.-Gen. Robertson, 1762–80.

1114–32. Entry books of the Board of Trade, 1696–1779.

1134. Grants of land, 1761–4.

1137–40. Secretary of State's entry books of in-letters, 1766–81.

1141. Secretary of State's entry book of out-letters, 1768–82.

1143–82. Acts, 1691–1775.

1184–220. Minutes of Council, Assembly, and Council in Assembly, 1694–1775.

1221. Miscellaneous, 1765–6. *New York Gazette*, no. 1201; printed speeches and pamphlets.

1232. Account of various Rights of New York, 1773. Concerning boundaries.

PENNSYLVANIA

1233. Miscellaneous. *Newport Mercury* for 7 October 1765; copies of orders and instructions to Thomas and Richard Penn regarding trade, 24 April 1767.

1235. Miscellaneous. Copies of military letters from Pennsylvania, Clinton –Germain letters, and a few intercepted letters, 1776–81.

1237–55. Acts, 1700–75.

PROPRIETARIES

1257–79. Original papers relating to the Proprietary Governments: Bahamas, Connecticut, Carolina, Maryland, East and West New Jersey, Pennsylvania, and Rhode Island, 1697–1776.

1280–6. Miscellaneous. Various papers relating to Connecticut, Rhode Island, Pennsylvania, and Maryland, mostly letters from Governors.

1287–97. Entry books of the Board of Trade, 1696–1776.

1299–1300. Secretary of State's entry books of in-letters, 1766–76.

1301. Secretary of State's entry book of out-letters, 1768–76.

RHODE ISLAND

1302. Miscellaneous. Mostly memorials and petitions, 1698–1782.

VERMONT

1304. Letters relating to Vermont, 1781. Includes Minutes of Council, 2 February 1781; Haldimand to Clinton, 28 February 1781; intelligence from Micah Townshend, 4 April 1781; intercepted letters of Ethan Allen to Samuel Huntingdon, 9 March 1781, etc.

VIRGINIA

1313–34. Original papers, letters, etc., to the Board of Trade from the Governors, 1701–74.

1336. Drafts of letters, 1753–74.

1344. Miscellaneous, 1722–80. Includes some letters of Virginia merchants trading with St Eustatius; abstracts of letters between Clinton and Arbuthnot concerning an expedition to the Elizabeth River in Virginia, July 1780.

1345–53. Letters to the Secretary of State from the Governors . . . 1762–77.

1358–69. Entry books of the Board of Trade, 1689–1774.

1372–3. Secretary of State's entry books of in-letters, 1767–77.

1374. Secretary of State Shelburne's entry book of correspondence, 1767.

1375. Secretary of State's entry book of out-letters, 1768–76.

1376–404. Acts, 1661–1773.

1406–40. Journals of Council, Assembly, and Council in Assembly, 1680–1774.

1449–50. Shipping returns, Naval Office lists, 1762–70.

C.O. 42. *Canada, Original Correspondence*, 1763–81. Correspondence with the Board of Trade concerning Indians, military operations against the Americans, troop distribution and returns, with many letters from Haldimand and James Murray to the Secretary of State.

C.O. 43. *Canada, Entry Books*, 1763–86. Correspondence with the Secretary of State, commissions, instructions, etc.

C.O. 44. *Canada, Acts.* 1764–83.

C.O. 45. *Canada, Sessional Papers.* Minutes of Council, 1764–80.

C.O. 47. *Canada, Miscellanea,* 1764–82. A few items relating to trade.

C.O. 137. *Jamaica.* Governors' letters to the Secretary of State. Contain much of interest, especially concerning American Loyalists, the activities of the Spanish, the campaigns in Florida, with many secret dispatches from Germain.

(See also **C.O. 138.** *Jamaica Entry Books,* 26–9, 40.)

C.O. 152. *Leeward Islands. Pieces 55–63, 1775–84.* Contain frequent references to the affairs of the American colonies and their influence in the islands, including the movement of American vessels, privateers, and prisoners; intercepted letters; the relationship of American vessels with the French, Danish and Dutch islands.

C.O. 194. *Newfoundland, Original Correspondence. Pieces 26–35.* Letters to the Secretary of State from the Governors, 1762–84.

C.O. 217. *Nova Scotia, Original Correspondence. Pieces 41–2.* Military dispatches to the Secretary of State from Lt.-Gen. Archibald Campbell, 1782–6. *43–57.* Letters to the Secretary of State from the Governors, 1762–84.

C.O. 239. *St Christopher, Original Correspondence. Piece 1.* Contains some intercepted American correspondence, 1780.

C.O. 246. *St Eustatius, Original Correspondence. Piece 1.* Includes some intercepted letters and petitions to the King concerning property destroyed, 1779–83.

C.O. 253. *St Lucia, Original Correspondence.* Dispatches from Germain to Maj. James Grant; letters and instructions to Grant from Clinton and other papers relating to the 1778 expedition.

C.O. 260. *St Vincent, Original Correspondence.* Letters to the Secretary of State, 1776–86, discussing the effect of the American example on the islanders; intercepted American letters; much information on movements of American privateers and reports of numerous engagements; aid from the French islands to the Americans.

C.O. 285. *Tobago, Original Correspondence. Piece 1, 1778–81.* Some comment on the activities of French spies and American raids.

C.O. 318. *West Indies, Original Correspondence.* A few relevant dispatches, 1778, and many Spanish papers from Cuba, *c.* 1778–9.

C.O. 323. *Colonies General, Original Correspondence. Pieces 1–33.* Correspondence of the Board of Trade and Plantations to 1780.

C.O. 324. *Colonies General, Entry Books of Commissions, Instructions,* etc., *Series I to 1783. Pieces 17–19, 21, 40–4, 52–4, 57,* 60. Relevant to the period and contain a wide variety commissions, warrants, reports, letters, and instructions.

C.O. 325. *Colonies General, Miscellanea. Vols. 1–4.* Tracts and historical sketches of the colonies, together with some letters and representations, 1753–77.

Vol. 5. Return of fees of offices compiled by the Governors in accordance with an instruction of 1764.

Vol. 6. Memoir on the West Indian trade, but only a few pages cover the period before 1783.

C.O. 326. *Colonies General, Registers.* Registers of Board of Trade papers, 1702–82.

C.O. 388. *Board of Trade, Original Correspondence. Vols. 51–74.* Various aspects of colonial trade, 1763–82.

Vols. 75–84. Expense accounts and other papers.

Vol. 95. Consular reports on the existing state of trade of British subjects in each consular district, 1765–6.

C.O. 389. *Board of Trade, Entry Books.* Entry books of correspondence, patents, conventions, expense accounts, and papers relating to Ireland, 1780.

C.O. 390. *Board of Trade, Miscellanea.* A few customs house statistics in *Vol. 5;* and some export-import statistics in *Vols. 9–10,* none later than 1771.

C.O. 391. *Board of Trade, Minutes.* Journals of the Board of Trade together with the original minutes of the proceedings, etc. (These have been printed in full, from April 1704 to May 1782, when the Board was abolished, as *Journals of the Commissioners for Trade and Plantations*, London, 1920–38, 14 vols.)

C.O. 412. *Duplicates, 1605–1863.* This class occasionally contains copies of documents which are missing in their original series. *Vol. 1.* Miscellaneous papers, America and West Indies, to 1794.

Vols. 3–26. Acts, dispatches, and sessional papers of the various colonies.

CUSTOMS AND EXCISE

The records of the Customs and Excise are in a number of locations, hence one main entry has been made in the London section, which describes the general body of these records.

HIGH COURT OF DELEGATES

The High Court of Delegates exercised an appellate jurisdiction from the Instance Court of the High Court of Admiralty, hence probably contains relevant material. The record classes are:

Del. 1. *Processes*, 1609–1834. Official copies of the proceedings of first instance in causes before the Court.

Del. 2. *Cause Papers, c.* 1600–1834. Unbound copies of the proceedings.

Del. 5. *Sentences*, 1585–1802.

Del. 6. *Assignation Books*, 1650–1829.

Del. 8. *Miscellanea.* Account books, bills seal accounts, etc., 1609–1866; draft instruments, 1760–1833; repertory books (list of cases before the Delegates, with brief notes of their commissions, their nature, etc.), 1619–1789.

EXCHEQUER

King's (or Queen's) Remembrancer's Department

The voluminous records of the Court of Exchequer contain certain references to the American colonies in the latter part of the 18th century, principally in suits between English and American merchants.

The most important series are: **E. 112.** *Bills and Answers:* **E. 130.** *Decrees;* **E. 131.** *Orders;* **E. 133.** *Barons' Depositions;* **E. 161.** *Minute Books;* **E. 194.** *Reports and Certificates;* **E. 140.** *Exhibits.*

Among the revenue records: **E. 190.** *Port Books.* Entry books kept in the various English ports of goods imported and exported, giving full descriptions of shipments, merchants' names, etc. (This class supercedes **E. 122,** *Customs Accounts*, which for the 18th century give only notes of seizures, tonnage rolls, etc.)

Lord Treasurer's Remembrancer's and Pipe Offices.

E. 351. *Declared Accounts (Pipe Office Series).* Duplicate of Audit Office, **A.O. 1.**

E. 368. *Memoranda Rolls.* Contains the enrolment of commissions, other letters patent and writs relating to Exchequer business.

EXCHEQUER AND AUDIT

(Lists and Indexes, II, 1893; XLVI, 1921)

A.O. 1. *Declared Accounts (in Rolls).* Contains the accounts of Richard, Viscount Howe, one of the Peace Commissioners to America, 1777–8; the accounts of various commissaries, barrack-masters, commanders, military governors, contractors, expeditions, agents and superintendents of Indian affairs, the stamp duties of 1765, etc. (Andrews II, 81–106)
This is a duplicate of **E. 351.**

A.O. 2. *Declared and Passed Accounts (in Books).* In addition to being a continuation of **A.O. 1,** this class includes the accounts of the Admiralty Court and some material on Loyalist claims.

A.O. 3. *Accounts Various.* Contains accounts of payments to foreign troops . . . Hessians, 1776–84; accounts of many governors, officials, and military officers in the American colonies and Canada; papers and books of many officers and officials; entry book of letters and reports, America, 1775–8, on commissariat matters; commissariat accounts, America, 1777–83; customs receipts at American plantations, 1777–86; hospitals, 1763–80; American stamp duties, 1765–72. (Andrews II, 66–81)

A.O. 12. *American Loyalist Claims,* Series I, 1776–1831. Entry books and ledgers containing evidence of witnesses, reports and other communicated documents, examinations, and decisions of the Commissioners.

A.O. 13. *American Loyalist Claims,* Series II, 1780–1835. Original claims and supporting documents, examinations, etc.

A.O. 16. *Miscellanea.* Exemplification of 1775–7 accounts of Lord Dunmore, Governor of Virginia.

A.O. 17. *Absorbed Accounts.* Comptroller of Army Accounts: minutes and reports contain material relevant to British forces in America, 1763–83.

FOREIGN OFFICE

The Foreign Office began as an independent department in 1782 with the appointment of a Secretary of State solely concerned with foreign affairs. The Foreign Office records continue the various series of State Papers Foreign in the State Paper Office and consist mainly of the dispatches of ambassadors and consuls abroad and the archives of embassies and legations.

F.O. 4. *General Correspondence, United States of America,* Series I, 1782–92. This series includes correspondence between David Hartley and the Secretary of State, 1782–4, with enclosed and supplementary letters concerning the peace treaty, many copies of American papers, resolutions of Congress, etc. There is also a bundle of petitions presenting various claims of British officers and American Loyalists, which supplements the Loyalist material in **A.O. 12–13** and **T. 79.** The papers of John Temple, Consul-General to America, though dated 1783–5, frequently contain useful retrospective material.

F.O. 9. *General Correspondence, Bavaria,* 1781–3.

F.O. 27. *General Correspondence, France,* 1781–3. *Vol. 557.* Contains various letters of Fox, Franklin, Grenville, Richard Oswald; advices and intelligences; letters and papers of the Duke of Manchester and Mr Fitzherbert in Paris relating to the negotiations.

F.O. 31. *General Correspondence, Germany, States,* 1781–3. Cologne and Hesse-Cassel.

F.O. 33. *General Correspondence, Hamburg and Hanse Town,* 1781–3.

F.O. 37. *General Correspondence, Holland and The Netherlands,* 1781–3.

F.O. 64. *General Correspondence, Prussia and Germany,* 1781–3.

F.O. 65. *General Correspondence, Prussia and Germany,* 1781–3.

F.O. 65. *General Correspondence, Russia,* 1781–3. Letters and papers of Sir James Harris and Consul Walter Shairp at St Petersburg to the Secretary of State, with draft replies, 1781–3.

F.O. 68. *General Correspondence, Saxony,* 1780–1783.

F.O. 72. *General Correspondence, Spain,* 1781–3. Letters and papers of the British Commander at Gibraltar, the Ambassador and various consuls in Spain, and Hussey, Munro, and Hunter in England to the Secretary of State. Many papers relating to the Hussey–Cumberland mission and to the attempt of Spain to seize the Floridas.

F.O. 73. *General Correspondence, Sweden,* 1781–3. Some letters from Sir Thomas Wroughton, Charles Keene, and Consul Thomas Erskine.

F.O. 83. *Great Britain and General. Vol. 1.* Admiralty reports concerning American prisoners and prizes, 1776.
Vol. 7. A few items on Hessian auxiliaries and rebel prisoners.
Vol. 8. Some Loyalist petitions.

F.O. 93. *Protocols of Treaties,* 1778–83. These are instruments recording the agreements reached by the negotiators.

F.O. 94. *Ratifications of Treaties,* 1782–3.

F.O. 95. *Miscellanea,* Series I. *Piece 2.* Large bundle including many intelligence letters from Paris, 1781; information on the French fleet under de Grasse, 1781; correspondence relating John Robinson to William Knox, 1781.
Piece 8. Letters, dispatches and enclosures between the Secretary of State and Carleton, but a few also of Haldimand and James Robertson.
Pieces 391–2. Admiralty northern letter books 1761–91.
Pieces 531, 535. Letters and papers concerning the peace between England and America, 1782–3, consisting of correspondence from Shelburne, Franklin, Strachey, Richard Oswald and others.

F.O. 97. *Supplement to the General Correspondence*, from 1780. *Vols. 1–5.* Letters, papers and intelligences from various persons at The Hague, 1781–3.

F.O. 148. *France, Miscellanea.* 1782–3. Correspondence and papers relating to special missions, conferences, trade, etc.

F.O. 353. *Jackson Papers.* Mainly post-date 1783, but *Vols. 2–7* and *30–4* contain letter books, 1772–82, with a few letters on the British efforts to hire Russian troops for service in America, 1775; but the bulk of the material pertains to the hiring of German troops. There is also some correspondence of Hugh Elliot with Stormont, Fox, Grantham and Suffolk, 1777–82, and some letters of William Eden, 1776.

HOME OFFICE

(Lists and Indexes XLIII, 1914)

The department which eventually became the Home Office was created in 1782 when the Secretary of State for the Southern Department became Secretary of State for Home Affairs. The Home Office records pertinent to the Revolution are continuations of the various classes in State Papers Domestic.

H.O. 28. *Admiralty Correspondence. Vols. 1–3,* 1782–3. Contain numerous letters on the problems caused by and the exchange of American prisoners, transport of German troops, recruiting in England, intelligence of French naval moves, etc.

H.O. 29. *Admiralty Entry Books. Vol. 1,* 1779–83. Consists entirely of warrants, commissions and instructions from the King to the Admiralty.

H.O. 32. *Foreign Office Correspondence. Vol. 1,* 1782–9. Contains some papers regarding German auxiliaries, with abstracts of the various treaties with the minor German princes, and a few papers pertaining to Loyalists and trade.

H.O. 35. *Treasury and Customs Correspondence.* Includes colonial correspondence, 1781–90.

H.O. 36. *Treasury Entry Books. Vols. 1–6,* 1776–89. Out-letters recording such parts of colonial administration as the Treasury turned over to the Secretary of State and correspond with **T. 1.**

H.O. 38. *Warrant Books. Vol. 1,* 1782–4. Shelburne's warrant book which contains, for example, the warrants for the commission of Richard Oswald to treat for peace in 1782.

H.O. 42. *Domestic Correspondence, George III. Vols. 1–3,* 40, 1782–3. Many in-letters and petitions concerning America, mostly of a routine nature, but there is also a number of letters from Richard Oswald to Townshend, a draft of a commercial treaty with America, etc.

H.O. 43. *Domestic Entry Book.* Out-letters, 1782–3

H.O. 49. *Law Officers' Letter Books.* Include correspondence about cases involving the American colonies and the war, 1771–84, dealing with prisoners, prizes, treason, etc.

H.O. 50. *Military Correspondence. Vol. 1*, 1782–6. Letters from the Commander-in-Chief, the Secretary at War, and other military officials relating to internal defence, the court martial of Major Stanhope, 1782, and some American Loyalist regiments.

H.O. 51. *Military Entry Books. Vols. 1–139*, 1758–88. Contain some American entries of commissions, appointments, and warrants relative to the militia, volunteers, ordnance, etc.

H.O. 55. *Addresses Miscellaneous.* Petitions and addresses to the Home Secretary, a substantial number bearing on the American rebellion, the war and the peace, and some seeking redress of grievances stemming therefrom.

H.O. 88. *Fees*, Series I. Entries of fees paid for royal grants and licences, military commissions, etc., and account books.

KING'S (OR QUEEN'S) BENCH COURT

The King's (or Queen's) Bench was the highest court of common law and dealt with matters directly concerning the King or the maintenance of the 'King's peace'.

It seems probable that **K.B. 27.** *Crown Rolls*, which are the main record for *quo warranto* proceedings in England, also contain cases in which the charters of American colonies were held in question.

The most important records to use in conjunction with the *Crown Rolls* are **K.B. 21.** *Rule or Order Books.*

PAYMASTER-GENERAL'S OFFICE

(*Lists and Indexes* XLVI, 1921)

P.M.G. 4. *Half Pay and Retired Pay Ledgers,* from 1737.

P.M.G. 14. *Miscellaneous Books.* These include the accounts of the Deputy Paymaster for America, 1755–72; accounts of extraordinary expenses in America, such as payments to Loyalists, the expenses of the various generals, etc., 1753–82; entry books of letters and powers-of-attorney from 1759 pertaining to the pay and affairs of British officers in America.

P.M.G. 2. *Ledgers*, from 1757. Yearly and half-yearly accounts of the expenditure and receipts of regiments, garrisons, etc.

PRIVY COUNCIL

P.C. 1. *Unbound Papers*, 1763–83. Various reports, letters, and other documents, arranged by year, pertaining to the affairs of the Council. The years 1765–6, 1770 and 1774 contain considerable material pertaining to the repercussions of the Stamp Act in the colonies, the Boston riots of 1774, and other disturbances.

P.C. 2. *Privy Council Register.* The register contains a record of the proceedings of the Privy Council, consisting of all references, instructions, approvals, confirmations, orders, etc., pertaining to business brought before it. Copies of documents and reports are also included.

P.C. 3. *Privy Council Minutes.* These supplement the register in that they record every matter that came before the Council and its committees, whereas the register only records those resulting in an order, letter, or other action.

P.C. 5. *Plantations Books.* Copies of colonial acts, confirmations, charters, instructions, letters, etc., issued to Governors and other colonial officials.

(The items of colonial interest to 1783 in the Privy Council Register, *Unbound Papers* and *Plantation Books*, have been calendared in James Munro, ed., *Acts of the Privy Council—Colonial Series*, London 1908–12, 6 vols.)

PRIVY SEAL OFFICE

IND. 6744–67. *Docquet Books* and **P.S.O. 3.** *Warrants for Privy Seal*, Series III. Both valuable for the issue of letters patent.

PUBLIC RECORD OFFICE

P.R.O. 30. *Gifts and Deposits*:

P.R.O. 30/55. *Carleton Papers.* Records of the British Army Headquarters in America, 1775–83, representing the official notes of Gage, Howe, Clinton and Carleton as successive commanders-in-chief. (Formerly in the Royal Institution of Great Britain. See HMC 59, 1904–9, 4 vols., for a calendar. Copies of these documents are in *The Stevens Transcripts* at the British Museum, *Additional Manuscripts* **42257–496.** See also Randolph G. Adams, *The Headquarters Papers of the British Army in North America during the War of the American Revolution*, Ann Arbor, Mich., 1926)

P.R.O. 30/8. *Chatham Papers.* Papers of William Pitt, 1st Earl of Chatham (1708–78) and his son William Pitt the younger (1759–1806).

P.R.O. 30/11. *Cornwallis Papers.* These include 59 bundles of official papers of Charles, 2nd Earl Cornwallis and 1st Marquis Cornwallis (1738–1805). The American papers are calendared and partially abstracted in George H. Reese, comp., *The Cornwallis Papers: Abstracts of Americana,* Charlottesville, Va., University Press of Virginia, 1970. Microfilms are held at the Library of Congress, Alderman Library of the University of Virginia, Virginia State Library, Virginia Historical Society, and Research Library of Colonial Williamsburg. Many documents have also been published in Charles Ross, ed., *Correspondence of Charles, 1st Marquis Cornwallis,* London, 1859, 3 vols.

P.R.O. 30/39. *Documents of Unknown Authorship.* Contains 15 letters of Surgeon Richard Hope to relatives in England from Quebec, Boston, New York, and the *British King* off Staten Island, 1770–82, with a copy of the *Noon Gazette and Boston Weekly News-Letter* for 17 August 1775.

P.R.O. 30/15. *Manchester Papers.* Included are the papers of George Montagu, 4th Duke of Manchester (1737–88), with many relating to his opposition to governmental policy and role in the peace negotiations of 1783. (See HMC 8, Appendix, Part II, 1881, 1–166)

P.R.O. 30/26. *Miscellaneous. Exchequer (?).* American Loyalist Claims Commission, warrant for payment to Archibald Hamilton, 18 March 1789.

P.R.O. 30/20. *Rodney Papers.* Miscellaneous journals and correspondence of Adm. George Brydges Rodney (1719–92), with notes and pedigrees relating to the Rodney and Harley families.

P.R.O. 31. *Transcripts*

P.R.O. 31/14. *Venetian Archives.* Transcripts of dispatches, diaries, and reports of Venetian ambassadors. *Vols. 157–8.* Benjamin Franklin and America to 1784.

SIGNET OFFICE

IND. 6801–28. *Docquet Books* and **S.O. 7.** *King's Bills.* Both valuable for the issue of letters patent.

STATE PAPER OFFICE

(*Lists and Indexes,* XIX 1904, XLIII, 1914)

Prior to 1782, the State Paper Office was the repository for the papers of the

Secretaries of State. Within the office papers were divided into *State Papers Domestic* and *State Papers Foreign*. In 1782, however, the Secretaries of State for the Southern and Northern Departments became Secretary of State for Home Affairs and Foreign Affairs respectively. After approximately 1782, therefore, the State Paper Office series end and are continued in the series of the Home and Foreign Offices.

State Papers Domestic

S.P. 37. *George III, 1760–82. Vols. 1–26*, 1761–81. Letters and papers on many subjects concerning America, many mercantile addresses, minutes of cabinet meetings, etc. (Most of these papers are detailed in *Calendar of Home Office Papers 1760–1775*, London, 1878–99, 4 vols., but due to rearrangement within the series, this calendar is not particularly useful)

S.P. 41. *Military. Vol. 26.* Contains plans for the relief of America and the West Indies, 1773–7; some letters concerning Burgoyne, the defence of England, John Paul Jones, American provincial troops; papers relating to the Stamp Act riots, munitions for North America, etc.

S.P. 42. *Naval.* Admiralty and supplementary letters, 1763–82, contain many on military operations, prizes, prisoners, dispatches of Germain; the law reports letters discuss some cases of American prizes.

S.P. 44. *Entry Books.* Drafts, copies and minutes of out-letters, most dealing with routine matters such as passes, petitions, accounts, etc.

S.P. 45. *Various.* Precedent Books, Proclamations, and Fee Books for the Revolutionary period.

S.P. 47. *Channel Island,* to 1782. Details of war materials ordered from Europe by America, abstracted from the papers of American ships taken into Guernsey.

S.P. 54. *Scotland to 1783*, Series II. Contains considerable American material.

S.P. 9. *Miscellaneous.* Letters patent appointing Governor Bernard a Baronet, 1769; original letter appointing Shelburne Secretary of State; pamphlet of instructions for English ships privateering against the Dutch, 1780.

State Papers Foreign

S.P. 78. *France, 1763–80.* Correspondence of the Ambassador, Lord Stormont, from 1772.

S.P. 81. *Germany, States. Vols. 154–7.* Correspondence with Cologne, 1775–80.

Vols. 181–96. Correspondence of William Faucitt and Charles Rainford, 1775–84. All the correspondence deals with German troops in America.

S.P. 82. *Hamburg and Hanse Towns,* to 1780.

S.P. 84. *Holland,* 1772–80. Mainly letters of Sir Joseph Yorke.

S.P. 89. *Portugal,* 1773–80. Letters of Robert Walpole.

S.P. 90. *Prussia,* 1777–80. Mainly letters of Hugh Elliot.

S.P. 91. *Russia,* 1775–80.

S.P. 94. *Spain.* Letters of Lord Grantham, 1774–9, and Richard Cumberland, 1780.

S.P. 100. *Foreign Ministers in England,* to 1780. Letters and memorials from foreign ministers accredited to the British Court, arranged chronilogically under countries.

S.P. 102. *Royal Letters,* to 1780. *Vol. 13.* Anspach and Baden; *Vol. 16.* Brunswick; *Vol. 17.* Cologne and Mentz; *Vol. 20.* Hesse Cassel; *Vol. 21.* Hesse Darmstadt; *Vols. 28–9.* Waldeck, Hanau, and Anhalt-Zerbst.

S.P. 104. *Entry Books,* to 1783. Official letter books and registers with copies or extracts of out-letters, but not a complete record.

BOARD OF TRADE

(*Lists and Indexes* XLVI, 1921)

The Lords of Trade and Plantations, whose main responsibility was the American colonies, were abolished in 1782 and their records ultimately incorporated into the archives of the Colonial Office. The modern Board of Trade was established by William Pitt in 1784, hence its records do not bear on the Revolution, with one exception.

B.T. 6. *Miscellanea.* Contains Custom and Excise Accounts, accounts of imports and exports, and of foreign tariffs, etc., 1780–1832, which include some material on British commercial intercourse with North America.

TREASURY

(*Lists and Indexes* XLVI, 1921)

T. 1. *Treasury Papers, In-Letters.* The American material for 1763–83 is detailed in Andrews II, 168–200, and reveals rich material on customs affairs, smuggling, the Molasses and Stamp Acts, the growth of American disaffection as viewed by British customs agents and revenue officials, as well as material on military and naval commissary problems during the war.

T. 2. *Registers of Papers*, from 1777. Brief entries of letters and papers, indicating subject and date, etc.

T. 3. *Skelton Registers*, from 1783. Useful for tracing transferred papers.

T. 4. *Reference Books*. Index to papers transferred to other departments.

T. 11. *Customs Letters*. Detailed lists of customs establishments, instructions to collectors occasioned by the Revenue Acts of the 1760s, etc.

T. 27. *Out-Letter Books—General*, 1763–83. Many letters relating to America and American correspondents.

T. 28. *Out-Letter Books—Various*, 1763–83. *Vols. 1–2*, 1763–97, known as 'the America Books', are colonial warrant and commission books.

T. 29. *Treasury Minute Books*, 1763–83. Record of the chief matters coming before the Board of Treasury. *Vol. 628*, for example, is Copies of Minutes relating to the American War, 1771–7.

T. 30. *Accounts General—Yearly*, 1763–83. Includes receipts on sugar and tobacco and returns of the $4\frac{1}{2}\%$.

T. 31. *Accounts General—Quarterly*. Quarterly revenue accounts from 1701, containing the plantation duty, expenses of the Board of Trade, cost of civil establishments in America, and salaries of British officials in America.

T. 33. *Accounts General—Declarations (Auditor's)*. Brief declarations of receipts and expenses, among which are occasional items relating to the colonies.

T. 34. *Accounts General—Plantations, Pells*, to 1783. These probably duplicate **T. 33.**

T. 38. *Accounts Departmental*. Contains colonial customs accounts, accounts of German troops in America, 1776–84, and Paymaster-General's accounts of extraordinary expenses, 1782–3.

T. 42. *Register, Establishments, Customs*. Quarterly establishment books for London and the outports, including names of American customs officials.

T. 47. *Register, Various. Vols. 9–12*. Contain details of emigrants from England and Scotland to America, 1773–6.

T. 50. *Documents relating to Refugees. Vols. 1–28, 31–56*. Accounts of colonial militia and compensation and pension lists for Loyalists, 1780–1836.

T. 52. *Warrants, King's,* to 1783.

T. 53. *Warrants Relating to Money,* to 1783.

T. 54. *Warrants Not Relating to Money,* to 1786.

T. 56. *Four and a Half Per Cent,* 1765–83.

T. 60. *Order Books,* to 1783. Brief entries of orders on the Tellers of the Exchequer resulting from the issue of warrants, Acts of Parliament, etc.

T. 64. *Miscellanea, Various.* Lists of provincial regiments, 1783; exchange of prisoners, 1779–82; shipping returns; customs fees; commissariat matters —correspondence and accounts; accounts of imports and exports to 1783. (Andrews II, 235–54)

T. 77. *East Florida Claims Commission.* Claims and compensation resulting from the cession of East Florida to Spain, 1783.

T. 79. *American Loyalist Claims Commission.* Mostly minute books of the commissioners with reports on individual claims. (Names of claimants are printed in *Lists and Indexes,* XLVI, 105–10. See also **A.O. 12–13**)

TREASURY SOLICITOR

The function of the Treasury Solicitor was to attend the King's Counsel in all revenue cases in the Exchequer, to inspect the offices in the Exchequer so that all proceedings would be carried out without delay, and to make strict inquiry into all warrants which might diminish the royal revenue. At one point, the Treasury Solicitor was also responsible for political prosecutions as well. (Andrews II, 266–9, notes 17 cases pertaining to America between 1756 and 1793 which have interest for the Revolution.) The papers are private and can only be inspected by permission of the Solicitor. The one exception is:

Records of the West New Jersey Society, **T.S. 12,** 1675–1921. Consisting of in-letters, entry books, minute books, ledgers, accounts, share registers, and a history of the Society.

WAR OFFICE

(*Lists and Indexes* LIII, 1903, for an alphabetical guide; XXVIII, 1908, for a listing of many of the classes)

W.O. 1. *In-Letters, Secretary at War,* to 1783. Much correspondence with Gage, Howe, Burgoyne, Amherst, Clinton, etc., on many subjects; departmental correspondence; statistics; parliamentary orders.

W.O. 2. *Indexes* to **W.O. 1,** usually with a brief abstract.

W.O. 3. *Out-Letters, Commander in Chief,* Series II, 1765–86. Contains drafts of routine letters to the colonies.

W.O. 4. *Out-Letters, Secretary at War,* 1756–84. Contains *inter alia* letters, instructions, and warrants to officers serving in America; the Press Act; 5 vols. of American letter books, 1763–84.

W.O. 5. *Marching Orders,* to 1783. Embarkation and disembarkation orders for America but no marching orders.

W.O. 7. *Out Letters, Departmental,* to 1783. Letters from the colonies and orders for the embarkation of troops to the colonies.

W.O. 12. *Muster Books and Pay Lists,* 1757–83. Listing of regiments and personnel serving in America.

W.O. 17. *Monthly Returns,* 1759–82. Distribution of each regiment in the Army.

W.O. 18. *Vouchers for Disbursements, Artillery,* from 1770. Contains pay receipts for nurses at American hospitals.

W.O. 24. *Registers of Military Establishments.* Troop lists for America and royal warrants authorizing the establishment of regular and militia regiments in America.

W.O. 25. *Registers Various.* Personnel registers of various kinds, such as Commission Books of officers, Notification Books, Regimental Succession Books, and embarkation returns.

W.O. 28. *Miscellanea,* 1775–83. *Vols. 1–10.* Headquarters Records, America containing garrison and regimental returns, general and field officers' letters, order books, petitions, etc.

W.O. 34. *Amherst Papers.* Papers of Jeffrey Amherst (1717–97) as Commander-in-Chief in America, 1753–63, Governor of Virginia, 1768, and Commander-in-Chief in Britain, from 1778.

W.O. 36. *American Rebellion Entry Books,* 1773–83. 4 small folio entry books:
    M.H. 334. 'Orders, America, from 10 June 1773 to [10 June] 1776', containing extracts of orders to the British Army in America.
    M.H. 335. 'Rhode Island, 1776–1779', extracts of orders from commanders in Rhode Island including Clinton, Lord Percy and Brig.-Gen. Smith.
    M.H. 336. 'Returns, America, 1776–1783', including Howe's force at Boston, 17 March 1776; comparative view of the expenditures in certain departments during the commands of Howe and Clinton; distribution of the British Army in America at various dates, etc.; list of the troops of the Hesse

Cassel Cavalry and Infantry, showing regiment, date raised, commanders, numbers, stations, etc.

M.H. 337. Volume of copies of capitulations during the revolutionary war, including St Johns, Saratoga, Pensacola, etc.

(Described by Andrews and Davenport, 188, as being in the War Office (now Ministry of Defence) library; but were transferred to PRO in 1927)

W.O. 40. *Selected Un-numbered Papers. Bundles 1–28,* 1753–83. Various petitions, memorials and applications to the Secretary at War concerning matters outside the routine of the office. There are, for example, several reports on disturbances at Boston, 1770 and 1773, and a report by Carleton on the condition of affairs at Quebec, 1776.

W.O. 42. *Certificates, of Births, Baptisms, Marriages, and Deaths. Vols. 59–63.* Loyal American and Canadian Corps, 1776–83.

W.O. 46. *Ordnance Office, Out-Letters,* 1762–83. Some references to America, especially in *Vol. 13.*

W.O. 47. *Ordnance Office, General Minutes and Journal of Proceedings,* 1763–81. A few American entries.

W.O. 48. *Ordnance Office, Ledgers.* Summaries of expenditures under various headings.

W.O. 49. *Accounts Various. Vols. 284–5.* Many papers relating to military operations in America, 1711–1800.

W.O. 51. *Ordnance Office, Bill Books,* Series II. Quarterly accounts, many of which pertain to America between 1763–83.

W.O. 55. *Ordnance Office, Miscellanea.* Letters, returns, estimates, etc., some of which pertain to America.

W.O. 60. *Commissariat Accounts.* Victualling of the Army and Navy in America, 1774–84.

W.O. 64. *Army Lists.* Miscellaneous series to 1783. Useful for tracing officers, usually gives some career details.

W.O. 65. *Annual Army Lists.* Printed lists, 1754–83. (Similar to **W.O. 64.**)

W.O. 69. *Artillery Records of Service,* 1765–83. Listings of non-commissioned officers and enlisted men.

W.O. 71. *Judge Advocate General's Records, Courts Martial.* Proceedings.

71/61. The trial of the Col. the Hon. Cosmo Gordon for neglect of duty at Springfield, North America, 1782. *Vol. 46* contains American Courts Martial Records.

There is related material in **W.O. 85, 89, 93**.

W.O. 76. *Records of Officers's Services*, 1771–83. Includes some personal as well as career details.

W.O. 81. *Judge Advocate General's Records, Correspondence.*
81/13. Lt.-Gen. John Burgoyne: failure of the Albany Expedition, 1778.

W.O. 97. *Regular Army Soldiers' Documents,* from 1760. Documents pertaining to enlisted men.

Royal Artillery Institution (The Library), Woolwich
London SE18

MS. 58. Sir William Howe, 5th Viscount Howe (1729–1814). 1 volume of general orders, 27 September 1777 to 21 February 1778, of his North American command.

MS. 19. 'Book of Returns, Etc. for the Corps of Artillery in Canada Commencing the 1st July 1778', 2 vols., 1778–83.
Vol. 1. Orders, monthly returns of forces, etc., and copies of letters, Quebec and elsewhere, Forbes Macbean to Pattison, Townshend and others concerning defences, supplies, etc.
Vol. 2. Lists ordnance and ordnance stores at various posts in Canada, 1778 and 1783.

MS. 57. 5 volumes of papers of James Pattison (1724–1805?), commander in New York, 1779–80. 'Brigade Orders, Royal Artillery, from September 28, 1777 till February 21, 1778 by Brigadier General James Pattison'.

MS. 11. 'Warrants, Bills of Lading. Record of Commissions, Day Book', containing warrants by Pattison, bills of lading for artillery supplies, 1779, record of commissions, 1779–80, day book for New York command, 1779–80. Also 'Orders and Regulations of the Superintendent General of the police of the city of New York . . . authorized by Major General Jones', 1778–9.

MS. 9. *Vol. 1.* Letters, mainly from New York, 10 January 1779 to 11 January 1781, to Amherst, Clinton, Germain, Townshend and others, concerning the progress of the war. (microfilm in Library of Congress)
Vol. 2. Letters, Philadelphia and New York, 10 July 1779 to 18 August 1780, to many correspondents, mainly concerning his administration of New York. (Microfilm in Library of Congress)

(Crick and Alman, 295–6)

Royal Society, Burlington House, Piccadilly
London W1

The large archives of the Society deal mainly with scientific matters (for their American material, Andrews and Davenport, 355–68). The only reference of interest for the Revolution is the letters of Sir Charles Blagden (1748–1820), a physician who served with the British forces in America and returned to England, 1780. A few letters from colleagues still in America comment on the military and naval situation, 1780, the peace negotiations, 1783, and the exodus of Loyalists to Nova Scotia.

Royal Society of Arts, John Adam Street
London WC2

Founded in 1754 for the encouragement of arts, manufacturing and commerce, the Society counted among its early objectives the development of potash and pearl-ash manufacturing and mulberry tree growing-silk manufacture in the American colonies. The Society has considerable records for the revolutionary period but the American material (Crick and Alman, 302–8) pertains mainly to the technical aspects of the development of colonial agriculture and manufacturing.

Royal United Service Institution, Whitehall
London SW1

MILITARY MANUSCRIPTS

Vol. 99. Proceedings of the general court martial held at Brunswick, N.J., 1778, by George Washington for the trial of Maj.-Gen. Charles Lee, 212 pp.

*Vol. 125, no. 91.*Lists showing the British Army in the retreat from Philadelphia, 1777, and at the 'Repulse of Stono Ferry, S.C.', 1779, 2 pp.;
    no. 110. 'America: State of the Provincial Army on the 31st May 1776', giving the number of men and the stations of various regiments, 6 pp.

(Crick and Alman, 309)

Sion College, Victoria Embankment
London EC4

The Pamphlet Collection, catalogued under 'Americana', contains a large number of 18th-century pieces, including some revolutionary ones. (Crick and Alman, 312)

Society of Friends (The Library), Friends House, Euston Road
London NW1

PENN MANUSCRIPTS, 1682–1779

Vol. II, 113. 'An Account of the Grant of Pennsylvania to William Penn Esquire with an Account of the Sales and other Dispositions of Land made by said William Penn the first Proprietor thereof and by other succeeding Proprietors from and between the 4th Day of March 1680–1 to December 1776, . . . Together with an Estimate of the value of various Articles of Property, which belonged to the Honorable John Penn Junior and the Honorable John Penn Senior in the year 1779: before the 27th Day of November in the same year, when the Act of Assembly was passed entituled "An Act for Vesting the Estate of the late Proprietories of Pennsylvania in the Commonwealth".

Vol. II, 114, c. 1779. Duplicate of a 'Form of an affidavit to be made by Mr. Physick, late receiver and agent of heirs and proprietors of Pennsylvania, and the schedule to be annex'd'.

(Andrews and Davenport, 354)

MISCELLANEOUS CORRESPONDENCE

Copies of letters, 1766–76, from Dr John Fothergill to William Logan and James Pemberton (originals in the Library of the Historical Society of Pennsylvania).

Copy of a letter, 13 March 1776, from David Barclay to Benjamin Franklin (original at the American Philosophical Society).

(Crick and Alman, 218)

QUAKER JOURNALS

Rachel Wilson (1720–75), journal of a visit to America, 1768–9, MS. and typescript copies. (Crick and Alman, 216)

Society for Promoting Christian Knowledge
Holy Trinity Church, Marylebone Road
London NW1

The Society undertook missionary work in America only from 1698–1701, after which it mainly sent religious material such as books and pamphlets.

Possibly relevant information could be found in the Salzburg Emigration Papers, 8 volumes and loose papers, consisting of accounts and correspondence relating to the settlement of German Protestant exiles in Georgia, 1731–71. (Crick and Alman, 312)

Society for the Propagation of the Gospel in Foreign Parts. See United Society for the Propagation of the Gospel

United Society for the Propagation of the Gospel
15 Tufton Street
London SW1

Formerly the Society for the Propagation of the Gospel in Foreign Parts, it amalgamated with the Universities Mission to Central Africa in 1965 to become the United Society. Founded in 1701, the American colonies were its chief field of work until the Revolution. The Society's archives and the Fulham MSS. in the Library at Lambeth Palace are the two basic collections for the history of the colonial church. The archives include many letters from colonial governors and officials, contain many insights into the conditions of colonial life, the effect of the Revolution on the church, and about the roles of leading Loyalist ministers, such as Samuel Seabury and Charles Inglis. There are 6 classes of records relevant to the revolutionary period:

'B' MSS

Letters received, 25 bound vols., 1709–99, and 16 boxes of unbound papers, 1701–1800. The later letters have some reference to the problems encountered by the Society's workers during and after the Revolution. (Microfilm in Library of Congress of bound material)

'C' MSS

Miscellaneous unbound MSS. relating to colonies, 16 boxes, 1630–1811. Much correspondence, most of it pre-Revolution, and treatises on the state of the church in various colonies.

'X' MSS

Letters sent (copies): *Vol. 141*, 1773–8; *Vol. 142*, 1778–84. Devoted almost exclusively to America, dealing especially with the affairs of the Church of England in the rebel colonies.

PRINTED REPORTS

Printed Reports of the Society, 1704–, give lists of missionaries in America up to the Revolution, and extracts of their letters and other material relating to the state of the church in the colonies.

JOURNALS AND MINUTES

Journal and minutes of the Society and its Committees, 1701–, 107 vols., 1714–1833.

Minutes of the meetings of the Standing (executive) Committee, 64 vols. rough copy, 1714–1819.

MSS. OF DR BRAY'S ASSOCIATES

Founded c. 1695, to provide support for the establishment of clerical libraries and the education of negroes in the plantations.

2 vols. of minute books, 1735–68, including abstracts of letters received from the plantations.

Account book, 1777–1800, with statements of salaries paid to schoolmasters in the plantations, etc.

(Crick and Alman, 313–15. Andrews and Davenport, 335. Some of the documents in the Society's archives have been published in Hawks and Perry, eds., and Perry, ed.—see *Lambeth Palace* entry)

University of London Library, Senate House
London WC1

GOLDSMITH'S LIBRARY OF ECONOMIC LITERATURE

The largest special collection in the University Library, Goldsmith's contains over 60,000 books and pamphlets covering the 16th–19th centuries and 400 manuscripts. Of special interest for the study of the Revolution is the large pamphlet collection which contains over 80 pamphlets directly related to the Revolution, especially for the years 1766–7 and 1775. (Margaret Canney and David Knott, *Catalogue of the Goldsmith's Library of Economic Literature, Printed Books to 1800* Vol. I, London, 1970, Vols. II and III forthcoming)

John Baker Holroyd, 1st Earl of Sheffield (1735–1821), MS. 139: French translation, 1784, of his *Observations of the Commerce of the American States*, London, 1783.

PORTEUS LIBRARY

150 uncatalogued volumes of pamphlets with extensive sections on the Revolution and on the West Indian slave trade, 1772–1807.

Sir Samuel Romilly, letter, 2 September 1785, to John Baynes, a fellow member of Gray's Inn, containing comment on the American Ambassador John Adams and his daughter.

Westminster, Archdiocese of, Archibishop's House
London SW1

Archives in the keeping of the Archbishop of Westminster.

Section A Main Series
Vol. 31, **208.** Supression of the Jesuits: names of the Jesuits in England and America, enclosed in a letter of submission by Thomas Saunders, 1773.
Vol. 40, **173–4.** Printed papers: *The* 'Defence of John Ury' and 'New Lightmen', Philadelphia, *c.* 1781.

Section B. **33–46.** 14 vols. of *c.* 1000 letters, unindexed, 1701–84, mainly correspondence of the agents in Rome of the English Vicars Apostolic, very few American references.

Section H. 26 bound vols. of pamphlets, including a few relating to Catholicism in America before 1824.

(Crick and Alman, 344–6)

MIDDLESEX

Middlesex County Record Office, 1 Queen Anne's Gate Buildings
Dartmouth Street
London SW1

Sessions Papers of the Sessions Gaol of Delivery at Newgate (Middlesex Prisoners), held at the Old Bailey, 1755–96. These records are fully listed but not yet indexed and contain minor information about American privateer attacks on British ships, confiscations, etc.

NORFOLK

Colonel Q. E. Gurney, Bawdeswell Hall
Bawdeswell

GURNEY AND BARCLAY FAMILY PAPERS, 1728–1809

Contain the papers of David Barclay (1728–1809), banker and merchant.

Commercial letters, 1769–72, are mainly general business correspondence with much reference to trade and include 2 letters, 1770, giving steps taken in view of the American non-importation resolution.

Banking letters, 1769–70, also contain some references to the tea trade as well as banking matters with his Philadelphia agent John Ashley.

Also 20 items concerning the peace negotiations, 1774–7, of Barclay, Dr John Fothergill and Lord Hyde with Benjamin Franklin.

(Most of these have been printed in R. Hingston Fox, *Dr. John Fothergill and his Friends*, Appendix A, London, 1919. An account of these negotiations also appears in J. C. Lettsom, *The Works of John Fothergill*, Vol. I, London, 1783. Crick and Alman, 352)

R. W. Ketton-Cremer Esq., Felbrigg Hall
Cromer

WILLIAM WINDHAM (1750–1810).

Draft of a protest, 28 January 1778, drawn up by William Windham and Thomas Coke, M.P., opposing the raising of a fund to help carry on the war in America. (Quoted in R. W. Ketton-Cremer, *Early Life and Diaries of William Windham*, London, 1930, 188. Crick and Alman, 352)

NORTHAMPTONSHIRE

Northamptonshire Record Office,
Delapre Abbey, London Road
Northampton

ELLESMERE PAPERS

Manuscript map of the 'Potowmack and James Rivers showing their several communications with the navigable waters of the New Province on the River

Ohio', n.d., and other printed maps of American ports and coastline, 1775–7. (Crick and Alman, 361)

SOTHEBY PAPERS

1 letter, 9 April 1778, from John Pilgrim to Ambrose Isted of Ecton, with comments on the war and its effects on stocks and shares. (Addenda 1963, 59)

FITZWILLIAM PAPERS

Papers of Edmund Burke: letters, notes, and draft speeches on American affairs, 1753–81. (These papers, dealing mainly with the Stamp Act and American war, are complementary to the group of Burke papers: YORK-SHIRE. *Central Library, Sheffield*, Fitzwilliam—Wentworth Woodhouse —Muniments)

Earl Spencer, Althorp
Northampton

GEORGE JOHN SPENCER, 2ND EARL SPENCER (1758–1834)

Various letters, 1774–83, including 6 letters from Sir William Jones, tutor at Althorp, concerning the parliamentary debates on the American question and a description of Franklin in Paris; letter from Patrick Campbell, 1777, on the military situation in America; other letters touching on American affairs to some degree. (Crick and Alman, 358)

GEORGIANA SPENCER, COUNTESS (POYNTY) (1737–1814)

6 letters, May 1774 to October 1777, from George Bussey Villiers, 4th Earl of Jersey, with various items concerning the debates on and battles in America.

25 letters, July 1775 to October 1778, from the Hon. Mrs Howe, sister-in-law to General and Admiral Howe, with various scraps about the war.

Filed with the Georgiana Spencer correspondence is the Asgill correspondence, consisting of 9 letters, 1782–3, pertaining to the case of Capt. Asgill, taken prisoner by the Americans.

(Crick and Alman, 359)

NORTHUMBERLAND

R. H. Carr-Ellison Esq., Hedgeley Hall
Alnwick

RALPH CARR

Merchant of Newcastle upon Tyne. There are 60–70 vols. of copy lette books, 1737–83, but most of the relevant business correspondence is in 2 separate volumes of American letter copies, 1748–75, concerning his American trade ventures. (Crick and Alman, 363)

Duke of Northumberland, Alnwick Castle
Alnwick

NORTHUMBERLAND PAPERS

Letter book of Hugh Percy (1742–1817), containing various letters and papers relating to the war in America: rebel orderly book covering 1–13 September 1776, taken at the island of New York, 1776; diary of operations of the Lords Howe fleet and army in America (Connecticut, Dutch Island, Goat Island, etc.), 29 July to 31 August 1778. Percy went to Boston in 1779 where he served under Gage. In 1776 he was promoted to general, but after many disputes with the Howes, he returned to England in 1777. (C. K. Bolton, ed., *Letters of Hugh Earl Percy from Boston & New York, 1774–1776*, Boston, 1902. Crick and Alman, 363)

NOTTINGHAMSHIRE

University of Nottingham
(The Department of Manuscripts, The Library) University Park
Nottingham

MELLISH MANUSCRIPTS

Papers of Charles Mellish (*c.* 1737–96), M.P.

Bundle of 54 letters, 1772–82, from various persons in England and North America on North American affairs, including the war.

9 letters, 1773, 1776–81, from Sir Henry Clinton on the war; list of pamphlets concerning America, etc.

(NRA 0893)

NEWCASTLE MANUSCRIPTS

44 bundles of letters, documents, etc., of Henry Fiennes Clinton, 2nd Duke of Newcastle (1720–94), which include over 100 letters, copies of letters, and documents from his cousin Sir Henry Clinton (1738–95), General and M.P. The majority of the letters are to the Duke but there are also copies of letters to Sir William Howe, Lord Germain, Lord Cornwallis, Lt.-Col. Webster, V.-Adm. Arbuthnot, some of Clinton's sisters, Richard Reeve, etc. Obviously regarded by Clinton as confidential correspondence to his political patron, these letters are a commentary on the course of the war and on Clinton's feelings, especially his dissatisfaction with fellow officers and his own position both before and after his appointment to the senior command in May 1778.

The Duke's papers also include 12 letters, 1775–80, of William Phillips (1731?–81), covering his service with Carleton and Burgoyne and his imprisonment at Saratoga, with some reference to Clinton's secret correspondence with Benedict Arnold and the execution of John Andre.

Also 2 letters, 1776 and 1777, from Richard Rigby and Edward Harvey with news of the war.

(NRA)

PORTLAND MANUSCRIPTS.

There is no specific material on the Revolution, but reports and comments are imbedded in the general correspondence, especially the papers of William Henry Cavendish Bentinck, 3rd Duke of Portland (1738–1809), during the period of the Revolution. (NRA)

OXFORDSHIRE
All Souls College Library
Oxford

While containing no manuscripts pertinent to the Revolution, the library does have a valuable collection of books and pamphlets, including:

John Bartram, *Description of East Florida, with a Journal*, 1769.

Amos Adams, *A Concise Historical View of the Difficulties, Hardships and Perils which attended the planting and progressive improvement of New England*, 1770.

Israel Maudit, *A Short View of the History of the Colony of Massachusetts Bay*, 1774.

13 vols. of American tracts, such as 'Observations of the Merchants at Boston in New England, upon several Acts of Parliament respecting American Commerce and Revenue', 1770, and Francis Bernard, *Select Letters on the Trade and Government of America*, 1774.

(Andrews and Davenport, 422–3)

Bodleian Library
Oxford

Although rich in 17th-and early 18th-century material, the Library contains only a few peripheral documents concerning the Revolution, as follows:

DASHWOOD PAPERS

1 printed piece, 'Narrative of Facts relative to American Affairs', 15 pp., a résumé based on official documents and on letters, principally from Sir Francis Bernard. The latest letters referred to are October 1768.

MISCELLANEOUS COLLECTIONS

Ms. Top. Oxon. d. **224.** Records of the campaigns of the 52nd (Oxfordshire) Light Infantry, 1755–1822. Summary description of its movements, casualties, promotions, extracts from dispatches and field orders. The regiment served in Canada, 1765–74, and America, 1774–8, including Lexington, Bunker Hill, Brooklyn, Pelham Manor, etc.

Ms. Eng. Hist. **c. 306,** *f. 5.* Le Fleming Papers. Letter, 17 December 1774, from Sir Michael Le Fleming to — Moore, on the rebellion and Lord North's attitude to it.

Mss. Eng. misc. **c. 132,** *ff. 42–3, 44–5, 53–6.* Letters from Lord Shelburne to Dr Richard Price, 2 n.d. and 1 24 September 1777, concerning the political and military aspects of the war.

Mss. Top. Oxon. **c. 386.** American account book, 1778–82, relating to the property of the father-in-law of the Rt. Hon. Willoughby Bertie, Earl of Abingdon.

NORTH PAPERS, 1702–78

The papers of the North family include a few of Lord North (1732–92), but most pre-date 1763.

a. 12. Papers relevant to the Revolution: complete list of ships engaged in American trade, 5 January 1772 to 5 January 1773, giving kind, tonnage, details of voyages, and a list of imports and exports of the colonies, with quantities for the same period.

ff. 260–78. Recommendations, 8 June 1763, from the Board of Trade to George III, concerning the future administration of newly acquired territory in Canada, Florida and the West Indies.

ff. 333–4. Statement of account of Lt.-Col. James Robertson, Deputy Quartermaster-General of H.M. Forces in North America, 1757–65, including amounts paid for provisions, etc.

f. 339. Extract letter, 13 January 1771, from Thomas Bishop of Boston stating that the Bostonians desire peace and concord.

ff. 380–2. Extracts from an unsigned letter; New York, 25 January 1778, complaining of Howe's dilatoriness in carrying on the war.

b. 69. Copies of all entries of goods and merchandise to Florida and Canada from England, 22 December 1775 to 13 May 1776, since the Act prohibiting all trade and intercourse with the colonies.

b. 78, *ff. 9–17.* Rated and unrated East India goods (tea excepted) exported from England, Christmas 1760 to Christmas 1776, to Africa, the West Indies and North America.

c. 83. Alphabetical list of goods imported into North America from Great Britain and Ireland, 5 January 1769 to 5 January 1770.

(Crick and Alman, 371–3)

Manchester College Library
Oxford

SHEPHERD MANUSCRIPTS Papers of the Rev. William Shepherd (1768–1847), Unitarian minister.

Vol. 28 contains copies of 16 letters, 1769–76, from Henry Hulton to Robert Nicholson, concerning the former's tenure as Revenue Comissioner in Boston, giving eye-witness accounts of the beginning of the war and the perils faced by revenue officials from the colonists. (Copies of these letters are also held by: LANCASHIRE, *McLachlan Library. Manchester.* Crick and Alman, 399)

Rhodes House Library
Oxford

NORTH PAPERS, 1756–1861

Most of the MSS. in the North Papers in the Bodleian Library relating to the British territories in North America and the West Indies have been transcribed and bound into a single volume (MSS. Brit. Emp. **s. 1.**) in Rhodes House.

DIARY OF THE SIEGE OF QUEBEC, 1775–6

Kept by an English soldier, 1 vol., 120 pp. (MSS. Can. **r. 2.**).

CALE AND CHUTTER

Letter book of 1030 letters, 1783–96, of London merchants and brokers with a large trade with the US, most letters addressed to American firms.

(Crick and Alman, 388)

RUTLAND

Earl of Gainsborough, Exton Park
Oakham

BARHAM PAPERS

Papers of Charles Middleton, 1st Baron Barham (1726–1813), Comptroller of the Navy, 1778–90.

Letters, 1780–2, concerning the West Indian and American Stations from Parker, Rodney, Graves, Prescott, Spry, Rowley, Hunt, Hood and Thompson.

19 miscellaneous papers, 1773–93, on the war.

Books A and B, 1779–83, containing 290 letters, drafts, lists and notes on victualling and convoys for America and Gibralter, including 26 letters and drafts by Middleton.

(Some of these papers have been published in *Letters and Papers of Charles, Lord Barham, Admiral of the Red Squadron 1758–1813* . . ., London, Naval Records Society, 1907–11, 3 vols. NRA 0315)

SHROPSHIRE

Corporation of Shrewsbury, Guildhall
Shrewsbury

MUNICIPAL RECORDS

Unanimous petition, 6 October 1775, to the King against the rebellion in America by the Mayor, Aldermen and Burgesses of Shrewsbury. (Crick and Alman, 403)

Salop Record Office, New Shirehall
Shrewsbury

SHIREHALL COLLECTION

Papers, 1733–74, relating to the Shrewsbury property of Thomas Bowers of Maryland.

SANDFORD HALL COLLECTION

Letters, 1776–7, relating to the appointment of Hugh Alexander Kennedy to the forces in America.

(Crick and Alman, 403)

SOMERSET

The American Museum in Britain, Claverton Manor
Bath

PETER CORNWALL

6 letters, 1778–86, from Flatbush, N.Y., to various relatives concerning, *inter alia*, problems with the officers quartered with him. (Addenda 1963, 60)

Lord Strachie, Sutton Court
Pensford

STRACHEY PAPERS, 1774–82

Large collection of papers relating to the American war and the Treaty of Paris of Sir Henry Strachey (1736–1810), Secretary to H.M. Peace Commissioners during the peace-making efforts.

Includes a series of letters, January 1774 to January 1776, from Governor Tryon of New York to Lord Dartmouth, describing the progress of the rebellion in New York province. (Crick and Alman, 405)

Fox Bros. & Co. Ltd, Tonedale Mills
Wellington

BUSINESS RECORDS, 1770–1821

This Quaker woollen firm, known as Were and Company until 1796, possesses Common letter books and Foreign letter books covering mainly the years 1770–1821, containing extensive references to the American trade, especially in the period 1783–1807. (The records were used by Herbert Fox, *Quaker Homespun*, London, 1958. Crick and Alman, 406–7)

STAFFORDSHIRE

University College of North Staffordshire (The Library)
Keele

RAYMOND RICHARDS COLLECTION

Business records of William Davenport and Co., 1746–82, Liverpool merchants involved in the triangular trade. Most material relates to the West Indies, but some to the mainland: bill of exchange book with some from New York, Virginia and South Carolina, 1769–75 and 1782; ships' logs and accounts concerning slave and rice trade, 1764–6. (Crick and Alman, 408)

Staffordshire Record Office, County Buildings
Stafford

DARTMOUTH PAPERS

Transferred from the William Salt Library. Papers of William Legge, 2nd Earl of Dartmouth (1731–1801), President of the Board of Trade and Foreign Plantations, 1765–6, Secretary of State for the American Department and President of the Board of Trade, 1772–5, and Lord Privy Seal, 1775–82. The bulk of the material is from his tenure as Secretary of State for the American

Department and is of the greatest importance for the study of the beginning of the Revolution.

There is, for example, in 1765–6, much material on the Stamp Act and its repeal; correspondence with Franklin and other American Agents; settlement schemes for Florida and west of the Allegheny Mountains; copies of inter- cepted letters from the American mails; and dispatches from the Royal Governors giving the situation in their respective provinces. (HMC 14 (10) is entirely devoted to the American papers; but see also NRA 5197 and Crick and Alman, 411–18)

Wedgwood Museum, Josiah Wedgwood and Sons Ltd, Barlaston
Stoke-on-Trent

WEDGWOOD FAMILY

Business and personal papers, 1765–. Occasionally permission is granted to researchers to inspect documents held by the firm, but such permission can only extend to a period of a day or two, since facilities for carrying out written work are limited.

Letters, 1762–95, of Josiah Wedgwood, on obtaining clay and on Anglo- American political relations. (most have been published in K. E. Farrer, ed., *The Letters of Josiah Wedgwood*, vol. I, 1762–80, vol. II, 1781–94, London, 1903–6

Thomas Griffith's journal, 1767–8, of a trip to Ayoree, in the Cherokee country of South Carolina in search of clay for Wedgwood.

Miscellaneous business papers, late 18th-century, which include material on the American relationships of the firm.

(Crick and Alman, 407–8)

SUFFOLK
Bury St Edmunds and West Suffolk Record Office, 8 Angel Hill
Bury St Edmunds

HENRY WATSON

Case book, *c*. 1745–74, concerning tithes in the estate of Henry Watson of Maryland and London, etc.

GRAFTON PAPERS, 1768–9

Papers of Augustus Henry Fitzroy, 3rd Duke of Grafton (1735–1811), containing a variety of letters concerning North America to and from William Pitt, Thomas Walpole, Jeffrey Amherst, etc.

(NRA 2567)

Miss T. Chevalier, 3 Sidegate Avenue
Ipswich

SIR WILLIAM JOHNSON (1715–74) AND SIR GEORGE JOHNSON (1742–1830)

Both men served as Superintendents of Indian Affairs in North America, while the latter commanded the Queen's Own American Regiment ('Johnson's Greens') during the Revolution.

Scrapbook, 1784–, containing letters, copies, and notes on family history.

Lady Johnson. 'Narrative of Lady Johnson', bound vol., n.d., concerning her adventures during the Revolution.

Johnson Family History, notebook, n.d., containing copies of old letters and some notes by Sir John Johnson.

(Crick and Alman, 421)

Ipswich and East Suffolk Record Office, County Hall
Ipswich

ALBEMARLE PAPERS

1 letter, 22 April 1766, from General Amherst to Viscount Barrington discussing military plans for America.

John Henniker (1724–1803), later 1st Baron Henniker: London day book, 1765–89, including business transactions as a merchant for provisioning ships through army and American contracts, adventures to New England, purchase and sale of ships and freight.

George Stansbury, 1 document, 1784. Testimony of Stansbury, 4 March 1784, in London concerning the arrangements of Benedict Arnold and Sir Henry Clinton; Stansbury decoded their correspondence.

(Crick and Alman, 422)

SURREY

Colonel A. C. Barnes, Foxholm, Redhill Road
Cobham

HAMMOND FAMILY PAPERS, 1763–1877

Documents concerning two prominent intermarried American Loyalist families, the deLancey's of New York and the Allens of Pennsylvania, mainly business papers and claims against the Crown, with a few genealogical notes. (Crick and Alman, 424)

C. S. Marris Esq., 7 The Fairway
New Malden

Crowther Family business and private papers, 1769–1825, of woollen manufacturers and merchants in Gomersal, Churwall and Leeds. Includes general business correspondence with American customers and agents and a specific body of correspondence relating to the 1772–5 American journeys of Benjamin Crowther, giving business matters and his impressions of Boston, etc. (See also: YORKSHIRE, *Brotherton Library, University of Leeds*, Crowther Family Letters. Crick and Alman, 427)

SUSSEX

Brigadier J. R. C. André, Church House, Sidlesham
Chichester

LETTERS OF MAJOR JOHN ANDRÉ, Soldier and spy

From North America, 1775–80, to his mother, sisters and uncle, telling of his personal experiences; of the progress of the war, including the operations on the Delaware River and his appointment as Adjutant-General to Sir Henry Clinton.

Letter to Clinton, 29 September 1780, telling of considerate treatment by the Americans and including a copy of his trial as a spy.

(NRA 4721)

Public Museum and Art Gallery (Muniment Room), John's Place
Hastings

Commission, 1779, for the privateer, the *Roebuck* of Hastings, to cruise against enemy shipping. (Crick and Alman, 432)

East Sussex Record Office, Pelham House
Lewes

SHIFFNER MANUSCRIPTS

Papers relating to estates in West Jersey and Pennsylvania owned by the Shiffner family, especially correspondence concerning the estates during and after the Revolution. (F. W. Steer, ed., *The Shiffner Archives: A Catalogue*, Lewes, 1959. Crick and Alman, 493)

WARWICKSHIRE
Assay Office, Newhall Street
Birmingham 3

MATTHEW BOULTON COLLECTION

Papers of Matthew Boulton (1728–1809), engineer, who corresponded with most of the leading men of the time on scientific and technologial subjects. In particular:

1 box labelled 'American disputes 1775', which contains notes, drafts of letters, and newspapers concerned with the Birmingham petitions of 1775. (Crick and Alman, 436)

University of Birmingham (The Main Library), Edgbaston
Birmingham 15

CORBETT COLLECTION

Autograph Letters. *Vol. I* contains a letter, Paris, 29 May 1777, in code but decoded, to George Carlting in London from George Chalmers, an English spy during the Revolution, mentioning an indiscretion of Lord Germain; desire of France and Spain to recoup their positions; negotiations with Baron

Schulenburg; visit of Beaumarchais to Dunkirk about artillery; in passing Franklin and Deane. (Crick and Alman, 440)

Earl of Denbigh, Pailton House
Rugby

DENBIGH PAPERS

1 letter, 6 October 1775, from Earl Sandwich to Denbigh, urging Denbigh to attend Parliament to support the Government's measures against America. Draft, 19 October 1775, from Denbigh to Dr Rochford, saying that loyal addresses in support of the Government are coming in slowly. (Crick and Alman, 442)

WILTSHIRE

Wiltshire Archaeological and Natural History Society
The Museum, Long Street
Devizes

HENRY WYNDHAM (1709–88)

A set of 25 draft letters, 1765–7, to his son Henry Wyndham (1736–1819), M. P. for Wiltshire, 1795–1812, which include accounts of the proceedings in Parliament concerning the American problem. (Crick and Alman, 445)

Earl of Pembroke, Wilton House
Salisbury

PEMBROKE PAPERS

Letter, 26 October 1780, from New York, from Augustus Reebkomp to Lord Herbert on the fleets of Rodney and Arbuthnot, the impending final defeat of the rebellion, Gates' defeat in Carolina, and Arnold's defection from the American side. (Crick and Alman, 446)

Marquess of Bath, Longleat
Warminster

BATH PAPERS

The papers of Thomas Thynne, 3rd Viscount Weymouth and 1st Marquis of

Bath (1734–96), contain 29 letters in an envelope labelled 'American Affairs, 1777–78, War of Independence'. (Addenda 1962, 57)

WORCESTERSHIRE

The Cathedral (Library)
Worcester

MUNIMENTS

1 letter, 28 August 1777, from W. Digby, Dean of Worcester, reporting rumours at Court that Philadelphia had been seized by Quakers for the Crown. (Crick and Alman, 447)

YORKSHIRE

East Riding Record Office, County Hall
Beverley

HOTHAM COLLECTION

Sir Charles Hotham Thompson (1738–92), c. 100 letters, 1771–9, from persons serving with the British forces and others, referring to American affairs.

William Hotham, 1st Baron Hotham (1736–1813), Commodore on the North American Station during the war, 23 letters, 1776–80, on naval affairs, including several from the Howe brothers.

Copy of a loyal motion passed by the Beverley Corporation relating to the war.

(Crick and Alman, 448)

Shibden Hall, Folk Museum of West Yorkshire
Halifax

LISTER FAMILY PAPERS, 1733–75

Correspondence during the Revolution between Gen. Sir William Fawcett (1728–1804) and the Lister family concerning the army service of his cousin and a brief account of the battle of Lexington.

Letters of Jeremy Lister, 1774–5, written while stationed in Boston, and his journal, 1770–83. (The journal, as well as a few of the Boston letters, has been partially published as Jeremy Lister, *Concord Fight*, Cambridge, Mass., 1931. Crick and Alman, 452–3)

Brotherton Library, University of Leeds
Leeds 2

CROWTHER FAMILY

1 letter, 1774, from Benjamin Crowther on his departure for North Carolina on business. (See also *Crowther Family papers* in the possession of *C. S. Marris Esq., New Malden,* SURREY. Crick and Alman, 455)

City Library (Archives Department)
Leeds 7

RAMSDEN FAMILY RECORDS

These letters are closely related to the Fitzwilliam Muniments in the Sheffield City Library.

Vol. 2 contains letters or copies of letters, 1773–1801, between Sir John Wentworth, Governor of New Hampshire and later of Nova Scotia, and his wife and Lord and Lady Rockingham concerning his posts and the American war. (Addenda 1962, 57)

Lord Bolton, Bolton Hall
Leyburn

BOLTON PAPERS

In the papers of Thomas Orde, 1st Baron Bolton (1746–1807), Secretary to the Treasury under Shelburne in 1782:

'List of Americans applying for allowances whose cases have not yet been considered', 3 June 1782. (Crick and Alman, 76)

Major George Howard, Castle Howard
Malton

CARLISLE PAPERS, 1754–83

These are mainly the papers of Frederick Howard, 5th Earl of Carlisle (1748–1825), head of the Commissioners sent out to America in 1778 to treat with the colonists. Includes:

Enumeration of the contents of the Commissioners' letter book, numerous letters to Howard from American Loyalists, some letters from Clinton, Cornwallis and Earl Cathcart. (Crick and Alman, 449)

Central Library
(Department of Local History and Archives), Surrey Street
Sheffield

BAGSHAWE COLLECTION

1 folder of business letters and documents, 1773 and 1785, of B. W. Wyatt, lead-mine owners of Derbyshire. The material relates to the duty on exported lead, including several MS. copies of an undated 3-page article entitled 'Observations on the tax or duty laid upon lead exported by an Act passed the last session of Parliament'.

FITZWILLIAM (WENTWORTH WOODHOUSE) MUNIMENTS

Letters and papers of Charles Watson Wentworth, 2nd Marquis of Rockingham (1730–82), Prime Minister, 1765–6 and 1782, and Leader of the Opposition in the House of Lords, 1768–81. This collection is of prime importance for the British side of the Revolution and includes over 2000 letters. (A full hand-list is given in NRA 1083)

Also various papers and letters relating to the stamp duties and colonial trade in general, and to the repeal of the Stamp Act.

Additionally, an important set of letters, 1769–75, from Joseph Harrison, Joseph Warren and Thomas Cushing, on the rising revolutionary temper of the colonies; letters from colonial governors, such as Sir Francis Bernard, John Wentworth, Samuel Ward, Stephen Hopkins, Thomas Fitch and Thomas Boone.

Also the letters and papers of William Wentworth Fitzwilliam, 2nd Earl Fitzwilliam (1748–1833), containing some correspondence with Governor John

Wentworth and a 'Copy of Mr. Champion's account of the state of America', 1785.

A further important section, some letters and papers of Edmund Burke, including many drafts of his speeches on American affairs and some letters on the same subject.

(T. W. Copeland and M. S. Smith, *A Checklist of the Correspondence of Edmund Burke, Arranged in Chronological Order and Indexed under the Names of 1200 Correspondents*, London, 1955. All letters from Burke and some to him have been edited and published in T. W. Copeland, gen. ed., *The Correspondence of Edmund Burke* London and Chicago, 1958–72, 10 vols.)

WILLIAM VASSALL

Merchant and resident of Boston and London. 2 letter books, 1769–99, containing copies of letters from Boston 1769–75, Nantucket, Mass., 1775, and London, 1775–99. Most of the pre-war letters concern his business, while the post-war tend to concern the confiscation of his farm in Bristol, R.I.

Guide to the Manuscript Collections in the Sheffield City Libraries, Sheffield, 1956. Crick and Alman, 461–6)

WALES

CARDIGANSHIRE

National Library of Wales
Aberystwyth

DILLWYN DIARIES AND PAPERS

William Dillwyn (1743–1824) was a Quaker of Philadelphia and especially concerned with the abolition of slavery.

The papers consist of the minutes of his voyage from Philadelphia to Bristol in 1774, diaries of his tour of Great Britain, his return in 1775, and a subsequent voyage to England in 1777. All told, there are 13 volumes of diaries, covering the period 1774–90. Also the war-time passports issued to him to enable him to travel through combat areas and visit England.

(Microfilm, Society of Friends, London, and of the diary only, Yale University Library. Crick and Alman, 483)

MISS F. N. NORMAN DEPOSIT

Notes on trade relations with the colonies, 1769.

Petition, 1778, from the merchants, traders, and other inhabitants of New York, to the Commisioners appointed to 'quieten the disorders' in the colonies.

(Crick and Alman, 484)

GLAMORGAN

Central Library, The Hayes
Cardiff

BUTE CORRESPONDENCE

Letters, 1752–90, mainly to, but a few from, John Stuart, 3rd Earl of Bute (1713–93). The largest number are from the 1760s and have some references to the growing American problem. For example:

c. 400 personal letters and notes of George III, mostly undated, with some comments on American affairs, as well as his 'Thoughts on the British Constitution', *c.* 1760.

Copy extracts of resolves of Providence, R. I., Maryland, Essex County, N.J., and Philadelphia, asserting the rights of local assemblies to levy taxes and objecting to the new stamp duties.

(Crick and Alman, 485–6)

SCOTLAND

ABERDEENSHIRE

Aberdeen Town Council, Town House
Aberdeen

COUNCIL REGISTERS OF THE CITY OF ABERDEEN

Vol. 64 of this 95-vol. MS. series contains various items pertaining to the Revolution, including a loyal address to George III on the outbreak of war, the offer by the Town Council to raise a regiment for service (refused), and preparations for defence if invaded. (Crick and Alman, 491)

University Library, King's College
Aberdeen

ATHOLL PAPERS

1 copy letter from Lt. Thomas Campbell to Lord Adam Gordon, describing his mission for Governor Johnstone of Florida to interview leaders of the Creek nation, November 1764 to June 1765.

2 letters, 1768, from James Grant, Governor of East Florida at St Augustine (to Lord Gordon?).

(Crick and Alman, 493)

OGILVIE FORBES OF BOYNDLIE (deposited in the King's College Library, Aberdeen)

AMERICAN PAPERS, 1778–1806

Mainly Empire Loyalist papers, with letters by George Ogilvie from South Carolina, to his wife and Mr Forbes of Pitsligo 1778–86. (NRA-Scotland 426)

Captain A. A. C. Farquharson, Invercauld
Braemar

Large collection of muniments which include 1 letter, 30 April 1777, from Aeneas Mackintosh at Perth Amboy, N.J., to James Farquharson of Invercauld, giving an account of the 71st Regiment's operations in America from 5 June 1776. (NRA-Scotland 0061)

Sir Francis Grant, Bt, Monymusk House
Monymusk

GRANT FAMILY PAPERS

Copy letter, 1767, from A. Campbell, with an account of the Creek Indians and their country. Charter and correspondence connected with land in Florida deeded to Sir Archibald Grant.

Copies of letters by Sir Archibald to the Secretary of State for the Colonies on the disputes with America, 1769.

(NRA-Scotland 0099)

ANGUS

Earl of Southesk, Kinnaird Castle
Brechin

2 vol., 1777–83, listing ships with details of cargoes, etc., permitted to land at New York after General Howe's proclamation of 17 July 1777.

Letters from George Washington, General Knox and Elias Boudinot.

(Printed in Sir William Fraser, *History of the Carnegies, Earls of Southesk . . .*, Edinburgh, 1867. NRA-Scotland 792)

AYRSHIRE

N.A. Cochran-Patrick Esq., Ladyland
Beith

Ledgers and waste books of merchants in Irvine trading with the West Indies and America, 1736–81. (NRA-Scotland 0038)

W. H. Dunlop Esq.
Doonside

Green deed box, *Bundle 2*. Contains the parole of William Hamilton, Captain of the Royal North Carolina Regiment, to go to New York and thence to Europe by permission of Washington. (NRA-Scotland 620)

BANFFSHIRE

Sir Ewan Macpherson-Grant, Ballindalloch Castle
Ballindalloch

A large collection of papers containing the following:

Bundle 129. Copy by Dr John Witherspoon, Princeton, of a note signed by Capt. John Macpherson of the 17th Regiment of Foot, captured wounded at the battle of Princeton, going to New York on parole by permission of Washington.

Bundle 203. Letter, 27 December 1781, from John Macpherson to Capt. Macpherson at Badenoch, reporting some news from America.

Bundles 242, 243, 244, 246, 250–4, 260, 262–4, 290, 293–4. Correspondence of Gen. James Grant, Governor of East Florida and active in the campaigns of 1775–7. Many of the bundles contain mainly correspondence relating to East Florida and Grant's various private ventures, but interesting letters of more general interest are scattered among these. See especially *250*, which has many letters concerning the war, and *290*, dispatches from Hillsborough, 1768–70.

Bundle 2. 'Papers in the office of Sir Ewan Macpherson-Grant', the copy letter book of Grant, 10 August 1775 to 21 March 1777, concerning his operations in the American war. Cardboard box, 'Hellmer's', contains a printed plan of St Lucia, with extracts of a letter from Grant to Germain, 13 December 1778.

(NRA-Scotland 771)

G. Gordon Esq., Letterfourie
Buckie

PAPERS OF GORDON AND CO.

Wine shippers, Madeira, including correspondence with customers in America, 1760–88. (NRA-Scotland 0096)

BUTESHIRE

Marquis of Bute, Mountstuart House
Rothesay, Isle of Bute

A large collection arranged by year. Items noted below are letters unless otherwise indicated.

1764, *Bundle 3*. ?Rodger to Gen. Gage, enclosing a long description of Florida and account of troop dispositions there.

Bundle 4. Several letters from James Campbell in New Orleans, describing the country, military affairs, and a trip to Mobile.

1765, *Bundle 3*. James Campbell from Arkansas, on the general situation and military dispositions; Thomas Hutchinson, member of the Massachusetts Assembly, describing his persecution for refusing to join the opposition to Parliament.

1766, *Bundle 2*. John Campbell from Illinois, describing the country and his intention of settling there.

1767, *Bundle 1*. John Brown from Niagara, on Indian affairs and the departure of Governor-General Murray.

Bundle 2. John Campbell from Illinois, asking to sell his commission and describing the settlement in general.

1772, *Bundle 3*. Gen. Lyman's proposed settlement on the Mississippi.

1773, *Bundle 1*. Same.

1774, *Bundle 4*. Earl of Stair, commenting on North's American policy.

Bundle 5. Col. James Abercrombie, commenting on the American situation.

Bundle 6. Capt. Andrew Barkly, H.M.S. *Scarborough* at Boston, relating events at Boston and the growing rebellion.

1775, *Bundle 6*. 6 letters, from various persons, giving news of America; Earl of Stair, justifying his opposition to the American war; Charles Mckinen from St Augustine, describing his treatment by the rebels.

1776, *Bundle 3*. Several letters of John Gillon, merchant of Dominica, describing the effect of the war on trade and the island.

1777, *Bundle 2*. Thomas Campbell, with news of the war in Canada.

Bundle 3. Copy letters of Robert H. Harrison and George Washington, published by order of Congress, describing events at Brandywine, 11 September; Germain on army operations in Canada.

Bundle 4. Various letters giving news of America and related papers.

1778, *Bundle 1.* Andrew Frazer, with intelligence from France and rumours of war; George Keir, on the state of the Loudoun Regiment in America.

Bundle 3. 2 letters of Lachlan Macintosh, merchant of Charleston, describing his treatment by the rebels; several lists relating to the British fleet in America.

Bundle 4. Several letters with news of America.

1779. George Keir describing the landing at Savannah, 13 and 15 July.

1780, *Bundle 1.* Gabriel Christie, on Rodney's action against the French, 3 November.

Bundle 3. 2 letters of Thomas Campbell, describing the Gordon riots in detail, and 1 describing the fall of Charleston, 15 June.

Bundle 4. W. A. Douglas on the Gordon riots.

(NRA-Scotland 631)

DUMFRIESSHIRE
A. M. Bell-Macdonald Esq., Rammerscales
Lockerbie

Volume containing the return of recruits levied at Glasgow for the Macdonald Regiment by Lt. Allan Macdonald, and copies of letters from him while serving on Long Island, 1781–2. (NRA-Scotland 139)

ISLE OF CANNA
J. L. Campbell Esq.
Isle of Canna

INVERNEILL PAPERS

Letters, letter books, accounts, etc., relating to various members of the Campbell family, in particular Sir Archibald Campbell (1739–91). Campbell

served with the British forces in America 1775–82. His papers contain correspondence with Germain, Howe and others, about his time as a pri-
soner-of-war, 1777–8, and information about the Georgia expedition,
1778–9. Later became Governor of Jamaica, and his papers for that period include references to American Loyalists in Jamaica and his tactical support of
the British forces to the north. (The William L. Clements Library, University
of Michigan, Ann Arbor, Mich., holds a list of the American material in the
Inverneill Papers. Addenda 1966, 64)

KINROSS

Captain C. K. Adam, Blair-Adam
Kinross

PAPERS OF WILLIAM ADAM (1751–1839)

M.P. and politician. Adam was a supporter of Lord North from 1779, very
active in the politics of 1779–83, and was the negotiator of the North–Fox co-
alition of 1782. His papers are an important source for the reign of George III.

Miscellaneous papers contain his personal notes and memoranda on the political events and episodes of the reign of George III.

70 boxes of his correspondence, including letters of Lord North on the 1782
resignation of Fox; the offer of independence to America, 1782; and other letters on American affairs. Other correspondents include Henry Dundas,
Richard Rigby, and most of the leading political figures of the time.

(NRA-Scotland 0063)

KIRKCUDBRIGHTSHIRE

Major Richard A. Oswald, Cavens
Kirkbean

RICHARD OSWALD (1705–84)

Merchant and shipowner of Auchencruive, owned estates in America and the
West Indies. A sympathizer with the American cause, during 1782 he played
an important role in bringing about the peace of 1783. (For his correspondence with Lord Shelburne, see HMC 5, LXX-LXXI, 'Report, Marquis
of Lansdowne Mss'.) Major Oswald possesses 3 letter books:

The first contains miscellaneous letters to Oswald, 1776–81, some of which report on military affairs in America.

The second contains letters to Oswald, mainly concerning business, 1765–84.

The third contains correspondence between Oswald and his wife, 1761–3.

(Crick and Alman, 500)

MIDLOTHIAN

Hunter, Harvey, Webster and Will, W. S., 7 York Place
Edinburgh 1

Deed box of miscellaneous manuscripts which include 'Journal of a detachment of the 42nd Regiment from Fort Pitt down the Ohio to the country of the Illenoise, 1765'. (NRA-Scotland 351)

National Library of Scotland, George IV Bridge
Edinburgh 1

(*National Library of Scotland Catalogue of Manuscripts*, 1938–68, 3 vols.)

BANKING AND SHIPPING IN SCOTLAND

List of sailings from Scottish and Northern English ports, giving cargoes, destination, and master's name for each ship, 1781. (MS. 1801)

WILLIAM CUNINGHAME AND CO.

Glasgow merchants with agents at Falmouth and Williamsburg, Va.

3 letter books, 1767–74. (Microfilm Acc. 2461)

ALEXANDER HOUSTON AND CO.

Glasgow merchants and shipowners trading with America

3 letter books, 1776–81, to the firm's agents and ship's captains. (Microfilm Library of Congress)

EARL OF MARCHMONT

Letters, 1773–8, of Hugh Home Campbell, 3rd Earl of Marchmont (1744–1818), to George Rose containing extensive comment on the politics of the day and in particular the course of the American war. (MSS. 3523)

ROBERTSON–MACDONALD PAPERS

Family papers of the Robertsons, a branch of the Robertsons of Strowan and the MacDonalds of Kinlochmoidart. William Robertson (1721–93), Principal of Edinburgh University, and his son William, of the College of Justice, are the chief correspondents. Also the materials for and a partial manuscript of Principal Robertson's *History of America* (London, 1777).

The journal of Col. George Croghan's journey down the Ohio River, 1765.

Letters, 1775–80, from Alexander MacDonald in America concerning his military experiences.
MSS. 3942–88. NLS Cat. II, 317–20)

STEUART PAPERS

Correspondence and papers, 1758–97, of Charles Steuart, Receiver-General of the American Board of Customs. There are some letters from Loyalists, mainly in Norfolk, Va., but the bulk of the correspondence is with customs officials, and in particular Nathaniel Coffin, Steuart's deputy in Boston. (MSS. 5025–46)

CHARLES STRACHAN (later Fullerton) trader in Mobile, Ala., 1763–70.

Letter book mainly concerned with business affairs. (MS. 119)

STUART OF TORRANCE PAPERS
These papers include:

'Thoughts on the Present State of America and Lord North's Late Declaration in the House of Commons', November 1775.

Copy of a petition to the Treasury by Maj.-Gen. James Robertson, Barrack-Master-General in North America, 1765–76, for compensation for losses caused by the fire in New York after the British occupation, n.d.

Letter from Brig.-Gen. James Hamilton to the Duke of (?Hamilton), stating that 'the misfortunes of Saratoga . . . hang round me'.

STUART STEVENSON PAPERS

Letters, 1776–7, of Maj. Charles Cochrane on the progress of the war.

Correspondence, 1777–84, of the Hon. John Cochrane, Deputy Commissary to the British forces in America.

(MSS. 5320–404)

YESTER PAPERS

Box VII (Acc. 1611). Contains several letters from John McColme and others with references to the Revolution.

MELVILLE PAPERS

Letter, 1782, from the Earl of Selkirk to Lord Townshend on the defence of Scotland. (MSS. 3835)

Scottish Record Office, H.M. General Register House
Edinburgh 2

(The Scottish Record Office has issued the following mimeographed lists: *Source List of Manuscripts Relating to the U.S.A. and Canada in the Scottish Record Office*, 1964, 77 pp.; *Material Relating to the U.S.A. and Canada in the Scottish Record Office, List No. 2*, 1965, 6 pp.; ibid., *List No. 3*, 1967, 22 pp.)

ABERCAIRNY COLLECTION

23 letters, 1760–97, to Sir William Stirling of Ardoch from his brother Thomas during his army career, relating to the campaigns in America. 12 letters, 1760–75, to Lord Kames from Benjamin Franklin (8 of which have been published in Jared Sparks, ed., *Works of Benjamin Franklin*, Boston 1836–40, 10 vols.)

Letter, 19 July 1778, from Alexander Dundas in Quebec, describing the campaign.

Letter, 3 July 1780, to Sir William Stirling at New York, informing him that his brother has been wounded.

AILSA MUNIMENTS

2 letters, 1767 and 1769, concerning settlement in East Florida.

Letter, 1776, from John McColme to the Earl of Cassillis on the success of Howe's campaign.

BREADALBANE PAPERS

Muster rolls, etc., of the 40th Regiment of Foot while serving in America and Canada, 1775–85.

BRITISH RECORDS ASSOCIATION

List of general and staff officers and of the officers in the several regiments serving in North America under command of Gen. Sir William Howe (printed at Philadelphia, 1778).

BROUGHTON AND CALLY MUNIMENTS

Copies of the Articles of Confederation of the Philadelphia Congress; address by New York to the Governor of the province; letter from the Narrows near New York, 1775; letters concerning naval and military operations during the war, including coastal defence against John Paul Jones.

BUCCLEUCH AND QUEENSBERRY MUNIMENTS (property of the Duke of Buccleuch)

Box VIII. Includes the papers of Charles Townshend (1725–67), Chancellor of the Exchequer in the second Pitt ministry, 1766–7. The following bundles are devoted to American affairs:

Bundle 2. War Office papers, mainly financial, and including the establishment list for the Northern Department of Indian Affairs, 1766.

Bundle 4. Military and political papers in Townshend's holograph, 1745–c. 1766.

Bundle 17. Papers relating to excise duties on linen, paper, leather and beer, and proposals for regulating North American trade, 1766–7.

Bundle 22. Papers on the army, agriculture, manufactures, imports and exports, and a list and extracts of papers laid before Parliament relative to disturbances in America due to the Stamp Act, 1761–6.

Bundle 25. American papers, 1765–7.

Bundle 27. Papers from the Board of Trade, including a draft Bill for recruiting in North America, 1766.

Bundle 28. Estimates of army expenses in North America and other papers, 1765–7.

Bundles 31, 34, 39. More American papers, 1765–7. Additionally, there are letters, returns, and other papers relating to the financial administration of

Britain and the colonies, evidently compiled or provided for the use of Town-shend while Chancellor of the Exchequer, and other papers relating to colonial trade, 1761–7.

(NRA-Scotland 0001. Crick and Alman, 502–3)

CAMPBELL OF BALLIVEOLAN MUNIMENTS

Orderly book, 1783, of a regiment (the 74th Argyllshire Highland?) at New York.

CARRON IRON COMPANY RECORDS

Letter books from 1759 or, containing correspondence of Glasgow merchants receiving iron ore from America and supplying iron goods to the American market.

COLLECTIONS DEPOSITED BY MESSRS TODS, MURRAY, AND JAMISON, W.S.

Miscellaneous business papers relating to Maryland, 1766–84.

COURT OF SESSION, UNEXTRACTED PROCESSES

These records include the account books of Jamieson, Lawson, and Sample, for the management of plantations in Maryland and Virginia, 1750–1817.

CUNINGHAME OF THORNTOUN PAPERS

13 notebooks, covering 1776–82, comprising the journal of Capt. John Peebles during the war.

4 letters, 1777–81, from Peebles to his father concerning the war.

Papers of Peebles' company in the 42nd Highlanders.

Copy of negotiations between the American Commissioners and the Six Nations, 1777.

CUNNINGHAM OF LAINSHAW MUNIMENTS

Business correspondence and letter books, 1761–78, of Messrs William Cunningham and Co., Glasgow.

CUSTOMS RECORDS, 1742–95

For each port is given the names of ships sailing and arriving, names of masters, ports of destination and departure, goods carried and duties paid.

DALGUISE MUNIMENTS

3 letters, 1779–80, to Lord Provost William Creich in Edinburgh from William Strahan in London, concerning Lord Kames and also the Gordon riots.

1 letter, 1779, from Col. William Robertson of Lude to his father, describing the fighting on St Lucia.

DRUMMOND CASTLE MUNIMENTS

Papers, 1775–9, of Thomas, Lord Drummond, in America. Some relate to his negotiations with the colonists, 1775–6.

DUFF OF BRACO PAPERS

1 letter, July 1775, from William Braco Gordon in Boston, describing military life in the army and the battle of Charles Town Heights.

DUNDAS OF OCHERTYRE MUNIMENTS

Letters, 1780–1, particularly from Capt. Ralph Dundas of the sloop *Bonetta* concerning naval operations off the American coast.

Also letters of Dr David Dundas and his wife, containing much news of military events during the war.

EXCHEQUER RECORDS

Exemplification of the state of account of Lt.-Gen. James Robertson, Barrack-Master-General in North America, 1765–76

Letters and papers, 1780–2, relating to the activities of Maj. George Hay, commissary for captures and agent for captured property, in procuring provisions for the forces and dealing with captured rebel property during the siege of Charleston.

GILCHRIST OF OPISDALE MUNIMENTS

Letters, accounts, etc., 1776–84, of Capt. John Ross of Auchnacloich with the 71st Highlanders in America.

HAMILTON BRUCE

Part letter, 3 January 1776, from Concord, concerning the writer's captivity.

HAMILTON-DALRYMPLE OF NORTH BERWICK

Letters, 1775, from Alison Cockburn, commenting on the American war

HAY OF BELTON MUNIMENTS

Letter, 6 April 1779, from J. Hay to the Hon. John Hay of Belton, giving an account of his journey from Rhode Island to St Lucia and its defence.

HENDERSON OF FORDELL

Papers of Gen. James Robertson (?1720–88), Governor of New York, 1779–83, and Commander in Chief for North America, 1782

5 bundles of papers dealing with American affairs and his large estates in New York and Florida.

1 letter book, 1780–3, in his capacity as Governor of New York.

1 order book, same capacity, 1781–3.

INGLIS PAPERS

Papers, 1777–87, of John Inglis, sutler and merchant in New York.

LEITH–ROSS MUNIMENTS

Letters and papers, 1775–90, of John Ross the younger of Arnage, relating to his residence in East Florida as a plantation factor and his ledger.

LEVEN AND MELVILLE MUNIMENTS

Papers, 1775–81, of Gen. Alexander Leslie and Capt. William Leslie in the war.

Letter, 1778, from Dr Benjamin Rush.

Letter, 1779, from John Donaldson in London on the war in America.

Note of a journey, 1780, from Charleston, S.C., to Petersburg, Va., to join Lord Cornwallis.

State of the troops at the Battle of Guildford, 15 March 1781.

2 letters, 1781, from Robert Skene with news of the war.

Letters, 1783, from Capt. Lichenbrodf and Gen. Bose, concerning the Hessian Regiment de Bose serving in America.

Part letter, 1784, from 'R.J.', describing how Capt. Asgill, a prisoner of the Americans, was set free by the intervention of the French Queen.

LOGAN HOME OF EDROM

Letter, 1775, from Adam Hunter in Fredericksburg, Va.

Letters, 1778–82, from William and James Howe, officers in the Royal Marines, West Indies Station, giving news of the war.

MACLAINE OF LOCHBUIE

Papers of Capt. Murdoch Maclaine, 2nd Battalion, Royal Highland Emigrants (84th Foot), 1775–84, mostly pertaining to service in Nova Scotia, but a few to service in South Carolina, 1781.

MELVILLE CASTLE MUNIMENTS

Papers of Henry Dundas, 1st Viscount Melville (1742–1811) and Lord Advocate of Scotland.

Various papers, 1775–85, relative to tobacco imports from America.

Correspondence, 1780–1, about the situation in America and peace terms, with the Lord Chancellor, Richard Rigby, and William Adam, M.P.

Memorandum by Maj.-Gen. Murray on the service of Maj.-Gen. Stirling in Canada and America.

MURRAY OF LINTROSE

Letters, 1777, from William Murray giving news of the campaign in America.

Letters, 1780, from Charles Willing in Philadelphia.

MURRAY OF MURRAYTHWAITE

Copy account of the attack, 28 June 1778, on Charleston, S.C., 'with remarks by a gentleman residing in Charlestown [sic] at that time'.

REGISTER HOUSE PAPERS

Various accounts of fighting and expeditions against the Indians, 1765, in the Ohio Valley and upper Mississippi areas.

List of transports carrying companies of the 42nd Regiment from Gourock to America, 1776 (microfilm).

Short account of movements and engagements of the 2nd Battalion of the 42nd Regiment in America, from 22 August to 16 December 1776 (microfilm).

Customs account book of goods exported from Scotland to Newfoundland, 1770–85.

ROBERTSON OF KINDEACE MUNIMENTS

Notebook, 1779–81, giving daily accounts of operations against the rebels, apparently by an officer (Charles Robertson?) of the 76th Regiment.

MESSRS SALT AND SON

5 business letters, 1780–94, to William Shedden at Bermuda and New York.

SEAFIELD MUNIMENTS

Copies of minutes of Council, proclamations, and other documents, forming a narrative of the riots in Massachusetts, 1765–6.

University Library, Old College, Southbridge Edinburgh 8

ANDREW BROWN (1763–1834), Scottish Presbyterian Minister

Unfinished manuscript, 'History of North America during the War of Independence'. (Crick and Alman, 514)

LAING MANUSCRIPTS

Part of a collection formed by David Laing (1793–1878), antiquary and librarian to the Signet Museum, these manuscripts include a number of items pertaining to the Revolution, for example:

A bundle of correspondence, 1775–6, concerning Gen. Simon Fraser's raising of the 71st regiment for service in America.

3 letters, 1777–8, from Lt.-Col. Patrick Ferguson, describing the beginning of the war.

'Address to His Excellency the President and other members of Congress, etc.', apparently drawn up by Prof. Adam Ferguson, *c.* 1778, on peace between Britain and America.

(Crick and Alman, 514)

MISCELLANEOUS AMERICAN MATERIALS

Letter, 11 December 1777, from David Murray, 7th Viscount Stormont, from America, to William Eden, Baron Auckland, on the war.

'Copy of an account laid before the Rt. Hon. Lewis Lord Sondes, Auditor of the Imposts', for the Province of Georgia, 1765–70, by John Campbell, Agent, 30 November 1770.

'Proceedings of H.M. Commissioners . . . to treat, consult, and agree upon the means of quieting the disorders in . . . North America', 1778–9, 366 pp. (partly in the hand of Adam Ferguson, the Secretary).

(Crick and Alman, 514. Addenda 1962, 62)

MORAYSHIRE

Sir Edward Dunbar, Bt., M.C., The Old Manse
Duffus, Elgin

Large collection of family muniments.

Letter, 17 January 1778, from Thomas Dunbar in Philadelphia, in which he notes that the army is in the best of spirits and the city well supplied.

Letter, 16 September 1778, from same from camp near Bedford, L.I., in which he refers to the appearance of the French fleet off the coast.

(NRA-Scotland 0065)

N. Brodie Esq., Brodie Castle
Forres

BRODIE FAMILY PAPERS

Letter, 18 October 1767, from St Michael's River, Md., from John Braco, on Maryland and its products.

Letter, 1778, from Lord North in reply to Brodie's offer to raise a company for service in America.

(NRA-Scotland 770)

ORKNEY

Orkney County Library, Laing Street
Kirkwall

BALFOUR OF BALFOUR AND TRENABIE PAPERS

Box 4, bundle 12. Contains many letters from Earl Ligonier to his sister and her husband Col. Balfour, with second-hand news of the war and comments.

Box 8, bundle 6. Contains papers relating to a complicated claim by William and John Chapman to the Commissioners of American Claims, 1783–91.

Box 9, bundle 3. Contains the Loyalist claim of William Manson of Georgia, 1783.

(NRA-Scotland 627)

PERTHSHIRE

Earl of Mansfield, Scone Palace
Perth

This collection of papers contains a number of boxes of correspondence and related documents of Viscount Stormont.

Box 13. 'Cabinet Meetings, Minutes [copies], 1779–82.'

Box 14. 'Letters to Viscount Stormont from King George III, Lord North, Lord Thurlow, 1779–83.'

Box 15. General correspondence, partly concerning military affairs and relations with Holland and Sweden, 1779–81.

Box 16. Copies of letters of Viscount Stormont to King George III, 1777–83.

Other boxes contain miscellaneous correspondence and papers relating to European affairs in the 1760s. There do not appear to be any papers relating to his tenure as Ambassador to France.

(NRA-Scotland 776)

RENFREWSHIRE

Major D. Crichton-Maitland, Houston House
Houston, Johnstone

Book store in the basement. Green deed box No. 1:

Bundle 5. Contains balance sheets giving details of the business and estate accounts of Alexander Speirs, merchant of Glasgow, mostly in the tobacco and sugar trade, with details of his Virginia ventures in land and money lent out to other business people, 1770–3, 1782, 1785 and 1788. Other boxes contain more business records of Speirs.

Bundle 6. Contains a letter from Judith Bell to Speirs, 1776, justifying the rebellion.

(NRA-Scotland 607)

Professor Robin Orr
Lochwinnoch

Log book apparently kept by John Dow of Saltcoats, 1764–8, of trading voyages to North America and from Virginia to the West Indies.

7 letters to his wife, 1762–74.

(Microfilm held by the Scottish Record Office. NRA-Scotland 438)

SELKIRK

Duke of Buccleuch, Bowhill House
Selkirk

BUCCLEUCH AND QUEENSBERRY MUNIMENTS

These papers include an apparently stray bundle of the Townshend papers, the remainder of which are in the Scottish Record Office. This bundle is mainly American correspondence, 1765–7. (NRA-Scotland 0001)

NORTHERN IRELAND

ANTRIM

Public Record Office of Northern Ireland
Law Courts Building, May Street
Belfast 1

(Reports of the Public Record Office of Northern Ireland 1954–9, 1960–5)

DOBBS PAPERS

Papers of Arthur Dobbs, Governor of North Carolina, 1754–65. Material pertaining to trade in the 1760s and the disposal of Dobbs' estates in North Carolina, 1764–75. (Desmond Clarke, *Arthur Dobbs Esquire, 1689–1765*, London, 1957. D.O.D. 162)

DOWNSHIRE PAPERS (Hillsborough Collection)

A large collection mostly of estate papers of Wills Hill, 1st Earl of Hillsborough and 1st Marquis of Downshire (1718–93), with no reference to his tenure as Secretary of State for the Colonies, 1768–72, and Secretary of State for the Northern Department, 1779–82. There is, however:

A memorandum, 21 June 1779, from Robert Hodgson, outlining a plan for the military and economic domination of North and South America, using the West Indies and Nicaragua as bases, and sketches, 1780, of the British siege operations at Charleston, S.C. (D.O.D. 607)

JOHN DUNLAP (1747–1812)

Printer to the Convention of 1774, to the Continental Congress, and of the Declaration of Independence.

About 12 letters, 1780s, mostly on family affairs, and a memorandum, *c.* 1800, describing his career. (T. 1136)

ANDREW FERGUSON (General merchant, Londonderry)

Out-letter books, 2 vols., 1775–80 and 1783–7, with some material on trade with Philadelphia. (D. 1130)

FLOYD PAPERS

Journal of Capt. Alexander Chesney (1755–1815), a Loyalist who served under Cornwallis and Hastings. (Published as E. D. Jones *et al.*, eds., *The Journal of Alexander Chesney, a South Carolina Loyalist in the Revolution and After*, Columbus, Ohio, 1921. T. 1095)

EARL OF GOSFORD PAPERS

1 letter, *c.* 1785?, from Lord Gosford to his son Arthur Acheson, containing a discussion of unrest in the American colonies in 1775.

There may be more material in this collection of 150 letters, 1745 to early 19th-century, as the correspondents include Cornwallis, Sandwich, Buckingham, Charlemont, Richard Rigby, Townshend, and Downshire.

(D. 1606)

DOWN

Mrs Terence Johnston
Castlewellan

1 volume of copy letters of Sir John (later Lord) Rawdon, which contains letters from Sir Thomas Bate in London, referring *inter alia* to the parliamentary debates on the American Bill of 1766. (T. 1839)

LONDONDERRY

V. McG. Greer Esq.
Moneymoore

In the correspondence of the Greer family of Dungannon, Co. Tyrone, are the papers of Thomas Greer (1724–1803), a linen merchant trading with America. Mentions how trade is hampered by the ill-feeling of the Americans over taxes on exports to America, *c.* 1770. (D. 1044)

MACARTNEY PAPERS

As Secretary for Ireland, 1769–72, George Macartney, 1st Earl Macartney (1737–1806), was not directly involved in American affairs, but his papers contain some references to American matters, mostly Commons debates in 1770. (D.O.D. 572)

MASSEREENE-FOSTER PAPERS

This huge collection contains the papers of John Foster, Baron Oriel (1740–1828), Chief Baron of the Exchequer, 1766–77, and those of his father Anthony, both closely connected with the Linen Board. There is much important material on trade with America in this period. (D.O.D. 562)

PERCEVAL-MAXWELL PAPERS

The American papers in this deposit mainly concern Richard Montgomery (1736–75), born in Donegal and appointed by Congress to lead the attack on Canada in 1775 when he was killed at Quebec (T. 1023).

A later deposit under the same name includes the correspondence of Lt. John Waring, serving in the 56th Regiment in Antigua, 1781–2.

(D. 1556)

TYRONE

J. B. and R. H. Twigg, Solicitors
Cookstown

An exceptionally good group of emigrant letters, 1771–5, discussing the tea tax, the possibility of armed conflict, the determination of Americans to defend themselves, and other salient matters. (D. 1140)

REPUBLIC OF IRELAND

DUBLIN

Irish Manuscripts Commission, 73 Merrion Square
Dublin

In 1928 the Commission was established to locate and report on collections of manuscripts and papers of literary, historical and general interest relating to Ireland, in public and private ownership, and to arrange for and supervise programmes of publication. In 1950 the Commission ceased its search function, which was taken over by the National Library of Ireland, but since 1961 the two organizations have worked together in locating and reporting on manuscript material in private keeping. The serial publication of the Commission is *Analecta Hibernica,* which calendars and prints manuscripts and includes the reports of the Commission. Apart from the following, the *Analecta* contains no references pertinent to the revolutionary period.

LONGFORD PAPERS

No. 15 (November 1944), p. 127, calendars the Longford Papers (property of the Earl of Longford, Pakenham Hall, Castlepollard, Co. Westmeath), which include:

21 letters, 1776–7–8, from Richard Pakenham, an officer in the British Army, from various places in America, to his brother Thomas Pakenham, describing the progress of the campaign and current affairs.

BAYLY PAPERS

No. 20 (1964), p. 111 ff., calendars the Bayly Papers (property of Mr E. A. R. Bayly, Ballyarthur, Woodenbridge, Co. Wicklow), which include:

Correspondence and diary, 1779–93, of Brig.-Gen. Richard Symes, Quartermaster-General of British Forces in North America, 1782; also 5 commissions, giving his progress from Adjutant, 1765, to Lieutenant-Colonel, 1782.

National Library of Ireland, Kildare Street
Dublin

The National Library holds what is probably the largest collection of historical manuscripts in Ireland, and conducts an active search and acquisitions programme in conjunction with the Historical Manuscripts Commission. Only the following material relates to the American revolutionary period.

BALFOUR PAPERS

3 letters, 1764–5, from James Pillson of New York to Harry Brabazon, merchant of Drogheda, Co. Louth, concerning the marketing of flax seed and butter.

MANSFIELD PAPERS

2 letters, 13 May and 18 June 1782, to Robert Snow from his brother William, describing his situation as a prisoner in New York.

Public Record Office of Ireland, Four Courts
Dublin

During the Civil War 1916–22, part of the Public Record Office was blown up, with the result that most of the 18th-century material, including the papers of the Chief Secretaries of Ireland, was lost. The surviving records are described in Margaret Griffith 'A Short Guide to the Public Record Office of Ireland', *Irish Historical Studies* VIII, March 1952, reprinted by the Stationery Office, Dublin, 1952. The only material pertaining to the American Revolution appears to be the following.

ABSTRACTS OF EXPORTS AND IMPORTS OF IRELAND, 4 vols., 1764–73, 1784–8

These are apparently complete returns of Irish trade, giving names of ports, countries of consignment, type of merchandise, amount and value. Destinations for exports were the Carolinas, New England, New Providence, Pennsylvania, Virginia, etc. (Crick and Alman, 543)

Royal Irish Academy, 19 Dawson Street
Dublin

CHARLEMONT MANUSCRIPTS

Papers of James Caulfield, 4th Viscount and 1st Earl of Charlemont (1728–99), which include his memoirs discussing the effect of the American war on Ireland and several letters with minor mention of the war. (Crick and Alman, 545)

State Paper Office, Dublin Castle
Dublin

Established in 1702, the State Paper Office, by an Act of 1867, transfers papers of more than 50 years' standing, when fully catalogued and indexed, to the Public Record Office of Ireland. By 1922, the papers down to that year had been transferred, and hence did not survive the explosion and fire. The State Paper Office thus contains nothing pertaining to the American revolutionary period.

LONGFORD

Earl of Granard, Castle Forbes
Newtownforbes

GRANARD PAPERS

Letters, 1776–81, of Francis Rawdon-Hastings, 1st Marquis of Hastings and 2nd Earl of Moira (1754–1826), which give details of his military career in America, 1773–81, including service at Bunker Hill, Monmouth, Charleston, and his celebrated victory over a superior force under Gen. Nathaniel Greene at Hobkirk's Hill, S.C. (Crick and Alman, 552)

TIPPERARY

Earl of Donoughmore, Knocklofty
Clonmel

DONOUGHMORE PAPERS

Letter, 16 March 1774, from Lord Townshend to John Hely Hutchinson on the blockade of Boston, the pending alteration of the Boston Charter, and criticisms of the Chatham and Rockingham factions.

Letters, 25 October 1775 and 6 March 1776, from Charles Jenkinson to John Hely Hutchinson on the rebellion and related parliamentary debates.

(Crick and Alman, 553)

PART II
THE NETHERLANDS, FRANCE, SPAIN

THE NETHERLANDS

INTRODUCTION

Unlike many of the other countries of Europe, no guide to historical material relating to America in the Netherlands has ever been produced; hence it is not possible to use earlier reference works as a basis for approaching the material concerning the American Revolution. Thus the editors feel that useful new ground has been broken by listing the principal sources for research on the American Revolution which exist in Holland. The following is in no sense a comprehensive survey. Such a task would have necessitated a visit to every library and archive in the Netherlands, as each conceivably could contain material of greater or lesser relevance to the subjects of trade and commerce during the revolutionary period. They have instead chosen to examine the most important archival repositories where most of the material is to be found. Researchers will find the bulk of their material in The Hague and Leiden, so it was in these two cities that the survey was concentrated.

Relations between the Netherlands and the United States were as complex as they were interesting, both from the American and the internal Dutch points of view. Although the Dutch lost their North American colonies to the English during the reign of Charles II, Dutch interest in trade with British North America continued throughout the 18th century. Because of the Navigation Acts much of this trade in both slaves and goods came under the general heading of smuggling. However, the profitability and success of Dutch trade with the colonies was influenced by the declining position of the Netherlands in terms of sea power and world influence after the War of Spanish Succession. The restrictions placed by the British on American trade with other nations after the Seven Years War tightened the enforcement of the Navigation Acts and supporting Acts of Parliament. For commercial reasons, therefore, the Dutch welcomed the opportunity presented by the American revolutionaries when hostilities broke out in North America. A market with enormous potential offered Dutch commercial interests new chances to make inroads if the British lost control over much, if not all, of the territory east of the Mississippi.

Dutch interest in the American Revolution, however, was not confined solely to opportunities for economic gain. Within the Netherlands an intellectual movement, growing in influence throughout the Republic at the time, sympathized with the ideals set forth in the Declaration of Independence. John Adams soon made contact with the pamphleteers and professors at the

147

heart of this movement, and converted these feelings into diplomatic recognition of the United States as well as providing solid loans and investment which helped to finance the revolutionary cause. The Dutch Republic was caught between two stools as this support of the US gained momentum. On the one hand, middle and upper middle class intellectuals, the professions, merchants and bankers, who wanted to gain some influence on events within the Netherlands, were among the early proponents of recognition and support of the United States. On the other, the Dutch Republic saw the opportunity presented by an alliance with France against the British which involvement in the American war would bring. However, support of the American independence struggle would only strengthen the hand of those same groups who wanted to increase their influence in the Republic at the expense of the oligarchy which ruled it. The result was initial support for the colonies using the so-called 'patriotic' movement, but soon afterwards the leaders of this movement were abandoned by the State. Many were forced to flee the country after the Americans had won their independence. Many, like van der Kemp, came to the United States, while others fled to France or Brussels. But during the Revolutionary War there was a community of interest within Holland whose purposes were served by active support of the American cause.

This support manifested itself in three ways. First, intellectual support, through pamphlets and newspapers, which proselytized the cause of democracy and reform throughout Europe, particularly the *Gazette de Leyde*. Second, naval support of the American cause by the government, which waged war against Britain on the high seas, not only in the North Sea and in the Caribbean, but in East Indian waters as well. Third, commercial support through loans by private firms to the American government. Three commercial houses risked their capital on the American cause in 1782: De la Lande and Fynje, Nicolaas and Jacob Staphorst, and the Willinks. These contracts, according to P.J. van Winter, became the cornerstone of American credit abroad for many years thereafter. In all, eleven major loans were floated between 1782 and 1794 on behalf of the US, which amounted to 29 million guilders. Unfortunately for the Dutch, however, Holland's declining influence as a financial centre and a lack of confidence on the part of Dutch merchants hampered the great opportunities for influence and further investment presented by American independence. American merchants required a long line of credit during and after the war, which Dutch traders were not keen to extend. Furthermore, many of the Dutch goods shipped to the US did not suit the American market, and in any event the Americans used a different system of weights and measures to those used in the various provinces of the Netherlands. The Dutch were not flexible enough to cope with new sets of price quotations based on American specifications. And finally, Americans were not averse to resuming old patterns of trade after the war. Thus, the struggles within the Netherlands to recognize the new republic, the propaganda emanating from Holland on behalf of the Americans, the naval war, and the loans did not result in the Dutch capturing even a significant part of the American market at the expense of the British after the war. Once this became clear, Dutch interest in North America, already well on the wane prior to the Revolution, reverted to its former state. Disillusionment and apathy on the part of the Dutch deepened after the Republic collapsed in the wake of the French Revolution.

Nevertheless, although the Dutch never were able to capitalize on the American Revolution, the American cause was vitally influenced by the efforts made by the Netherlands. The naval war, combined with the French efforts, diverted the British Navy from a concentration on the blockade of American ports. The loans financed the US government at a time when French money was evaporating. Propaganda from Holland influenced intellectual circles in both France and Britain where it mattered most.

The Dutch archives, therefore, reflect the various interests of the Netherlands in the American Revolution. The voluminous pamphlet material in The Hague and Leiden is a rich source for any scholar interested in the intellectual history of Europe prior to the French Revolution. The records of the States-General, the Admiralty and the *Liassen*, dealing with the international diplomacy of the Dutch Republic, are key sources for the student of naval and diplomatic history. The commercial relations of the Netherlands with the United States are spread throughout a variety of sources, especially the private papers housed at the Rijksarchief and elsewhere. An examination of the diversity and volume of primary source material in the Netherlands indicates that the archives of the Netherlands, particularly those in Leiden and The Hague, are a rich fund of documentation which are more than worthy of new research and fresh assessments by historians.

Dutch central and provincial governmental archives have been incorporated into a national archive system since 1880. For a survey of these archives, see *De Rijksarchieven in Nederland: Overzicht van de inhoud van de Rijksarchiefbewaarplaatsen* ('S-Gravenhage, Ministerie van Onderwijs, Kunsten en Wetenschappen, 1953). Very brief, but more recent, is W.J. Formsma, *Gids voor de Nederlandse archieven* (Bussum, 1967). L. Thomas and D. Case, *Guide to the Diplomatic Archives of Europe* (Philadelphia, University of Pennsylvania Press 1959, 158–78), have a short discussion but a good bibliography. Another useful work for the researcher is W.J. Formsma and B. van't Hoff, *Repertorium van inventarissen van Nederlandse archieven* (Groningen, 1965, 2nd ed.). *Verslagen omtrent 's Rijks oude archieven* (1878–1927) has inventories appended, but from 1928 the inventories are published separately as *Inventarissen van Rijks—en andere archieven*.

Several Dutch scholars have turned their attention to Holland and the American Revolution. For a survey of the relations between the Continental

Congress and the Netherlands, see the unpublished doctoral dissertation of F.W. van Wijk, *De Republiek en Amerika, 1776–1782* (Leiden University, 1921). P.J. van Winter, *Verkenning en onderzoek* (Groningen, J.B. Wolters, 1965), is a recent analysis well worth noting on the diplomatic and commercial relations between the two countries.

AMSTERDAM

Gemeentelijke Archiefdienst, Amsteldijk 67
Amsterdam

Of the many repositories in Amsterdam, only the Municipal Archive has any real relevance to the study of the American Revolution. As with so many of the other local archives and libraries in the Netherlands, most of the relevant material is in the nature of important commercial family papers and some company records. (The published guide is P. Scheltema, *Inventaris van het Amsterdamsche Archief*, Amsterdam, Stadsdrukkerij, 1874, Part 3. This guide has been updated by inventories in the archive. The following summary of material bearing on the American Revolution is based on the guide and these more recent inventories.)

I

.9. *Resolutions of the States-General,* 1682–1793, 120 vols.

.14. Nouvelles van Staat of Missiven van Nederlandsche ambassadeurs, residenten, enyoyés, en consuls aan de Hoog Mogende Heeren Staten-Generaal der Vereenigde Nederlanden, 6 January 1682 to 4 November 1793, 160 vols.

(These two references duplicate material of a similar nature mentioned under THE HAGUE, in the entry dealing with official papers of the *Rijksarchief*.)

.73. Plakhaten en ordinanciën van de Staten-Generaal der Vereenigde Nederlanden en der Staten van Holland en West-Friesland, 1751–85.

.74. *Idem*, 1771–94.

III

.1. Notes of the meetings of the Seventeen of the VOC (Dutch East India Company), 1602–1796, 76 vols. An invaluable aid to the study of the affairs of the East Indies, and useful for the role of trade and naval policy in the Indies insofar as these influenced the British relationship with America. The connection between these seemingly disparate issues was considerable, as the British were obliged to fight a naval war on several fronts while they conducted their operations in North America during the Revolution.

.2. Notes of the meetings of the Seventeen of the VOC, held in Amsterdam and Middelburg, 1766–74, 16 vols.

.3. The Hague 'verbaal' of the commissions of the East India Company, 1770–94, 21 vols.

XII

Ships registers from the Arrondisement Amsterdam, pp. 84–9.

XIV

Guilds (and their effect on international trade) in Amsterdam, pp. 91–105. These notes should be consulted when dealing with any subject concerning Dutch economic history.

Guilds were almost at their nadir during the Revolution, but nevertheless had some considerable influence. For any study of shipping and trade with North America during the revolutionary period, the student should consult I.H. van Eeghen, *Inventarissen der Archieven van de Gilden en van het Brouwerscollege*, Amsterdam, Stadsdrukkerij, 1951, for a complete inventory of all the records, including trading of the Amsterdam guilds. This work can be found, with the records, at the Municipal Archive in Amsterdam, and references to North America are scattered throughout the text. There are similar records of local guilds and provincial trading with North America in the provincial archives of the Netherlands. Taken as a whole, they are of considerable interest to economic historians, but taken singly they are of only regional or local interest.

BRANTS ARCHIEF

The Brants family was one of the first to trade with the US under the aegis of several companies: Quirijn Brants en Zoon, Couderc and Brants; Couderc, Brants and Changuion; Couderc, Brants and Co.; Compagnie de Ceres; 't Hoen en Brants, and others. These companies dealt primarily with Pennsylvania during and after the American Revolution. For an inventory of the holdings in the Brants collection: I.H. van Eeghen, *Inventaris van het Familie-Archief Brants*, Amsterdam, Stadsdrukkerij, 1959. This is the only collection of private papers in the Municipal Archive which has any direct relevance to trade and commerce with North America during the revolutionary period.

Tropenmuseum, Linnaeusstraat 2
Amsterdam

The other repository in Amsterdam containing material pertaining to the American Revolution which is not duplicated elsewhere is the Tropenmuseum. Here can be found many periodicals and contemporary books concerning trade with the East Indies as well as items dealing with trade, especially the slave trade, with Surinam and the Dutch Caribbean islands. Although the Dutch West Indies trade has relevance to the supply of the rebels, most of this material would have but a peripheral interest for the student directly concerned with the American Revolution.

THE HAGUE

Algemeen Rijksarchief, Bleyenburg 7
The Hague

Algemeen Rijksarchief is the largest repository of historical documentation in the Netherlands. Being the principal archive for government papers, it is safe to say that most of the material in Holland relevant to the American Revolution is to be found here. The material is almost exclusively in Dutch, a knowledge of which is essential to the use of this as well as most other repositories of historical source material in the Netherlands. Like its counterparts in Britain and the United States, the Algemeen Rijksarchief is also the repository of a large number of collections of private papers. It is vital that any scholar interested in the Dutch role in the American Revolution should visit this national archive first if not exclusively, since far more material exists here than in all the other archives and libraries put together. The same might be said of other historical periods, with the sole exception of World War II and post-war periods, in which the Rijksinstituut voor Oorlogsdocumentatie, in two locations in Amsterdam and a subsidiary in The Hague, excels.

I

RESOLUTIONS OF THE STATES-GENERAL

The States-General was and is the Parliament of the Netherlands. Under the Republic, which held sway from the origins of an independent united Netherlands until the French conquest of 1795, the States-General played a different role than it was to play under the Monarchy of the House of Orange in the post-1815 period. In the period of the American Revolution the States-General was declining in power and influence, despite the fact that all companies which hoped to trade abroad received their ultimate permission from the States-General and the Stadhouder. The Resolutions were, in effect, acts of Parliament and are divided into several catagories:

2nd series of ordinary resolutions

These are fully registered for the 1637–1795 period.

For the period January 1763 to Index 1783 the numbers run from **3559** up to and including **3624**. There are 3 for each year, 1 from January–June, 1 from July through December, and 1 index.

'First Minutes'

These are divided into 12 volumes per annum, 1 each month.

1334–45 cover the period January–December 1763; December 1783 is **1586**.

Résumés of minutes of the notes of the meetings of the States-General

These would be equivalent to a précis of Hansard. They are divided as the above, in 12 volumes per annum, 1 per month.

January 1763 is **2697**; December 1783 is **2948**. The appropriate month can easily be calculated.

Published resolutions of the States-General

These were printed annually until 1780; thereafter 2 per year were published.

Thus 1763 is **3818**, and the second half of 1783 is **3841**. One must remember that **3836–41** cover only the years 1781–3; whereas **3818–35** cover the 1763–80 period on an annual basis.

Résumés of minutes of the secret notes of the States-General

These appeared 4 times per year, once every 3 months for the 1763–83 period.

January–March 1763 is **4460**; the last volume of 1783 is **4522**.

Registers of secret resolutions of the States-General

Indices of persons and cases raised in secret resolutions. This extraordinary group of documents covers the 1634–1796 period in 238 parts. They appeared on an irregular basis as circumstances required.

The 1763–83 period is covered in **4733–74** inclusive.

II
LIASSEN

The collection known as the Liassen includes all incoming letters addressed to the States-General as well as correspondence and minutes from outgoing letters. They represent, in effect, a rough equivalent to the British FO series at the Public Records Office, as all foreign affairs were handled and catalogued in this manner. However, relations on an official level between the various states of the Dutch Republic were also collected in the Liassen, which would also make this the rough equivalent of the Home Office papers.

1a–b. *Inland Liassen* (ordinary)

This vast collection covers internal intra- and inter-state relations during the 1550–1796 period.
    The period January 1763 to December 1783 is held in **5344–406.**
    A sub-category of incoming secret letters and other pieces is held in a 'secret' file. These were few in number and the 1763–72 period is listed in **5475**; while the 1773–89 period is covered in **6476.**

2a–b. *Admiralty Liassen*

The ordinary material in this equally vast collection is held for the 1613–1795 period.
    The early part of the revolutionary period in America is covered annually from **5684** onwards, but from 1780 onwards there is much more, collected in as many as 3 volumes per annum. The August–December 1783 volume, **5699,** completes the series for the revolutionary period.
    Like the *Inland Liassen*, there is a secret sub-category, which includes incoming secret letters and other pieces for the 1700–95 period. **5721–2** cover the revolutionary period: the first dealing with 1752–77, the second from 1778–95.

3. *Liassen of the Treasury,* 1616–1794 (ordinary)

By the time of the American Revolution these become few in number, largely because of the increasing bankruptcy of the Treasury of the Republic and the fact that most of the individual states and companies dealt with their American counterparts directly.
    5732–3 cover the period: the first dealing with 1744–67, the second from 1774–94. The intervening period contains no Treasury Liassen.

4a–b. *Liassen of the East India Company,* 1623–1795 (ordinary)

This is a most valuable collection, chiefly for the 17th century. By the mid-18th century the East India Company was near bankruptcy, and became defunct after 1795.

5746–7 cover this period: the first for 1753–67; the second for 1768–84.

A secret file was also kept for the East India Company (VOC), covering the 1703–95 period under **5750.**

5a–b. *Liassen of the West India Company* (ordinary)

This collection is marginally more important for America-oriented scholars because of the dealings of the West India Company (VWC) with the slave trade in the Americas.

5789–805 cover the 1763–83 period.

A secret sub-category is covered in **5816–17,** the years 1704–80 and 1781–95 respectively.

6. *Liassen: Maastricht and its relations with the Republic*
It holds little of relevance for America-oriented scholars.

7.18. *The Foreign Liassen*

7a–b. *Liassen England* (ordinary)
This collection holds the diplomatic relations on a formal level between Britain and the Netherlands.

The first and most vital of this equivalent to the British FO series is covered by **5979** (1763) to **5995** (1781–3).

The secret sub-category is covered in **6014–15** (1759–77, 1778–94, respectively).

8a–b. *Liassen of Upper Germany* (ordinary). Covering the 1578–1796 period, this collection includes relations with the following areas of the Germanies: Cologne, Danzig, Frankfurt, Hamburg, Hanau, Hanover, Hessen, Liège, Mannheim, Mainz, Prussia, the Holy Roman Empire, Saxony, Switzerland, and others which include smaller principalities within the Empire.

6788 (Jan–March 1763); **6546** (July–Dec 1783).

The secret sub-category is covered in 3 volumes: **6618** (1760–3); **6619** (1764–5, 1766–80); **6620** (1781–3).

Incoming letters from German princes are held in **6634** (1751–96).

Incoming secret letters from Dutch diplomatic representatives in Germany, with the exception of Brandenburg–Prussia during the 1700–96 period, are covered in **6669–74** inclusive (1763–83).

Incoming secret letters from Dutch diplomatic representatives in Brandenburg–Prussia for the 1700–96 period are held under **6689–90** (1763–83). However, in this last grouping three years of correspondence are missing: 1768, 1776, 1779.

9a–b. *Liassen: relations with Emden and East Friesland.* Of peripheral importance to the study of the American Revolution.

10a–b. *Liassen France*, 1588–1796.
The ordinary correspondence is covered in **6836–49** (1763–83).
The secret French Liassen deal with the 1700–96 period, and the 2 relevant volumes are **6882–3** (1758–70, 1771–83, respectively). The peace negotiations at Paris are included here.

11a–b. This collection includes the Liassen for relations with Italy, Savoy, Constantinople, Venice, the Barbary Coast of Algiers, Morocco, Tripoli and Tunis, in their ordinary and secret categorizations and are of peripheral importance.

12a–b. *Liassen Portugal*, 1641–1795. These are of especial interest to those concerned with the Dutch seizure of Portuguese posessions in the 17th century, starting with Portugal's independence from Spain. This entire file is far less useful for the revolutionary period than for the previous century, but should be consulted if matters of trade and commerce, especially the slave trade, are of interest.
The ordinary correspondence for the period 1762–85 is covered in **7029–33**.
The secret file is in **7040** for the 1752–86 period, but unfortunately large gaps appear: 1757–9, 1763, 1766, 1768–79, 1780–1 and 1783 are missing.

13a–b. *Liassen Spain.* The Dutch had no ordinary diplomatic relations with Spain until they had formally been granted their independence through the Peace of Westphalia (1648), so this file begins in 1649 and ends with the Dutch Republic in 1796.
The ordinary file covers **7149–55** (1761–84) and deals with naval and commercial affairs as well as the Paris Peace of 1783.
The secret sub-category is in **7167–8** (1739–70, 1771–96, respectively). Like the Portuguese file, several key years are missing in the secret category: 1763–5, 1767–9 and 1779–83 for the revolutionary period.

14a–b. *Liassen Sweden.* The ordinary file covers the 1591–1796 period. There is only peripheral information on the Revolution, largely dealing with the Armed Neutrality in the Baltic, in **7216–21,** (1763–89).
The secret file is **7231–6** (1757–90).

15a–b. *Liassen Denmark* (1579–1796). This file contains material of great interest for the 17th century but little for the period under examination here.

The ordinary file **7292–8** (1759–85).

The secret sub-category is **7308–9** (1761–72, 1773–89, respectively). The files for the 1775–9 period are missing in the secret category.

16a–b. *Liassen Poland.* Both the ordinary and secret files are of peripheral interest.

17a–b. *Liassen Muscovy.* The same is true here, except for the Baltic trade.

18a–b. *Liassen Brussels.* At this time the rough equivalent of Belgium was under the control of the Hapsburg Empire. This file has little relevance to the American Revolution in either its ordinary or secret files.

19a–b. *Liassen America.* The ordinary and secret categories apply here as well, but relations of a formal nature were not established until after independence. The 1784–94 period is covered here, but the files for 1785–7 period are missing. One would only consult this group of documents if one were treating problems of the post-Revolutionary War period.

22. *Liassen Requests received,* 1600–1796. Collected on about a 4-per-year schedule, this group of additional manuscripts, **7868–958** covers the years 1763–83. This file should be consulted as a check against missing information in the above files.

III

1. *The States at War on Land and Sea*, 1595–1795

An invaluable collection for any period of the Dutch Republic, and no less so for the 1763–83 period (**8234–75**). Military, naval and commercial policy merge in this, as in other periods, and therefore all scholars are advised to consult these files in dealing with any transatlantic question.

2. *Reports of Dutch representatives abroad*

8827–52 should be looked at with special reference to the notes made by Pieter Johannes van Berckel in his mission to the USA, 4 June 1783 to 27 February 1789.

7. *Reports concerning the defence of and war in West and East India*

9219–24 include the fortification of Curaçao during the American Revolution as well as naval struggles in East Indies waters during the 1779–83 period.

8a. *Notes from Commissions of the States-General concerning the Admiralty*

9251–7 cover the 1763–83 period.

IV

11161–669. Ordinary in-letters dealing with internal and external affairs. 1763 begins with **11446** in what is called the German register; **11575** completes the French register for 1783. These volumes are only useful as a cross-reference for material mentioned above.

11670–833. Registers of secret in-letters, 1672–1794. The 1763–83 period is covered in **11795–816.** These again are cross-reference material to the secret correspondence in the Liassen mentioned above.

11924. Special file of Registers of ordinary in-letters concerning America for the 1782–9 period.

11925–30. Register of in-letters from the Admiralty for the 1777–90 period. Divided in 6 parts, **11925–7** deal with the war period, 1777–84.

11934–2082. Registers of out-letters, 1646–1795. The 1763–83 period is covered in **12050–70.** This again is for cross-referencing against the more important material listed above.

12083–145. The publications called 'News of Dutch Envoys in Foreign Countries'. **12115–32** cover the 1763–83 period, and a special file, **12149** deals with additional material of a general nature gathered in the 1760–83 period.

12161–231. Printed posters, placards and leaflets from the 1590–1785 period. **12212–31.** dealing with the 1763–85 period, are of special interest.

12237–69. The Minutes of the Acts of the States-General, 1623–1794. Only **12264–5** (1762–75, 1776–82) have any relevance to the American Revolution.

VI

VII.B.7.**4287.** Act of ratification after preliminary discussions at the Paris Peace Conference between the King of England and the States-General, 2 and 10 September 1783.

VII.B.15.**4354**. Act of ratification of a treaty of commerce between the USA and the States-General, 8 October 1782 and 23 January 1783.

De Archieven der Admiraliteitscolleges

This is a reference, published in The Hague by the Algemene Landsdrukkerij in 1924, compiled by Dr J. de Hullu. It catalogues a number of sundry documents, only two of which contain items of interest:

239. Trade and Naval Relations with the USA, 1780–3. Deals with matters of emigration, trade and commerce, with particular reference to Pennsylvania.

250. Extracts from resolutions of the States-General concerning trade with France and the seizure of Dutch ships by the British in the 1778–80 period. This collection is only support material for *Admiralty Liassen* and the *Liassen England* mentioned above.

The following documents are of peripheral interest:

XXXI.E.

.251. Extract of Resolutions of the States-General concerning the exchange of Prisoners-of-War with England, 1782.

.252. Letter from Ambassadors Lestevenon van Berkenrode and Brantsen in Paris during the Peace Treaty negotiations in 1783.

.253. Extracts of Resolutions from the States of Holland concerning the secret relations of the Magistrate of Amsterdam with the US Congress, 1780–1.

XXXVII.A.j.

.102–35. Notes on the equipment of the Navy, 1746–94. The period 1762–83 is covered in Nos. **111–26.**

.137. Annual equipment of a warship to Guinea and the American coasts, 1766–8.

XXXVII.E.

.485. Notes on the Armed Neutrality, the selling of ships to the Dutch Republic, recruits from America and the Battle of Dogger Bank, 1781.

.486. Extracts of Resolutions of the States-General over trade with English colonies in North America, including the case of John Paul Jones and others, 1775–9.

.487. Continuation of the above, 1778–80.

XVIII.f.

Collection of Van Kinckel. **.64** is a copy-journal of the English warship *Victory*, during the period 16 May to 8 September 1778.

XXXI.G.

.265. Concerning casualties in the capture of the Dutch ship *De Vrouw Machtelina* by the British near Curaçao in June 1782. Covers 1782–3.

XXXVII.B.f.

.422. Admiralty records of the surrender of the *Castor* to the English under Capt. P. Melvill, 31 July 1781.

XXXIX.I.A.i.

.40. Placards of the States-General in the war with England, 1781–3.

.41. Plans of the campaign of the Dutch and the French against the English fleet, 1782.

.41a. Concerning a convoy commanded by Count van Bylandt in his surrender to the English off Texel, 1779 (dated 4 January 1780).

.42. Letter to Prince Willem V from Capt. P. Melvill and Lt. J.A. Bloys on the capture of the *Castor* by the English, 27 June 1781.

.43. Copy letter to Prince Willem V from J.A. Zoutman on the Battle of Dogger Bank, 7 August 1781.

.144. Exchange of prisoners-of-war and negotiations with Lord Wentworth in 1782 (1780–2).

.45. Support of prisoners-of-war in England, 1782–92.

.46. Letters between van der Hoop and R. Diggins in Chichester on exchange of prisoners, 10 April 1782 to 19 November 1792.

XL.III.

.33. Memoir of a journal of the French fleet under Lt.-Gen. de Grasse during its voyages in the Antilles, Santo Domingo and New England, 1781–2. Also the journal of Admiral de Suffren in the East Indies, 1781.

PRIVATE PAPERS

COLLECTION OF J. DERK VAN DER CAPELLEN TOT DEN POL (1741–84)

In September 1971 P. Wander made a complete inventory of this collection, which appears in *Leeszaal* **319** in the Rijksarchief. Van der Capellen dealt with Franklin, Adams, Livingston and other American agents who passed through Holland during the revolutionary period. This collection is a particularly rich source on the slave trade and diplomacy. Despite the fact that the early part of the collection covers internal affairs, the last parts are extremely valuable for all American revolutionary dealings with the Netherlands, including the question of loans and recognition.

ARCHIVE OF THE FAGEL FAMILY

Inventory made by N.M. Japikse and published in The Hague by the Ministry of Education, Arts and Sciences in 1964. This covers a famous family whose record of public service was surpassed by none in the Netherlands at the time of the American Revolution, as well as in other periods. The most important member of the family during the revolutionary period was François Willem Baron Fagel (1768–1856), who served in the Battle of Dogger Bank as a young boy.However, Hendrik Fagel de Oude, François Fagel de Jonge, Hendrik Baron Fagel de Jonge and Jacob Baron Fagel also hold important places in Dutch history. All the family papers are deposited in the Rijksarchief. The relevant papers for this period are not numerous: they are listed on pp. 128–33 of the inventory; and cover **1420–80** in the archive. This collection should be examined, particularly for the period after the Revolution.

PAPERS OF C. W. F. DUMAS (1721–96)

An agent of both France and the US in the last quarter of the 18th century. There are 34 packets of documents of his papers at the Rijksarchief. Dumas dealt with the first American diplomats and first US Ambassador to the Netherlands, John Adams. The relevant papers begin with an exchange of letters with Franklin in London in 1768, with whom he struck up an immediate friendship and sympathy for the American cause. He was employed as an American agent on 9 December 1775 and worked in that capacity in Holland thereafter. He was one of the first political agents working for the US in Europe apart from those in the United Kingdom. He was also used by the French, as they recognised their community of interest with the American cause. There is much correspondence with both Adams and Livingston in these papers, leading up to and following Adams' recognition as the first

American Ambassador to The Hague on 14 May 1778. On 26 June 1783 Dumas became the American *Chargé d'Affaires* in The Hague and later lived for a period in the United States. An invaluable source.

PAPERS OF LAURENS PIETER VAN DE SPIEGEL (1736–1800)

In 1780 he was the Secretary of State of the Province of Zeeland, which always had more interest in shipping and foreign trade than virtually any other Dutch province. Some of these papers deal with van de Spiegel's relations with the East Indies, shipping and naval campaigns there, as well as shipping to and from the USA during the Revolution.

VAN HOGENDORP PAPERS

This was another great family whose record of public service to the Netherlands is unsurpassed. All papers reside in the Rijksarchief. The most important individual for this period was Gijsbert Karel van Hogendorp, who visited the USA in 1783. Several documents dealing with the war against England, 1780–2, exist in this collection, as well as the diary of Gijsbert Karel van Hogendorp for 1777–85, which is particularly useful. Van Hogendorp went on to play a leading role in the reconstruction of the Dutch State after the French period and was one of the triumvirate which restored the State and established the Monarchy under the House of Orange in the 1813–15 period. His exploits in the US are catalogued here.

PAPERS OF RAADPENSIONARIS STEIJN

Steijn was involved in trade with America prior to the War of Independence. His papers cover the period 1749–83, but only a few deal directly with American affairs.

INVENTORIES

Several inventories of peripheral collections should be noted. Among these are:

R. Bijlsma, *Het Oud-Archief van de Gouvernements-Secretaire der Kolonie Suriname*. This contains information on the slave trade and relations with the USA before, during and after the Revolutionary War.

R. Bijlsma, *Het Oud-Archief van Curaçao en Onderhoorige Eilanden Bonaire en Aruba*. This collection deals with the rest of the Dutch West Indies and contains material on the slave trade for the entire period under examination here. *Het Archief van de Nederlandse Bezittingen ter Kuste van Guinea*. This contains further information on the slave trade between West Africa, the Dutch islands and North America.

Inventory of the West India Company and its successors.

Inventory of the Direction of Berbice and of the Surinam Society.

These last two items have peripheral information on trade with the United States, particularly the slave trade, during the 1763–83 period. The sections covering the Second Dutch West India Company, in the first of these two volumes, pp. 12–87, are of some interest.

Koninklijke Bibliotheek, Lange Voorhout 34
The Hague

The Koninklijke Bibliotheek, or Royal Library, is located within five minutes walk of the Rijksarchief. One of the Netherlands' most valuable archives, it has only some relevance for the revolutionary period. Its interests are largely literary and humanistic, and it is based on the Crown Collection which forms its heart. Records of the Royal Family are kept here, but no public papers are held in the Royal Library. Only official government publications, mostly of the 19th- and 20th-centuries, are to be found. Nevertheless, it should be noted that it holds the largest newspaper collection in the Netherlands. Most of these newspapers and some pamphlets are kept in the annex to the library at Korte Lombardstraat 15.

PAMPHLET COLLECTION

The locations combine to form one of the most extraordinary collections of pamphlets in the world. Literally tens of thousands concern the period of the American Revolution, the war, and its effect on trade and sea power. The Revolution created enormous interest in both commercial and intellectual circles in Holland, an interest which is reflected in this pamphlet collection. Although the collection is far more complete for the post-1830 period, these pamphlets contain a wealth of contemporary opinion which should not be overlooked. The relevant collections for this period are found under **677** in the catalogue. The periods covered are:

X. 1758–9	XIII. 1782–3
XI. 1780–1	XIV. 1783–5
XII. 1781–2	

The whole question of pamphlets and their cataloguing requires further comment, which will follow in the next entry dealing with the Library of the University of Leiden.

NEWSPAPER COLLECTION

It is clear that once the Dutch became involved in the war, interest mush-roomed. The newspapers of this period reflect the same interest indicated in the pamphlet collection, and there are many examples of provincial news-papers. Mostly only bits and pieces, with no real run of daily or weekly news-papers to examine. However, there are some key exceptions, among which are the following:

Amsterdam, *Nouvelles d'Amsterdam*, 16 May 1732 to 18 December 1792. Lar-gely complete.

Amsterdam, *Amsterdamsehe Courant*, 6 February 1672 to 31 March 1903. Very incomplete, but useful for this period.

Buyksloot, *De Noordhollandsche Courant*, 1 January 1779 to 6 August 1783. Extremely useful, despite the fact that the village where it was published was small, in the neighbourhood of Amsterdam. It reflects the most important period under examination here.

Delft, *De Hollandsche historische Courant*, 1735–87. Very incomplete.

Groningen, *Geoctrojeerde Groninger Courant*, 4 January 1743 to 30 October 1857. Incomplete but useful.

The Hague, *s'Gravenhaegse Courant*. Only a few for 1767.

The Hague, *Gazette de la Haye*, 24 April 1744 to 30 December 1778. Incom-plete with the 1749–70 period completely missing.

Leiden, *Leidsche Courant*, 1721–1889. Very useful.

Leiden, *Nouvelles extraordinaires de divers endroits*, 1764–1811. This publi-cation was issued twice weekly, and like so many pamphlets and newspapers appeared in French, which was the recognised second language of the literati of Holland and the rest of Europe. Publication of journals in French gave them currency throughout Europe.

Utrecht, *Gazette d'Utrecht*, 1769–79, 1783 and 1787. Incomplete.

LEIDEN

Bibliotheek der Rijksuniversiteit, Rapenburg 70–74
Leiden

The University of Leiden Library is one of the oldest and largest in the Netherlands. Leiden is Holland's foremost university city, equivalent to

Oxford or Harvard. Its tradition of scholarship, with particular emphasis on colonial affairs, is matched by none in the Netherlands. Without slighting the Universities of Amsterdam or Utrecht in any way, it is fair to say that in terms of material relevant to the American Revolution, Leiden's place is second only to The Hague in the quality and quantity of its reference and historical materials. However, for this period most of the material is of a secondary source nature. There are no documents to speak of, and only a few published sources available. Those extant are listed below; the library call numbers are placed alongside each reference.

PUBLISHED SOURCES

395. *E.1.* Lodewyck Theodor Grave van Nassau La Leek, *Brieven over de Noord-Americaansche onlusten den waarschijnlijk uitslag dien oorlog enz,* Utrecht, G.T. van Paddenburg, 1777–9.

1015. *G.27.* Richard Price, *Observations on the nature of civil liberty, the principles of government, and the justice and policy of the war with America,* London, 1776, 3rd edition.

1150. *G.24.* Richard Price, *Nadere aanmerkingen over den aart en de waarde der burgerlijke vrijheid en eener vrije regeering,* Leiden, L. Herdingh, 1777.

480. *E.10. Mémoires historiques et pièces authentiques sur M. de Lafayette, pour servir à l'histoire des révolutions,* Paris, an II, 1793.

395. *E.–4.* George Washington, *Official Letters to the American Congress, written during the war between the United States and Great Britain,* London, Cadell, Jr. etc., 1795, 2 vols.

1352. *D.10–21.* Jared Sparks, ed., *The Diplomatic Correspondence of the American Revolution. Being the letters of Benjamin Franklin, Silas Deane, John Adams, John Jay, etc., concerning the foreign relations of the United States during the whole revolution,* Boston, N. Hale, etc., 1829, 12 vols.

395. *C.9–12.* Jared Sparks, edited from original MS., *Correspondence of the American Revolution, being letters of eminent men to George Washington, from the time of his taking command of the army to the end of his presidency,* Boston, Little, Brown and Co., 1853, 4 vols.

PAMPHLET COLLECTION

The real value of the University of Leiden Library lies not in its published works or documents but in its pamphlets. Taken together with the Royal Library in The Hague, mentioned above, and the Bibliotheca Thysiana, also on the Rapenburg in Leiden, these pamphlet collections are invaluable.

In order to deal with the vast amount of material available, the student should first consult W.P.C. Knuttel, *Catalogus van de Pamfletten —Verzameling berustende in de Koninklijke Bibliotheek bewerkt, met aantee- keningen en een register der schrijvers voorzien,* The Hague, F.J. Belinfante, 1905. Although described as a catalogue of material in the Royal Library, this huge work of course includes material duplicated elsewhere, such as Leiden, and is the basic starting point for work with pamphlet material. For the period of the Revolution, Vol. 5 (1776–95), pp. 1–220, should be consulted: **19114–20718** include the key works in The Hague.

However, also vital to an understanding of this period is a close perusal of the *Gazette de Leyde*, a periodical to be found in the University of Leiden Library (**1416.** *D. 1–11).* Edited by Jean Etienne *Luzac* (1746–1807) and pub- lished during the period 1760 until its demise on 4 May 1798, it was without question the most important journal in Holland and one of the most import- ant in Europe in terms of its influence, which went well beyond the confines of the Dutch Republic. Among its contributors were Thomas Paine and other revolutionaries of the time. For an understanding of the growing spirit of rev- olution, both in Europe and America, and their interrelationship, outlined so well in R.R. Palmer, *The Age of the Democratic Revolution* (Princeton, 1959, 2 vols.), a reading of the *Gazette de Leyde* is a must. A Professor at Leiden during the American Revolution, Luzac was a friend of John Adams and cor- responded with most of the leading American (and French) revolutionaries of the time. As a pamphleteer he was second to none. His only rival in Holland at the time appears to have been a Mennonite preacher, François Adriaan van der Kemp (1752–1829), who wrote under many pseudonyms, including EHJ, Junius Brutus and Kemp. His autobiography and correspondence, edited by Helen Lindlean Fairchild, (published in New York, 1905) appears in the Leiden Library (**482.** *F.30).* Many of his pamphlets appear in the Leiden col- lection as well. Van der Kemp was a pamphleteer in defence of the American cause who emigrated to upper New York State in 1787. Before he left the Netherlands he had an enormous influence on John Adams during his stay in Holland and gained an audience through the *Gazette de Leyde* and his own publications.

A catalogue of the pamphlets which are available in the Bibliotheca Thy- siana was edited by Louis D. Petit and published in Leiden in 1925 by A.W. Sijthoff. This catalogue, entitled *Bibliotheek van Nederlandsche Pamfletten, versameling van de bibliotheek van Johannes Thysius te Leiden,* is the key to works held in the University's sister library across the canal. For the period of the Revolution, Vol. 3 (1703–1800), pp. 142–87, **6844–7230**, should be con- sulted.

An examination of these resources in Leiden and The Hague should exhaust most of the material available in pamphlet form in the Netherlands. The Thysiana also contains a considerable number of newspapers and other periodicals, such as *Nouvelles extraordinaires de divers endroits*, 1753–98 **(1729)**. However, much of this material is duplicated in the Royal Library in The Hague.

PROVINCIAL ARCHIVES

The archives of virtually all cities of any size in the Netherlands contain material which may have a bearing on trade with the British North American colonies. Of these perhaps the most interesting records are to be found in Zeeland, whose trading patterns were of greater international scope than those of most other provinces. (The published guide to the Provinciale Bibliotheek van Zeeland, Abdijplein 9, Middelburg, is J. Brockema, *Catalogus van de Pamfletten, Tractaten, enz. aanwezig in de Provinciale Bibliotheek van Zeeland*, Middelburg, 1892. **2034–782**, pp. 422–563, contain the material most relevant to the American revolutionary period.) Private papers of interest for study of trade and commerce may also be found here and in other provincial libraries and archives. The provincial archives of Zwolle and Leeuwarden would probably be of more interest than others. Each has a catalogue, but like the materials at Middelburg, much may be of only local interest, with the newspapers and pamphlets duplicating those found in The Hague and Leiden.

FRANCE

INTRODUCTION

When France openly intervened in the Anglo-American conflict in 1778, the character of the struggle was changed from a provincial rebellion to an international maritime war. The harsh terms of the Treaty of Paris in 1763 had left France with a strong desire for revenge. Throughout his term of office the Foreign Minister Choiseul had concentrated on rebuilding and expanding the French navy with a view to recouping France's losses at Britain's expense when the right moment arrived. Together with his Spanish counterparts, first Choiseul and then Vergennes watched with acute interest the growing split between Britain and her American colonies. When the actual outbreak of hostilities occurred in 1775, France was the first country to which the rebellious colonists turned as a potential ally. A clandestine French agent had been in the colonies in 1775, while the first American agent arrived in Paris in 1776. The American cause was immediately popular in France and a number of French officers, most notably the Marquis de Lafayette, volunteered for service in the rebel army.

French policy from 1775 to 1778 had three basic aspects. First was covert aid to the rebels in the form of munitions, funds and a sympathetic reception for American privateers in French ports. Second was the unsuccessful attempt to convince Britain that France was strictly uninvolved in the affair. Third was the effort to persuade France's ally Spain to join France's effort to aid the American cause.

Negotiations with the United States began to founder in 1777, partly because of the insistence by America's plenipotentiary to France, Benjamin Franklin, that France could only take territorial compensation from Britain in the event of a military victory outside the bounds of North America. After American military viability was proved at the Battle of Saratoga, Franklin was able to persuade the French court that the United States would be a competent and potentially victorious ally, if given sufficient quantities of arms, French naval support, military advisers, and, above all, diversionary tactics by France and other maritime nations outside North America which would diffuse British military and naval strength.

A treaty of friendship, commerce and amity was initialled in February 1778 between the US and France, which brought France into the war militarily on a significant scale. It has often been stated that the American Revolution was an important cause of the French Revolution of 1789. This is undoubtedly true, but the ideological impetus the American Revolution gave to French intellectuals was by no means the most important result of the war for France. State bankruptcy, for so many decades a real possibility in France, was hastened by the expenditures and efforts put forth by France ostensibly on America's behalf. The Treaty of Paris of 1783 brought few tangible results for France which would have justified, in actuarial terms, the costs of the war. The reacquisition of rights and territories in the Senegal and India were hardly sufficient compensation for a state which, more than any other, made the existence of the United States possible. The addition of sugar islands in the Caribbean at a time when the slave and sugar trade was beginning to decline could not bring sufficient profit to the empty French treasury that additional European territory, for example, would have provided. For the United States, French aid at the diplomatic table was as valuable as France's first function as a supplier of arms and naval assistance. But neither Franklin, America's chief negotiator, nor the British were anxious to see France returned to a significant position in North America, and, as a result, France had to take territorial compensation for victory elsewhere.

France maintains a network of centralized national or departmental archives and a decentralized system of municipal archives. The records of the central government before 1789 are almost entirely in the Archives Nationales in Paris, the bibliography of which is discussed under that heading. Records not in the Archives Nationales for the period before 1789 will usually be found in the archives of the Foreign Ministry, the Ministry of Marine and the Ministry of Colonies. The departmental archives are under central administration but contain the regional archives. These archives usually have an individual printed guide but a general survey can be found in *Etat général par fonds des archives départementales* (Paris 1903). The more important towns have their own communal archives which sometimes possess family and commercial papers from the region. Departmental and communal archives are open to the public but it is always wise to write in advance. Permission to work in the Archives Nationales must be applied for in advance. Foreign researchers must present a letter from their embassy or a leading French citizen. There is a list of national, departmental and communal archives in *Archivum* V (1955).

There is a network of public libraries in France which has the Bibliothèque Nationale as its centre. The greatest amount of relevant material lies in the Bibliothèque Nationale but there is also a certain amount in the municipal libraries. Access to municipal libraries is generally unrestricted but a permit is necessary for the Bibliothèque Nationale. The catalogues of the Bibliothèque Nationale are discussed under that heading. The two main catalogues for public libraries are *Catalogue général des manuscrits des bibliothèques publiques des départements* (Paris 1849–95, 7 vols.) and *Catalogue général des manuscrits des bibliothèques publiques de France, Départements* (Paris, 1886 to date), cited below as 'CG'. David M. Matteson, *List of Manuscripts concern-*

*ing American History preserved in European Libraries and noted in their Pub-
lished Catalogues and similar Printed Lists* (Washington, D.C., Carnegie
Institution, 1925), has surveyed the latter catalogue series to CG 45(1915) for
material relating to American history, while the present editors have carried
the survey to CG 58(1971).

The Carnegie Institution of Washington published a guide to American
material in France: Waldo G. Leland *et al., Guide to Materials for American
History in the Libraries and Archives of Paris* (Carnegie Institution, 1932–43, 2
vols.). This work covers the Bibliothèque Nationale, some other libraries and
the archives of the Foreign Ministry. Leland reportedly was preparing to pub-
lish several more volumes dealing with other sections of the central government archives, but these have never appeared, although the manuscripts exist.
Henry P. Beers has provided a useful reference, *The French in North America:
A Bibliographical Guide to French Archives, Reproductions, and Research Missions* (Baton Rouge, La., Louisiana State University Press, 1957), which has
an extensive bibliography. The Canadian National Archives have published a
number of surveys and inventories of material in French archives pertaining
to Canada, some of which would also be relevant to the American Revolution. References to these Canadian reports can be found in Beers, op. cit.,
but they have not been utilized by the present editors. The Lafayette Papers
Project, Cornell University Libraries, Ithaca, N.Y. 14850, has undertaken to
locate, list and copy all known manuscripts of the Marquis de Lafayette.

AIX-EN-PROVENCE

Bibliothèque de Méjanes, Hôtel de Ville
13 Aix-en-Provence

1628. Pièces et documents réunis par E.-J. Genest sur la marine anglaise.
Various documents on the state of the British Navy, 1754–77. (CG 49(1951),
9)

Bibliothèque municipale, Hôtel de Ville
13 Aix-en-Provence

530. (R.A.48). 'Journal de la campagne du vaisseau *la Provence*, armé à
Toulon en 1776, commandé par M. de Barras.' 'Journal de la campagne du
vaisseau *le César*, armé à Toulon en 1777, commandé par M. de Barras, capitaine des vaiseaux du Roi.' 'Journal de la campagne du vaisseau *le Zélé*,
commandé par M. de Barras, armé en 1778, dans l'escadre commandé par M.
le comte d'Estaing, vice-amiral.' (CG 16(1894), 255. Matteson, 2)

AMIENS

Bibliothèque et archives municipales, 50 rue de la République
80 Amiens

881–95. Papiers du général de Vault, directeur du Dépot de la Guerre. Tome XIV. Mémoire du comte de Rochambeau pour l'histoire de la guerre en Amérique, commençant à l'arrivée du corps de troupes françaises, en 1780. Publié dans la *Revue Anglo-Française.* (CG 19(1893), 435. Matteson, 3)

ANGERS

Bibliothèque municipale, 10 rue du Musée
49 Angers

482.(466). 'Plan de guerre contre l'Angleterre, rédigé par les ordres du feu Roi, dans les années 1763–1766, par M. le comte de Broglie, et refondu et adapté aux circonstances actuelles, pour être mis sous les yeux de S.M., à qui il a été envoyé le 17 septembre 1777.' At the end is a letter of transmission to the King which is signed 'Le comte de Broglie.' (CG 31(1898), 350. Matteson, 17)

483.(467). Mémoire du comte de Grasse sur le combat naval du 12 avril 1782, avec les plans des principales positions des deux flottes. À la suite, plusieurs pièces de 1782 et 1784, relatives du même affaire, dont une réplique du marquis de Vaudreuil touchant la discussion au conseil de guerre, une réplique du comte de Grasse et une discussion entre M. de Vaudreuil et M. d'Albert de Rions. (CG 31(1898), 351. Matteson, 17)

ARRAS

Bibliothèque et archives municipales, Palais Saint Vaast
rue Paul Doumer
62 Arras

299.(186–91). 'Oeuvres manuscrites de Mr. M.D.S.M. (Médéric-Louis-Elie-Moreau de Saint-Méry, avocat au parlement et au Conseil supérieur du Cap). Tome III.-13° 'Mémoire pour les Amériquains, touchant l'achat des syrops et taffias aux colonies, 27 mars 1782,' 4 pp. (CG 40(1902), 254. Matteson, 18)

AVIGNON

Bibliothéque municipale et Musée Calvet
65 rue Joseph-Vernet
84 Avignon

2750. 'Journal de la campagne du vaisseau *le Marseillois*, de 74 canons, commandé par M. de la Poïpe Vertrieux, capitaine des vaisseaux du Roy et brigadier des armées navales, commandant la compagnie des gardes de la marine à Toulon, (armé le 6 fevrier 1778), sous les ordres de M. le comte d'Estaing, vice-amiral, par M. de Saint-Laurent, garde de la marine. 1778 et 1779' (action at Savannah and Grenada). (CG 28(1895), 640. Matteson, 20)

BESANÇON

Bibliothèque et archives municipales, 1 rue de la Bibliothèque
25 Besançon

1453. Géographie. Voyages. Guerre d'Amérique et expedition de Saint-Domingue. *f. 90* 'Journal des campagnes de l'Amérique, depuis le 5 juillet 1781 jusqu'au 12 avril 1782.' (CG 45(1915), 173. Matteson, 29)

BREST

Bibliothèque de la Marine, Préfecture Maritime
29N Brest

Formerly the Bibliothèque du Port de Brest, access to this library is restricted to naval staff and individuals authorized by the Préfet Maritime.

34. Correspondance originale des administrateurs de la Martinique avec le ministre de la marine, 1773–9. Letters of Bouillé and other officials, some of which relate to Anglo-French naval operations in the Caribbean.

35. *idem,* 1780–3. (Charles de la Roncière, *Catalogue général des manuscrits des bibliothèques publiques de France, bibliothèques de la marine,* 1907, 286–7)

161. Recueil de pièces originales sur la marine de guerre, signées de divers officiers généraux. . . . 16 dispatches from Sartine to Orvilliers, Ruis, Hector, and La Prévalaye, 12 September 1774 to 18 July 1780.

174. Correspondances et papiers des officiers généraux des armées navales
. . . Pierre Landrais. Various documents concerning this officer who served
aboard the *Bonhomme Richard.*

176. Quittances, billets, procès-verbaux et dépêches pour la plupart relatifs à
la marine et aux opérations militaires. . . .

76. 'Etat des matières fournis par Masson et Chauveau à Philadelphie pour le
service de la frégate du Roy *la Gloire,* commandée par M. le chevalier de
Valongne et en vertu des ordres de M. de Marbois, consul-général', Philadelphia, 18 March 1783.

(CG 46(1924), 135, 177, 205)

Bibliothèque municipale, 22 rue Traverse
29N Brest

FONDS LANGERON

7 cartons of material containing many items dealing with the sending of
French forces to America and the French army in America, 1778–83. (CG
22(1893), 453. Matteson, 40)

CALAIS
Bibliothèque municipale, Hôtel de Ville, 1 rue de Vic
62 Calais

90. 'Journal de navigation, pour le service de la frégate *l'Amazone,*
commandée par le vte de Monguiot, commencé le 15 mars 1782, . . .'. Récit
naïf et sans pretention d'une campagne navale sur les côtes d'Amérique, vers
la fin de la guerre de l'independance américaine. (CG 41(1903), 19. Matteson,
43)

CLERMONT-FERRAND
Bibliothèque municipale et universitaire, 1 Boulevard Lafayette
63 Clermont-Ferrand

564. 'Journal des opérations de l'escadre du comte d'Estaing en Amérique.
1778–1779' (copy). (CG 41(1903), 188. Matteson, 47)

DIJON

Archives départementales de la Côte d'Or, 8 rue Jeannin
21 Dijon

Foreigners must show a letter from a diplomatic agent to gain access.

95.(F. Portefeuille n° 5). Relation des opérations de la flotte française dans les Isles du Vent, 1780–1. (*Catalogue des MSS. conservé dans les Dépôts d'archives départementales, communales, et hospitalières,* Paris, 1886, 58. Matteson, 59)

GIRONDE

Archives départementales de la Gironde, 13 rue d'Aviau
33 Bordeaux

46. Mélanges politiques et litéraires: 'Lettre de M. Linguet à M. de Vergennes . . . à Londres 1777' (copy). (CG 51(1956), 191)

GRENOBLE

Bibliothèque municipale, Place de Verdun
38 Grenoble

1627.(Nouv. acq.). 'Très humble et très-respecteuses remonstrances que présentent au Roy, nostre très-honoré et très-souverain seigneur, les gens tenant son grave conseil.' Au sujet de recueil intitulé: 'Suite de la justification du sïeur de Beaumarchais', 16 February 1777.
2065.(Nouv. acq.). Note sur la citoyenne Romand, 'veuve d'un ancien officier d'artillerie qui a été au service des Etats-Unis pendant leur guerre avec l'Angleterre.'

(CG 7(1889), 546, 642. Matteson, 79)

ILLE-ET-VILAINE

Archives départementales d'Ille-et-Vilaine, 2 place Saint Melaine
35 Rennes

184.(I F 2163). 'Histoire de Saint-Pierre-et-Miquelon de 1763 à 1815', 53 pp. (CG 51(1956), 210)

LA ROCHELLE

Bibliothèque municipale, rue Gargoulleau
17 La Rochelle

401.(7382). 'Mémoire de M. le marquis de Vaudreuil au conseil extra-ordinaire de guerre et de marine à l'Orient', sur le combat du 12 avril 1782, avec responses marginalles de comte de Grave (?Grasse), 1783.

650. *f. 222.* Inventaire du navire *le Fier Rodrigue*, appartenant M. Caron de Beaumarchais, 1783.

677. Dossier et pièces concernant les Rigaud, comte et marquis de Vaudreuil, célèbres marins. Various documents and memoranda pertaining to the of-ficial inquiry into the battle of the Saintes, 12 April 1782, including several submitted by de Vaudreuil and de Grasse.

(CG 8(1889), 229, 400, 527–8. Matteson, 84–5)

LUNEL

Bibliothèque municipale, Place des Martyrs de la Résistance
34 Lunel

30. 'Voyage du général Lafayette aux Etats-Unis, poëme inédit et autographe, par Aug. Rigaud..., orné d'une lettre de Lafayette, datée, signée et apostilée.' (CG 31(1898), 175. Matteson, 100)

LYON

Bibliothèque municipale, 4 Avenue Adolphe Max
69 Lyon

The Bibliothèque du Palais des Arts was merged with the Bibliothèque muni-cipale in 1912.

123. Sur la révolution des colonies anglaises en 1776, par de Précy. (CG 31(1898), 68. Matteson, 102)

MANTES LA JOLIE

Bibliothèque municipale Georges Duhamel, Square Brieussel
78200 Mantes la Jolie

COLLECTION CLERC DE LANDRESSE

Contains about 60 items related to the battle of Ouessant (Ushant) in July 1778.

CORRESPONDANCE DES COLONIES

Contains 8 letters from de Crèvecoeur and 4 unsigned letters to La Rochefoucald concerning the campaign of d'Estaing in 1778.

MÉMOIRES ET RELATIONS

Includes 14 letters to La Rochefoucald, with 3 items by Filippo Mazzei, 1781–2, commenting on the American war.

(CG 20(1893), 557, 559, 561–2. Matteson, 107–8)

NANCY

Bibliothèque municipale, 43 rue Stanilas
54 Nancy

697. Recueil de mémoires sur la marine (par Dessalles). *f. 1.* 'Compilation de toutes les guerres de mer depuis 1512 jusqu'en 1762, suivie d'un journal des campagnes de mer depuis 1778 . . .,' 456 pp, liste des auteurs consultes.

698. *f. 117(–127).* 'Extrait d'un mémoire de M. de Broglie de 1778'; *f. 228(–161).* Recueil de pièces qui ont paru à Paris concernant le combat du 12 avril 1782; *f. 162(–188).* 'Journal d'un officier de l'armée navale en Amérique, 1781–1782.'

(CG 4(1886), 228. Matteson, 122)

NANTES

Bibliothèque municipale, 37 rue Gambetta
44 Nantes

882. (français 718). 'Extrait detaillé et abrégé des événemens arrivés au vaisseau *la marquis de la Chalotais,* capitaine le sieur de Foligny, officier des maréchaux de France pendant le cours du voyage qu'il vient de faire en Amérique', *vers 1780.*

1137. (français 975). Le lieutenant général marquis du Langeron: 'Reflexions politiques. 1783'; 'Mémoire politique et militaire sur l'état présent de la guerre avec l'Angleterre, 17 novembre 1778'.

1319. (français 1158, 1191). *f. 200.* Nouvelles de Toulon depuis 1778. Guerre d'Amérique.

1398. (français 1238). Venant de M. de Langeron. Préparation de la guerre d'Amérique; armements du Havre, de Hanfleur et de Saint-Malo; troupes qui doivent s'embarquer en Bretagne, 1777–9, 17 pp.

1452. (français 1292). Vicomte de Pontèves. Lettre à une dame sur le conseil de guerre maritime tenu à Lorient en 1784 (affaire de l'amiral de Grasse).

(CG 22(1893), 123, 156, 179, 190, 197. Matteson, 123)

33. J.B.D. de Vimeur, comte de Rochambeau, à M. de Saint-Paul, St. Malo, 6 août 1779.

2308. (français 2154). 'Marine militaire. Événements pendant les guerres navales, 1740, 1755, 1778' (copy), 94 pp.

2335. (français 2181). Tableau de l'armée combinée de France et d'Espagne, 1779.

2344. (français 2190). Guerre de l'Independance. Rapport sur le combat du *Triton,* commandé par le comte de Ligandés-Rochefort, avec le vaisseau *le Jupiter* et une frégate anglaise à 8 lieues de cap Finistére, le 20 octobre 1778.

2933. L'Esprit de Saint-Domingue. Manuscrit de 32 p. portant au-dessus du titre la date 1780, et le nom de Lory, en marge, et au bas de la page 32 'à Saint-Domingue, 1781.'

(CG 58(1971), 162, 171, 174, 175, 220)

The *Table alphabétique des pièces autographes* contains *inter alia*:
2 letters of Benedict Arnold, 1767 and 1773; Beaumarchais to Dorat, 1779;

Cornwallis, 1782; Thomas Fitzsimmons, 1779; 4 letters of Franklin to various correspondents, 1770–84; John Habersham, 1781; Alexander Hamilton, 1780; John Hancock, 1781; John Hanson, 1782; John Jay, 1779; John Paul Jones to President Kean, 1781; de La Motte Picquet, 1779; Henry Laurens to Mackintosh, 1768; MacIntosh (?Lachlan or John), 1777; Robert Morris, 1782; Général Saint-Claire, 1775; Gen. Schuyler to Col. Dayton, 1776; Gen. Sullivan to John Langdon, 1780; 3 letters of Washington, 1779 and 1784; General Wayne, 1779.

ORLÉANS

Bibliothèque municipale, 1 rue Dupanloup
45 Orléans

535.(422). 'Journal de la campagne du vaisseau royal *le Magnanime*, aux ordres du M. le comte de Le Bègue, capitaine de vaisseau, faisant partie de l'armée de M. le comte de Grasse, sortie du port de Brest, le 22 mars 1781.' Contains the state of the forces of de Grasse, the capitulation of Yorktown and Tobago, the naval battle of 29 April 1781, and 'Journal de ma campagne sur *le Glorieux*, aux ordres de M. le vicomte d'Escars, capitaine de vaisseau employé dans l'armée du général M. le comte de Grasse.' (CG 12(1889), 240. Matteson, 130)

536. (423). 'Recueil des mémoires présentés au conseil de guerre extra-ordinaire de marine, assemblé à Lorient, en 1783, pour juger la conduite des officiers de la marine du Roy, dans l'affaire du 12 avril 1782.' On y trouve des mémoires du M. le baron d'Artois, d'Albert de Rions, du marquis de Vaudreuil et de Bougaineville. (CG 12(1889), 240. Matteson, 130)

PARIS

Archives de la Bastille. See *Bibliothèque Nationale*

Archives du Ministère des Affaires Etrangères
(Service des Archives Diplomatiques), 37 quai d'Orsay
75007 Paris

Access to these archives is unrestricted and the staff will often prepare documents in advance upon request. The archives are divided into three main series: *Correspondance politique, Mémoires et documents,* and *Correspondance consulaire.* The *Correspondance politique* consists of the following: drafts and copies of communications from the Foreign Ministry to agents abroad; the reports and letters of those agents; correspondence between foreign diplomatic representatives in France and the Foreign Ministry; notes, minutes, and memoranda originating in the Ministry, and enclosures from agents abroad. *Correspondance politique: Supplément* contains some duplicates and enclosures detached from original dispatches or later acquired. Now a closed classification extending only to 1897, *Mémoires et documents* consists of documents and papers acquired by government order, legacy or purchase. These are mainly the papers of ministers and diplomats. There are also reports and memorials drawn up by the staff of the Foreign Ministry and documents sent by agents abroad which were not a part of their original correspondence.

The *Correspondance consulaire* prior to 1792 is housed in the Archives Nationales and is described under that heading.

The America-related material in the Foreign Ministry archives has been surveyed in detail in Leland II, from which the following survey has been drawn.

CORRESPONDANCE POLITIQUE

This is the main series of the archives and is described in the following works. *Etat numérique des fonds de la correspondance politique de l'origine à 1871* (Paris, 1936). *Inventaire sommaire des archives du Département des Affaires Etrangères, correspondance politique*, Vol. I: Allemagne, Angleterre, Argentine, Autriche (Paris, 1903); Vol. II: Bade à Espagne (Paris, 1908); Vol. III: Etats-Unis (n.d.).

Angleterre (Leland II, 135–236)

451. August–October 1763. Correspondence of Praslin with d'Eon, Choiseul and Guerchy. *ff. 23, 140.* British colonial difficulties; extracts from British newspapers with news of the colonies and Indian problems.

452. November–December 1763. *f. 28.* Extract of British newspapers of 4 November on the fur trade with the Indians in America.

457. May–June 1764. Correspondence of Praslin, Guerchy, Milner, Choiseul, Halifax, Hertford, d'Abbadie, Chabert, Ford. *ff. 316, 333.* British charge that French officers are encouraging Indian hostilities in ceded territories.

458. July–September 1764. Correspondence of Praslin, d'Abbadie, Choiseul, Guerchy, Hertford, Blosset, Penfold, Fénélon. *ff. 39, 40, 42, 48, 50, 90.* British charge against d'Abbadie of stirring up Indian trouble.

462. January–February 1765. *f. 247.* Abstract of Stamp Act of 6 February 1765; *ff. 255, 312.* text of Stamp Act.

463. March–April 1765. Correspondence of Choiseul, Guerchy, Praslin. *ff. 195–7*. Accounts of British colonial trade in sugar and coffee.

464. May–June 1765. Correspondence of Dangeac, Girard, Guerchy, Halifax, d'Herlye, L'Averdy, Macleane, Palisser, Praslin, Trecesson. *ff. 102, 106*. Commerce between the West Indies and British North America.

465. July–October 1765. Correspondence of Blosset, Boulet, Bretel, Bussy, Choiseul, Conway, Cramond, Dangeac, Fontanieu, Guerchy, Hume, Palisser, Praslin. *f. 265*. Commerce between the French West Indies and British North America.

466. November–December 1765. Correspondence of Choiseul, Conway, Dangeac, Fontanieu, Galliot, Girard, Guerchy, Palisser, Praslin, Watson. *f. 62*. Stamp tax disturbances in America; *f. 180*. conversation between Conway and Guerchy on troubles in America; *ff. 205, 206, 211, 225*. 17 December speech of George III to Parliament; *f. 229*. News from America.

468. August–December 1765, Supplement. *ff. 275–8*. memoir on British commerce in North America, 1765.

469. January–April 1766. Correspondence of Bretel, Choiseul, Conway, Fontanieu, George III, Guerchy, L'Averdy, Praslin, Richmond, Watson. Parliamentary debates on American affairs and the stamp tax; George III's speech to Parliament; British forces on land and sea; situation of England and attitude of ministers to possibility of war in the near future.

470. May–July 1766. Correspondence of Choiseul, Durand, Guerchy, Praslin. *f. 227*. Repeal of Stamp Act; *f. 133*. copy of George III's speech to Parliament.

471. August–December 1766. Correspondence of Choiseul, Durand, Guerchy, Porter, de Vaudreuil, Shelburne. Information from Pont leRoy on his mission to America; American news and politics; conversations of Durand and Shelburne on America; Chatham's plans for America; Durand's observations on Chatham; intelligence from America.

473. January–April 1767. Correspondence of Choiseul, Grimaldi, Guerchy, Hocquart, Ossun, Stanislas, Vialars. *ff. 188, 331, 372*. American affairs in Parliament; *f. 176*. differences of Chatham and Townshend over American policy; *f. 141*. desire of New Yorkers for free trade.

474. May–August 1767. Correspondence of Choiseul, Durand, Guerchy. Parliamentary debates on American affairs; Durand's comments on possibility of revolt in the colonies and their influence on the prosperity and commerce of Britain.

475. September–December 1767. Correspondence of Choiseul, Durand,

Lemere, Palisser, Praslin, Shelburne. Durand's observations of the American colonies, ability of England to go to war, American preparations to resist England, rumour that the Americans have sent an emissary to London to dispute over the Stamp Act and with instructions to go to France for support against England, etc.

476. 1767 Supplement. *f. 192.* Decision of Boston to prohibit import of certain British merchandise, consternation of British Ministry.

477. January–March 1768. Correspondence of Châtelet-Lomont, Choiseul, Durand, Kalb, Praslin, Rohan. Choiseul on three possible causes of war with Britain; much comment on the American colonies and British politics; plan for French agents to encourage revolt in America.

478. April–May 1768. Correspondence of Châtelet-Lomont, Choiseul, Rochford, Stevens. *f. 188.* Revolt in Boston against customs duties; *f. 256.* Gomicourt, 14 May, reflections on present condition of Britain.

479. June–July 1769. Correspondence of Châtelet-Lomont, Francès. Many reports and letters on the turbulence in Boston and the British reaction; *ff. 350, 360.* discussion of French policy alternatives to exploit the situation.

480. August–September 1768. Correspondence of Choiseul, Francès, Franklin, Praslin, Walpole. French pleased with news of British troubles in America; speculation concerning use of force to subdue colonies; effect of American troubles on Corsican question; extracts from American newspapers; various documents reporting events in Boston and Philadelphia; colonial policy of Grenville and its opposition.

481. October–March 1768. Correspondence of Châtelet-Lomont, Choiseul, Francès, Kalb, L'Averdy, Praslin, Rybot, Walpole. Events in Boston; speeches by George III; plan to secure American grain for France; Francès on the British idea that a foreign war may be necessary to settle the American troubles; Kalb on American disturbances; Choiseul on the importance of observing closely the American troubles, etc.

482. December 1768. Correspondence of Châtelet-Lomont, Choiseul, Francès, Kalb, L'Averdy, Law, Latt, Marville. British war expenditures; possibility of grain from North America; American affairs in Parliament; Châtelet-Lomont on the chances of separation of the colonies from Britain; Choiseul on British policy toward the colonies; Francès—numerous items on America; Kalb on the Stamp Act and its consequences; the Stamp Act Congress; Indians in the west.

483. Supplement, 1768–9. *f. 150.* 9 May 1769, speech of George III at close of Parliament.

484. Supplement, 1768–70. *ff. 157, 250.* Plans to import New England grain.

ff. 281–5. French policy toward the American colonies; news from America; Choiseul on the weakness of the British Ministry in dealing with the Boston revolt.

f. 451. French council decides on plan concerning America, July 1770; Kalb to Choiseul from Boston and New York; index to correspondence of Francès with the French court.

485. January–February 1769. Correspondence of Bretel, Châtelet-Lomont, Choiseul, Harcourt, Invault, Ossun, Praslin, Walpole. Châtelet-Lomont's plan for Franco-American commerce and detaching the colonies from England; parliamentary debates on American affairs; revolt in Louisiana and resulting British satisfaction; letters and extracts relating to America and Parliament.

486. March–April 1769. Correspondence of Bretel, Châtelet-Lomont, Choiseul, Hanson, Harcourt. Troubles in Boston; persistence of colonial union; attitude of England; Châtelet-Lomont's plan for commercial relations with America and the latter's separation from England; memoir on English exports to North America.

487. May–June 1769. Correspondence of Châtelet-Lomont, Choiseul, Guinand, Harcourt, Invault, Lennan, Praslin, Walpole, Weymouth. News from Virginia, Pennsylvania, South Carolina; speeches of George III; French abandonment of notion of direct trade with American colonies; extracts from Virginia and Pennsylvania assembly resolutions.

488. July–September 1769. Correspondence of Bretel, Châtelet-Lomont, Choiseul, Francès, Walpole. Actions of Virginia and Massachusetts assemblies; proposal to revoke objectionable Acts; reasons for relaxation of attitude of British Ministry toward the colonies; Dutch trade with the colonies.

489. October–December 1769. Correspondence of Châtelet-Lomont, Choiseul, Cléonard, Francès, Walpole. Condition of British naval forces; accounts submitted to House of Commons of use made of appropriations for services, 1763–8; *ff. 173–4.* Cléonard's memoir proposing formation of Franco-American commercial company to engage in direct trade between France and American colonies.

490. January–February 1770. Correspondence of Bretel, Châtelet-Lomont, Choiseul, Fatio, Harcourt, Praslin, Terray. Obstacles to Cléonard's plan; American affairs in Parliament; Chatham's attitude toward the Americans; speech of George III on the colonies.

491. March–April 1770. Correspondence of Châtelet-Lomont, Choiseul, Fatio, Fox, Garnier, Hammond, Harcourt, Palmerston, Praslin, Spencer,

Terray, Weymouth. American affairs in Parliament; revolt in Boston; Cléonard's project.

492. May–August 1770. Correspondence of Beaujon, Châtelet-Lomont, Choiseul, Fatio, Francès, Terray. Revolt in Boston; American affairs in Parliament; proposal to import American rice; Hillsborough's plan against the Bostonians; American politics.

493. September–October 1770. Correspondence of Choiseul, Fatio, Francès. *f. 11.* Possible British actions against the colonies; *ff. 270–1.* Expenses of British artillery in the colonies for 1770.

494. November–December 1770. Correspondence of Francès, de Guines. Documents concerning condition and strength of the British forces in America; parliamentary debates on regiments for America.

495. January–February 1771. Correspondence of Francès, de Guines. General account of the British Navy and lists of vessels.

496. March–May 1771. Correspondence of Genet, de Guines, Harcourt, Terray. *f. 129.* General account of the British Navy on 5 April and vessels in North America; *ff. 214–15.* expenditures for colonial governments in America.

497. June–December 1771. Correspondence of d'Aiguillon, Anson, Blaquière, Boynes, Francès, Garnier, de Guines, Hales, La Vrillière, Terray. Memoirs of Francès on the situation of England, difficulties in America, Chatham's attitude, England's ability to conduct a war, and military forces in America.

498. Supplement, 1771–2. Various notes and memoirs on the practical independence of the British colonies; British armament; rumoured project of Lord Bute; Dumesnil St Pierre's plan for a settlement in North Carolina.

499. January–May 1772. Correspondence of d'Aiguillon, Blaquière, Boynes, Garnier, de Guines, Harcourt, Hocquart, Rochford, Terray. *f. 97.* Importation of North American grains; *ff. 30–6, 132.* strength of British Navy; British expenditures for the American colonies for 1772.

501. January–April 1773. Correspondence of d'Aiguillon, Boynes, de Guines, Hocquart, Lotbinière. *f. 76.* Promise of reduction of tax on tea exported to America.

502. May–September 1773. Correspondence of d'Aiguillon, Boynes, Bretel, Garnier, de Guines. *ff. 197–249.* Memoir of de Guines on England, including the means of freeing the American colonies; *f. 140.* complete list of the British Navy on 30 June; *ff. 286, 306.* committees appointed by colonies to investigate conduct of Parliament and reasons for this action; British attitude toward the colonies.

503. October–December 1773. Correspondence of Boynes, Bretel, Garnier. *ff. 281, 285, 286.* American resolutions against the importation of East India Company tea.

504. January–February 1774. Correspondence of Garnier, Vergennes. *f. 112.* Boston Tea Party; *ff. 170, 193, 251.* intentions of the British Ministry toward the colonies;ff. *186, 236.* dismissal of Franklin as Postmaster-General; *ff. 17–18.* account of the British Navy on 3 January.

505. March–June 1774. Correspondence of Boynes, Garnier, Lauraguais, Moustier, Vergennes. Proceedings in Parliament concerning America; attitude of the Americans; *ff. 166, 185.* desire of Louis XVI to see peace in America; influence of the American problems on whale fisheries.

506. July–September 1774. Correspondence of Garnier, MacDermott, Vergennes. British and American attitudes; intelligence of events in America; various extracts of letters and resolutions from America.

507. October–December 1774. Correspondence of Garnier, Gontier, Herries, Hocquart, MacDermott, Mante, Vergennes. First Continental Congress, turbulence in America; British reactions; attitude of France to England; Chatham's plan for the colonies; British desire that French ships should not enter British colonial ports; much intelligence concerning the British Navy.

508. January–February 1775. Correspondence of Bretel, Garnier, Melivier, Périgord, Rochford, Sartine, Senat, Turgot, Vergennes. Attitude of French Government on American affairs; French secret service in London; American petitions to George III; American affairs in Parliament; British ministerial policy.

509. March–April 1775. Correspondence of Bull, Colden, Dartmouth, Desrivierre, Dunmore, Eden, Garnier, Penn, Rochford, Vergennes, Wallace, Wentworth, Wright. French attitude toward the colonies; neutrality and contraband trade; arrival of American merchant ships; British policy and parliamentary debates; American resolutions and petitions; much military and naval intelligence.

510. May–June 1775. Correspondence of Desrivierre, d'Eon, Garnier, de Guines, Sartine, Saudray, Vergennes. French attitude toward the American colonies; events in America; British attitude to the colonies, hostility of British public opinion; proposal for hiring German mercenaries; complaints about the Dutch munitions trade with the colonies.

511. July–September 1775. Correspondence of Astier, Beaumarchais, Bonvouloir, Bourdieu et Chollet, Gage, Duke of Gloucester, Grimaldi, de

Guines, Louis XVI, Rochford, Sartine, Turgot, Bishop of Verdun, Vergennes, Villère. British attitude to America; de Guines advises sending secret agent to America; mission of Bonvouloir; entente between French and Spanish Ambassadors in London; intelligence of events in America; British seizure of American ships; purchase of New England grain ordered by the Abbé Terray; numerous British and American documents.

512. 26 September to 20 November 1775. Correspondence of de Guines, La Croix, Perrée, Sartine, Turgot, Vergennes. Bonvouloir's mission; reception of American ships in French ports; danger of war between France and England; purchase of New England grain by Abbé Terray; much intelligence from America and England; copies of many petitions favouring Americans.

513. 21 November to December 1775. Correspondence of Bausset, Beaumarchais, l'Espérance, de Guines, Legge, Mistral, Rodney, Sartine, Stormont, Vergennes. Reception accorded American vessels in French ports and prohibition of shipment of war supplies to America; Beaumarchais mission in England; intelligence of British and American affairs; Rodney to Germain on American contraband trade.

514. January–February 1776. Correspondence of d'Anglemont, Bayard-Jackson and Co., Beaumarchais, Fitzherbert, Garnier, Greville, de Guines, Hillsborough, Jenyns, Northey, Palliser, Sartine, Stormont, Earl of Suffolk, Vergennes, Weymouth. French attitudes to American insurrection; prohibition of shipment of war supplies to America; Bonvouloir's mission in America; American military operations; political and military intelligence from Britain; copies of British treaties for the hiring of German mercenaries.

515. March–April 1776. Correspondence of d'Argout, Bayard Jackson and Co., Beaumarchais, Garnier, George III, Landelles, Lauraguais, Louis XVI, Montaudouin Frères, Saint Germain, Saint Paul, Sartine, Vergennes, Villiers et fils aîné. Roubaud's proposal for Anglo-French alliance to effect the submission of the colonies; Lauraguais' mission to London; Bonvouloir's mission; Francy going to America; Garnier's insinuations that the French furnish supplies to the Americans; political and military intelligence from Britain and America; capture of Dutch vessels bound for America; affair of the *Dickinson*.

516. May–June 1776. Correspondence of Beaumarchais, Carleton, Doyard, Dubourg, Du Pont, d'Ennery, Garnier, de Guines, Howe, Lauraguais, Le Bégue, Lombard, Montaudouin Frères, Peire, Saint Paul, Sartine, Vergennes, Weymouth. Affair of the *Dickinson*; Beaumarchais' mission; peaceful intentions of Spain; freedom of American commerce in France save in war supplies; Francy's mission to America; Du Pont's offer to be secret agent and relations with Franklin; Bonvouloir's mission; political and military intelligence from America and Britain.

517. July–August 1776. Correspondence of Beaumarchais, Choiseul, Clugny, Dubourg, Garnier, Girard, Hopkins, Richard Howe, Julien, Lauraguais, O'Gorman, Parker, Pic de Pere, Pancet, Poterat, Sartine, Vallière, Vergennes. British uneasiness with regard to Spain; Beaumarchais and Deane; American commerce with French islands; Dubourg's mission; supply of armament to the Americans; Lauraguais' mission; French contraband trade with America; political and military intelligence from Britain and America.

518. September–October 1776. Correspondence of Beaumarchais, Bourelly, Brethé, Deane, Garnier, Hamilton, Hopkins, Lauraguais, Masserano, Noailles, Planta, Saint Germain, Sartine, Vergennes. American ships at Bordeaux; correspondence between Hamilton and the French Ministry; Beaumarchais' mission; conduct of Dubourg; Lauraguais' mission; Bonvouloir's mission; British opinion of French policy; political and military intelligence from Britain and North America.

519. November–December 1776. Correspondence of Aranda, Beaumarchais, Deane, Garnier, Richard and William Howe, Keith, Louis XVI, Masserano, Noailles, Renaudeau, Saint Germé, Sartine, Stormont, Vergennes. Mission of Beaumarchais; Lafayette joins Washington; Vergennes and Stormont concerning contraband; Deane's mission; arrival of Franklin; Noailles' cooperation with Masserano; political and military intelligence from Britain and America.

520. Supplement, 1776–7. This volume contains only copies of documents in the preceding and succeeding volumes.

521. January–February 1777. Correspondence of Beaumarchais, Clinton, Deane, Garnier, Grantham, Grimaldi, Masserano, Maurepas, Noailles, Sartine, Stormont, Vergennes. Reception of American merchant vessels and privateers in French ports; French sentiments on the American insurrection expressed to Britain; activities of Beaumarchais and attitude of Coudray; Franklin's conduct; Suffolk to Masserano on the help furnished to the Americans by the French; Germain's sympathy for the Americans; political and military intelligence from Britain and America.

522. March–April 1777. Correspondence of d'Argout, Audiffren, Beaumarchais, Boisbertrand, Bouchet, Deane, Farmers General, Garnier, Grimaldi, William Howe, Hutchinson, La Brosse, Magnières, Masserano, Maurepas, Noailles, Sartine, Stormont, Taboureau, Thiric, Vergennes, Wuibert. Utility to Holland of American independence; British spy service in France; operations of Beaumarchais; American activities in Martinique; capture of French officers in America; Noailles' reasons for favouring American independence; Vergennes and the departure of Lafayette; political and military intelligence from North America and Britain.

523. May to 15 July 1777. Correspondence of Angeron and Rolland, Audrin, Bausacourt, Beaumarchais, Bouillé, Budd, Bulkeley, Burgoyne, Byrne, Collier, Ferry, Frazer, Germain, Grand, Guichard, de Guines, William Howe, Linguet, Mistral, Montdenoix, Noailles, Raynach, Robecq, Saint Germain, Sartine, Stormont, Tiphaigne, Tort, Vergennes, Weymouth. Linguet's journal of his stay in America; British spies in French ports; final departure of Lafayette; Vergennes' resolve to await events; protection accorded to American vessels trading with French ports; operations of Beaumarchais; Deane at Havre; return of Bonvouloir; shipment of French supplies to America; political and military intelligence of Britain and North America.

524. 16 July to 25 September 1777. Correspondence of the Admiralty of Bordeaux, Amelot, Beaumarchais, Continental Congress, Cunningham, Deane, Du Chaffault, Farmers General, Franklin, Gautier fils et Rey, Grand, Guichard, Guys et Cie., La Baume, Mme La Baume, Lacombe, Lauraguais, Laureau, Arthur Lee, Lenoir, Marchegay, Néville, Noailles, Parcieux, Pissy, Robecq, Saint Germain, Sartine, Stormont, Ternizien, Tiphaigne, Vergennes, Weymouth. French and Spanish preparations for eventual war with England; British desire to compromise France in American eyes; French censure of political works concerning America; missions of Jenkinson to France; operations of Beaumarchais; arming of American ships at Bordeaux and Martinique; misunderstanding among Franklin, Deane, and Arthur Lee; political and military intelligence from North America and Britain.

525. 26 September to 20 November 1777. Correspondence of the Admiralty of Bordeaux, Amelot, d'Arbaud, d'Aubarède, Bazillohemieux et Bouchard, Beaumarchais, Berthelot, Bourdieu, Burgoyne, Burt, Du Lion, Franklin, Grand, Gruel, Guichard, Richard Howe, William Howe, La Carière, Louvel, Mauduit, Maurepas, Mongelas, Noailles, Robinot, Saint Léger, Sartine, Sayre, Stormont, Vergennes, Weymouth. Sayre's mission to Berlin; British seizure of French ships; American privateers and French ports; operations of Beaumarchais; Vergennes on duration of the war; political and military intelligence.

526. November 21 to December 1777. Correspondence of Argilier, d'Argout, d'Aubaréde, Beaumarchais, Berranger, Bertin, Biddle, Botton, Bourdieu et Chollet, Brown, Burt, Carmichael, Chaumont, Crahton, Desjoutières, Funcks, Gale, Garnier, Grand, William Howe, Lauzun, Marchegay, Mayne, Morisse Pliarne Penet et Cie., Noailles, Puyabry, Rayneval, Sartine, Stormont, Vergennes, Vincent. British spies in France; British visit and seizure of French vessels; activities and conduct of American privateers; influence of Saratoga on French policy; operations of Beaumarchais; Stormont's apparent knowledge of the Franco-American treaty; political and military events in Britain and America.

527. Supplement, 1777–8. Mostly duplicates.

528. January–February 1778. Correspondence of d'Adhémar, Aussenac, Beaumarchais, Berthelot, Bertin, Bourdieu et Chollet, Chaumont, Dantani, Dubourg, Escarano, Floridablanca, Forth, Francès, Galatheau, Garnier, Grand, Jenkins, Lauzun, Maurepas, Montagu, Noailles, Rey, Rézeville, Sartine, Verdelet, Vergennes, Weymouth. British visit and seizure of French ships; French espionage in England; Spanish attitude to America; American privateering; operations of Beaumarchais; Stormont's suspicions of the treaty; Garnier's mission to America; political and military intelligence from Britain and North America.

529. March–May 1778. Correspondence of J. Adams, d'Ageno, Beaumarchais, Boisbertrand, Bourdieu, Castillon et Rey, Chaulieu, Dumont, Escarano, Franklin, Garnier, Grand, William Howe, La Thiolais, Lauzun, La Vauguyon, Arthur Lee, Lenoir, Mitchell, Montbarey, Noailles, Rayneval, Robecq, Rodney, Sartine, Smithe, Sorèze, Stormont, Vanderhey, Vergennes, Weymouth. British seizure of French ships; threat of war between France and England; Spanish attitude to Franco-American alliance; operations of Beaumarchais; announcement of Franco-American treaty; rupture of Anglo-French diplomatic relations; measures to protect French and American traders; political and military events in America and England.

530. June–December 1778. Correspondence of Almodovar, Beaumarchais, Dodet, Escarano, l'Espérance, Evans, Garnier, Grand, Hamilton, Hennin, Lauzun, Loré, MacDermott, Parcieu, Vanderhey, Vergennes. British seizure of French ships; British conditions for peace with France; summary of French complaints against Britain; operations of d'Estaing; plan for attack on India to aid the Americans; operations of Beaumarchais; American envoys in Paris; British espionage; Stormont's complaints; events in America; British actions in America.

531. January–July 1779. Correspondence of d'Ageno, Anisson-Dupéron, Aranda, Beaumarchais, Bessière, Bossu, Caryll, l'Étang, Francès, Hamilton, Kersaint, La Houlière, Maurepas, Noailles, d'Orvilliers, Richardson, Vergennes. Military and naval operations; disgrace of Garnier; Caryll's mission in France; secret correspondence with London through d'Ageno; operations of Beaumarchais.

532. August–December 1779. Correspondence of A. J. Alexander, W. Alexander, Amelot, Anisson-Dupéron, Beaumarchais, Bessière, Bulkeley, Choiseul, d'Estaing, Franklin, Genet, Hamilton, La Thoison, Maurepas, Néville, Nivernais, d'Orvilliers, Praslin, Richard, Sartine, Vergennes, Walpole. Prizes and privateering; exchange of prisoners; military and naval operations; events in America; operations of Beaumarchais.

533. 1780. Correspondence of Amherst, Aranda, d'Aubarède, Beaumarchais, Castries, Chaumont, Creutz, Cumberland, Hillsborough, Holker, Izard, Marsh, Mazille, Moriès, Néville, d'Orvilliers, Sartine, Stormont, Surloville, Vergennes. Prizes; operations of Beaumarchais; the mission and intrigues of Holker père et fils; events in America; attitude of Spain; military and naval operations.

534. 1781. Correspondence of d'Aubarède, Baxon, Baudouin, Bertrand, Bonne de Regnauvalle, Calonne, Castries, Croy, Dumouriez, Dupont, Genet, Hamilton, Herries, Maurville, Néville, Saint Martin, Servières, Thurne (alias Lerchenberg), Vergennes. Events in America; exchange of prisoners; Hutton–Franklin negotiations; Dupont's proposals to Hutton; Cumberland–Floridablanca negotiation; Hussey's intrigues; d'Aubarède's offer to serve as peace agent.

536. January–April 1782. Correspondence of Aubigny, Baudouin, Bouillé, Castries, Cologne, Dupont, Fitzherbert, Grand, Gros Préville, Lenox, Mary, Richmond, G. Smith, Thurne (Lerchenberg), Vergennes. French guarantee of Dutch loan to America; events in America; Dupont's peace proposals to Hutton; Fitzherbert–Vergennes talks; Franklin–Burke correspondence; Grenville's mission to France; mediation of Russia and Sweden; Dutch recognition of American independence.

537. May–July 1782. Correspondence of d'Argenson, Lady Aggill, Baudouin, Beaumarchais, Mme Boisgérard, Brefny (O'Reilly), Bruny, Castries, Chardon, Colbert, Crèvecoeur-Baussy, Croy, Des Roches, Dumouriez, Dupont, Fleury, Fox, Francès, Franklin, George III, Grant, Grantham, de Grasse, Grenville, Hamilton, Kerguelen, Lardimalie, Lauzun, La Valinière, Le Boucher, Lenoir, Lessart, Louis XVI, Maillebois, Maurice, Menou, d'Ogny, Parcieu, Robertson, Rutledge, Thurne, Vergennes, Washington. Grenville's mission; military and naval operations; prisoner exchange; Franklin's peace negotiations; plans for invasion of England; correspondence of Hutton; French peace overtures to Britain.

538. August to 20 November 1782. Correspondence of d'Ahémar, Aranda, Lady Asgill, Bariatinsky, Baudouin, Bertrand, Brefny, Castries, Charost, Croy, Dumouriez, Dunilac, d'Estaing, Fitzherbert, Fréville, Goyon, Grantham, de Grasse, Kerguelen, Lambert, Langeron, Lux, Maillebois, Moracin, Peinier, Polignac, Rayneval, Shelburne, Soliva, Thurne, Valette, Vergennes. Military and naval operations and plans; various diplomatic missions and correspondence—Oswald, Fitzherbert, Rayneval, comte de Chateigner, Beurelin, Abbé Morcelet; Anglo-Spanish negotiations.

539. 21 November to December 1782. Correspondence of Baudouin, Caffieri, Castries, Charost, Dorset, Dupont, Fitzherbert, Franklin, George III, Grantham, de Grasse, Jerningham, Le Mort, Le Vaigneur, Maillebois, Melfort,

Mentelle, d'Orly, Oswald, Picquelin, Rayneval, Reboul, Shelburne, Smith, Mrs Swinburne, Thowsend, Thurne, Vaudreuil, comte de Vergennes, vicomte de Vergennes. Apart from the usual papers relating to prizes, planned and actual military and naval operations, etc., this volume deals mainly with the various aspects of the peace negotiations and the missions related to them, including that of Fitzherbert and Rayneval's second mission to London.

540. January to 15 February 1783. Correspondence of Anisson-Dupéron, Baudouin, Beaumarchais, Castries, Chardon, Chaumont, Du Moustier, Favier, Fitzherbert, Franklin, Genssane, Grantham, Haumont, Mme de La Salle, La Tour, Lepinoy, Louis XVI, Mauvoir, Mazille, Moustier, Périer, Préville, Rayneval, Robinot, Mme de Vitré. This volume is similar to the preceding in make-up and deals largely with the conclusion of the preliminary peace.

541. 16 February to 10 April 1783. Correspondence of d'Adhémar, Aubert, Baudouin, Browne, Castries, Cazeneuve, Chanetié, Chardon, Couradin, Digby, Dumas, Dupont, Fitzherbert, Fleury, Fox, Genet, Grandmont, Grantham, Howe, Lenoir, Magnières, Miroménil, Moustier, d'Ogny, Rayneval, Richemont, Ryan, Schweighauser, Ségur, Seymour, Shelburne, Thurne, Todd, Vergennes, Vial. Many miscellaneous documents concerning trade matters, prizes, reparations, etc. Of more interest are papers concerning Moustier's mission to London, d'Adhémar's mission in England, and the official declarations of peace.

542. 11 April to 15 June 1783. Correspondence of d'Adhémar, Barry, Baudouin, Beaufort, Beaumarchais, Bienassisse, Candau, Castries, Coppens, Duvautenet, Fitzherbert, George III, Grand, Grantham, Grenville, Gustave III, Hamilton, La Pérouse, Manchester, Millet, Mitchell, Moustier, North, d'Ormesson, Queen of England, Rayneval, Ségur, Shelburne, Thurne, Vergennes. This volume deals with the definitive peace treaty and the adjustments resulting from it, such withdrawal of forces, re-establishment of trade, claims, subsidiary negotiations on specific issues arising from the war, etc.

543. 16 June to 10 August 1783. Correspondence of d'Adhémar, Aranda, Aussenac, Bertin, Bruny, Caffieri, Candau, Castries, Chardon, Fitzherbert, Fox, d'Impfer, Ingram, Mme Lejeune, Macdonagh, Maddison, Manchester, Morellet, Prince of Nassau, d'Ormesson, Pirovani, Rayneval, Robinet, Vergennes, Washington. Embassy of d'Adhémar in London; Anglo-Dutch negotiations; embassy of Manchester; Anglo-Spanish negotiations; definitive treaty of peace; other matters such as reparations, hostages, postal service, trade, etc.

544. 11 August to 20 September 1783. Correspondence of d'Adhémar, Aranda, Baudouin, Baussay, Bertin, Bossenet, Castries, Chardon, Coffyn,

Fletcher, Fox, George III, Harries, Kent, Lenoir, Louis XVI, Manchester, d'Ormesson, Rayneval, Smith, Shelburne, Thurne, Vergennes. Documents pertaining to the conclusion of peace and related negotiations as well as the other matters mentioned under **543**.

545. 21 September to 10 November 1783. Correspondence of d'Adhémar, Anisson-Dupéron, Candau, Castries, Chambard, Cooper, Dacier, Fox, George III, Grantham, Hills, Manchester, Jonathan Nesbitt and Co., Rozel, Steel, Stephens, Thurne, Vergennes. Similar in nature to the preceding several volumes.

546. 11 November to December 1783. Correspondence of d'Adhémar, d'Auberteuil, d'Aubigny, Barentin, Breteuil, Briansiaux, Calonne, Castries, Chardon, Dacier, Dumas, Lafayette, Lenoir, Manchester, Mauvoir, Shelburne, Storer, Vergennes. Similar in nature to the preceding volumes.

Autriche (Leland II, 306–9)

332. 6 February 1777 to **336**. May–July 1778; **339**. 1779–80 to **340**. 11 April to December 1779. Correspondence of Vergennes and Breteuil concerning the stance of Austria vis-à-vis the Anglo-American conflict and the role of Austrian diplomacy in this period. There are also some papers of Barthélemy included.

Danemark (Leland II, 315–17)

162. 1779 to June 1780. Correspondence of Blome, Caillard, La Houze, Sartine, Vergennes. Largely concerned with prizes and privateering, contraband trade, and the neutral league proposed by Catherine II.

163. July 1780–1. Correspondence of Bernstorff, Blome, La Houze, Stormont, Vergennes. Danish attitudes to American and British policies; the neutral league; trade and prizes.

164. 1782–3. Correspondence of Blome, La Houze, Martin, Vergennes. Problems caused by privateers, the neutral league, and the peace treaty.

Espagne (Leland II, 431–98)

540. January–July 1764. *ff. 44–8*. French trade in Virginia tobacco.

548. January–May 1767. *ff. 323–6, 343–6, 408–11, 427, 463–70*. News from British North America.

427, 463–70. News from British North America.

549. June–September 1767. News from British North America.

550. October–December 1767. News from British North America; possible defence measures against British attacks on French and Spanish colonies in America.

551. January–March 1768. News from British North America; British threat to French and Spanish security in America.

552. April–June 1768. News from British America.

553. July–September 1768. News from British America; defence measures.

554. October–December 1768. News from British America; Spanish advantage derived from British difficulties in America.

555. Supplement, 1768–72. *ff. 35–59*. Need for Franco-Spanish unity in face of British designs on their possessions in America.

556. January–May 1769. News of British America; projected trade between New England and French and Spanish colonies.

557. June–September 1769 to **560.** July–September 1770. These volumes contain only news of events in America.

561. October–December 1770. News of British America; Franco-Spanish defence plans.

562. January–June 1771 to **567.** September–October 1772. These volumes contain mostly news of British America, except **564.**, which has some reference to contraband trade with Cuba as well.

569. January–March 1773. Spirit of independence in North America; unease of Nozières regarding British actions in North America.

570. April–June 1773. News of America; Franco-Spanish defence plans.

571. July–September 1773. Affairs of the American colonies.

572. Supplement, 1773. This volume contains the regular correspondence for the last three months of 1773. Topics pertaining to the Revolution are trade of British and Dutch colonies; possibility of French trade with American colonies via New Orleans.

573. January–July 1774. News of the American colonies.

574. August–December 1774. Disturbances in Boston; troop movements; first Continental Congress.

575. January–April 1775. News of the situation in America; British and Spanish suspicions over their respective naval preparations.

576. May–July 1775. British embarrassment over the situation in America; Spanish reaction to the naval build-up of Britain; Spanish naval preparations.

577. August–September 1775. Correspondence of Aranda, De Muy, Grimaldi, Masserano, Ossun, Vergennes. The Anglo-American conflict and the British view that war with France and Spain a means of ending the trouble in America; Franco-Spanish policy.

578. October–December 1775. Correspondence of Aranda, Grimaldi, Le Bretton, Ossun, Sartine, Vergennes. British negotiations with Russia; military operations in America; Franco-Spanish defences; Spanish fear that British forces in America will be used against Spanish colonies.

579. January–March 1776. Correspondence of Aranda, J. Delaire, Grimaldi, Macnamara, Ossun, Sartine, Turgot, Vergennes. Anglo-Russian negotiations; hiring of German mercenaries; news from London; Spain not yet asked for help by Americans; opportunities offered by the American revolt.

580. April–June 1776. Correspondence of Aranda, Du Bouchet, Grimaldi, Mongelas, Ossun, Sartine, Vergennes, Secret assistance to the Americans; news from America; French policy toward Spain; British threat to French and Spanish colonies in America.

581. July–September 1776. Correspondence of Aranda, Grimaldi, Malouet, Ossun, Sartine, Vergennes. British strength and Spanish distrust of British arming as unnecessary; question of encouraging colonies in revolt.

582. October–December 1776. Correspondence of Aranda, Boyetet, J. L. Duval, Grimaldi, P. C. Jouet, Maxent, Ossun, Sartine, J. Thouron, Vergennes. Danger of eventual war with British; American vessels in French and Spanish ports; events in America and Britain; French and Spanish policy toward Britain; Franklin's mission to Europe; fear that Britain will seek to recoup losses in the colonies by war with Spain and France.

583. January–March 1777. Correspondence of Aranda, Floridablanca, Grimaldi, P. C. Jouet, Kersaint, Louis XVI, Masserano, Ossun, Sartine, Vergennes. Relations with American agents; joint militarr preparations; secret aid to colonies; Spanish policy toward Britain, France and America.

584. April–June 1777. Correspondence of Aranda, Dufourcq, Floridablanca, Ossun, Paulze, Sartine, Vergennes. Joint action against the British in connection with the Americans; news from America; British reconciliation proposals to Congress.

585. July–August 1777. Correspondence of Aranda, directors of Caracas Company, Floridablanca, Muzquiz, Ossun, Sartine, Vergennes. War news; Franco-Spanish attitude toward insurgents; joint action against British.

586. September–October 1777. Correspondence of Aranda, Dufourcq, Duplessix, Floridablanca, La Tournelle, Ossun, Vergennes. Joint preparations against England; war news; French and Spanish attitudes toward Americans; Spanish policy toward France.

587. November–December 1777. Correspondence of Aranda, Deane, Dufourcq, Floridablanca, Franklin, Arthur Lee, Montmorin, Ossun, Vergennes. Joint preparations against Britain; French and Spanish agents in the colonies; American privateers; American agents in Europe; war news.

588. January–March 1778. Correspondence of Aranda, Blosset, Floridablanca, Montmorin, Sartine, Vergennes. British attempted negotiations with American agents in Paris; French negotiations with American agents; Spanish displeasure at Franco-American treaties; war news.

589. April–June 1778. Correspondence of Aranda, Bourgoing, Floridablanca, Humbourg, Montmorin, Poirel, Rayneval, Sartine, Vergennes. Spanish opposition to Franco-American alliance; Spanish proposal of mediation; Hartley's proposals to Franklin and Vergennes; British offer to Americans.

590. July–September 1778. Correspondence of John Adams, Almodovar, d'Amon, Aranda, Bertin, Continental Congress, Descloseaux, Floridablanca, Franklin, La Tournelle, Arthur Lee, Montmorin, Poirel, Sartine, Senneville, Vergennes. Ratification of Franco-American treaties; failure of Anglo-American negotiations; refusal of Spain to negotiate with the Americans; American agent in Madrid; war news; British attempts to disrupt Franco-American alliance.

591. October–December 1778. Correspondence of Almodovar, Aranda, d'Augnac, Floridablanca, Fonteneau, Magnières, Montmorin, Muzquiz, Sartine, Vergennes. Spanish refusal to join war; Spanish attempts to mediate; American agent at Madrid; British agents in America; Miralles sent to America by Spain; Spanish fear of American development; truce proposed to Franklin by Hartley; war news.

592. January–February 1779. Correspondence of Almodovar, Aranda, Coriolis, Floridablanca, Montbarey, Montmorin, Paulze, Sartine, Vergennes. War plans against England; war preparations; Spanish dissimulation against England; French efforts to bring Spain to declare against England; war news.

593. March–April 1779. Correspondence of Almodovar, d'Espinouse, Floridablanca, Franklin, Hartley, Montmorin, Vergennes. Spanish mediation; Franco-Spanish convention; joint plans and preparations against England; uncertainty of British policy; Spanish unwillingness to guarantee independence of American colonies.

594. May–July 1779. Correspondence of Almodovar, Aranda, Bancroft, Bessière, Breteuil, Castejon, Catherine II, Charles III, Floridablanca,

Gérard, Hartley, La Haye, La Tournelle, Louis XVI, Montbarey, Montmorin, Necker, d'Orvilliers, Rayneval, Sartine, Vergennes, Weymouth. Spanish mediation; joint preparations and plans for specific operations; Franco-Spanish convention; Spanish resentment of British attitude; mediation offer by Catherine II not acceptable to Charles III; Gérard in Philadelphia; British offers to Americans; American agent in Ireland; war news.

595. August–September 1779. Correspondence of Aranda, Bessière, Castejon, Du Chaffault, Floridablanca, Louis XVI, Montmorin, d'Orvilliers, Sartine, Vergennes. Florida project against British; British peace proposals to France; Spanish aid to Americans; Miralles in America; La Luzerne in Boston; Spanish manifesto against England; refusal of Austrian mediation; war news.

596. October–December 1779. Correspondence of Aranda, Bessière, Cordoba, Dufossat, Floridablanca, José de Galvez, Heredia, Kantoffer, La Luzerne, La Pérouse, Montmorin, Poirel, Rions, Sartine, Vergennes. War news; Spanish subsidies to America; John Adams made plenipotentiary for peace; French aid to America; desire of Vergennes to confine war to America; Spanish difficulty in furnishing subsidies to Americans.

597. January–February 1780. Correspondence of Aranda, Bausset, Bessière, Chardon, Cordoba, Floridablanca, La Luzerne, Montbarey, Montmorin, Sartine, Vergennes. Joint attack on Florida; French desire to confine war to America; Spanish refusal to recognize America and related negotiations; Russian mediation; French aid to America; activities of Gérard.

598. March to 25 April 1780. Correspondence of d'Amou, Aranda, d'Ayen, Bausset, Bourgoing, Charles III, Floridablanca, Jay, Le Comte, Louis XVI, Malet, Montmorin, Rayneval, Rougier, Sartine, Vergennes. Franco-Spanish differences over military policy; Spanish refusal to recognize American independence; Anglo-Spanish negotiations in Lisbon; question of neutrals; British proposals to Spain.

599. 26 April to 20 July 1780. Correspondence of d'Amou, Aranda, Bausset, Charles III, Cumberland, Fernan Nuñez, Floridablanca, Guichen, Jay, La Luzerne, Louis XVI, Malet, Montmorin, Normandez, Sartine, Ternay, Vergennes. Monetary needs of Americans; Dalrymple–Cumberland negotiations in Spain; Spanish fears of American independence; Franco-Spanish policy differences.

600. 21 July to 21 September 1780. Correspondence of Aranda, Bausset, Bessière, Bouillé, d'Estaing, Floridablanca, José Galvez, Gardoqui, Jay, La Luzerne, Malet, Montbarey, Montmorin, Necker, O'Dunne, Sartine, Vergennes, Vigny. Spanish financial aid to Americans; Cumberland negotiations; Jay in Madrid; western boundary questions; Spanish fear that the American example will encourage revolt in Spanish colonies.

601. 22 September to December 1780. Correspondence of Aranda, Bessière, Castries, Chardon, Duchesse de Crussol, d'Estaing, Floridablanca, Guichen, La Luzerne, Marbois, Maurepas, Montmorin, O'Dunne, Sartine, Vergennes. Cumberland's mission to Spain; Jay in Spain; Spanish aid to America; Russian offer of mediation; Spanish interests in the war; Spanish fear of the future conduct of the Americans.

602. January–March 1781. Correspondence of d'Amou, Aranda, Bessière, Bonnaire, de Forges, Castries, Duchesse de Crussol, Fleurieu, Floridablanca, José Galvez, Gardoqui, Kaunitz, Lacaze et Mallet, Laclède, La Luzerne, Livingston, Maurepas, Mongelas, Montmorin, Necker, Vergennes. Hussey –Cumberland mission; Austrian and Russian mediation; boundary issues; Spanish coolness to American independence; Franco-Spanish joint operations.

603. April–June 1781. Correspondence of Amelot, d'Amou, Aranda, Castries, Florence, Floridablanca, Guichen, d'Hector, Jay, Laclède, La Luzerne, Louis XVI, Maurepas, Montmorin, O'Dunne, Vergennes. Jay, the congressional drafts, and negotiations in Madrid; joint plan of campaign in America; Austrian and Russian mediation; Floridablanca's policy contrary to American independence; French financial aid and guarantee of Dutch loan; Cumberland in Spain; war news.

604. July–September 1781. Correspondence of Aranda, Castejon, Castries, Caupenne, Cordoba, Fleury, Floridablanca, José Galvez, W. Jackson, Jay, Joseph II, La Luzerne, Marbois, Mongelas, Montmorin, O'Dunne. Projects for joint Franco-Spanish operations; situation in America; nomination of peace plenipotentiaries; Austrian and Russian mediation; Mississippi navigation issue; war news.

605. October–December 1781. Correspondence of Aranda, Castries, Caupenne, Chardon, Fleury, Floridablanca, Franklin, José Galvez, Grand, La Luzerne, Louis XVI, Maurepas, Montmorin, Rochambeau, Ségur, Simoline, Torris, Vergennes. Franco-Spanish campaign plans; Spanish recognition of America; Jay's mission; treaty negotiations; Mississippi navigation issue; Austrian and Russian mediation; Spanish financial problems; war news.

606. January–April 1782. Correspondence of Aranda, Castejon, Castries, Creutz, Floridablanca, José Galvez, Grand, Iranda, Jay, Malet, Montmorin, Vergennes. Franco-Spanish campaign plan in America; American dissatisfaction with the attitude of Spain; Spanish opposition to American independence; French monetary grant to America; peace overtures by Forth and

Oswald; opposition of Franklin and Adams to conclusion of a separate peace; war news.

607. May–June 1782. Correspondence óf Aranda, Mme Aubert, Bellecombe, Castries, Charles III, Croy, Floridablanca, B. Galvez, Jay, La Luzerne, Montmorin, Saavedra, Vaudreuil, Vergennes. Oswald's negotiations; Jay and Aranda in Paris; British decision to recognize and treat with the colonies; Grenville's negotiations; La Luzerne and Congress; Mississippi navigation issue; British emissaries to America; Franco-Spanish campaign plan; war news.

608. July–September 1782. Correspondence of Aranda, Bellecombe, Cabanes, Castries, Charles III, Floridablanca, Montmorin, Polignac, Shelburne, Vergennes. Grenville's mission to Paris; Shelburne's efforts to separate America and France; Oswald's appointment; French negotiations with Fitzherbert; Spanish peace terms; war news.

609. October–December 1782. Correspondence of Aranda, Bessière, Castries, Charles III, d'Estaing, Floridablanca, La Luzerne, Marbois, Montmorin, Polignac, Vergennes. Negotiations of Fitzherbert and of Rayneval; Franco-Spanish negotiations over peace terms; military and financial condition of Americans; military and naval movements.

610. January–June 1783. Correspondence of Aranda, Bessière, Cabanes, Charles III, d'Estaing, Fleury, Floridablanca, Lafayette, Louis XVI, Montmorin, Vergennes. Boundary issue between Spain and Americans; Mississippi navigation issue; efforts to reconcile Spain and Americans; peace negotiations and the preparation of a definitive treaty; movement of forces.

611. July–December 1783. Correspondence of Aranda, Bourgoing, Calonne, Castries, La Luzerne, Montmorin, Vergennes. Definitive conclusion of peace; American commerce flourishes; progress of the American negotiations; Floridablanca's disdain for the Americans; settlement of Franco-Spanish accounts relative to the war.

Etats-Unis (Leland II, 560–612)

1. 1774–6. Correspondence of Clugny, Deane, Dubourg, J. Emerson, Falquières, Franklin, Garnier, Gérard, Kalb, La Luzerne, Arthur Lee, W. Lee, Lenoir, Lotbinière, Magnières, T. Morris, O'Reilly, Penet, Pfeffel, Planta, Saint Germain, Vergennes. Memoirs of Silas Deane; French secret aid to colonies; pro-American sympathy in France; American agents in Paris; affairs in America.

2. 1777. Correspondence of David Allen, American Commissioners, Aranda, d'Ayen, Bancroft, Beaumarchais, Broglie, Carmichael, Deane, Dubourg,

Duportail, Eyriès, Franklin, Gérard, Gourlade, Grand, Holker, Holtzen-dorff, Kalb, Lafayette, Arthur Lee, Lenoir, Leray de Chaumont, Maurepas, Montaudouin, T. Morris, Paulze, Pont-de-Vaux, Pulaski, N. Rogers, Rulhière, Sartine, Stormont, Taboureau, Vergennes, Wicks, Jonathan Williams. French policy toward America and Britain; negotiations and relations with the American Commissioners; French officers in America; secret aid; activities of Deane and Beaumarchais; Kalb in America.

3. January–June 1778. Correspondence of John Adams, Amelot, American Commissioners, Beaumarchais, Bondfield, Breugnon, Capitaine, Chateau, Chazerat, Courten, Deane, Eyriès, Flavigny, Fleurieu, Francès, Franklin, Garnier, Genet, Gérard, Guy, Hartley, Holker, Izard, James Jay, J. P. Jones, Lauraguais, Lauzun, Le Camus de Neville, Le Tillier, Arthur Lee, Leray de Chaumont, Louis XVI, Lovell, Maurepas, Montbarey, Necker, Noailles, d'Ogny, Pont-de-Vaux, Texier, Thaxter, Vergennes, Jonathan Williams. Franco-American treaties; British proposals to Americans in Paris; policy of Spain; recall of Deane and appointment of Adams; Beaumarchais and aid to the colonies; military and naval operations; instructions to Gérard.

4. July–September 1778. Correspondence of John Adams, American Commissioners, Anisson-Dupéron, Bersolle, Bertin, Boisbertrand, British Peace Commission; Broglie, S. Chase, Continental Congress, Damas, Duportail, d'Estaing, Franklin, Gérard, Grand, d'Herbault, Holker, Izard, Kalb, La Bove, H. Laurens, A. Lee, W. Lee, Leray de Chaumont, Lloyd, Mauroy, Miroménil, Montbarey, Necker, Pont-de-Vaux, Sartine, Vergennes, Weissenstein, Jonathan Williams. Franco-American relations generally; American financial operations in Paris; operations of Beaumarchais; proposals of Weissenstein; American Commissioners and agents in Paris; Gérard's reports and instructions; events in America.

5. October–December 1778. Correspondence of John Adams, Amelot, American Commissioners, Anisson-Dupéron, Breugnon, Broglie, Chardon, Abbé de Clermont-Tonnerre, Continental Congress, Creutz, Doumers, Du Moley, d'Estaing, Fleury, Franklin, Gérard, Gontaut, Grand, Joshua Johnson, Kalb, La Salle, H. Laurens, A. Lee, R. H. Lee, W. Lee, Lenoir, Leray de Chaumont, Louis XVI, Miroménil, Montbarey, Necker, Vicomte de Noailles, Rayneval, Sartine, Vergennes, Jonathan Williams. Activities of Americans in Paris; publication of the Franco-American treaties; Spanish policy; news from America; loans; Gérard's mission in Philadelphia; Deane affair; accounts of Beaumarchais; Mississippi navigation.

6. 1778 to July–September 1779. Duplicates only.

7. January–March 1779. Correspondence of John Adams, Samuel Adams, American Commissioners, Berkenhout, Bourron, Breugnon, Chardon, Durival, d'Estaing, Farley, Franklin, Genet, Gérard, Grand, Patrick Henry, Holtzendorff, Izard, John Jay, Lafayette, La Rochefoucald, Henry Laurens, Le Camus de Néville, Arthur Lee, Meunier, Montbarey, Vicomte de Noailles, Pont-de-Vaux, Roulhac, Saint Pierre, Sartine, Vergennes. Activities of Americans in Paris and relations with the French Ministry; attitude of other European powers; conditions for negotiation of peace; trade and convoys; Gérard's mission and the French in America; Mississippi navigation; American agents in Europe.

8. April–June 1779. Correspondence of John Adams, d'Annemours, Chardon, Continental Congress, Durival, d'Estaing, Feutry, Franklin, Gérard, Grand, Hartley, Holker père, John Jay, Jefferson, Lafayette, La Luzerne, Le Camus de Néville, Arthur Lee, Leray de Chaumont, Louis XVI, Meyer, Necker, Neuville, Rayneval, Risteau, Roulhac, Saint Maur, Sartine, Valnais, Vatteville, Vergennes, Wharton. Franco-American dealings in Paris; American finances; Holker in America; Americans in France; preparation of the French expeditionary force; news from America; Gérard's reports and instructions; Franco-American trade; Franco-American relations in Philadelphia; Spanish policy.

9. July–August 1779. Correspondence of Almodovar, Breugnon, Cazotte, Chardon, Chavannes, Continental Congress; Cuzey, d'Estaing, Forsters, Franklin, Mme de Gannes, Gérard, Holker père, James Hutchinson, John Jay, Lafayette, La Luzerne, Le Camus de Néville, Arthur Lee, Louis XVI, Matlack, Montbarey, Necker, Niccoli, O'Gorman, Pont-de-Vaux, Rayneval, J. Reed, Roulhac, Jean Rousseau, Sartine, Tiran, Valnais, Vergennes. Franco-American relations in Paris and Philadelphia; commercial affairs; Spanish attitude; French expeditionary force; French in America and Lafayette; Gérard's reports and instructions; Mississippi navigation; military and naval operations; exchange of prisoners; Spanish proposal for a long truce.

10. September–December 1779. Correspondence of d'Acosta Frères, Beaumarchais, Benezet, Bernstorff, Boucheporn, Chamber of Commerce of Dunkirk, Chardon, Continental Congress, Deane, Du Luc, d'Estaing, Famin, Franklin, Gérard, A. Hamilton, Holker fils, Huntingdon, Lafayette, La Luzerne, Arthur Lee, Lemoyne, Leray de Chaumont, Louis XVI, Maillebois, Meyer, Montbarey, Montmorin, Maréchal de Noailles, d'Ogny, Pfeffel, Pont-de-Vaux, Rayneval, Sartine, Vergennes, Wittgenstein. Military and naval operations; end of Gérard's mission and beginning of La Luzerne's; news from America; Mississippi navigation issue; American attitude to Spain; truce issue; Indian affairs; Spanish policy; American-Dutch relations.

11. January–April 1780. Correspondence of John Adams, Arendt, Beaumarchais, Brandt, Choin, David, Floridablanca, Francy, Franklin, Gérard, Goltz, de Grasse, Holker fils, Huntingdon, John Jay, Lafayette, Marquise de Lafayette, La Luzerne, La Rocatelle, Arthur Lee, Lenoir, Leray de Chaumont, Le Tellier, Louis XVI, Maurepas, Abbé de Mauroy, Montbarey, Maréchal de Noailles, Pascal et Thoron, Rochambeau, Roulhac, Sartine, Ternay, Vergennes. Mission of J. Laurens to France; problems of Arthur Lee; La Luzerne in Philadelphia; events in and comments on America; American finances; American relations with Spain; French aid; Mississippi navigation and Florida boundary issues; American-Dutch relations.

12. May–June 1780. Correspondence of John Adams, Beaumarchais, Berkenroode, Chardon, Charet et Ozenne, Choin, d'Estaing, Franklin, Garson Bayard et Cie., Gérard, Gerry, Goltz, Holker fils, Huntingdon, John Jay, Lafayette, La Flotte, La Luzerne, La Tagnerette, Leray de Chaumont, Marbois, Melfort, Montbarey, Montmorin, Necker, Rayneval, Sartine, Torris, Van der Oudermeulen, Vergennes. John Adams in Paris; events in America; Adams' attitude to the French alliance; American finances; La Luzerne in Philadelphia—reports from and instructions to; Miralles and Spanish policy; currency manipulation; Dutch loan; French and British propaganda.

13. July–September 1780. Correspondence of John Adams, Berkenroode, Bertrand, Castries, Chardon, F. Dana, Deuxponts, Durival, Franklin, Garner, Garson Bayard et Cie., Genet, Grand, Guichen, Holker fils et père, Huntingdon, E. J. Jones, J. P. Jones; Lafayette, La Luzerne, La Tagnerette, Leray de Chaumont, Lion J. Lovell, Marbois, Matty, Maurepas, Monistral, Montmorin, Najoc, Rayneval, Rochambeau, Roker, Sartine, Schweighauser, Ternay, Vergennes. Reports from and instructions to La Luzerne and Marbois; American finances; military and naval operations; Spanish policy; Searle's mission; J. Laurens' mission; arrival of French fleet and expeditionary force in America; Miralles replaced by Gardoqui; neutral league, Cumberland in Spain; Jay in Spain.

14. October–December 1780. Correspondence of Beaumarchais, Bertin, Bertrand, Castries, Cazotte, Clinton, Continental Congress; Deane, d'Espagne, Franklin, Grand, F. Grand, Holker père et fils, Huntingdon, John Jay, Lafayette, Mme de Lafayette, La Luzerne, Leray de Chaumont, Louis XVI, Marbois, Maurepas, Miroménil, Montbarey, Necker, Vicomte de Noailles, Rasquin, Rayneval, Rochambeau, Roulhac, Sartine, J. Searle, Ségur, Tarlé, Ternay, Valory, Vergennes, Jonathan Williams. Military and naval affairs; reports of and instructions to La Luzerne and Marbois; treason of Arnold; American finances; neutral league; Mississippi navigation and western boundary issues; anti-French faction in Congress; American spy system; Dana in Russia.

15. January to 19 March 1781. Correspondence of John Adams, d'Argainaratz, Beaumarchais, Castries, Continental Congress, Destouches,

Deuxponts, Desverneys, Dumouriez, Franklin, Genet, Greene, Jefferson, Jenifer, Lafayette, La Luzerne, La Millière, J. Laurens, Le Camus de Néville, W. Lee, Leray de Chaumont, Louis XVI, Mercier, Miroménil, Montbarey, Mourel de Basterans, Necker, Rochambeau, Tarlé, Valory, Vergennes, Washington. Military and naval operations; reports from and instructions to La Luzerne; Dana in Russia; American politics and the anti-French faction; American finances; H. Laurens in captivity; Prussian interest in American trade; Spanish policy; Indian affairs; French propaganda in America.

16. 20 March–May 1781. Correspondence of d'Annemours, d'Argainaratz, Castries, Chamillard, Continental Congress, Coulongnac et Cie., Dana, Destouches, Galatheau, Greene, Huntingdon, John Jay, Lafayette, La Luzerne, La Rouerie, J. Laurens, Leray de Chaumont, Louis XVI, Montmorin, Mourel de Basterans, Necker, d'Ormesson, Rasquin, Rochambeau, Roquebrune, Roulhac, Ségur, Tarlé, Veimerange, Vergennes. Reports from and instructions to La Luzerne; military and naval operations; French financial and naval assistance; congressional politics; American finances; J. Laurens in France; British peace propaganda in America; American-Dutch relations; Anglo-Spanish relations; Austro-Russian mediation; America and the Armed Neutrality; Dana in Russia.

17. June–July 1781. Correspondence of John Adams, d'Argainaratz, d'Auberteuil, Barras, Castries, Continental Congress, Fleury, Franklin, Galatheau, Grand, de Grasse, Greene, Hartley, Holker père et fils, R. Howley, Huntingdon, La Luzerne, La Pérouse, J. Laurens, H. Lee, Lenoir, Leray de Chaumont, Louis XVI, G. Mason, G. Mason Jr., Miroménil, R. Morris, Necker, d'Ormesson, Rayneval, Sabatier fils et Desprez, Veimerange, Vergennes. American finances; La Luzerne and Marbois—reports and instructions; military and naval operations; French trade with America; America and the neutral league; France and the Hussey–Cumberland mission; Dana in Russia; politics in America; American-Dutch relations; J. Laurens in France.

18. August–September 1781. Correspondence of d'Agay, B. Arnold, T. Barclay, R. Butler, Castries, Clinton, Corny, Dautun, B. Deane, S. Deane, d'Estaing, Fleury, Franklin, Grand, de Grasse, Holker fils, Mme de Kalb, Lafayette, La Luzerne, Le Camus de Néville, Lenoir, Leray de Chaumont, R. Livingston, Marbois, Mauduit, Maurepas, Mazzei, McKean, T. Monford, Monteil, R. Morris, Pasdeloup, Pioger, Rayneval, Sabatier fils et Desprez, Schweighauser, Ségur, H. Shields, Tarlé, J. Thaxter, Veimerange, Vergennes, Washington. La Luzerne and Marbois—reports and instructions; American finances; military and naval operations; military and diplomatic manoeuvres preceding Yorktown; Franco-American consular convention; American-Dutch treaty; peace preliminaries; American relations with Spain; Indian affairs.

202   FRANCE

19. October–December 1781. Correspondence of d'Argainaratz, Beniowski, Bersolle, Castries, Chastellux, Continental Congress, Du Fresne, Fleury, Grand, de Grasse, Gros Pléville, B. Harrison, Holker père et fils, Lafayette, La Luzerne, Lamarque et Fabre, Leray de Chaumont, Létombe, R. Livingston, Louis XVI, Maurepas, Melfort, Mercy-Argenteau, R. Morris, Mourel de Basterans, Rayneval, Raze, Sabatier fils et Desprez, Saint Simon, Ségur, Stahremberg, Veimerange, Vergennes, Washington. La Luzerne—reports and instructions; American finances; military and naval operations; neutral league; peace preliminaries; Franklin in Paris; Adams in Holland; American-Dutch relations; American trade with Britain via third countries; Mississippi navigation issue; politics and events in America.

20. January–March 1782. Correspondence of Alexander, d'Argainaratz, Bancroft, Blome, E. Burke, Castries, Dumouriez, Duportail, d'Eon, Fleury, Franklin, Goltz, Gros Préville, Harcourt, B. Harrison, Col. Hartley, Holker père, John Jay, Lafayette, La Luzerne, Le Camus de Néville, W. Lee, Létombe, R. R. Livingston, Marbois, Mercy-Argenteau, Rayneval, Ridley, Roulhac, Ruker, Ségur, Shelburne, Strange, Tingry, Veimerange, Vergennes, Jonathan Williams. La Luzerne—reports and instructions; American finances; military and naval operations; Mississippi navigation issue; American troubles with Spain; Dutch loan; politics and events in America; defection of Deane; peace negotiations—mainly Hartley–Franklin correspondence.

21. April–July 1782. Correspondence of John Adams, d'Argainaratz, Beaumarchais, Beniowski, Blome, Bouillé, Carleton, Castries, Coulongnac et Cie., Davau, Digby, Fleury, Franklin, Abbé Giroud-Soulavie, Gordon, Grand, Nathaniel Greene, B. Harrison, Hartley, Herouard, Baroness de Kalb, La Luzerne, La Motte, La Touche, H. Laurens, A. Lee, Létombe, R. R. Livingston, Marbois, Maupeou, Melfort, R. Morris, Ogle, O. Pollock, Rayneval, Rochambeau, Ségur, Shelburne, Veimerange, Vérac, Vergennes, Washington, Watson et Cossoul, Jonathan Williams. La Luzerne and Marbois —reports and instructions; American finances; congressional politics; military and naval operations; American policy—Jay in Spain; defection of Deane; Dana in Russia; French, Spanish and American policies in the peace negotiations.

22. August–December 1782. Correspondence of John Adams, d'Argainaratz, Auty, Barclay, Countess Beniowski, Carleton, Marquise de Cossini, Castries, Chrestien et Cie., Continental Congress, Cooper, Cuming and Macarty, Digby, d'Estaing, Fleury, Franklin, Goltz, Grand, N. Greene, B. Harrison, Hartley, Holker père, John Jay, Lafayette, La Luzerne, A. Leslie, B. Lincoln, R. R. Livingston, R. Morris, Nixon and Foster, Rayneval, Rochambeau, Abbé Romand, Ségur, Solano, Steuben, Terrason, Vaudreuil, Vergennes, Viomesnil, Washington, A. Wayne. Reports of and instructions to La

Luzerne; American finances; military and naval operations; Jay in Spain; congressional politics; British emissaries in America; western ambitions of Americans, boundaries; terms of peace; Dana in Russia; Rayneval in England; American-Swedish relations; peace negotiations in Paris.

23. January–March 1783. Correspondence of d'Aligre, d'Artus, Beaumarchais, Boudinot, Cadet de Vaux, Calonne, Castries, Chamber of Commerce of Aunis, Continental Congress, Coulongnac et Cie., Gazan, Ginette Frères, Goyon d'Arzac, Guirard, Hennin, Holker père, Hortal, Mrs. R. Izard, Lafayette, La Luzerne, Lanney, La Vauguyon, Le Camus de Néville, Lemaire, Le Tort, Livingston, Lotbinière, Malsherbes, Martin, Mazzei, Mercy-Argenteau, Miroménil, R. Morris, Rayneval, Ridley, Saint-Dizant, Ségur, Tascher, Vergennes, Vignon, Vilevault, Washington, J. Wilson. La Luzerne —reports from Philadelphia; Congress and peace; American financial problems; American-Dutch treaty; recall of American privateers; politics and events in America; British, French and American trade; American attitude to Spain; American public opinion and the peace terms; peace negotiations in Paris.

24. April–June 1783. Correspondence of Amelot, Barclay, Besson de Salomone, Cadet de Vaux, J. Carter, Castries, Chardon, Conti, S. Cooper, Dupont de Nemours, Fitzherbert, B. Franklin, W. T. Franklin, Friol Roux et Cie., Gazan, Grand, B. Guérard, Holker père et fils, Hortal, John Jay, Jouvenal, Laage, Lafayette, La Luzerne, La Vauguyon, Le Camus de Néville, Lenormant, d'Etoiles, Louis XVI, Mailly, Marbois, Mazzei, Miroménil, Noailles, d'Ormesson, Pauly, Pierre, Pignon, Rayneval, Reverseaux, Ricquebourg, Ridley, Saint-Dizant, Saint-Ouen, Ségur, Vergennes, J. Wadsworth, J. Williams. La Luzerne's reports from Philadelphia; American finances; American desire for peacetime subsidy from France; cessation of hostilities in America; congressional politics and administration; American-Swedish commercial treaty; French, British, and American trade; American claims against France; claims of French merchants against America.

25. July–September 1783. Correspondence of John Adams, Comtesse d'Auterroche, Barclay, Bayard, Burral, Cambray, Carleton, Castries, Chardon, Continental Congress, Corny, Cussac, Demouville, Dupont de Nemours, Fleury, Forsters, Frères, B. Franklin, W. T. Franklin, Grubb et Cie., Holker père et fils, James Jay, John Jay, Baroness de Kalb, Lafayette, La Luzerne, La Rigaudière, La Rochefoucald, Lauzun, Lenormant, d'Etoiles, Leray de Chaumont, Lotbinière, Louis XVI, Marbois, Milligan, Montholon, d'Ormesson, Pierre, Poisson, Rayneval, Ricquebourg, M. Ridley, Sabatier fils et Desprez, Ségur, Steuben, Texier, Thiériot, Tholménil, Veimerange, Vergennes, White, J. Williams. La Luzerne—letters and enclosures; American finances; Congress and foreign affairs; Dana leaves Russia; French subsidies and loans to America; Mississippi navigation and western boundaries issues; Anglo-Dutch negotiations; Franco-American trade.

26. October–December 1783. Correspondence of John Adams, Alexander, Comtesse d'Auterroche, Barclay, Calonne, Cambray, Carayon, Castries, Chardon, Cicé, Conti, Coulongnac de Coste Belle, Fleury, Franklin, Grand, Guérard, Holker père, Lafayette, La Luzerne, Létombe, Melartic, Marbeuf, d'Ormesson, Paulze, Rayneval, Reine, Rochambeau, Schaffer, Schweighauser et Dobrée, Ségur, Thévenard, Thiériot, Vergennes, Vilevault, Washington. La Luzerne—letters and enclosures; American finances; political situation in America; weakness of Congress; Indian affairs; American commercial legislation; French and Spanish commercial policy toward America; American-Spanish relations; definitive peace treaties; failure of Dana's mission.

Hambourg (Leland II, 686–7)

101. 1775 to **104.** 1785. Correspondence of La Houze, Vergennes, Lagau, and Viviers, dealing mainly with British recruitment of German troops for service in America and occasionally with matters of commerce and privateering.

Hesse (Leland II, 699)

14. 1775–6. Correspondence of Grais and Vergennes concerning mainly the British purchase of mercenary troops, rumours of a British purchase of Russian troops and a Russian alliance.

Hollande (Leland II, 720–2)

540. January–April 1780. Correspondence of Bleiswyck, Chardon, Deghels et Cie., Dubroeuil, Grand, Groult, La Vauguyon, Louis XVI, Necker, Sartine, Vergennes, Vlierden. The two main subjects are the Armed Neutral League and Dutch relations with Britain, France, Russia and America.

541. May–August 1780. Correspondence of Aranda, Berkenroode, Grand, La Vauguyon, Montaran, Necker, Sartine, Van de Oudermeulen, Vergennes, Vlierden. Dutch commerce; abrogation of the Anglo-Dutch alliance; Armed Neutral League; Dutch naval preparations.

542. September–December 1780. Correspondence of Bérenger, Berkenroode, Castries, Grand, Guitton, Holker père, La Vauguyon, Mercede, Sartine, Vergennes, Vlierden. Armed Neutral League; naval operations; naval supplies; news and intelligence from Britain and America.

543. January–March 1781. Correspondence of Bérenger, Berkenroode, Castries, Grand, La Vauguyon, Necker, Vergennes, Vlierden. Mainly dispatches of Vergennes, La Vauguyon, Bérenger, concerning the Armed Neutrality.

544. April–June 1781. Correspondence of John Adams, Bérenger, Berkenroode, Boers, Castries, Chardon, Fleury, La Vauguyon, Louis XVI, Vergennes, Vlierden. Similar to **543.**, but also dealing with the negotiation of a Franco-Dutch convention.

545. July–August 1781. Correspondence of Berkenroode, Castries, Fabry, Fleury, Grand, La Vauguyon, Louis XVI, Nadaillac, Receveur, Ségur, Van de Perre, Vergennes, Vlierden. Mainly the correspondence of Vergennes and La Vauguyon concerning the Armed Neutrality and Dutch cooperation in the war against Britain.

546. September–December 1781. Correspondence of Bérenger, Berkenroode, Boers, Castries, Chardon, Fleury, Grand, La Vauguyon, Louis XVI, Roffignac, Ségur, Vergennes, Vlierden. Mainly the correspondence of Vergennes with Bérenger and La Vauguyon concerning Dutch participation in the war against Britain.

Portugal (Leland II, 773–7)

106. 1776 to **113.** 1782–3. Volumes containing chiefly the correspondence of Blosset, Vergennes, d'Anville, Sa, Sartine, d'Augnac, O'Dunne, Souza. The chief subjects are news of the war and of commercial problems; Portugal and the privateering of the various belligerents; and a small amount of material in **113.** on Portugal's participation in the Armed Neutrality.

Prusse (Leland II, 778–9)

194. 1776 to **196.** January–June 1778. Correspondence of Gaussen, Grim, Pons, Rulhière, Vergennes. The main topics are the attitude of Frederick II toward the British difficulties and reports on the activities of British and American agents in Berlin.

Russe (Leland II, 783–90)

98. April–December 1775 to **111.** July–December 1783. Main correspondents Bariatinsky, Catherine II, Chotinsky, Coberon, Panin, Vérac, Vergennes. The principal topics are intelligence of the Anglo-Russian negotiations; Russian efforts at mediation; development of the Armed Neutrality; Vérac's reports on Dana's mission; Catherine II's attitude toward Britain and the American problem.

CORRESPONDANCE POLITIQUE: SUPPLÉMENT

Angleterre (Leland II, 829–30)

18. 1773–91. Various documents, dated 1775–9, including papers relating to Silas Deane; reflections on American and French policy by Rayneval, Turgot and Vergennes; a report by Bonvouloir; Franco-Spanish discussions of joint policy toward England.

Espagne (Leland II, 832–3)

15. 1753–65 to 17. 1768–95. A few documents relating to the Family Compact; Franco-Spanish policy toward Britain; the possibility of mediation; Spanish war objectives.

Etats-Unis (Leland II, 837–9, 847–50, 854–8)

1. 1777–87. Almost entirely draft letters of Gérard to Borda, d'Estaing, and others, on naval affairs, with replies; enclosures sent by Gérard with his regular dispatches.

3. 1778–80. Correspondence of Gérard with Sartine and Vergennes. The Sartine correspondence is original while the Vergennes correspondence is copied from *Correspondence Politique, Etats-Unis,* **3–12.**

4. 1776–89. Chiefly dispatches from French consuls in America with enclosures, dealing with politics and internal events in America.

11. March 1778 to December 1784. Drafts and minutes of ministerial correspondence concerning consular affairs, including appointments of consuls, instructions to consuls, correspondence concerning consular affairs. All this material is relative to the American Revolution.

12. 1778–84 (Second Series, 1) (Military Operations, 1). Combined Franco-American military and naval operations; correspondence of Choin with Gérard, 1778; correspondence of the French officers in American service with the French ministers at Philadelphia.

13. 1779–83 (Second Series, 2) (Military Operations, 2). Similar to **12.**

14. 1779–85 (Second Series, 3) (Military Operations, 3). Military and naval operations; problems of French officers in American service; correspondence of Lafayette and La Luzerne, 1780–2; correspondence of Gérard and d'Estaing, 1779.

15. 1780–3 (Second Series, 4) (Military Operations, 4). Mainly the correspondence of Rochambeau with La Luzerne, Washington, Lafayette, and others, June 1780 to July 1783.

16. 1775–85 (Second Series, 5) (Exchange of Prisoners). Exchange of prisoners, 1779–83, including letters from prisoners.

17. 1780–4 (Second Series, 6) (Intendant of the Army). Mainly commissariat, logistic and financial aspects of French forces in America.

18. 1781–7 (Second Series, 7) (Finance, 1). Franco-American financial relations and American financial problems.

19. 1783–97 (Second Series, 8) (Finance, 2). A few documents of 1783 on Franco-American loans.

26. 1772–94 (Second Series, 15) (Memoirs, 1). Various observations, 1776–80, on American affairs, British policies, French policy alternatives.

27. 1775–89 (Second Series, 16) (Memoirs, 2). Several miscellaneous documents, 1775–8, consisting of sketches of British statesmen, notes of an American traveller, etc.

29. 1778–84 (Second Series, 18) (War and Marine). Naval supplies to America; consular convention; French naval forces in America; etc.

30. 1778–94 (Second Series, 19) (Marine and Colonies). French consular representation in America; capture of French colonies in America by the British; commercial mission of Meade and Dupuy.

Hollande (Leland II, 866)

20. 1774–80. Effect of the war on Dutch commerce; means of detaching Holland from Britain.

21. 1781–91. 7 October 1782, Lettre et Mémoire remis par Son Altesse . . . le Prince d'Orange et de Nassau . . . à Leurs Hautes Puissances . . . Contenant un exposé détaillé de son Administration, en qualité d'Amiral Général de l'Union.

MÉMOIRES ET DOCUMENTS

Amérique (Leland II, 894–901)

11. 1713–71. These are documents from the proceedings of the British Parliament which contain some material on the Anglo-American dispute for 1766–8.

13. 1680–1777. Some correspondence between d'Ennery and Vergennes, 1775–6, with news of events in America and comment on British policy.

16. 1664–1783. A few documents on commerce between the French and American colonies; present state of the war with Britain, 1780; provisioning the French colonies from America, 1783.

Angleterre (Leland II, 928–44)

1. 1604–1779. Considerations by Vergennes on British problems and the policy to be followed by France and Spain, 1776.

2. 1782–1805. Memoir by d'Albon on the status of Britain 1781?.

6. 1554–1794. Various memoirs planning attacks on British commerce, 1776–80; fear that Britain really plans to attack France.

10. 1697–1810. 2 memoirs of 1776, 1 on British prize law and the French attitude toward American prizes brought to French ports; the other on the conflict of European and American commercial interests.

46. 1713–1811. Discussion of British commerce, 1774; list of British loans, 1776–83.

47. 1763–1805. Memoir on Lotbinière's proposed mission to Canada, 1778; La Valinière's memoir inciting Canadians to insurrection, 1782.

48. 1762–1810. 4 February 1783. Printed royal French ordinance, concerning the cessation of maritime hostilities.

52. 1740–93. Several memoirs by de Guines, Du Pons, and others, on French interest in the Anglo-American problem, 1773–9.

53. 1743–1813. Broglie's war plan against Britain of 1763–6, revised and submitted to Louis XVI, 1778.

54. 1666–1776. Ricard's memoir, 10 December 1776, on the necessity of utilizing all resources against Britain and what France, Spain and America should gain from the war.

55. 1734–95. Various military plans, 1778–80.

56. 1750–1810. Various memoirs, 1770–83, speculating on ways to increase the French advantage over Britain and replace her as the dominant European power.

59. 1763–1803. Memoir on Britain and her North American possessions, 1773.

61. 1765–1832. Documents relating to British naval strength and intelligence, 1778 and n.d.

73. 1749–1822. Memoir on the British colonial system and the reasons for American progress, 1783.

Espagne (Leland II, 951)

208. 1776–82. Several memoirs on Spanish policy toward Britain and America and the value of the Franco-Spanish alliance against Britain.

Etats-Unis (Leland II, 953–64, 976)

1. 1766–80. Various memoirs on British possessions and considerations of policy by Vergennes, Rayneval, Malouet, Gérard, and others; other miscellaneous documents.

2. 1767–95. Memoirs on the American colonies prepared by Bourdieu, Rayneval, Ricard, Fleury, Juigné, Lafayette, and others, submitted to Vergennes.

3. 1775–94. Memoirs on the war with Britain by Bertrand.

4. 1776–83. Memoirs on American commerce, finances, and productions, by d'Eon, Valnais, Marbois, n.s.

5. 1778–81. Memoirs by Favier on the origin and course of the war and on the Armed Neutrality.

6. 1780–91. 86 original letters of Washington, most to La Luzerne, taken from the files of the French legation in the United States. (All are printed in J. C. Fitzpatrick, *The Writings of George Washington . . . 1745–1799*)

7. 1781–9. Various memoirs on the state of the war and possible peace moves; also a memoir on John Holker fils, general agent of the French marine in Philadelphia, 1781–2.

10. 1783–1812. General observations on America and how France can secure American commerce, 1783, n.s.

17. 1781–5. D'Annemours on Maryland and the prospects of French commerce there, 14 February 1781; Marbois on Franco-American trade, August 1782; Marbois and Toscan on commerce, 1783.

France (Leland II, 985–1033)

410. 1648–1806. 2 letters by Favier and a memoir by Beaumarchais on various aspects of French participation in the war, 1778.

446. 1700–82. 2 memoirs by Vergennes on French foreign policy, 1782.

463. 1715–1813. Various documents on the military and political situation of Britain and America.

495. 1726–1810. Memoir, 20 September 1780, by Bertrand, which is supplementary to the preliminary draft of the peace terms of October 1779.

518. 1744–1800. 2 circulars from Vergennes to French agents, announcing the signing of the preliminary and definitive peace treaties respectively.

530. 1771–4. News of Anglo-American problems.

531. 1775–9. Mostly reports of military operations in America, with a few documents on Spanish policy.

582. 1767–89. French censorship imposed on political treatises, some of which pertain to America.

584. 1774–88. Miscellaneous documents giving war news; memoirs on peace plans; memoirs on political events in Europe.

586. 1777–81. Military and naval situation of various European powers, 1777–9.

587. 1781–92. Several memoirs, 1 by Rayneval, on the political situation in Europe and the effect of peace on it, 1781–3.

1385. 1778. Various printed royal ordinances and decrees of the council of state, mostly concerning prizes.

1387. 1779. Printed ordinance and regulations concerning maritime prizes.

1389. January–August 1780. Printed letter of Louis XVI concerning American prizes brought to French ports.

1393. 1783. Various printed ordinances and regulations concerning the cessation of hostilities and the establishment of a packet service with the United States.

1897. 1774–87. Exclusively the political correspondence of Vergennes, some of which concerns joint Franco-Spanish policy.

2005. 1739–80. Various memoirs on French trade and finance, 1778–80.

2011. 1781–4. Several memoirs on the possibility of Bayonne as a free port for Americans.

2012. 1774–1785. 2 memoirs, 1782–3, on French commerce and commercial treaties to be negotiated.

2022. 1758–95. Various ordinances and documents relating to maritime prizes, the Armed Neutrality, maritime commerce.

2027. 1659–1800. Printed ordinances and regulations concerning maritime prizes, 1778–82.

Hollande (Leland II, 1038)

48. 1778–1810. Gérard de Rayneval's observations 'of a citizen of Amsterdam' on Sir Jos. Yorke's memoir of 22 July 1779 presented to the States General. Memoir, 1788, n.s., on the Franco-Dutch alliance and the American war.

CORRESPONDANCE CONSULAIRE
See *Archives Nationales*

Archives de la Ministère de la Guerre. See VAL DE MARNE

Archives du Ministère de la Marine. See *Archives Nationales*

Archives Nationales, 60 rue des Francs-Bouregeois
75003 Paris

The Archives Nationales are the central repository for governmental records in France. They are open to the public on presentation of a diplomatic or university letter of introduction. The records are divided into two sections: *Ancien* (prior to 1789) and *Moderne*. Within each of these sections are subsections designated by letters. In addition to the general collection, there are documents deposited by particular ministries, notably foreign affairs, navy and overseas territories.

There are two general published guides to the Archives Nationales, but a new guide is reportedly in the planning stage. *Inventaire sommaire et tableau méthodique des fonds conservés aux Archives nationales (1er partie, Documents antérieures à 1789)* (Paris, 1871) is a general survey of documents and series. More precise information and more exact references are found in *Etat sommaire par séries des documents conservés aux Archives nationales* (Paris, 1891). The finding aids available at the Archives Nationales are surveyed in *Etat des inventaires des Archives nationales, départementales, communales et hospitalières au 1er janvier 1937* and *Supplément* to 31 July 1955. There is also a useful *Guide du Lecteur* (1964) and published inventories for some of the subseries. The Archives Nationales has embarked on an active programme of publication, hence new inventories and catalogues appear periodically.

SECTION ANCIENNE: ANCIEN RÉGIME

G. *Administrations financières et speciales*

5. Amirauté et conseil des prises:

216. Jugements du Conseil des prises, 1695–1782.

264. Enregistrement des procédures des prises pendant la guerre de 1778.

FONDS SPÉCIAUX

AD7. *Marine et Colonies*

2ª. Colonies en général; 2ª–3 Colonies: Canada, 'Saint-Domingue, troupes coloniales; 7ᵇ–8 Prises et course.

MUSÉE DE L'HISTOIRE DE FRANCE

AE3. *Traités*

217–22. Amérique: Etats-Unis, 1776–1803.

FONDS DES COLONIES

Virtually all the colonial records before 1789 are now in the Archives nationales. There is a manuscript inventory and several of the sub-series have their own published inventories. (N. M. Millèr Surrey lists some of the documents from the Fonds des Colonies in her *Calandar of Manuscripts in Paris Archives and Libraries relating to the History of the Mississippi Valley to 1803*, Washington, D.C., Carnegie Institution, 1926)

A. *Actes du pouvoir souverain*

B. *Correspondance envoyé-ordres du Roi,* 1665–1789.

(For this series, Etienne Taillemite, *Inventaire analytique de la correspondance générale avec les colonies. Départ. Séries B, Paris, Service des Archives, 1959, is in progress; but only Vol. I, 1654–1715, has appeared to date)*

C. *Correspondance générale-lettres reçues*

Cᵃ ᵇ. *Guadeloupe*

C8ᵃ ᵇ. *Martinique*

This series covers primarily Martinique, but with many documents concerning other French possessions in the Caribbean. (A complete published inventory in Etienne Taillemite, *Inventaire de la série Colonies C8ª Martinique*, Paris, SEVPEN, 1967–71, 2 vols.)

Martinique served as the base for the French fleet during the American war, hence **76–83** (1777–83) contain documents dealing with French naval operations which complement the documents in Série B4, *Campagnes,* of the Archives de la Marine. There are many documents on the military situation in the Caribbean, defence of the French islands, convoys, privateering, and movements of Rodney's squadron.

C9A[a b c]. *St Domingue*

C10[a e]. *Antilles*

D1. *Correspondance relative aux troupes des colonies*

D2A. *Recrues des colonies*

D2C. *Matricules et revues des troupes des colonies*

D2D. *Personnel militaire et civil; listes générales*

E. *Personnel individuel*
These are dossiers on personnel, mainly naval, giving information on salaries and positions but occasionally other details. There is a card inventory (**972**), but it is essential to know the name of the person to locate relevant material.

F1, 2. *Commerce aux colonies; comptes, dépenses, compagnies*

F3. *Collection Moreau St Méry*
This series is known to contain documents concerning the Caribbean in the 18th century. (A printed inventory is expected soon)

ARCHIVES DU MINISTÈRE DE LA MARINE

The central marine archives prior to 1870 are housed at the Archives Nationales, but belong to the Ministère de la Marine. Permission to consult these archives must therefore be applied for through the Ministère des Affaires Etrangères. The Service historique de la marine, 3 avenue Octave-Gréard, 75007 Paris, is helpful on general approaches.

The archives are divided into series A-G, with B. *Service général* the largest and most important. The only printed guide to the archives is Didier Neuville, *Etat sommaire des archives de la Marine antérieures à la révolution* (Paris, 1898), which is cited below as 'ES'. Within the B series some of the sub-series also have published inventories, which are indicated below where relevant. The Salle d'Inventaires of the Archives Nationales contains a duplicated book by Waldo Leland, John J. Meng and Abel Doysié, in English, but titled

Sources d'histoire américaine, Fonds Marine, with the following note on the title-page: 'Volume 3 (unpublished) of Guide to Materials for American History in the Libraries and Archives of Paris, vol. 1, 1932; vol. 2, 1943'.

The naval ministry also maintains depots in Brest, Cherbourg, Lorient, Rochefort and Toulon, the libraries and archives of which are noted where relevant under the headings for those cities.

A. *Actes du pouvoir souverain* (ES 15–25)

A1. Recueil général des ordonnances, édits, arrêts, lettres patentes, etc., sur la Marine.

111. 1773 to **132.** 1783.

A2. Recueils particuliers d'ordonnances, édits, arrêts, lettres patentes, etc., sur la Marine.

37–41. Recueil des règelements, décisions et ordonnances rendus sur le fait de la Marine, sous le ministère du maréchal de Castries, 1780–7.
36. Contains the ministry of Boynes, 1771–4.

There is nothing listed for 1775–9.

A3. Inventaire ou table chronologique des édits, déclarations, arrêts, ordonnances et autres pièces faissant loi pour ce concerne la Marine, le Commerce et les Colonies.

10. 1767–83.

B. *Service général* (ES 27–308. *Inventaire des Archives de la Marine: Série B, Service général*, Paris, 1885–1963, 8 vols., covering B1–B3, cited as 'IS')

B1. *Décisions* (ES 38–44. IS I, 141–84)

79–87. 1773–7. Scattered items concerning French and American defences.

88–98. 1778–83. Much material on all aspects of French naval activity in this period.

B2. *Ordres du Roi et dépêches de la marine* (ES 45–78. IS III, 458–522)

400–25. 1773–83. Naval orders and dispatches.

B3. *Lettres reçues* (ES 130–46. IS VIII, 54–156)

In-letters of the Ministry.

610. begins 1774; **753.** ends 1783. Much of the correspondence is from the *intendants* of Brest, Havre, Dunkirk, Bordeaux, Rochefort, etc., with occasional volumes from other ministries.

800–1. Supplements 1763–84. Topics of interest generally concern the navy's role in the American war, transport and supply of the French expeditionary force, and related matters.

B4. *Campagnes* (ES 188–219)

111. Amérique du Nord, Antilles, 1766–7. On the British colonies in North America.

128. Amérique du Nord, Antilles, 1776. Operations of de Grasse in the Caribbean.

129–30. Côtes de France, 1777. Coastal defence; prizes taken by the British before the opening of hostilities.

132. Amérique du Nord, Antilles, 1777. War plans against Britain; British prizes; Fagan's mission to New York.

135. Côtes de France, Méditerranée, 1778. War plans against Britain; letters of Kerguelen; reflections of an American on the present declaration of war.

136. Côtes de France, 1778. Battle of Ouessant (Ushant); prizes; defences; letters of de Grasse, de La Motte-Picquet, d'Orvilliers, Guichen.

137–8. Côtes de France, 1778. Memoirs of de Grasse on the war; naval actions.

140. Antilles, 1778–9. Naval and military operations; letters of d'Estaing.

141. Antilles et Etats-Unis d'Amérique, 1778. Observations on America; correspondence of d'Estaing.

142–8. *idem*, 1778–9. Mostly the operations and correspondence of d'Estaing.

151. *idem*, 1778–9. Prizes; prisoners.

152. *idem*, 1778–9. State of d'Estaing's squadron.

153. Sénégal, Antilles, Amérique du Nord, 1778–82. On the Marquis de Lafayette.

154–5. Côtes de France, d'Angleterre, d'Espagne, 1779. On the Franco-Spanish naval force under d'Orvilliers.

156. Côtes de France et d'Angleterre, mer du Nord, 1779–80. Projects for the invasion of Britain; naval encounters.

157. Côtes de France, 1779. Convoys, etc.

158. Côtes d'Angleterre et d'Espagne, mer Baltique, mer du Nord, 1779. On John Paul Jones; naval actions.

159. Angleterre, Iles Jersey et Guernsey, Irelande, Espagne, Açores, Amérique du Nord, 1779. Explanation of French policy toward Britain; plans for attacks against Britain and British shipping; memoir on North America.

161. Antilles françaises, 1779. Correspondence of Bouillé and d'Estaing.

162. *idem*, 1779. Correspondence of d'Estaing.

163. Antilles anglaises et hollandaises, et possessions espagnoles, 1779. Correspondence of d'Estaing; memoir of the attack on St Vincent; account of the engagement of 6 July near Grenada.

164. Antilles et terre ferme d'Amérique, 1779. Correspondence of French naval officers, arranged alphabetically, A–G.

165. *idem*, 1779. I–T; correspondence of d'Estaing with British officers.

166. *idem*, 1779. A–T; frigate actions; siege of Savannah; concerning d'Estaing's actions.

167. Amérique du Nord, 1779. Correspondence of army officers at Savannah, arranged alphabetically, B–T; orders of d'Estaing.

168. *idem*, 1779. Siege of Savannah: correspondence of d'Estaing, of diplomatic and consular agents, and of British and American officers and agents.

169–70. Antilles et terre ferme d'Amérique, 1779. Paroles given to d'Estaing's squadron—notes and dossiers in alphabetical order by ship name, A–V; debarkation of troops.

171. Espagne, 1779–80. Joint enterprises against Britain; escorts for merchant ships; correspondence of d'Estaing; correspondence of the French Ambassador in Spain.

172. Antilles et Amérique du Nord, 1779–80. D'Estaing's squadron; capture of Charleston; letters of Lafayette; French expeditionary force in America; operations of John Paul Jones; observations on America.

173. Côtes de France, 1780. Mostly single actions between French and British ships.

174. *idem*, 1780. Letters of Guichen; Chaffault's force; state of the fleet preparing for America; escorts for merchant ships.

177. Espagne, 1780. D'Estaing's journal.

178. *idem*, 1780. Correspondence of d'Estaing, of French diplomatic and consular officials in Spain, and of the Spanish authorities.

180. Antilles, 1780. Letters of naval officers, arranged alphabetically, A–I; Guichen's engagements of 17 April, 15 and 19 May; Guichen's correspondence with the commander of the Spanish naval force.

181. *idem*, 1780. Letters of naval officers, arranged alphabetically, K–V; translations of British letters.

183. Amérique du Nord, 1780. Correspondence of de Ternay's squadron; Hudson Bay expedition; correspondence of Rochambeau; protection of American commerce; American documents.

184. Antilles, Amérique du Nord, 1780–1. Captures of Yorktown and Pensacola; operations against St Christopher and St Lucia; journal of de Grasse's squadron.

185. Amérique du Nord, 1780–2. Letters of de Ternay; copies and extracts of Rochambeau's correspondence; Hudson Bay expedition; prisoners; minor actions.

186. Espagne, 1780–3. Actions of d'Estaing; letters of Montmorin to Castries and d'Estaing; articles of the preliminary peace.

187. Amérique du Nord, France, 1781. Escort of convoys; expedition against Jersey.

188. Côtes de France et d'Espagne, Antilles, mer du Nord, 1781. Escort of convoys; capture of British privateers; letters and memoirs of Hamilton; battle of Dogger Bank.

189. Espagne, Côtes de France, 1781–2. Letters of Montmorin to Castries; letters of de La Motte-Picquet.

191. Amérique du Nord, 1780–1. De Ternay's death; battle of Chesapeake Bay; letters of Rochambeau and Barres; Hudson Bay expedition; journals of various ships.

192. Amérique du Nord, Antilles, 1781. Various naval engagements; de Ternay's death; letters of British officers on the war; letters of Lafayette.

193. Antilles, Guyane, 1781. Letters of Bouillé; various naval and military operations.

195. Antilles et terre ferme d'Amérique, 1781–2. Letters of Bouillé; battle of the Saintes; situation of the French forces in America.

199–201. Côtes de France, d'Espagne, d'Angleterre, 1781–3. Mostly convoy escorts and single-ship actions.

204. Espagne, 1782–3. Operations of the Franco-Spanish fleet; conduct of d'Estaing.

205. Antilles et terre ferme d'Amérique, 1781–2. Correspondence of officers, arranged alphabetically, A–G; convoy escorts; correspondence of de Grasse; battle of the Saintes.

206. *idem*, 1782. Correspondence of officers, arranged alphabetically, K–V; letters of Lapérouse; battle of the Saintes; correspondence of de Vaudreuil.

208–9. Espagne, Amérique, 1782–3. Lists of naval, military and civil officers.

210–11. Espagne, 1782–3. Correspondence of d'Estaing.

213. Amérique, Angleterre, Espagne, Méditerranée, 1782–4. Council at Lorient concerning the battle of the Saintes and its judgment; paroles given to the French forces in America; prisoners.

214. Amérique, Côtes d'Angleterre, 1774–80. Letters, memoirs and notes concerning the navies of France, Spain and Britain; instructions for de Grasse.

215. Amérique, Côtes d'Angleterre, de France, d'Espagne, 1780. Letters, memoirs and notes on many naval matters; instructions for de Ternay, de Grasse and de La Motte-Picquet.

216. Côtes de France, et d'Espagne, Amérique, 1780–2. Instructions for Guichen, de La Motte-Picquet and de Vaudreuil.

217. Côtes de France, Amérique, 1780–3. Correspondence between the Minister and d'Estaing; signing of the peace.

218. Amérique, Espagne, 1782–3. Situation of the French forces in the American colonies; instructions for d'Estaing; signing of the peace.

219–20. Côtes de France, 1780–3. Letters of Hector to Castries.

221–64. These volumes all deal with the *Conseil de guerre* held at Lorient to enquire into the débâcle of the battle of the Saintes. Included are ships' journals, testimony, other documents submitted as evidence, and deliberations of the Council.

266. Amérique, 1782–3. Hudson Bay expedition; convoy escorts; single-ship actions; signing of the peace; correspondence of de Vaudreuil.

267. Amérique du Nord, . . . 1783–4. De Vaudreuil's squadron; troop transport.

B5. *Armements* (ES 226–9)

10–25. Bâtiments du Roi, 1771–84. Contains various lists, inventories, etc., of the state, extent and disposition of the navy.

11. Contains Tableau des forces maritimes de France, d'Espagne et d'Angleterre en 1777.

B7. *Pays Etrangers, Commerce et Consulats*

The American material in this series is calendared in A. P. Nasatir and G. E. Monell, *French Consuls in the United States: A Calendar of their Correspondence in the Archives Nationales*, Washington, D.C., Library of Congress, 1967, 329 ff. An inventory of this series is in progress but does not yet cover the post-1778 period: see Etienne Taillemite, *Inventaire des Archives de la Marine: Sous-série B7* (*Pays Etrangers-Commerce-Consulats*), Paris, Imprimerie Nationale, 1964–. For related consular material, see *Correspondance Consulaire* below.

517. Consuls, Listes générales, etc. (All information concerning North America, 1748–91, is given in Nasatir and Monell, op. cit., 332–3. This includes salaries and dates of entry into service of officials

518. Lists of consuls, vice-consuls, etc., in North America, with salaries and other documents related to appointments.

C. *Personnel*

This series deals entirely with various aspects of naval personnel matters. (The only printed guide is ES 349–575)

C1. *Officiers militaires*

Contains royal orders, dispatches, in-letters, lists, reviews, rolls and other documents concerning naval officers.

C2. *Officiers civils*

Similar material concerning civilian administrators, inspectors, comptrollers, doctors, etc.

C3. *Troupes*

Dispatches, memoirs, regimental rolls, rolls of artillery units, etc., of the marines who served mainly on shipboard and at arsenals.

C4. *Classes, Amirautés, Police de la navigation*

Mainly concerned with personnel administration of seamen and others, containing rolls, dispatches, orders, etc.

C6. *Roles d'équipage*

Ships' musters. (ES 473–566 lists each ship included)

C7. *Personnel individuel*

Individual dossiers on persons in naval service.

F. *Invalides et Prises* (ES 645–62)

Fl. *Invalides*

Documents on disabled persons and on pensions.

F2. *Prises*

1–5. Décisions, all dealing with the war of 1778–83.

45–9. Ordres et dépêches, 1779–82.

68–70. Various aspects of prizes, 1778–81.

71, 72, 74. General documents on prizes, 1668–1823.

76. Prises anglaises: liquidations (A–Z).

77 Instructions, assurances, contentieux, 1778–83.

78–81. Guerre de 1778–83: état des prises par port.

82. Etat général de liquidation, prisonniers anglais, liquidations des prises, colonies, 1778–88.

94–101. Prisoners-of-war, 1770–91.

G. *Mémoires et documents divers* (ES 663–83)

165. Letters of Choiseul, Boynes, Castries, 1760–86.
166. Correspondence of Fleury, Castries, 1778–82.

167–9. Letters of d'Estaing, 1772–80.

170. Letters and notes of d'Estaing, n.d.

171–2. Letters to d'Estaing, n.d.

CORRESPONDANCE CONSULAIRE (ARCHIVES DES AFFAIRES ETRANGÈRES)

In the Treaty of Amity and Commerce, 1778, France and the Continental

Congress agreed to accredit consuls, vice-consuls and agents. As a result of the signing of a consular convention in 1778, Conrad Alexandre Gérard arrived in July of that same year as the first French consular agent. The consular correspondence thus complements the regular series of diplomatic correspondence in the Archives du Ministère des Affaires Etrangères, but the series prior to 1792 are housed at the Archives Nationales.

The material is located in the series *Affaires Etrangères,* Série B1, and *idem,* Sous-série BIII. A complementary series is Marine Série B7, (see *Archives du Ministère de la Marine* above). A detailed calendar of the American material in these series is A. P. Nasatir and G. E. Monell, op. cit., on which the following summary is based. A multi-volumed inventory of Sous-série B7 is being issued but the revolutionary period has not yet been covered. This material is also covered by carton, in ES and Leland II, but the carton numbers given in each case are no longer accurate since the papers have now been bound into volumes. The researcher should therefore rely on the authoritative work of Nasatir and Monell.

Affaires Etrangères, Série BI. *Correspondance Consulaire*

209. Boston, Vol.1, 1779–85. Main correspondents are Valnais and Létombe, with the first letter from Valnais to Sartine, 16 June 1779. Topics are generally the movements of the French squadron under d'Estaing, French prisoners and deserters, provisioning the French army and navy, and American politics.

909. New York, Vol. 1, 1783–7. Contains, for 1783 only, 2 routine letters from Crévecoeur to Delisle and 1 to Castries, mostly concerned with Franco -American commerce.

945. Philadelphia, Vol. 1, 1778–83. Chiefly letters of La Luzerne, Barbé -Marbois and Holker père et fils, from 25 August 1778 to 31 December 1783. Topics generally are the activities of the Holkers, American financial problems, activities of and supplies for French squadrons, negotiations with Congress, etc.

Affaires Etrangères, Sous-série BIII

440. Etats-Unis, 1664–1829: Traités et Conventions de Commerce, Tarifs et Douanes. Largely concerned with 1783 and after, this volume has much correspondence concerned with commerce and navigation, translations of acts of the states and Congress, lists of duties and tariffs, and material concerning the negotiations relating to consuls.

441. Mémoires sur le commerce. Reports and correspondence of Valnais, Barbé-Marbois, Létombe, and others, concerning contraband trade, money problems, establishment of consulates, American commerce, the Luxembourg affair, etc., 1777–85.

444. Etats-Unis: Tableaux de Commerce. Contains only a list of Maryland exports for 1774 and 2 lists of French ships arriving at Baltimore from France and the French colonies, 1783.

445. *idem.* A continuation of **444.** This volume has a few documents concerning American trade, 1772–6, and others concerning Franco-American trade, 1781–3.

446. Etats-Unis: Tableaux de Commerce et du Statistique Général. Lists of ships, exports and imports in America for 1776.

447. Etats-Unis: Affaires Particulières, 1778–82. Mostly letters and supporting memoirs requesting positions as consuls or vice-consuls in America.

448. A continuation of **447.**, covering 1783 onwards.

457. Etats-Unis, 1783–1870. Contains 2 documents, 1778 and 1781, pertaining to the establishment and functions of consuls in the US.

MANUSCRITS

There is a body of manuscripts at the Archives nationales which do not form a part of any of the collections of the archive. (These manuscripts are listed in *Catalogue des manuscrits conservés aux Archives nationales*, Paris, 1892, which is supplemented by a card index. This last has not been examined by the present editors)

74. (C11, 8¹⁴⁸) 'Tableau historique des événements politiques, militaires et intérieures qui se sont passés dans les différentes cours de l'Europe depuis la mort de Louis XV jusqu'à la paix de 1783', 270 pp.

421. (F⁶⁰, 6). Notes et relations concernant les opérations militaires pendant la guerre d'Amérique (1 bundle). Relation d'un voyage en Amérique et aux Antilles, 1782, 42 pp.

553. (K, 147, no. 3). *1.* 'Traduction en abrégé de l'Histoire de la guerre de l'Amérique entre l'Angleterre et ses colonies, et dont l'origine est au commencement de l'année 1764; imprimée à Londres en 1780.' *2.* 'Evénements qui ont rapport à la guerre d'Amérique depuis la fin de l'année 1779, lesquels sont tirés de l'annual registre', 1780.

573. (K, 157–9, no. 2). 'Conjectures raisonnés sur la situation actuelle de la France dans le système politique de l'Europe, et réciproquement sur la situation respective de l'Europe à l'égard de la France, enfin sur les nouvelles combinaisons qui doivent ou peuvent résulter de ces différentes rapports, aussi dans le système politique de l'Europe,' par le comte de Broglie, 16 avril 1773, 237 pp.

912. (K, 1231, no. 8). *f. 1r°.* 'Précis des opérations de l'escadre du M^r. le comte d'Estaing'. *f. 9r°.* 'Journal de la campagne du comte d'Estaing en Amérique, 1778–1779'. *f. 57r°.* 'Voyage de la Grenade à l'isle espagnole de la Trinité, en juillet 1783', 61 pp.

2478. (MM 849). 'Extrait du Journal des services principaux de Paul Jones dans la Révolution des Etats-Unis d'Amérique, écrit par lui-même et présenté avec un profond respect au très illustre prince Louis XVI.'

SECTION D'OUTRE-MER.
See *Ministère d'Outre-Mer*

Bibliothèque de l'Arsenal. See Bibliothèque Nationale

Bibliothèque de la Chambre des Députés
Palais Bourbon, 126 rue de l'Université
75007 Paris

Access reserved for deputies and scholars.

293. Recueil des Mémoires établissant les inconvéniens du Commerce des Fraudeurs Anglois pendant les hostilitiés; ensemble la nécessité du rendre les armateurs français armant sous pavillion américain justiciables des juges de leur domicile. Par M'e Poirier, Avocat en Parlement à Dunkerque, 1779 à 1782.' 20 March 1780, case of the privateer *Prince Noir.* Memoir presented to Sartine, on the question whether a French subject fitting out a privateer under American flag is 'justiciable' in French or American courts. 10 August 1780, letter from the King to the admiral concerning adjudication of prizes brought into French ports by American privateers. 11 August 1780, Sartine to admiralty officers of Dunkirk, French courts to exercise jurisdiction in the cases of the *Prince Noir* and the *Princesse Noire* since the letters of marque granted to them by the Congress of the colonies have been withdrawn. (Leland I, 251)

Bibliothèque du Dépôt des Cartes et Plans.
See *Service hydrographique de la Marine*

Bibliothèque du Dépôt des Fortifications—Archives du Génie
39 rue de Bellechasse
75007 Paris

Formerly the Dépôt Général des Fortifications, this library contains bound memoirs and atlases concerning fortresses and fortifications. There is no restriction on access and no printed catalogue. The only item concerning the American Revolution is *Atlas de la Guerre d'Amérique 1774–1783* (shelf-mark Atlas 224 MS.), containing 82 coloured engraved or hand-drawn plates.

Unbound archives are kept in the Dépôt des Archives du Génie at the Château de Vincennes (see below, VAL DE MARNE) and consist of memoirs and maps of battles and sieges involving French and foreign fortresses. There is no restriction on access and no printed catalogue. The handwritten catalogue lists:

'Article 15—7, Guerre d'Amérique 1775 à 1783', which contains a number of items such as Charles Henri d'Estaing, 'Journal du siège de Savannah 1779', and Armand Charles Augustin de la Croix, 'Journal de ma voyage en Amérique 1780'.

Bibliothèque du Dépôt Général des Fortifications.
See *Bibliothèque du Dépôt des Fortifications—Archives du Génie* and *Ministère d'Outre-Mer*

Bibliothèque historique de la Marine, 3 avenue Octave-Gréard
75007 Paris

This library is part of the Service historique de la Marine. Its contents were originally catalogued in Charles de la Roncière, *Bibliothèques de la Marine* (Paris, 1907) and CG 46 (1924), which contain a few documents of interest. Unfortunately la Roncière's work is no longer valid because shelf-marks have been changed and documents moved. To trace the documents listed below from la Roncière, it is necessary to use the *concordances* at the Service historique, and even then it is sometimes difficult.

4. Protocole des provisions, commissions, brevets expédiés en faveur des officiers de marine, 1684–1780. *P. 47.* An order recalling Chaffault to court and giving command of the combined Franco-Spanish fleet at Brest to Guichen. (la Roncière, 3)

16. 'Droit maritime; recueil de pièces et notes critiques,' Thomas-Pierre -Adrien Groult, procureur du tribunal de l'amirauté à Cherbourg (1771–1808). Contains several memoirs on prizes taken by French privateers in 1779. (la Roncière, 15)

41. 'Liste générale des vaisseaux de guerre des royaumes de France et Espagne, et la récapitulation des vaisseaux de guerre, jointe celle des Anglais pour l'année 1781', 21 pp. (la Roncière, 25)

49. 'Recueil de pièces authentiques sur les colonies,. . .' (1699–1804). 6. 'Mémoire concernant les Etats-Unis de l'Amérique septentrionale, écrit vers l'an 1780.' (la Roncière, 27)

55. Recueil de textes sur la jurisprudence maritime, par Groult. Contains several tracts on the application of maritime law to the war of 1778–83. (la Roncière, 29)

122. 'Recueil sur la marine militaire.' 'Observations de M. le marquis de Vaudreuil addressées au conseil de guerre tenu à Lorient, relativement au combat naval du 12 avril 1782', followed by 'Lettre du M. d'Albert de Rions à M. le marquis de Vaudreuil'. (la Roncière, 78)

142. Portefeuille de plans de batailles navales livrées pour la plupart par des flottes françaises, 1607–1795. Includes Ouessant (Ushant), 1778; la Manche, 1779; Grenada, 1779; Chesapeake Bay, 1782; Saintes 1782. (la Roncière, 91)

376. (C.7). Recueil de pièces originales relatives au navigateur Louis-Antoine de Bougainville. . . . Letters and memoirs concerning his career, including some for his service in America, 1777–80. (CG 46(1924), 62–3)

Bibliothèque de l'Institut de France, 23 quai Conti 75006 Paris

Access is restricted to members of the Institut, those introduced by members, and foreigners presented by their embassies.

838. French translation of an essay by Francis Wharton on the negotiations for peace in 1782–3 (revising Jay's treatments in the light of the Stevens collection of French alliance papers now in the Library of Congress and printed in Vol. III of Wharton's *Digest of International Law,* app., Section 150).

857. Papers of Condorcet. Dossier, 'Oeuvres et fragments politiques antérieurs à 1789', including a draft essay, 'De l'influence de la Révolution d'Amérique sur les opinions et la legislation de l'Europe', 1804.

1619. MSS. Labéne. 'Histoire ancienne et moderne jusqu'à la chute de Napoléon I.' Contains numerous references to American history.

1689. Correspondence of Henri Doniol relating to his *Histoire de la Participation de la France à l'Etablissement des Etats-Unis d'Amérique.* Correspondents include Henry Vignaud, Francis Wharton, Worthington C. Ford, John Bigelow, Charlemagne Tower, 1888–95.

1871. French translation of John Jay's essay on the negotiations for peace, 1782–3 (printed by the New York State Historical Society, 1884). See also **838.** above.

2050. Papers of the Duke of Orléans in the Collection Beugnot. Letters from Sartine to the Duke on board the *St. Esprit*, 1776–8, relating to naval affairs, John Paul Jones, etc.

2222. Papers of Abbé P. L. Lefebvre de la Roche. 'Au C. Pierre Didot, Imprimeur du Sénat, Sur Franklin.' Biographical fragment containing personal recollections of Franklin's sojourns in France and England.

2314–19. Miscellaneous memoirs on geography by Buache and others, including the naval operations of 1778.

(Leland I, 255–7)

Bibliothèque Mazarine, 23 quai Conti
75006 Paris

Access unrestricted.

1833. History of France, England, and the United States. Course of lectures by Professor Koch of Strasbourg(?). The section on the United States presents a general view of American history from 1607 to 1783.

2404. List of vessels, officers, troops, etc., composing the expedition against Great Britain, under the command of the comte de Vaux, at St Malo, 1779, 129 pp.

3749. 'Réflexions sur la guerre des Anglais, envoyées à M. de Choiseul en 1767.' 'Observations sur l'armement de l'Espagne', 13 juillet 1775—fortification of Pensacola by the English; revolt of the English colonies; inadvisibility of Spanish aid to the insurgents. 'Mémoire sur la formation et le recrutement des troupes des colonies', 30 July 1775.

(Leland I, 265–7)

Bibliothèque municipale du XVIᵉ Arrondissement
71 Avenue Henri-Martin
75016 Paris

Access unrestricted.

10. Facsimile of a fragment of a letter from Lapérouse, relating to naval affairs of the American War of Independence, with annotations by de Castries and Fleurieu. Facsimile of a letter, 20 October 1781, from Lapérouse to his mother relative to the surrender of Cornwallis.

13. Letter, 14 July 1780, Necker to Sartine, relating to flour intended for the colonies and held at Cadiz following the declaration of war. (Leland I, 278)

Bibliothèque Nationale, 58 rue de Richelieu
75004 Paris

Access restricted to those engaged on specific projects and able so to prove. The Bibliothèque Nationale is the largest and most important of the libraries of France. It is organized into four sections but only the *Départment des Manuscrits* is here surveyed. The *Départment des Imprimés, Cartes et Plans*; the *Départment des Medailles, Pierres Gravées, et Antique*; and the *Départment des Estampes* fall outside the scope of this work due to the nature of their holdings.

DÉPARTMENT DES MANUSCRITS

This contains one of the largest collections of manuscript material in the world and is organized in various categories or *fonds*, according to language. The bulk of the material pertaining to the American Revolution and France's role therein lies in the Fonds Français. This *fond* contains two series, the first of which is a closed series (nos. **1–33264**) called *Manuscrits Français*. The second is an open series, designated *Manuscrits Français, Nouvelles Acquisitions*, with its own numbering.

The *Manuscrits Français* are described in the *Catalogue des manuscrits, anciens fonds* 1868–1902, 5 vols. and the *Catalogue général des manuscrits français* 1895–1918, 13 vols. Vol. X of this latter work begins the *Nouvelles Acquisitions*, which are continued in *Nouvelles acquisitions du départment des manuscrits pendant les années 1911–1931* (1913–32); *Nouvelles acquisitions du départment des manuscrits pendant les années 1924–1928: Inventaire sommaire* (1929); *idem*, 1929–31 (1932); *idem*, 1932–5 (1936); 1941–5 (1947); 1946–57 (1967). Leland I, 1–220, covers the American material until about the late 1920s.

Manuscrits Français

4586. *f. 122.* Register of the destruction of Canadian paper and card money, in accordance with decrees of 29 June 1765 and 17 January 1776.

6431. *Papers of Abbé Guillaume-Thomas Raynal.* Memoirs relating to commerce. *ff. 188–97.* Extracts from replies by —— Payte to queries by the Earl of Dartmouth respecting the English possessions in America, . . . (in English).

6680–7. 1763–89. 'Mes Loisirs', by Siméon Prosper Hardy. These volumes are a daily record of events by Hardy, a bookseller of Paris. (The MS. is fully described and abstracts from it, 1764–73, are printed by Maurice Tourneur and Maurice Vitrac in *Siméon Prosper Hardy: mes loisirs*, Paris, 1912. Another account of the MS. is Charles Aubertin, 'Le Bourgeois de Paris au XVIII siècles', *Revue des Deux Mondes*, 1 November 1871.) From 1775 on, the journal contains frequent references to American events which indicate the form in which American news circulated in Paris.

8306–7. 'Précis par ordre de matières des mémoires, pièces et rapports de Commissions déposés au greffe des États (de Bretagne).' Includes memoir respecting foreign commerce in the colonies (1770) and another on excessive duties laid on products from Santo Domingo (1780).

8978. *ff. 115–33.* 'Mémoire pour faire connoitre la Situation du commerce maritime.' Losses in the trade with the colonies and America, capture of vessels by the English, lack of protection; Canadian trade and its losses since the capture of Louisburg and the Newfoundland fisheries.

10764–70. *Papers of Beliardi.* (Beliardi was an Italian, who served as French Chargé des affaires de la marine et du commerce de France at Madrid from 1758–70.) Correspondence and memoirs which contain some references to American affairs, including American contraband trade, American disaffection with England, and possible Franco-Spanish alliance against England. (See also **13417–19.**)

11056. *ff. 119–32.* Extracts from the proceedings of the Chambre des Comptes, 1749–77.

11061. *ff. 373–82.* Extracts from *procés-verbaux* of the Chambre des Comptes, 1690, 1718, 1773.

11300–1. Correspondence and original documents relating to the marine and to artillery, 1716–78.

11344. *ff. 2–24.* Journal of Jean-François de La Pérouse, 31 October 1779 to 18 April 1780. Contains the end of his campaign with de Rions and the beginning of his campaign with de Ternay. *ff. 29–31.* Biography of La Pérouse, with references to the destruction of English establishments in the Hudson Bay area in 1782.

11907. *f. 282.* Address of John Adams to Louis XVI on presentation of his credentials as Minister of the United States, and response of the King.

12763. Autograph letters. *f. 279.* Franklin to the Abbé de la Roche, 7 December 1778.

12768. Autograph letters. *ff. 233–53.* Letters to Barbé-Marbois from Washington, Jefferson, Adams.

13090. Lists of vessels passing through the Sund, 1780–2, including American ships.

13417–19. *Papers of Beliardi.* These include a copy of the American 'declaration of rights', observations by the Abbé de Mably on the American constitution, and material on the state of the French navy. (See also **10764–70.**)

13862. *f. 33.* La Grande Victoire remportée en Amérique sur les Anglois, tant sur terre que sur mer, par les troupes du Roi avec le journal des opérations du Corps Français sous le commandement du comte de Rochambeau depuis le 15 août 1781 (Boston, imprimé du Congrès, 8 pp., 4to).

14609. 'Traité de la défense et de la conservation des colonies par M. Dumas, Brigadier des Armées du Roy, ancien commandant des Isles de France et de Bourbon, 1775.' References to the loss of Canada, the importance of Louisburg, commerce of the former American colonies, etc.

14610. A copy of **14609.**, including an autobiography of the author.

14611. 'Principes sur l'administration, l'amélioration, et le commerce des Colonies françaises de l'Amérique, selon les suites prévues de la guerre présente des Colonies', by the Chevalier de Ricard, colonel of infantry, 1 January 1778.

14612. 'Mémoires politiques et militaires sur la situation respective de la France et de l'Angleterre à l'occasion de la guerre des colonies', by the Chevalier de Ricard, 1776–7, 293 pp.

14694. 'Relation du Prince de Broglie', of his travels with the Chevalier de Lameth in the United States and Venezuela, 1782–3. (See 'Journal du Voyage du Prince de Broglie . . . aux États-Unis D'Amérique et dans l'Amérique du Sud, 1782–1783' in *Société des Bibliophiles Français, Mélanges*, Part 2, Paris, 1903; translation in *Magazine of American History*, I, 1877).

14695. 'Voyage au continent américain par un Français en 1777, et réflexions philosophiques sur ces nouveaux républicains', 108 pp. Draft of a narrative by an unidentified civilian traveller with interesting comment on people, manners, visits, and the American army.

21013–60. Archives de la Chambre Syndicale de la Librairie et Imprimerie de Paris.

22014–16. Censorship reports on works for which licence or permission was requested, 1767–88. A number relate to the American Revolution, such as *ff. 41–3. De la France et des États-Unis ou de l'importance de la Révolution de l'Amérique pour le Bonheur de la France* ... by Etienne Clavière and J. P. Brissot de Warville, 1787, etc.

22102. *no. 17. Arrêt* ordering destruction of *Apologie du Commerce*, 21 December 1778; *no. 26. Arrêt* of the *Cour de Parlement* condemning the *Histoire Philosophique ... des Établissements ... dans les deux Indes* of the Abbé Raynal, 25 May 1781.

22180. *no. 64. Arrêt* against printers of the abstract of Raynal's *Histoire Philosophique ...* , 13 June 1777.

Manuscrits Français, Nouvelles Acquisitions

1307. *f. 245.* An XII, Frim. 26. Rochambeau to the Minister of War concerning his son's dispute with the Minister of Marine; negligence of French ministers during his service in the United States; 'miracle du blocus et de la prise de Cornwallis'.

1479. 'Armées de Terre et de Mer en 1779 et 1780' by J. A. Du Coudray. *f. 4.* Table of changes in the French and British navies, 1779, with a list of the American islands conquered and lost; *f. 6.* comparative table of the French and British navies, 1 January 1780, with a list of officers serving in the colonies.

1908. Autograph MS. of the *Histoire de Beaumarchais* by Gudin de La Brunellerie, Maurice Tourneur, ed., Paris, 1885.

5001–2. *Procés-verbaux* of the censorship books, 1811–13 (cf. *Manuscrits Français* **22061–193**). There are a few relevant works discussed, such as Botta's *Histoire de la Guerre de l'Independance des États-Unis d'Amérique*, trans. by Sévelinges.

5398. *ff. 24–39.* 'Apperçu sur l'état présent de l'Amérique. Journal de notre conduite; quelques observations sur ce continent, le Congrès, caractères [de] quelques généraux, et les principaux événemens de la campagne de 1777.'

5944–64. Registres de la Régie-Générale des Vivres et Subsistences Militaires, 1778–90.

5945–51. Various accounts of the expeditionary forces of Rochambeau in America, 1779–83.

6360–3. MS. copy of the memoirs of Talleyrand.
6360. *ff. 143, 197.* References to the American War of Independence.

6464–97. Collection of notes, extracts and transcripts made by Henri Doniol for his *Histoire de la Participation de la France à l'Établissement des États-Unis d'Amérique.* The collection covers the years 1774–85 and is composed mainly of the documents printed by Doniol in whole or in part. While Doniol breaks up most of his documents, here the unity of the documents is preserved with the arrangement in the order of the originals in their repositories. The volumes of documents and their respective repositories are:
6464–9. Archives, Ministère des Affaires Étrangères, Correspondance Politique, Angleterre, 1774–83.

6470. Extracts and transcripts from British archives and collections. (*British Museum,* LONDON: *Additional Manuscripts* **24163, 24173–6, 24321, 29237;** *Egerton* **2135.** *Public Record Office,* LONDON: *Foreign Office, France,* **2, 3;** *State Papers Foreign, Spain,* **207**)

6471–81. Archives, Ministère des Affaires Étrangères, Correspondance Politique, États-Unis, 1775–85.

6482–92. Archives, Ministère des Affaires Étrangères, Correspondance Politique, Espagne, 1774–82.

6493. Archives, Ministère des Affaires Étrangères, Correspondance Politique, Prusse, Vienne, Russie, Hollande, Suède, 1776–82.

6494. Archives, Ministère des Affaires Étrangères, various series; Archives Nationales; Bibliothèque Nationale; miscellaneous, 1774–95.

6495. Archives, Ministère de la Marine, especially Series B4, 1776–82.

6496–7. Archives, Ministère de la Guerre, Correspondance; correspondance de Rochambeau.

6577. Correspondence of Mme Dupont de La Motte. *ff. 153, 155, 163–.* Verses on Franklin and American independence 'Invocation à la Liberté'. *ff. 162, 166, 171.* Biographical notes on Franklin, Penn, Washington.

6946–71. Résumés of and extracts from the dispatches of the impérial (Austrian) ambassadors in France, 1715–92, and inventories of various series in foreign archives relating to the history of France, 1416–1792. Formed by Jules Flammermont, the collection has three parts:
6946–51. Résumés of the dispatches of the Austrian ambassadors in France, 1715–92. These are fairly full, in German, and contain, for the years 1776–83, many references to American affairs as observed at the French court and reported to Prince Kaunitz by the ambassador Mercy-Argenteau.
6952–64. Extracts from the same dispatches, but relate much more to purely French matters.

6965–71. Inventories and miscellaneous, with apparently no reference for American matters.

9255–510. *Collection Margry.* This collection of documents and extracts was formed by Pierre Margry (1818–94) for the purpose of writing the history of French navigation, exploration and colonization.

9409. Journal of Bougainville for 1776–8, 1781–2, describing his service aboard various ships in the fleet of de Grasse. Also various papers concerning the charges brought against Bougainville by de Grasse for the former's conduct in the battle of the Saintes, 12 April 1782.

9414–25. La Pérouse and the marine, 1771–1807. Letters, orders, memoirs and plans relating to French naval participation in the American war.

9426. Chevalier de Ternay. March–December 1780, copies and extracts of letters from de Ternay to the Minister of Marine; journal by Des Hayes of the expedition under de Ternay, 2 May 1780 to 4 January 1781.

9427. Marine of Louis XVI: de Ternay and La Pérouse. *f. 122.* 'Mémoire du Roi pour servir d'instruction particulière à Mr. le Ch'er de Ternay, chef d'escadre des armées navales;' *ff. 134–51.* March–April 1780, copies of letters from de Ternay to the Minister of Marine; *ff. 175–294.* March–August 1780, copies and extracts of the correspondance of Rochambeau; *f. 318.* plan of M. de St Aubin for an expedition against the Hudson Bay.

9428. Marine of Louis XVI: d'Estaing, numerous orders and documents relating to naval operations, 1778–80.

9429. *ff. 106–337.* Copies, extracts, rough notes, etc., of the correspondence of d'Estaing with Washington, Lafayette, Bouillé, John Laurens, Vergennes, and others.

9430. More correspondence and notes concerning d'Estaing.

9431. Copies and extracts of letters of Suffren, capitaine de vaisseau, commanding the *Fantastique* in the fleet of d'Estaing, July–September 1778.

9434–5. Miscellaneous naval papers which include prize inventories; extracts of instructions and a note by Beaumarchais (*ff. 49–53*), 'Réflexions sur les secours à donner à l'Amérique'.

10573. Extracts from the admiralty archives of Brest, relating to vessels in the West Indies, capture of vessels from or by the British, privateers, etc., 1777–9.

21081. *f. 80.* Photographic copy of a letter of marque against American vessels issued to the British ship *Anna Gally*, London, 26 September 1778; *f. 84.* photographic copy of a letter of the King of France to the Admiral of France explaining the motives of the war against England, Versailles, 5 April 1779.

21510. *ff. 51–60.* 5 October 1780 to 24 January 1781, Newport, R.I., 6 letters from the Vicomte de Tressan, relating to personal affairs, return of Rochambeau's son to France, general disgust of all except those who made their fortune in America, etc.

22101. Papers of M. d'Hermand, French Consul at Lisbon, Madrid, and elsewhere, 1763, 1777–98.

22738. *f. 6.* Lafayette to Louis XVI, 19 February 1779, Paris, setting forth the reasons that decided him to espouse the American cause and excusing his disobedience.

22762. *ff. 75–7.* 'Mémoire donné par M. d'Estaing dans le mois de Mars 1769 à l'instant qu'on apprit en France que les Français de la Louisiane avaient chassé les Espagnols', 10 March 1769, Versailles. Suggests the example of New Orleans should aid the separation of America from England.

23349. Correspondance officielle, et en partie autographe, de William Henry de Nassau de Zuylestein, duc de Rochford, ambassador d'Angleterre en France, avec Etienne-François, duc de Choiseul, ministre des affaires étrangères, 1766–8.

23666. 26 autograph letters of Charles-Eugène-Gabriel de La Croix, marquis de Castries, maréchal de France, and Minister of Marine, 1771–88. Most unaddressed.

23800. Mélanges and pièces historiques. Ordres du vice-amiral Henri d'Estaing et du baron de Wimffen, 1783.

COLLECTION JOLY DE FLEURY

(The catalogue of this collection is A. Molinier, *Inventaire sommaire de la collection Joly de Fleury*, Paris, 1891. Leland I, 212ff., lists the American material).

503. 'Avis et mémoires sur les affaires publiques.' Printed copies of the treaty of alliance between France and the United States, 6 February 1778, and of arrêts, ordinances, and regulations relating to privateering, prizes, neutral vessels, etc., as well as manuscript correspondence of de Fleury, Sartine, and others.

2437. *f. 195.* 'Recueil de lettres, documents historiques, et nouvelles à la main, 1687–1789', *Exposé des Motifs de la Conduite du Roi relativement à l'Angleterre*, Paris, 1779. Statement of French policy concerning the American colonies and England.

ARCHIVES DE LA BASTILLE

The Archives de la Bastille are housed in the Bibliothèque de l'Arsenal (see below). (Its holdings are covered in Leland I, 246–50; *Catalogue des manuscrits de la Bibliothèque de l'Arsenal*, Paris, 1885–94, Vol. 9)

12453. Dossier of the Chevalier de Lannay, 1782. A brief document indicating his connection with a Franco-Anglo-American gazette published at Maestricht, and his correspondence with Swanton.

12478. Ordres du Roi. *Lettres de cachet* for the imprisonment of William Hodge of Philadelphia, 10 August 1777 and 24 September 1777.

BIBLIOTHÈQUE DE L'ARSENAL
(1 rue Sully, 75004 Paris)

This library became a part of the Bibliothèque Nationale in 1935. Access is unrestricted. (Its holdings are covered in Leland I, 240–6; *Catalogue des manuscrits de la Bibliothèque de l'Arsenal*, Paris 1885–94, 9 vols.; CG 45(1915)

4518. *f. 210*. 28 October 1778, Boston Harbour. Proclamation of d'Estaing to the former French subjects of Canada. *ff. 218 ff.* Relation of the capture of Grenada, 1779, followed by letters on the same subject.

4565. 'Plan de guerre contre l'Angleterre, rédigé par les ordres du feu Roi, dans les années 1763, 1764, 1765, et 1766, par M. le comte de Broglie, et refondu et adapté aux circonstances actuelles pour être mis sous les yeux de Sa Majesté, à qui il a été envoyé le 17 decembre 1778', 269 pp.

4789. 'Extrait de l'Histoire de l'Origine du Commencement et du Progrès de la Guerre en Amérique entre l'Angleterre et ses Colonies depuis l'année 1763', to 1779, 216 pp.

6056–103. Papers of Gabriel Brizard.
6100. *ff. 379–81*. A few notes on Anglo-French rivalry, 1783.

6402–3. Papers of Pierre Lucien Joseph Dreux, secretary to the comte de Vergennes.
6402. Some verses concerning the American war.

6871–81. Papers of Paul Ph. Gudin de la Brenellerie, 1738–1812.
6880. 'Histoire Politique et Philosophique', containing fragments, notes, etc., with frequent references to the American Revolution, French participation in the war, preliminaries of the treaty of 1783, summary of the history of the American war, treason of Benedict Arnold, etc.

7054. Letter, 10 January 1779, from John Jay in Philadelphia.

7587. A miscellaneous volume containing, on p. 264, the reasons for the refusal of Spain to join France in aid of the American rebels.

7588. Another miscellaneous volume containing, on pp. 282–90, material concerning the revolt of the American colonies.

7593. An autograph notebook of Mirabeau entitled 'Pensées diverses et anecdotes sur l'administration', with notes on Beaumarchais and the insurgents; connection with Leray de Chaumont in supplying them; financial disorder; criticism of d'Estaing; attitude of Vergennes, d'Aiguillon, Maurepas, Turgot, etc.

9027. *Gazette d'Utrect*, nos. 7 and 13, 15 September 1769 and 8 September 1775, containing news from New England; *Courrier de L'Europe*, no. 9, 28 June 1776, with American news.

Bibliothèque Sainte-Geneviève, 10 place du Panthéon 72005 Paris

Access unrestricted.

2088. 'Mémoire sur l'état actuel du Canada', *c.* 1777. Memoir by a missionary who served in Canada from 1754. Chapter VI: Raisonments politiques sur tout le continent septentrional, que le Canada s'unisse aux Insurgents, reste à l'Angleterre, ou revienne à la France, 20 pp.

Ministère d'Outre-Mer, 27 rue Oudinot 75007 Paris

When the Inspection du Génie absorbed the Dépôt Général des Fortifications, documents concerning colonial fortifications were sent to the Ministère d'Outre-Mer where they are designated *Archives Nationales, Section Outre-Mer, dépôt des fonds des fortifications des colonies*. These documents may contain material pertaining to Anglo-French military operations in the Caribbean during the American war. There is no restriction on access and no printed catalogue.

Service historique de la Marine, 3 avenue Octave-Gréard 75007 Paris

The Service historique contains the Bibliothèque historique de la Marine (see above) and the central marine archives after 1870. The staff is helpful on general approaches to topics dealing with the marine and colonies.

Service hydrographique de la Marine, 13 rue de l'Université 75007 Paris

The Service hydrographique replaced the Bibliothèque du Dépôt des Cartes et Plans but some of the contents of the former have been dispersed to the

Archives Nationales and the Archives du Ministère de la Marine (above). (There is no printed catalogue or inventory, although it may be noted in passing that the Map Division, Library of Congress, contains Abel Doysié's manuscript 'Inventory of the Archives of the Service hydrographique de la Marine . . .', n.d. The material listed below is drawn from la Charles de la Roncière, *Catalogue général des manuscrits des bibliothèques publiques de France, bibliothèques de la marine*, 1907, and CG 46, as illustrative of what was once in this library and may still be there.)

22–40. (176). 'États abrégés de la marine', 1778–83. (la Roncière, 166)

51. (274). 'Tableaux des vaisseaux de la marine royale' en 1786. Attached is a list entitled 'bâtiments en station à l'Amérique, 1777 et 1778', with the names of their commanders; also 'relevé des Etats envoyés par M. de La Porte pour faire connaître le nombre et l'espèce de marins de levée arrivées à Brest à compte du 1er janvier 1779'. (la Roncière, 171)

177. (2847). Recueil de plans de sièges et de positions fortifiées, durant la guerre de l'independance aux Etats-Unis, 1780–2. There are 9 maps: Rhode Island; the route of march from Newport to Yorktown; the camp at Philipsburg at White Plains occupied by French and American forces in July –August 1781; reconnaissances at Kingsbridge; northern West Point; the siege of Yorktown; West Point in Virginia; the French camp at 'Pisk-Kill' in September 1782 and that of Washington in 1780; the French camp of September–October 1782. (la Roncière, 218)

260. (125m). 'Mémoires, rapports sur plusieurs parties de Marine', 1779–86.
Various documents concerning strengthening the navy and its condition in 1779.
Recueil de documents relatifs aux constructions navales, 1768–1817.
'Relation de la prise de la Grenade', par le comte Charles-Hector d'Estaing; 'Relation du combat naval de la Grenade donné entre l'armée du Roi et celle du roi d'Angleterre, le 6 juillet 1779 . . .'.

(CG 46(1924), 66)

374. (7228ᵇ). 'Journal de la campagne de 1778 aux ordres de M. le comte d'Estaing'. Journal du *Guerrier*, commandé par Louis-Antoine de Bougainville. (CG 46(1924), 85).

376. (7249ᵉ). Journaux de bord de Denis Decrès, plus tard duc, vice-amiral et ministre de la Marine . . . 1780–1803. Includes his service under de Grasse in 1781. (CG 46(1924), 112)

377. (7263ᵃ). 'Journal du siège de Savannah avec des observations de M. d'Estaing', par l'ingénieur O'Connor (septembre–octobre 1779). (CG 46(1924), 114)

QUIMPER

Bibliothèque municipale, Place Toul al Laer
29S Quimper

12H. Recueil de pièces et de mémoires sur l'histoire de la marine et des colonies françaises au XVIIIe siècle. *f. 201.* Sur la prochaine guerre avec l'Angleterre.

40. Journal de bord du vaisseau *le Languedoc* de l'escadre commandée par le comte de Grasse, du 22 mai 1781 au 23 août 1782.

(CG 22(1893), 432, 439. Matteson, 135)

RHEIMS

Bibliothèque municipale, 2 place Carnegie
51 Rheims

Vol. 39, carton 18. Lettre, en anglais, non signée, de Joseph Wharton à Joseph Dobson, 'at the King's Head Tavern', à Londres; il lui donne des nouvelles des événements d'Amérique et des détails sur son genre de vie à Nantes (Nantes, 15 décembre 1778). Billet, en anglais, de Benjamin Franklin, priant M. Grand, banquier, rue Montmartre, à Paris, de payer à M. Vital une somme de 1150 livres pour des frais de table (Passy, 1 mai 1781). (CG 39(1904–6), 367, 374. Matteson, 138)

ROUEN

Bibliothèque municipale, 3 rue de la Bibliothèque
76 Rouen

1100.(0.38ᵃ). Adrien Pasquier, de Rouen, '. . . Ode à la nation anglaise sur la guerre d'Amérique'. **1956.**(662). Mémoires politiques, 'Etat de toutes les forces navales qui se trouvoient réunies au fameux combat du 12 avril 1782, commandé par M. de Grasse, avec les plans de bataille et pièces justificatives'.

1964–5.(155). 'Balance du commerce', (1753–9 et 1773–81). Statistique du commerce de la France avec les colonies et l'étranger.

1974.(292). 'Mémoire sur le commerce entre la France et les Etats-Unis'.

(CG 1(1886), 272, 515, 517, 519. Matteson, 140–1)

3357.(5838). Lettres originales, en grande partie autographes, de maréchaux de France, lieutenants généraux et officiers supérieurs, . . . relatives à l'exercice de leurs fonctions, notamment au service de la marine des côtes pendant la guerre des Etats-Unis d'Amérique, 1773–88. Includes Richelieu, Broglie, Mouchy, Ségur, Croy, Mailly, Rochambeau, Harcourt, etc. (54 pièces).

3358.(5839). Correspondance originale, en grande partie autographe, de maréchaux de France, officiers généraux et ministres de Louis XVI, sur le service de la marine des côtes pendant la guerre d'Amérique, 1777–84. Lettres et mémoires . . . d'Aubeterre, Croy, Harcourt, Mouchy, Mathan, Sartine, etc. (62 pièces).

3359.(5840). Correspondance originale, autographe ou signée, de ministres, maréchaux de France, officiers supérieurs, intendants, agents de services publics [sic], et pièces visées par Louis XVI, relatives au personnel de la marine et à la guerre maritime, 1779–84. Includes Montbarey, Vergennes, Harcourt, Montmorency, Joigny, de Grasse, Saint-Simon, Mailly, etc.

(CG 2(1888), 140. Matteson, 142)

1158. (Montbret 850). 'Récapitulation de la valeur de toutes les marchandises entrées dans le royaume venant des pais étrangers tant par mer que par terre pendant l'année 1780'.

1181. (Montbret 908), *23 Procès-verbal* de publication à Paris du traité de paix avec la Grande-Bretagne, 1783.

11821. (Montbret 901). Documents sur la guerre navale. *3–4.* Rapports sur la prise de la frégate anglaise *l'Active*, le 1er septembre 1778. 5. Relation du combat naval de M. le comte de Grasse contre l'amiral anglais Rodney en Amérique, 27 avril 1782.

(CG 48(1933), 196, 201)

TOULON

Port de Toulon, Bibliothèque principale, Place d'Armes
83 Toulon

3. Recueil de la correspondance originale des gouverneurs et intendants de la Martinique avec le ministre de la marine, 1759–82. Includes 16 dispatches of Bouillé, 1779–82, as well as several of Montdenoix, 1779. (la Roncière, 450)

9. Evolutions navales, 1778–9, atlas par Fournier de Clusines de Paris. . . .

Plans 1–11. Battle of Ouessant (Ushant). *Plan 12.* Mouillage de l'armée à Brest, 1778, par le capitaine de vaisseau Thévenard, sour-directeur du port. *Plans 13–36.* Mouvements de la flotte depuis sa sortie de Brest, en juin 1779, jusqu'à sa rentrée, en septembre. . . . *Plan 37.* Mouillage de l'armée combinée en rade de Brest, par le lieutenant de vaisseau de Tromelin. (la Roncière, 454)

VAL DE MARNE

Archives de la Ministère de la Guerre, Château de Vincennes
Vincennes

These archives are located at the Château de Vincennes, Salle de Communication, and are under the administration of the Service historique de l'Etat-major de l'Armée. Access is generally unrestricted for researchers, although examination of some material remains subject to the authorization of the Minister of War.

The archives are divided into four sections: *Archives des opérations militaires, Archives des corps de troupes, Mémoires historiques et reconnaissances (Manuscrits des Archives de la Guerre)*, and *Archives administratives*.

ARCHIVES DES OPÉRATIONS MILITAIRES

This section of the archives contains the correspondence of the ministers of war with generals, of the generals themselves, documents on the state of the various forces in action, military justice, etc. This material is divided into series A–L, with each letter designation corresponding to a specific period and each period further subdivided by theatres of operations. Series A designates the period before 1789 and hence is the location of material pertaining to the French forces in America. (The published guide to this section of the war archives is the *Inventaire sommaire des archives historiques (Archives anciennes—période antérieure à 1792—Correspondance)*, Paris, 1898–1930, 7 vols. The following listing is drawn from the *Inventaire sommaire*, Vol. 5, 356–541)

Unless devoted to specialized subject, virtually all the volumes in this section contain correspondence of the ministers of war, marine, and foreign affairs, as well as general officers, intendants, commissaires, etc. Some volumes are devoted entirely to subjects such as Corsica, finances, administration, artillery, engineering, etc. Most of the topics are very routine in any given volume.

3704. 1772–7. Contains 'précis sur l'administration et l'état actuel de la marine en Angleterre'.

3712. May–December 1779. Table of war expenses for 1779; numerous items on the movement of troops.

3716. 1780. Circular concerning troops to be sent to America; documents given by Washington to the Marquis de La Rouerie for his service in the American army; letters of Montbarey, Castries, La Luzerne.

3724. 1781–2. Instructions concerning infantry detachments sent to the colonies as reinforcements.

3726. Marine, 1778–82. Coastal defences; projects against Britain; battle of Ouessant, 27 July 1778; accounts of several ship-to-ship actions; memoir of 1779 entitled 'Considerations sur les dispositions et les mouvements qui doivent terminer la campagne'; movements and state of the British fleet; battle order of Rochambeau's forces.

3728. Affaires diverses, surtout diplomatiques. Diplomatic ciphers, with keys; memoirs concerning the military, colonial, commercial and political condition of Spain and Franco-Spanish relations; news of Austria, Holland, Italy, Prussia; 'détail des places et pays conquis et restitués par les puissances belligérantes à la paix de 1783'; correspondence of Vergennes and French ministers at European capitals.

3731. Marine et colonies, 1778–83. 3 accounts of the seizure of Grenada; many documents concerning the condition and defence of Santo Domingo.

3732. Angleterre, Amérique, Gibraltar, 1767–83. Correspondence of Choiseul and Kalb concerning the latter's American mission; account of Kalb's mission; political and military news of America and Britain; naval engagements; embarkation of French troops at Havre and St Malo; regimental orders; letters of Ségur, Castries, Lafayette, Washington, Marbois, Keppel, Montmorin, and others.

3733. Amérique, mars 1780 à mai 1781. Letters of Montbarey, Ségur, Necker, Sartine, Castries, Lafayette, Rochambeau, Vioménil, Destouches, Washington, Huntingdon.

3734. Amérique, mai 1781 à août 1782. Letters of Louis XVI, Ségur, Castries, Vergennes, Choisy, Vaudreuil, Barras, de Grasse, La Pérouse, Rochambeau, La Luzerne, Duportail, Greene, Washington, George Germain, Kean, Trumbull. Journals of the operations of the French expeditionary force.

3735. Amérique, août 1782 à février 1784. Letters of Ségur, Castries, Choisy, Vaudreuil, Rochambeau, La Luzerne, La Valette, Washington, Greene. Journals of the operations of the French expeditionary force.

3736. Amérique, juin 1780 à janvier 1783. Letters of de Grasse, La Pérouse, Rochambeau, La Luzerne, Marbois, Tarlé, Gates, Sumpter, Jefferson. Other miscellaneous documents.

3750. Marine et commerce, 14 décembre 1779 à 10 novembre 1786. Letters of M. Chardon, procureur général près le Conseil des prises.

Séries Supplémentaires, Fonds divers

A. *Volumes reliés*

54. Registre alphabétique et analytique des lettres de la Cour, 1775.

62. *idem*, 1783.

B. *Cartons*

46. 1778. Documents on America, Antilles, Britain; letters of Montbarey, Castries, etc.

47. 1778a. Documents on America, Antilles, Britain, Spain; letters of Louis XVI, Harcourt, Necker, etc.

47a. Minutes de la correspondence ministérielle (Montbarey).

47b. 1779. Documents on America; journal of the siege of Savannah; letters of Montbarey, Harcourt, Langeron, etc.

48. 1780. Documents on the American war; embarkation and debarkation of troops; operations; navy; Spain; Martinique; Guadeloupe; letters of Montbarey, Rochambeau, Washington, Langeron, etc.

48a. & b. 1780. Minutes de la correspondance ministérielle.

49. 1781. American war; embarkation of troops; operations; siege of Yorktown; letters of Ségur, etc.

49a. 1782–4. Documents on coastal defence; navy, colonies; American war; operations; letters of Langeron, d'Estaing, etc.

50. 1783. Documents on the American war; embarkation and debarkation of troops; coastal defence; etc.

50a. 1783. Minutes de la correspondance ministérielle (Ségur).

74. 1781–6. Marine et colonies. Embarkation of the expeditionary force to America.

83. 1765–78. Etats de troupes, contrôles, tableaux d'emplacement.

84. 1779–89. *idem.*

ARCHIVES DES CORPS DE TROUPES

The focus of this section of the war archives is the organization and composition of the Etat-Major and the various corps. It includes a complete collection of regimental histories. (The general published guide is Marc-André Fabre *et al., Inventaire des archives conservés au Service historique de l'Etat-Major de l'Armée (Château de Vincennes), Archives modernes*, Paris, 1954, 2e ed.) The following are series bearing on French participation in the American war.

X^A. *Etat-Major de Places*

21–7. cover the years 1773–84.

X^B. *Infanterie*

Records of infantry regiments and their formation at various dates.

X^C. *Cavalerie*

Records of cavalry regiments and their formation at various dates.

X^D. *Artillerie*

Records of artillery units.

303–6. Artillery in the colonies, 1765–93.

X^I. *Troupes maritimes et coloniales*

1. Documents généraux, 1768–81. Noms des vaisseaux, frégates, corvettes et autres bâtiments de l'Etat armés en 1781, qui ont à leur bord des détachements de troupes de terre, ... Etat des régiments, bataillons et détachements qui ont été embarqués à Brest en 1780. Régiment de la Guadeloupe, 1779: prises de la Grenade et de Savannah. Rapports, états, correspondance, règlements et ordonnances, classés par armés. Embarquement des troupes pour les colonies en 1781 (registre).

2. Documents généraux, 1781–3. Etat des troupes qui ont participé aux prises de Savannah et de la Grenade, et leurs prises. Armée de M. le marquis de Bouillé. Armée de M. le comte de Rochambeau. Détachements embarqués à Brest en 1782. Correspondance général par armées.

34. Documents généraux. Procès-verbal de l'examen des comptes relatifs au payement des campagnes des gens de mer et du produit des prises, à compter du 1er janvier 1778 au 1er octobre 1790. Tableau des campagnes de la flotte française.

The following may also contain some marginal material:

92. Artillerie, divers, 1775–1834;

93. Artillerie, directions et sous-directions, 1774–1828;

95. Génie, sapeurs de la Guadeloupe et de la Guyane;

96. Génie, sapeurs de la Martinique;

97. Génie, directions et sous-directions, 1752–1812.

MÉMOIRES HISTORIQUES ET RECONNAISSANCES (MANUSCRITS DES ARCHIVES DE LA GUERRE)

(This material is catalogued in Louis Tuetey, *Catalogue général des manuscrits des bibliothèques publiques de France: Archives de la Guerre*, Paris 1912–20, 3 vols.; 'Supplément à l'inventaire des manuscrits des Archives de la Guerre établi par Louis Tuetey', in Marc-André Fabre *et al.*, op. cit., 257–66. The latter reference lists no material of interest for the American Revolution, hence the page citations below refer only to the former catalogue)

Mémoires historiques

238. 'Histoire de la guerre d'Amérique, 1775–1783, rédigée au Dépôt de la guerre d'après les documents officiels par M. de Rostaing; étant directeur le général Blondel', 471 pp. (I, 42)

248. This volume contains the following documents:

'Chronologie des événements les plus intéressants de la guerre d'Amérique', de 1774 à 1781, 9 pp.

'Journal du voyage de M. de Fagan, major d'infanterie et aide de camp de M. le marquis de Bouillé . . . (Opérations militaires dans l'Amérique septentrionale de 1775 à 1777), 16 pp.

'Mémoire sur l'affaire de Sainte-Lucie' en 1778, par M. de Micoud . . , 38 pp.

Observations, variantes et rectifications du comte d'Estaing, relatives à son rôle pendant la campagne de 1779 en Amérique . . . 62 pp.

'Journal des campagnes de 1777 et 1778 au service des colonies unies de l'Amérique', par Prudhomme de Barre . . . , 35 pp.

Notes sur la guerre d'Amérique pendant les années 1777, 1778, et 1779, 15 pp.

'Note des principaux événements de la campaign de 1779' contre l'Angleterre, 4 pp.

'Observations sur l'expedition de la Georgie et les événements qui ont suivi la prise de la Grenade', 1779, 27 pp.

'Journal du siège de Savannah en 1779, par O'Connor, ingénieur du Roi', 66 pp.

Mémoire sur la campagne de 1780 en Amérique, par Duportail, officier français commandant la génie à l'armée de Washington, 17 pp.

'Instructions pour M. Ethis de Corny, 5 mars 1780', 7 pp.

'Précis du siège de Charlestown . . . , attaquée le 21 février et prise le 12 mai 1780 par les anglais', 30 pp.

Mémoire officiel relatif aux renforts à envoyer à l'armée du Roi en Amérique, aux fonds à fournir pour son entretien, au service de ses subsistences, 10 pp.

Mémoire sur la campagne du corps français aux ordres du comte de Rochambeau in 1780 et 1781 . . . , 48 pp.

Résumé des événements qui se sont passés à Boston de 1764 à 1776, et journal de navigation de la flotte française commandée par M. de Vaudreuil, en 1782, janvier et février 1783, 57 pp.

(I, 48–9)

Colonies françaises

1105. Mémoires généraux et collectifs: Afrique, Amérique, 1720–85 et sans date. A few documents, 1764–76, concerning the state and defence of the French possessions in the Caribbean. (I, 313–15)

1107. Saint-Domingue, 1713–87. A few documents, 1770–80, relating to the defence of Saint Domingo. (I, 320–1)

Reconnaissances, Plans, Projets: Pays Etrangers

1414. Various plans for attacks on Britain, including those of Durand, 1765; la Rozière, 1778; de Wall, 1778; La Luzerne, 1779; Kerguelen, 1780. Also, 'Mémoire sur l'Angleterre' by de Guines, 1773; mémoire by La Luzerne, 1778; 'Mémoire contenant plusieurs observations politiques concernant la présente guerre entre la France et l'Angleterre' par Dubuisson, 2 decembre 1780. (II, 175)

1415. 'Plan de guerre contre l'Angleterre, rédigé par ordre de Louis XV dans les années 1763–1766 par M. le comte de . . . [Broglie], refondu et adapté aux circonstances actuelles pour être mis sous les yeux de Sa Majesté à qui il a été envoyé le 17 decembre 1778', 157 pp. (II, 176)

1416. Another copy of **1415.**, but including a 'Mémoire sur la manière dont la France peut disposer une descente en Angleterre . . .', 18 July 1778, and 2 'ordres de marche'. (II, 176)

1417. More duplicates of **1415.** and 4 letters from la Rozière to Broglie, 1763–73. (II, 176)

1418. Projets de descente en Angleterre; mémoires de Grant de Blairfindy et d'autres, 1759–80. All documents relate to attacks on England and Ireland, 305 pp. (II, 177)

1422. Isles Britanniques, 1749–1840. A few documents, with military and naval intelligence concerning Britain, 1776–81. (II, 183)

1681. Etats-Unis, 1757–1871. 'Mémoire sur un projet pour porter la guerre dans les colonies anglaises de l'Amérique septentrionale . . . ,' par de Marassé . . . , 23 pp.
'Observations sur la Caroline du Sud', 4 pp.
'Quelques observations sur l'ensemble des Etats-Unis de l'Amérique', 15 pp.
'Mémoire sur la défense de Westpoint', par Duportail, 20 août 1779, 21 pp. (II, 349)

Donation Perret

1797. Donation Perret, III. Trois notes sur la guerre d'Amérique, 1778. (II, 499)

ARCHIVES ADMINISTRATIVES

The Archives administratives contain four main series dealing with the general organization of the various corps, lists of officers and men, individual documents, etc. (The published guide is André Cambier, *Inventaire sommaire des archives administratives (Archives anciennes jusqu'en 1791 inclusivement)* in Fabre *et al.*, op. cit., 267–319)

Y ^A. *Documents collectifs ou d'interet général*

This series deals mainly with the organization of the various corps and related personnel matters. The items most pertinent to the French participation in the American war are:

228–30. Agents secretes. Dossiers alphabétiques.

307. Amérique. Guerre d'Amérique. Documents relatifs au personnel du corps de Rochambeau. Gratifications, grâces, officiers français restés au service des Américains.

97. Colonies. Troupes des colonies. Documents généraux, 1767–92.

179. Corps de troupe. Etats des corps de troupes avec les noms des officiers de l'état-major pour les années 1775–7 et 1779. Evaluations annuelles des dépenses pour l'entretien des corps de troupe, 1720–90.

21–7. Généraux. Papers concerning the nomination, promotion, assignments, pensions etc., of general officers.

73–105. Légions. Documents généraux et documents par corps. **156–88.** Officiers généraux. Lists of infantry and cavalry officers.

204. Officiers généraux de la marine. Dossiers on Bausset, Chaffault, Fabry, de Grasse, Hector, La Pérouse, Orvilliers, de Rions, and others.

420. Troupes. Registre des emplacements et mouvements de troupes de 1763 à 1791.

Y [B]. This series deals entirely with the nominations of officers, listing by regiment, registers of individual regiments, formation of new regiments, etc.

Y [1–14C] *Contrôles de la Troupe*

This series contains the registers of enrolment of all the regiments of infantry, cavalry, grenadiers, dragoons, artillery, etc.

Y [1D].*Maréchaux de France.* Dossiers on individuals.

Y [2D].*Lieutenants-Généraux.* Dossiers on individuals.

Y [3D].*Maréchaux de Camp.* Dossiers.

Y [4D].*Brigadiers.* Dossiers. (Cambier gives a full listing by name of individual dossiers, 305–19.)

Y [5D].*Ancien Régime.* Contains documents on 46 notables, among whom can be noted Rulhière, d'Alembert, Delmas, Fersen, etc.

VENDOME

Bibliothèque municipale, 41 rue Poterie
41 Vendome

368. 'Interrogatoire de M. Franklin, député de Pensilvanie au parlement de la Grande Bretagne, commencé le 6 mai 1775; traduit de l'anglais par Charles de Hirschberg, maitre de langue angloise à Strabourg.' (CG 3(1885), 490. Matteson, 159)

SPAIN

INTRODUCTION

The American colonies had three important European allies during their struggle against Britain. France was early and active in her support, but Spain and Holland were later, more reluctant and more calculating allies. Spain had suffered the loss of Florida to Britain during the Seven Years War as a result of the Family Compact alliance with France, but in return had received Louisiana from France as compensation. Like the French, the Spanish nursed a desire for revenge to regain lost territory, but the revenge motive was not as strong as it was in France. After the Seven Years War the Spanish began to rebuild and expand their navy but again not on the scale undertaken by France. The events in the American colonies were watched carefully by Spain which was concerned that the American troubles might be a prelude to new attacks on the Spanish possessions in America. Spain also shared France's view that Britain might embark on a new war with France and Spain to recoup possible losses in America if the revolution against Britain were successful.

The Spanish attitude towards the American rebels was throughout very cool as Spain was genuinely concerned at the effect the American example could have on her own possessions in the Americas. Spain thus resisted French efforts to engage her in a tripartite alliance with the United States against Britain until 1779. Having carefully calculated the alternatives, Spain entered the war with the specific goals of obtaining Florida and Gibraltar and the general expectation that the Americans would in the long run prove weaker and more tractable neighbours in North America than the British.

The Spanish military role in the war was limited to some naval activity in European waters in conjunction with the French and campaigns to drive the British from Florida and the lower Mississippi valley. Successful campaigns were conducted against Pensacola, Mobile, and some British posts on the Mississippi. The 'Natchez Rebellion' is also of interest in this period.

Throughout the war Spanish relations with Congress were tense as Spain refused to recognize the colonies until late in the struggle. Unlike France, Spain had genuine issues which had to be negotiated with Congress. Foremost among these were the questions of boundaries and navigation rights on the Mississippi. In the end, Spain received Florida back and retained Louisiana but failed in her bid for Gibraltar.

The resources for the study of Spanish diplomatic and military involvement in the American Revolution are divided between the three main Spanish historical archives: the Archivo General de Indias, the Archivo General de Simancas, and the Archivo Histórico Nacional. There are other repositories but the material they contain is insignificant, hence this introduction to Spanish sources for the American Revolution has been focussed on the three main archives and includes only short entries on two other institutions.

There are a number of references concerning Spanish repositories to which the student can turn. Although an older work, Francisco Rodríguez Marín, *Guía Histórica y Descriptiva de los Archivos, Bibliotecas y Museos arqueológicos de España* (Madrid, 1916), covers the three historical archives in the best detail. Lino Gómez Canedo, *Los Archivos de la historia de America*, (Mexico, D. F., 1961 2 vols.), provides similar treatment in Vol. I. L. Thomas and D. Case, *Guide to the Diplomatic Archives of Europe* (Philadelphia, University of Pennysylvania Press, 1959), 213–62, has shorter coverage but a good bibliography. Material for American history in the three main archives are briefly surveyed in William R. Shepherd, *Guide to the Materials for the History of the United States in Spanish Archives* (Washington, D.C., Carnegie Institution, 1907). Conceived as a companion volume to Shepherd, but now very outdated, is James A. Robertson, *List of Documents in Spanish Archives relating to the History of the United States, which have been Printed or of which Transcripts are Preserved in American Libraries* (Washington, D.C., Carnegie Institution, 1910). Francisco Sintes y Obrador, *Guía de los archivos de Madrid* (Madrid, Dirección General de Archivos y Bibliotecas, 1952), is useful for quick introductions to archives in Madrid other than the Archivo Histórico Nacional.

Short introductions to the libraries in Madrid can be found in *Guía de las Bibliotecas de Madrid* (Madrid, Dirreción General de Archivos y Bibliotecas, 1953). Manuscripts pertaining to the Americas in Spanish libraries are surveyed in José Tudela de la Orden, *Los manuscritos de América en las Bibliotecas de España* (Madrid, Ediciones Cultura Hispanica, 1954), but none pertaining directly to the American Revolution were noted.

MADRID
Archivo Histórico Nacional, Calle Serrano 115
Madrid

Established in the mid-19th century, the Archivo Histórico Nacional generally continues the collections found at Simancas, but with much overlap. The archive is divided into 12 sections, according to historical criteria, but only Section III, *Estado*, and XII, *Diversos*, contain material relating to the American Revolution as far as can be determined from the catalogue. Section X, *Ultramar*, might be thought to have relevant material as well, but in fact contains only 19th-century papers relating to Cuba, Puerto Rico and the Philippines.

The most recent general guide to the archive is Luis Sánchez Belda, *Guía del Archivo Histórico Nacional* (Madrid, 1958). See also Rodríguez Marín, op. cit., 3–128, and Gómez Canedo, op. cit., 149–59. Faustino Gil Ayuso, *Catálogo de los papeles que se conservan en el Archivo Histórico Nacional* (Madrid, 1934), was not available to the present editors. The material for American history is covered in very summary fashion in Shepherd, op. cit., 29–53.

SECCIÓN DE ESTADO

There is no printed inventory (other than Gil Ayuso), but see Shepherd, op. cit., 35–6, and Sánchez Belda, 83–94. Another detailed but limited catalogue is Miguel Gómez del Campillo, *Relaciones diplomáticas entre España y los Estados Unidos, según los documentos del Archivo Histórico Nacional* (Madrid, 1944–5, 2 vols.), which, combined with Jules Flammermont, *Les Correspondances des agents diplomatiques étrangers en France avant la révolution. . .* (Paris, 1896), 456–7, gives some idea of the diplomatic correspondence relating to the American war.

The series in this section known to or suspected of containing material relevant to the American Revolution are as follow.

Consejo de Estado

17th to 19th centuries, mainly council consultations and related papers concerning diplomatic matters.

Papeles del Conde de Aranda . . . legajos **2831–72**

2841. Copies of dispatches from Aranda to Floridablanca, 1776–83.

2846. Personal papers of Aranda, 1777–84.

2850. Contains a small part of the correspondence of Grimaldi and Floridabeanca with Aranda and Vergennes concerning the American war, 1776–83.

Expedientes Varios

3123–265. Mainly records of military, diplomatic and consular personnel.

Tratados y negociaciones diplomáticas

3266–489. 1701–1869.

Embajadas, legaciones y consulados

3479–5050 Original correspondence of embassies, minutes of the Council of State and related papers. The series includes Britain, 1747–98; France, 1730–1849; Germany, 1780–1805; Hamburg, 1779–99; Portugal, 1765–1825; Russia 1761–1838.

Gómez del Campillo inventories the following few *legajos*:

3883. 1766–7. Many documents relating solely to Louisiana, but also the American Declaration of Independence; voyage of A. Lee to Paris; Lee's proposals of 11 March 1777 to Floridablanca; much correspondence of Grimaldi and Floridablanca with Aranda, including instructions concerning the American agents.

3884. *File 1.* Concerns the recovery of Florida 1777–8.

File 3. Contains 147 documents, consisting of the correspondence of Aranda concerning the American colonies, including copies of dispatches of Vergennes to Ossun on the proposals of Franklin, Deane and Lee and correspondence between Aranda and Floridablanca discussing Spanish policy.

File 4. Contains 156 documents concerning Spanish financial aid to the Americans, 1777–82.

3884 *bis. Files 1–5.* Contain various miscellaneous documents transmitting copies of resolutions to Floridablanca, mostly by Arthur Lee.

File 6. Partly the letters of Miralles to José de Gálvez, 1778–80, with a few letters of Rendón and a few extracts of letters and instructions to La Luzerne from Paris.

File 7. Contains documents concerning Indian affairs in Louisiana, 1777–86.

File 8. Contains documents pertaining to Jay and Carmichael in Madrid, 1780.

File 11. Concerns the acquisition of ships built in America for the Spanish navy.

File 13. A few documents concerning Jay's proposals to Floridablanca for a treaty of friendship and alliance, 1781.

There are more papers of a miscellaneous nature in other files.

3885. *File 1.* Concerns Aranda's conferences with the American plenipotentiaries as reported to Floridablanca, 1782–4. Topics treated are the boundaries and Mississippi navigation issues—included is Aranda's diary of his conversations with Franklin, Jay and Vergennes concerning boundaries. There is also a report on the preliminary peace treaty.

File 2. A few documents on American pressure on the Mississippi, 1782.

File 16. The personal file of the American *chargé d'affaires* William Carmichael but only 6 documents fall within the 1779–83 period.

File 17. Contains 3 minutes of Floridablanca on the Mississippi navigation issue, 1782. Other files contain more documents of a routine nature.

3966. Correspondence of Aranda, 20 December 1773 to April 1774.

4066. Correspondence of Aranda with Grimaldi from September 1773 to 1775, except for the period covered in **3966**.

4062, 4072, 4116, 4143. Continue the correspondence of Aranda for 1776–80 and 1782.

Gobernadores de plazas y puertas, 1704–1833

This may also hold some relevant material.

Presas marítimes, 1690–1800

Protests and negotiations concerning the seizure of ships. The countries involved are Britain, France, Portugal, Prussia, Sweden and the United States.

In addition to the correspondence of Grimaldi, Floridablanca and Aranda, there is also known to be in the series listed above letters of Gardoqui, Campo, Muzquiz, Castejon, Ricla, Bernardo de Gálvez, José de Gálvez, Masserano, Almodóvar, Escarano, Miralles, Rendón, Vergennes, Ossun, Montmorin, Grantham, Cumberland, Hussey, Jay, Lee, Franklin. The range of topics includes military and naval matters; reception of American privateers and disposal of their prizes in Spanish ports; the 1779 alliance with France; observations of Miralles and Rendón from America; the campaigns of Bernardo de Gálvez; the Cumberland mission; the negotiations of Lee and Jay in Spain; relations between Aranda and the American envoys during the peace negotiations; Hussey in London; Spanish aid to the Americans; Spanish-American trade; policy disagreements between Floridablanca and Aranda; the Spanish attempt at mediation; and Aranda's views on the possible effect of the independence of the United States on the Spanish colonies in America.

SECCIÓN DE DIVERSOS

The following document is noted by María del Carmen Pescador de Hoyo, *Documentos de Indias, Siglos XV–XIX: Catálogo de la Serie existente en la Sección de Diversos* (Madrid, 1954), 182–3.

12 May 1782, Pensacola. 'Diario. De las operaciones de la expedición contra

la plaza de Panzacola concluida por las armas de S. M. Católica, baxo los
órdenes de Mariscal de Campo D. Bernardo de Gálvez.' Appended are the articles of capitulation for Pensacola.

Biblioteca Nacional, Avenue de Calvo Sotelo 20
Madrid

The Biblioteca Nacional is the largest and most important library in Spain. Its manuscript holdings are catalogued in *Biblioteca Nacional: Inventario general de manuscritos* (Madrid, Dirección General de Archivos y Bibliotecas, 1953–1970, 9 vols.). Manuscripts pertaining to the Americas are surveyed in Julián Paz, *Catálogo de manuscritos de América existentes en la Biblioteca Nacional* (Madrid, 1933), and in Tudela de la Orden, op, cit., 25, which covers the accessions from 1933 to 1952.

The following items have been noted for the American Revolution, but searching at the Biblioteca Nacional would surely reveal many more.

3174. *f. 74*. Establishment of the Republic of the United States in North America, preceded by an account of Florida, n.d.

10818. *f. 72*. 2 letters, 15 and 25 January 1783, to José de Gálvez and Floridablanca, accompanying the project for a force of Americans.

10952. *f. 184*. American Declaration of Independence.

12779. Contains an incomplete copy of **3174**.

12966. Secret memoir presented to the King of Spain by Count Aranda on the independence of the English colonies since the Treaty of Paris in 1783.

13228. *f. 4*. Another copy of **12966**.

17617. *f. 72*. Account of the fall of Pensacola, 10 May 1781.

17619. *f. 60*. Plan of Pensacola by Col. Langoria, 14 February 1781.

18579, 18761. Letters of the commander of Pensacola concerning British attack, 1781.

19246–8. Documents on Louisiana, 1767–92, contain scattered pieces concerning defence, the Natchez expedition, etc.

19509. *f. 76*. A decree concerning government in Louisiana, Pensacola and Mobile, 1782.

Biblioteca y Archivo del Palacio Real, Palacio Real
Madrid

Jesús Domínguez Bordona, *Catálogo de la Biblioteca de Palacio, vol. IX: Manuscritos de América* (Madrid, 1935), 134, lists the following document:

LXVI. *f. 269 ff.* Account of the British expedition of 1780 from Jamaica against the Spanish possessions in America.

SEVILLE

Archivo General de Indias, Queipo de Llano
Sevilla

This archive was formed in the late 18th century specifically to bring together the documents relating to the Spanish empire in the Indies. By royal command, papers were sent from the archive at Simancas and various departments of state. Although this is the largest collection of papers in Spain relating to Spanish America, many more papers have remained in other archives.

The archive is divided into twelve sections according to the provenance of the records. Of the twelve sections, V. *Gobierno* and XI. *Papeles de Cuba* contain considerable material which is partially listed below in accordance with the availability of catalogues. IX. *Papeles de Estado* and X. *Papeles de Ultramar* are briefly discussed.

The best guide to this archive is José María de la Peña y Cámara, *Archivo General de Indias de Sevilla; Guía del Visitante* (Madrid, Dirección General de Archivos y Bibliotecas, 1958). Other discussions of varying usefulness are Gómez Canedo, op. cit., 3–136; Rodríguez Marín, op. cit., 375–468; Pedro Torres Lanzas and German Latorre, *Cuadro General de la Documentación del Archivo General de Indias: Catálogo* (Sevilla, 1918); José Torre Revello, *El Archivo General de Indias de Sevilla: Historia y Clasificación de sus fondos* (Buenos Aires, 1929). Materials relating to North America are surveyed in Shepherd, op. cit., 55–95.

GOBIERNO

This section is referred to by various names in the guides and catalogues, including 'Audiencias y Indifferente' and 'Consejo de Indias y Ministerio de Hacienda'. The series *Florida y Luisiana* in the sub-section *Audiencia de Santo Domingo, 1512–1858* contains such material as pertains to the American Revolution. The series *Cuba* may also contain some material but there is no printed catalogue or inventory of it. The Louisiana material in *Florida y Luisiana* is the object of an excellent catalogue by José María de la Peña y Cámara, Ernest J. Burrus, et al., *Catálogo de Documentos del Archivo General de Indias, Sección V, Gobierno, Audiencia de Santo Domingo sobre la Epoca Española de Luisiana* (Madrid, Dirección General de Archivos y Bibliotecas and New Orleans, La., Loyola University, 1968, 2 vols.). Prior to the appearance of this work, there was only a sketchy manuscript inventory not always accurate in dates. Although the Florida material is generally not treated, this catalogue is the best place for the student to begin and the source of the following brief survey. The *legajos* or bundles of this series generally contain documents pertaining to all aspects of Spanish administration in Louisiana.

2530. Consultas La. y Fla., 1731–88. *ff. 24–9*. Capture of two English ships on the Mississippi, 11 August 1780; *ff. 30–6*. Confiscation decrees for eleven English ships on the Mississippi.

2532. Remisiones al Consejo, Cámara y Ministros, 1773–1815. *ff. 1–11*. 5 confidential letters from Martín Navarro concerning American settlers, 10 September to 15 December 1781.

2534. Provisiones de empleos, mercedes y graçias, 1730–78. *ff. 288–450*. Letters of Alejandro O'Reilly to José de Gálvez on military matters, June 1776 to December 1778; *ff. 451–78*. letters of Bernardo de Gálvez to José de Gálvez on political and military affairs, March 1777 to July 1779; *ff. 479–509*. proposals of Luis de Unzaga on military matters, July 1776; *ff. 510–54*. royal dispatches, 1777–8, containing some material on the state of forces in Louisiana, May 1778.

2535. Provisiones de empleos, mercedes y gracias, 1779–84. *ff. 1–167*. Letters of O'Reilly, February 1779 to February 1782; *ff. 168–336*. letters of Bernardo de Gálvez to José de Gálvez, September 1778 to February 1783; *ff. 353–69*. letters of Navarro to Bernardo de Gálvez, 1783; *ff. 496–561, 593–665*, papers on the Louisiana infantry regiment and other papers concerning promotions and concessions.

2539. Títulos varios, 1613–1818. Includes a few given 1779–83, including Martín Navarro and José Otrero.

2543. Correspondencia oficial con los Gobernadores, 1769–87. *ff. 573–728*. Papers concerning the Pensacola expeditions, 1779–80, and are the letters of Miró, Bernardo de Gálvez, Ezpeleta, Unzaga and Navarro, mostly to José de Gálvez.

2547. Duplicados de los Gobernadores e Intendentes, 1766–80. Letters of Unzaga to Arriaga, Council of the Indies, and José de Gálvez in 1776. Letters of Bernardo de Gálvez to José de Gálvez and the Council of the Indies, 1777–80.

2548. *idem*, 1781–2. Bernardo de Gálvez to José de Gálvez, with attention to Pensacola in 1781–2. Other correspondence to José de Gálvez from Victorio de Navia and Miró, 1781–3. Various maps of battles, 1781–2.

2549. *idem*, 1783–4. *ff. 286–430.* Letters of Bernardo to José de Gálvez, with mention of military affairs, 1781–3.

2572. Duplicados de Ministros y particulares, 1780–1821. *ff. 1–71.* 7 letters from the commissariat and fiscal officer of the Mobile expedition, Esteban Gayarre, to José de Gálvez, 31 May to 12 June 1780.

2596. Confidential papers and orders to the Governor of Louisiana, concerning the happenings in the British colonies, 1776–9. Contains letters of Unzaga, 1776; Bernardo de Gálvez, 1777–9; Urriza, 1778–9; de la Torre, 1777; Romá y Rosell, 1777.

2597. Letters of Commissioners Juan Miralles and Francisco Rendón, 1779–84.

2598. *idem*, 1779–85.

2628. Cuentes de Real Hacienda de Luisiana, 1769–80. Contains some army accounts.

2629. *idem*, 1781–4. Contains some army accounts.

2637. Cuentes de Real Hacienda de Panzacola y Mobila, 1780–1823. Commercial accounts of Pensacola and Mobile, 1780–3.

2655. Military patents and commissions, 1592–1815. Contains commissions of the Louisiana infantry regiment, 1781–1804.

2656. Asuntos de guerra y expedientes militares, 1767–84. *ff. 510–50.* Letters of Navarro to José de Gálvez, 1 March 1781 to 13 January 1783; *ff. 551–7.* Papers relating to the Natchez rebellion and campaign, 1779–81; *ff. 598–649.* supply of Pensacola, 1782–3.

2660. Fortificaciones, pertrechos de guerra y situados de tropa de la Florida, 1761–87.

2661. Fortificaciones, pertrechos de guerra, situado, tropa y sus incidencias, 1771–9. Letters and enclosures generally dealing with the state and numbers of troops, and some service records.

2662. Fortificaciones, pertrechos de guerra y situados de tropa de Luisiana, 1779–87. Correspondence of Bernardo de Gálvez, Navarro, Miró, and others, as well as papers on routine military matters.

2664. Quartermasters' accounts for Pensacola, 1781–3.

2666. Various papers relating to commerce, 1768–86.

2678. *ff. 303–18.* Concern monies paid to the American agent Oliver Pollock.

PAPELES DE ESTADO

This section of the archive is also divided into *audiencias,* of which the *audiencia* of Santo Domingo, Cuba, Puerto Rico, Louisiana, Florida and Mexico contains any documents relative to the American Revolution. These papers are catalogued in Cristobál Bermúdez Plata, *Catálogo de Documentos de la Sección Novena de Archivo General de Indias* (Seville, 1949), Vol. 1.

Legajos **1–19.** Santo Domingo, Cuba, Puerto Rico, Louisiana and Florida and constitute Series 1. The documents in these *legajos* represent certain but by no means all the matters taken up with the Council of State by the Council of the Indies. Although it would be expected to find some relevant papers in this series, the catalogue lists no *legajos* at all for the years between 1775 and 1785.

PAPELES DE ULTRAMAR

This section contains records relating to Cuba, 1740–1864; Puerto Rico, 1761–1854; Louisiana and Florida, 1717–1822; Philippines, 1630–1868; and America in general, 1605–1868.

Legajos **506–13.** Louisiana and Florida. Dispatch of funds and commodities, 1717–1822, and are unlikely to be very fruitful in terms of the American Revolution.

Cuba may contain some possibly relevant documents.

(There is no published catalogue for this section)

PAPELES DE CUBA

The papers in this section have been catalogued in some detail by Roscoe R. Hill, *Descriptive Catalogue of Documents relating to the History of the United States in the Papeles Procedentes de Cuba deposited in the Archivo General de Indias at Seville* (Washington, Carnegie Institution, 1916), on which the following survey is based. There are 23 series in this section, of which the following contain pertinent documents.

Series 1. *Archivo de Guerra, Florida Occidental. Legajos* **1–227**

1. 1775–9. 700 letters of Bernardo de Gálvez, many of which deal with relations with Britain, France and the colonies; progress of the war; plan for the conquest of Mobile; expeditions against Mobile and British posts on the Mississippi.

2. 1780–6. 700 letters of Bernardo de Galvez. The main topics are the expeditions against Mobile and Pensacola and the establishment of Spanish rule in the conquered areas. There are also letters concerning the 1783 Illinois expedition, agents of Georgia at Natchez, navigation of the Mississippi, Indian affairs, etc.

3. 1781–5. 1000 letters of Estevan Miró with de Gálvez and others. There are some, in 1781, on the capture of Pensacola; on military supplies and Indian affairs, 1782; on Indians and slaves, 1783.

9. 1781–3. 900 letters, mostly to Miró from subordinates in Louisiana, concerning the rebellion at Natchez, American immigrants, militia lists, Indian affairs, Mississippi shipping.

36. 1781–4. 600 letters of Arturo O'Neill, Governor of Pensacola, with de Gálvez and others. Mainly the state of Pensacola after its capture but also Indian affairs and military matters for all years.

40. 1781–93. 900 documents, mostly letters to O'Neill from other Spanish officials on routine military matters, Indian affairs, British prisoners, etc.

81. 1769–85. 400 letters of Unzaga, Governor of Louisiana, to various people, containing much on Indian affairs and the posts of St Louis and Natchitoches.

82. 1766–80. 700 letters of Unzaga to various people, mostly concerning finances but also Indian affairs and expeditions against the British.

83. 1779–84. 850 letters of Navarro, intendant of Louisiana, concerning *inter alia* the treaties with the British at Baton Rouge in 1779 and Mobile in 1780; expeditions against Pensacola and Natchez.

101. 1766–1805. 575 letters of de Gálvez and other officials. *Series b.* Important for the 1780 and 1781 expeditions against Mobile and Pensacola; *Series c.* Finances of the army and navy with lists of officers rewarded for meritorious service.

104. 1768–1815. 500 letters of consuls and ambassadors containing notices of the war, 1782; letters of Rendón, 1782; Aranda to Miró, 1777; and Machado to de Gálvez, 1779.

105. 1781–1810. 713 documents containing the correspondence of the Captain-General of Havana and others to officials in Louisiana and Florida: movements of the navy, 1781; Indian affairs, 1783; many letters of de Gálvez and others to O'Neill, 1781–3.

107. 1768–85. 500 letters of the commander of the Fort of Arkansas to the Governor of Louisiana, with reports on Indian affairs and notices of the attack on Pensacola, 1781.

112. 1776–9. 500 letters of the Governor of Louisiana, mostly to Unzaga and de Gálvez, concerning neutrality, regulation of commerce on the Mississippi, relations with the British at Fort Manchak, and the commission of Jacinto Panis to Mobile and Pensacola.

113. 1780–1803. 450 in-letters to the Governor of Louisiana, the main theme of which is the expedition against Pensacola, including signals, staff of de Gálvez, use of Indians, truce, paroles, etc.

114. 1781–1801. 800 in-letters to the Governor of Louisiana, dealing with *inter alia* the surrender of Natchez to the British; Mississippi navigation; supplies and military matters; list of troops, officers and ships of de Gálvez's force.

149–1. 1765–92. 536 documents containing the correspondence of the Viceroy of Mexico to the Governor of Louisiana. A few letters: 1778, on the war between Britain and her colonies; congratulations on the successes at Mobile and Pensacola; 1771–80, 1783, on the general situation.

151–1. 1782–9. 546 documents containing the correspondence between the captains-general of Cuba and the governors of West Florida. Mostly routine military matters and transmission of royal orders, some on Indian affairs.

173. 1782–1818. 50 files of *Causas Civiles* which in 1781 contains the criminal case against 'Juan Blommart Reo' as leader of the Natchez rebellion.

174. 1765–79. 677 documents containing royal orders transmitted by Grimaldi and Arriaga, including *inter alia* precautions in view of the American revolt; incitement of the Americans to attack British posts on the Mississippi and Florida; and contraband and commerce.

175. 1780–4. 418 documents containing various royal orders concerning the war against the British; Indian affairs; promotions for service in the expeditions against British posts; instructions for carrying on the war; plans for the war, 1781–2; movements of the fleets.

177. 1780–92. Letters to the Ministers has one long letter with many enclosures from Bernardo de Gálvez to José de Gálvez, reporting on the Pensacola expedition.

180–1. 1772–80. 166 documents containing royal decrees, including trade in British goods, 1779, and approvals of confiscations, 1780.

182. 1765–1812. Miscellaneous documents, mostly 1779–83, with important papers on the Pensacola expeditions.

186. Indexes to correspondence and royal orders.

188–3. 1757–1807. Correspondence of the Governor of Louisiana with foreign officials. Includes papers relating to the capitulations of Pensacola and Fort George.

191. 1772–1803. 700 letters of the Governors of Florida, containing letters on general affairs, 1778; relations with the British at Pensacola and on the Mississippi concerning prizes and prisoners.

192. 1768–99. *idem,* 1000 letters on general administration, Indian affairs, and a letter of Oliver Pollock to the people of Natchez concerning Spanish recognition of the US.

193. 1770–89. *idem*, 800 letters, with *inter alia* the parole of captured British prisoners; capitulation of Mobile; confiscation of the property of the Natchez rebels.

194. 1771–98. *idem*, 650 letters. 1781 contains general affairs, notices of the surrender of Pensacola, copy of the journal of Delavillebeuve.

197. 1770–1811. *idem,* 700 documents, containing *inter alia* the articles of capitulation between Bernardo de Gálvez and Alexander Dickson at Baton Rouge in 1779.

200. 1771–90. *idem*, 600 documents, containing *inter alia* the oath of allegiance of the British at Mobile and a list of householders of Mobile at the time of capitulation.

222–6. Copies of official letters, 1722–1825.

227. 1763–1823. Printed documents including: declaration of war against Britain, 1779; extension of free commerce, 1778; definitive peace treaty, 1783.

Series 2. *Florida Occidental.* **228–82**

The documents in this series mostly post-date 1783 and deal with commerce, supplies and accounts.

Series 3. *Florida Oriental.* **283–487**

Similar to Series 2, but note **462.** 1780–3, Register of the personnel of the convoy of the Marqués de Camacho, containing 100 documents and 7 volumes, all relating to the expeditions of Bernardo de Gálvez.

Series 4. *Luisiana.* **488–668**

Also similar to Series 2 and 3, but note the following:

563. 1765–1804. Miscellaneous papers containing *inter alia* lists of men, officers and ships for the Pensacola expedition.

569. 1766–85. Royal orders, including grants to Oliver Pollock, regulation of commerce, and declaration of war against Britain.

570. Also contains the declaration of war.

577. Contains the list of ships chartered for the naval expedition of 1779.

593. 1779–1810. Official correspondence, including the capture of Baton Rouge and Natchez, 1779; dispersion of the expedition against West Florida, 1780; attack on Mobile, 1781; money for Oliver Pollock.

600. 1778–1812. General correspondence containing *inter alia* references to money for Oliver Pollock.

610. 1780–8. Official correspondence containing for 1781 many letters concerning the capture of Pensacola.

624. 1780–1812. *Series a.* Letters of Urriza, intendant of Havana, to Navarro, intendant of Louisiana, with drafts of replies. Some of these concern the captures of Mobile and Pensacola.

Series 5. *Nueva Orleans.* **669–706**

This series concerns administrative, financial and judicial matters.

Series 15. *Archivo de Guerra, Captanes Generales.* **1049–2264**

1232. 1777–80. Letters of Bernardo de Gálvez to various people concerning Oliver Pollock, military matters, prisoners, American possession of Illinois, fears of British attack on Louisiana, capture of Fort Manchak, etc.

1233. 1780–1. Similar to **1232**, but also contains de Gálvez's diary of the attack on Pensacola.

1281. 1779–80. Correspondence with the Spanish commissioners in the American colonies; letters of Miralles and Rendón to Navarro, with draft replies, concerning supplies for Havana, war news, arrival of the French squadron, and the death of Miralles.

1282. 1780–1. *idem,* letters of Rendón to Navarro concerning commerce between the US and Havana, Clinton's embarkation at New York, plan for Spanish attack on St Augustine, and military operations of the Americans.

1283. 1778–81. Correspondence of the Spanish commissioner in the American colonies with the secretary of the Captain-General of Havana. Letters of

Miralles and Rendón to del Valle with draft replies. Most concern expenses of Miralles and Rendón but some concern US–Cuban trade.

1290. 1777–80. Confidential orders of the Council of the Indies and related papers. Includes news from the American colonies; order to drive the British from the Gulf of Mexico, 1779; expedition of 1780 against Pensacola; and death of Miralles.

1291. 1779–81. Correspondence with the Ministry of the Indies, including the war in the colonies, 1779; plans for the attack on the British in the Gulf, 1780; Mobile and Pensacola expeditions; war news; death of Miralles; correspondence of Rendón and charter of ships to carry it.

1301. 1777–81. Parliamentary dispatches . . . and correspondence, concerning *inter alia* the exchange of prisoners, 1780; death of Miralles; joint Spanish –American plans against East Florida and Georgia.

1304, 1309, 1318. Mostly contain papers concerning routine military matters, prisoners, letters of recommendation, etc., 1781–2.

1319. 1781–2. Commission of Francisco Rendón in Philadelphia: letters of Rendón to Cagigal, Captain-General of Cuba, 12 June 1781 to 10 October 1782, generally reporting on the war and American affairs.

1330. 1781–2. Drafts of letters from Cagigal to José de Gálvez, concerning exchange of prisoners, the expedition against New Providence, and Bernardo de Gálvez in Guarico.

1354. 1782–4. Correspondence of Francisco Rendón mainly to Cagigal and Unzaga, 12 September 1782 to 12 May 1784, reporting on American affairs and the war.

2317–1. 1777–86. Orders and reports containing *inter alia* expenses of the expeditions against Manchak, Baton Rouge and Natchez, and the 1782 payment to Oliver Pollock.

2351. 1746–84. West Florida and Mississippi. Includes British designs against Louisiana, 1778; relations with the British, 1779; expeditions against the British, 1780; progress of the American war, 1781.

2358. 1775–9. Spanish Louisiana miscellaneous. Includes possible British attack on Louisiana; notices of the American revolt; Indian affairs; relations with Britain—the captures of Fort Manchak and Baton Rouge, and British prisoners, 1779.

2359. 1780–2. *idem,* concerning Pensacola, British prisoners, progress of the war, use of Indians, and the Natchez rebellion.

2370. 1769–89. *idem*, concerning the plan for commerce between Louisiana and Virginia, 1776; Spanish aid to the Americans and British protests; prizes; fighting in Illinois; passage of American troops through Spanish territory.

VALLADOLID

Archivo General de Simancas, Simancas
Valladolid

The Archivo General de Simancas is the oldest of the Spanish archives and contains documents from the 6th to the 19th centuries. The bulk of the material lies between the middle of the 15th and the end of the 18th centuries. The papers are generally classified according to the main department of government to which they pertain: the Crown, the councils or the secretariats. Each general classification is further divided into sections according to provenance of the papers, the nature of the business, and persons and localities involved. The sections in turn are divided into series.

The *Guía de Archivo General de Simancas* (Valladolid, 1958) supercedes earlier official guides. See also Rodríguez Marín, op. cit., 129–372, and Gómez Canedo, op. cit., 139–49. Catalogues of the various sections of the archive are published in *Catálogo del Archivo General de Simancas* (Vol. 1, 1904 et seq.). Material for American history is cursorily surveyed in Shepherd, op. cit., 15–28.

The main papers for the American Revolution are in the following sections: *Secretaría de Estado, Secretaría de Guerra, Secretaría de Marina,* and *Secretaría y Superintendencia de Hacienda.*

SECRETARIA DE ESTADO

This section contains royal correspondence; royal acts and decrees; instructions to ambassadors; proceedings, reports and correspondence of the Council of State; routine papers of the Spanish embassies, legations and consulates. Most of these papers relate to the 16th and 17th centuries, but a fair number pertain to the 18th. For the American Revolution, the main materials are in the *negociaciones* of the correspondence of the Council of State and the Spanish ambassadors to France and Britain.

Negociaciones de Inglaterra (Catálogo XVII: Secretaría de Estado, Documentos relativos a Inglaterra. 1254–1834)

Legajos **6954–7039.** Diplomatic correspondence with Britain, cover the years 1763–79.

6958. 1764–5. Correspondence of Masserano, containing scattered references to British politics and the American question.

6959. 1765. Routine correspondence, including the political situation in Britain and disturbances in Boston over the Stamp Act.

6960. January–July 1766. Routine correspondence on the tumult in the British colonies over the new impositions; discussion of colonial affairs in the ministry and Parliament; parliamentary affairs; Pitt's position on the colonies; repeal of the Stamp Act; British political situation; second Pitt ministry.

6961. August–December 1766. Routine correspondence on the British political situation; repeal of the Stamp Act; parliamentary affairs; British naval strength.

6963. 1766–71. *Inter alia,* reflections on British military strength and politics by Don Martín de Mello, envoy of Portugal to London.

6964. January–June 1767. Routine correspondence with news of Parliament; naval preparations in British ports; dissension between Britain and the colonies; parliamentary discussions on the disobedience of the colonies; British politics.

6965. July–December 1767. Routine correspondence on news of Parliament; state of the British navy; British politics; prohibition of the import of European goods into Boston; punitive measures for the colonies.

6968. January–June 1768. Correspondence of Masserano on parliamentary proceedings; British politics; British financial situation; value of British imports and exports 1761–6; conversations of Masserano and Shelburne on foreign policy.

6969. July–December 1768. Routine correspondence on Spanish-British relations; unrest in America and news of Boston; suspicion that France is encouraging this unrest; British reaction to the American disturbances; dispatch of troops to Boston; strained relations between France and Britain; conferences of Weymouth and Masserano, British political situation; separatist tendencies in the American colonies.

6972. January–June 1769. Correspondence of Masserano concerning the American ban on British imports; parliamentary proceedings; disturbances in America; probable repeal by Parliament of Acts obnoxious to the colonies; British political situation.

6973. July–December 1769. Routine correspondence concerning the American ban on British imports; news from Boston—complaints of the provincial assembly to Bernard; exchange between the Governor and a deputation of citizens in Virginia.

6976. January–June 1770. Correspondence of Masserano on the disturbances in Boston and extracts of parliamentary proceedings.

6977. July–December 1770. *idem*, on the arming of ships in British ports; level of strength and distribution of the British navy.

6980. January–June 1771. *idem*, on the state of the British navy.

6981. July–December 1771. *idem*, on British naval preparations; state of the British navy; maritime incidents between the British and Spanish in America.

6984. January–June 1772. *idem*, on parliamentary proceedings; reflections on British naval and military strength; incidents in America between Spanish and British ships.

6985. July–December 1772. Routine correspondence on the movement of British naval squadrons; bloody events at the isle of Rod near Boston; British political situation—dismissal of Hillsborough; incidents between British and Spanish ships; parliamentary proceedings; dispatch of troops to America discussed in Parliament.

6986. 1773. Correspondence of Escarano, *chargé d'affaires* in London, on parliamentary proceedings, incidents between British and Spanish ships in America; state of the British navy.

6988. 1774. *idem*, on the grave situation in Boston and Philadelphia; spirit of independence in America; British troops in America; burning of the house of the Governor of New York; the American question in Parliament; punitive measures against Boston; changes in the government of Massachusetts; more incidents in Boston; measures concerning the government of Canada; Congress at Philadelphia; petition of Boston citizens to Gen. Gage.

6989. January–May 1775. Routine correspondence with news of the situation in Boston and measures of Gage; parliamentary proceedings; measures of the British ministry concerning the American colonies; troop increases to subdue the revolting colonies; American affairs in Parliament; orders for detention of Spanish ships carrying munitions to the American colonies; prohibition of New Englanders fishing in Newfoundland; Dutch trade with the colonies; position of the London guilds in favour of the colonies; concern about Spanish naval preparations.

6990. May–July 1775. Correspondence of Masserano with various reports on the situation in America; fighting in Massachusetts; seizure of Ticonderoga by the rebels; Gage's proclamation in Massachusetts; desire of Britain for cordial relations with Spain.

6991. August–December 1775. Routine correspondence on the dispatch of troops to America; arrival of Mr Penn, Governor of Philadelphia, and his peace proposals; recall of Gen. Gage and Adm. Graves; appointment of Howe; offer of 3000 Irish Catholics to serve in America; measures for subduing the colonies; desertion of British officials and soldiers to the American side; attitude of the Canadians; fears in Britain of a war against other countries; close relation between the Spanish and French Ambassadors; detention of a French ship carrying arms to the rebel colonies; request for Russian troops to serve in America; Masserano's opinion on the conflict.

6992. 1775–7. Official letters and related documents of Lord Grantham, British Ambassador to Spain. *Inter alia,* on maritime incidents and the sale of munitions to the colonies.

6993. January–April 1776. Correspondence of Masserano concerning registration of British and American ships by the Spanish authorities to avoid contraband; Rochford's plan for a Franco-Spanish-British convention to guarantee their respective possessions in America; parliamentary proceedings; American attacks on Quebec; arrival of a Spanish merchant ship at Charlestown; consequences of the use of German troops; British contracts for German troops; City of London petition supporting colonies; fall of New York city to General Lee.

6994. April–July 1776. Routine correspondence on parliamentary proceedings; British fears of French and Spanish naval preparations; dispatch of troops to America; considerations on the brothers Howe; peace mission of the Howes; new American attacks on Quebec; British withdrawal from the Carolinas; Franklin's activities; closure of Portuguese ports to American ships.

6995. July–December 1776. Routine correspondence on military operations in America; British activities in Canada; Declaration of Independence; British request for closure of Spanish ports to American ships; American question in Parliament; conference of Lord Howe with Congress; recruiting of German troops; Franklin's arrival in Paris.

6996. January–May 1777. Routine correspondence reporting conversations with the British ministers; military and naval preparations for the campaign in America; French aid—conferences of Franklin and Deane; parliamentary proceedings; peace mission of the Howes; rumours of the dispatch of 20,000 Russians to America; official presentation of the British Ambassador in Paris to the French ministry concerning the American colonies.

6997. May–September 1777. Routine correspondence on suspicions between Spain and England—conversations of Masserano with Suffolk and other British ministers about mutual disarmament; parliamentary proceedings; proceedings of the British ministry over friction between Spain and Portugal; maritime incidents between Spanish and British ships; French aid to the Americans; British military successes in America.

6998. September–December 1777. Routine correspondence reporting protestations of friendship by George III to Spain; Howe's campaign in America; reinforcement of French possessions in America; Burgoyne's campaign; conversations with Lord Mansfield on Anglo-Spanish relations; Russian troops in British service; parliamentary debates on America; Richmond's plan for a 'Family Compact' with the colonies.

7000. January–April 1778. Correspondence of Escarano on conferences with Weymouth; parliamentary proceedings; situation in America; London petition to the King to end the war; rumours of the Franco-American treaty and the rupture of Anglo-French relations; British naval and military preparations; British politics; Chatham's opposition to American independence; North's plan for reconciliation with the colonies; minutes of dispatches of Floridablanca.

7001. May–August 1778. Routine correspondence on Burgoyne's arrival in England; movements of the British fleet; defensive measures in England; military news from America; Howe's arrival in London; British eagerness to preserve peace with Spain; minutes of dispatches of Floridablanca.

7002. July–October 1778. Correspondence of Almodóvar concerning British naval preparations; arrival of the British peace commissioners in Philadelphia and their proposals; military operations in America; situation of the armies in America; messages of the ministers of Sweden, Denmark, and Prussia concerning British seizures; minutes of dispatches of Floridablanca.

7003. November–December 1778. Routine correspondence on incidents between French and British ships in Spanish waters; French expedition against Dominica; incidents with British ships in American waters; news of the colonies; operations of Washington and Clinton; Dutch protest against seizures; journals of Parliament; Congress accepts British proposals; failure and return of the British peace mission.

7004. 1778–9. Official letters and related documents of Lord Grantham as British Ambassador to Spain. These mostly concern privateers, incidents with neutrals, etc.

7005. 1779. Condidential correspondence of Almodóvar concerning British forces in America; British commerce 1761–77; journals of Parliament; possible Russian naval aid to Britain; correspondence with Hussey; plans for the attack on St Lucia; state of the British navy.

7016. 1770–7. Letters of Grimaldi to Masserano and Escarano (confidential papers from the estate of Masserano).

7020. January–October 1779. Correspondence of Almodóvar with Floridablanca: with news from America; British politics; fall of St Lucia; disgust of neutrals at ship seizures; British naval forces in America; parliamentary debates; military operations in America; rupture of Anglo–Spanish relations; letters of Floridablanca.

7021. 1778–9. Various papers, including Spanish mediation between France and Britain; letters of Aranda in Paris and Herrería in Holland to Almodóvar and his replies; ire of Sweden, Denmark, Holland and Prussia at seizures of their ships by Britain.

8133–67. Papers of the Spanish Embassy in London for the years 1760–96, but most contain nothing of interest. The following are noted:
    8136. 1783–9. Contains *inter alia* expenses of Spanish and British prisoners during the last war.
    8138. 1783–95. Various papers pertaining to Florida; reflections of the new United States; Anglo-American commerce.
    8139. 1781–4. Contains the definitive peace treaty and commercial treaty; Anglo-American commerce; foreigners in Florida; internal and political state of Britain; fortification of the banks of the Mississippi by the Americans; news of the British court and other British affairs.
    8156. 1783–8. Correspondence with the Spanish ministers in Sweden, Vienna, Russia, France, Portugal, and Gardoqui in New York.
    8157, 8158. May also contain marginal material.

Negociaciones con Francia

The most important diplomatic series for the American Revolution at Simancas is *Negociaciones con Francia*, which is inventoried in *Catálogo IV: Secretaría de Estado. Capitulaciones con Francia y negociaciones diplomáticas de los embajadores de España en aquella corte . . .* (Madrid, 1914), Vol. I, 1265–1714. Vol. II was never published hence this important series lacks a published guide for most of the 18th century. Shepherd, op. cit., 24, reports that material concerning the American Revolution is in some 35 *legajos* and 20 letter books containing the correspondence of Aranda, the Spanish Minister in Paris. Slightly more detailed description is given in Flammermont, op. cit., 480–6, which was originally published in *Nouvelles Archives des missions scientifiques,* VIII, 480 ff.

The correspondence of Aranda in Paris begins in August 1773 in **4590**, while **4606** (1775) contains the first papers concerning possible Franco-Spanish action against Britain.

4632. Contains Aranda's correspondence for the year 1783.

4650–68. Copies of Aranda's dispatches, 1773–83.

4673. Confidential correspondence of Aranda with Floridablanca, 1776–83.

4675–7. Copies of the general correspondence of Aranda, 1775–8.

The various guides to Simancas mentioned at the beginning of this section are of no use for this level of detail.

Negociaciones with Prussia, Germany, Saxony, Austria and Holland

The series detailed in *Catálogos* II and III contain no relevant material except as below.

Correspondencia de Alemania (Catálogo II: *Secretaría de Estado, Capitulaciones con la Casa de Austria y negociaciones de Alemania, Sajonia, Polonia, Prusia y Hamburgo, 1493–1796* Madrid, 1942, 2nd ed.)

6518. 1780–4. *Inter alia*, Austrian support of the Armed Neutrality.

6519. 1767–88. Routine and confidential correspondence of the Austrian imperial family with the Spanish King.

6520. 1781. *Inter alia*, signing of a treaty of friendship and defence between Austria and Russia.

6521. 1782. *Inter alia*, rumours of Russian recognition of American independence; peace talks between Britain and Holland; Austrian support of the principles of the Armed Neutrality.

6522. 1781–2. Letters and protests of Count Kaunitz, Austrian Ambassador to Spain, over British seizures of ships and mistreatment of Austrian subjects.

6525. 1782–4. Seizure of the British brigantine of Captain John Sibley.

Negociaciones con Portugal, 1478–1784

There is no published catalogue, but brief summaries can be found in Mariano Alcócen y Martínez, *Guía histórica y descriptiva de los archivos, bibliotecas y museos de España* (Madrid, 1921), 216–22.

SECRETARÍA DE GUERRA

This section contains papers concerning military affairs, 1700–1830. Documents concerning the Revolution are most likely to be found under the headings of *Hojas de Servicio, Florida y Luisiana, Generalidad de Indias*, and *Varios de España e Indias*.

Series 50. *Hojas de Servicio*

Catálogo XXII: Secretaría de Guerra (Siglo XVIII) Hojas de Servicios de América (Valladolid, 1958) contains a personal index, a regimental index, and a brief inventory of material relating to America in the 18th century.

Series 40. *Florida y Luisiana*

There is no published catalogue, but Shepherd, op. cit., 25, briefly describes documents concerning the conquest of Mobile and British posts on the Mississippi and rewards for service in these campaigns, 1779–85. *Catálogo* XXII, 348, contains a brief listing of these *legajos* aswell.

6912, 6913. Contain the diaries of Bernardo de Gálvez, describing the expeditions against Pensacola and Mobile and other documents pertaining to the Pensacola campaign, the Natchez Rebellion, the articles of capitulation between de Gálvez and Chester, and cooperation with the French naval forces in the West Indies, 1780–3.

Series 48. *Generalidad de Indias*

There is no printed catalogue, but *Catálogo XXII*, 351, notes that **7234** contains administrative details relative to the American expedition of d'Estaing, 1782–3.

Series 52. Varios de España e Indias

Catálgo XXII, 352, notes **7303** with correspondence relating to the campaigns of Bernardo de Gálvez and Victorio de Navia, 1780–2.

SECRETARÍA DE MARINA

These papers cover the period 1633–1783 and deal with such topics as munitions and artillery, personnel matters, prisoners and privateering, ministry of marine, expeditions in Europe and the Indies, etc. Shepherd, op. cit., 27, states that 25 *legajos* relate to Spain's share in the war against Britain, 1779–83, giving details of organization, equipment, movement of fleets, engagements, prizes, prisoners, etc. There is no printed catalogue.

SECRETARÍA Y SUPERINTENDENCIA DE HACIENDA

These papers are entirely 18th-century and contain some documents relating to the financing of the war against Britain under various general categories such as artillery; contraband; wars with France, England and Portugal; military orders; America. There is no printed catalogue.

PART III
AUSTRIA, GERMANY, ITALY, RUSSIA, SWEDEN

AUSTRIA

INTRODUCTION

Although a neutral state, the Hapsburg Empire played some role in the European diplomacy surrounding the American Revolution. Like the other European states, the court of Vienna was concerned with the effects of the American war on the pattern of power relationships in Europe. Specific Austrian involvement with the American Revolution centered on the three issues of British recruiting, Austrian mediation, and the Armed Neutrality.

Although Austria did not enter into diplomatic relations with the insurgent colonies, rebuffing the mission of the American agent William Lee in 1778, aid of a sort was given to the American colonies by the refusal to allow Austrian subjects to enter into mercenary service. As she had with other neutral European states, Britain early approached Austria for recruits to serve in the American colonies. This approach was unsuccessful as Austria wished to protect its own supply of recruits and to prevent desertion from its own forces. Even so, a few Austrians joined the Anspach troops hired by Britain. In 1780 and 1781 German troops passing through Austrian territory en route to embarkation for America were examined for Austrian subjects and deserters. In 1782 there was a clandestine attempt by Britain to secure Austrian recruits which provoked preventive measures from the Austrian government. This Austrian policy denied Britain much needed access to one of the largest supplies of recruits in Europe, although the motivation behind the policy had nothing to do with assistance to the insurgents. Some records relating to the recruiting issue are to be found in the Kriegsarchiv.

In conjunction with Russia, Austria embarked on several attempts at mediation, all of which were unsuccessful. The papers relating to these efforts are an important part of the Austrian diplomatic records relating to the American war as are the records of the Austrian relationships with the Armed Neutrality. The most important of the Austrian material relative to the American Revolution thus concerns Austrian policy and diplomacy and is found in the Wiener Haus-, Hof-und Staatsarchiv. Some miscellaneous material concerning trade with the American colonies lies in the Kriegsarchiv and the Wiener Hofkammerarchiv. Strictly forbidden by decree, emigration to America was not an issue in the later 18th century but some decrees concerning this matter at the time of the Revolution are noted in the Haus-, Hof- und Staatsarchiv.

VIENNA

The known material in Austria relating to the American Revolution is all located in the archives of the former Hapsburg capital of Vienna. All the archives in Vienna are under the administration of the:

Österreichisches Staatsarchiv,
1010 Wien I, Minoriten Platz I

to which all enquiries should be addressed. Although there are a number of published catalogues and inventories of the various individual archives in Austria, there is no overall survey of any significance. The material relating to America in the archives of Vienna, Salzburg and Innsbruck has been surveyed in Albert B. Faust, *Guide to the Materials for American History in Swiss and Austrian Archives* (Washington, D.C., Carnegie Institution, 1916). In terms of the American Revolution, however, this survey is unfortunately defective in that it ignores the diplomatic records concerning the mediation and the Armed Neutrality.

Kriegsarchiv

The printed guides to this archive are *Inventare Österreicher Archive, VIII: Inventar des Kriegsarchiv Wien* (Vienna 1953, 2 vols.); Faust, 237–46.

SCHRIFTENARCHIV

Faust, 238–40, notes no materials prior to 1780 but from that year lists the following:

1780

G. 756. *Nr. 1433.* Rekruten werden von Reiche-Ständen an Engelland überlassen, u. nach Amerika abgeschickt. Frankfurt, 23 February 1780. Report that perhaps twenty Austrian subjects are among the recruits for the Anspach troops to be sent to America. *Nr. 1434.* 'Major Grün und Hauptmann La Sollaye und den aus dem Reich gebürtigen Kaiserl. Soldaten Urlaub erteilt.' Inquiry added on whether it is possible to get the Austrians back.

G. 1724. *Nr. 3355.* 'Feldmarschall Lt. Prinz von Nassau-Usingen, den 31. May 1780, zeigt an, dass bei Höxter auf der Weser 1000 Recrouten nach Amerika vorbei passiret synd.'

G. 2677. *Nr. 5113.* Report from Lt. Prinz von Nassau-Usingen, Erfurt, 29 August 1789, concerning British recruiting in Germany.

B. 880. 'Dass die Kayserl. Untertanen mit ihren Schiffen von dem Französischen Droit de Frèt befreyt seyen' (an das Karlstädter General Commando).

B. 1187. Further information bulletins to the Karlstädter General Commando.

1781

B. 247. Requests to trade in salt with France and America referred to the Karlstädter General Commando.

G. 1543. Lt. Prinz Nassau reports further movements of Hessian, Anspach and Hannau recruits along the Weser near Höxter, 10 May 1781.

G. 1767. Acknowledgement of preceding.

G. 2137. Report of Lt. Prinz Nassau that the British are extending their recruiting and that the French plan to begin as well, 14 July 1781.

G. 2197. Erledigung des Exhibiti: 'Das mit der Reichs Canzlei do. 1777 verabredete Hilfsmittel bestehe darin, dass bey den Chur- und Oberrheinischen Creisen, hauptsächlich bey Chur Pfalz, auch andern am Rheine liegenden Ständen erwürket werde, dass sie dem Volksauszuge Schranken setzen, den durchziehenden Transporten Unterthanen und Deserteurs abnehmen, allenfalls hierzu den Kayserl. Beystand aufrufen, zu welchem Ende diesseitige Werb Officiers ohne Aufsehen zu machen, auf alle Fälle, wo Reichs Unterthanen auswandern mögen, aufmerksam zu seyn, und davon im vertraulichen Wege, jene Stände, in deren Bezirke sie sich befinden, noch in Zeiten zu verständigen haben', Kriegshof Kanzlei, 2 August 1781.

G. 2319. Acknowledgement of preceding.

G. 2368. 'Werbungen für die englischen Truppen in America werden im Reich aufgestellt, und wird wegen deren Abschaffung das Nöthige veranlasst.' 'Werb Depot will in einigen Reichsstädten v. allda für die zum dienst der englisch-ostindischen Compagnie allda v. in der Schweiz aufgebrachte Recruten errichtet werden, und wie diesfalls Abhülf zu treffen wird die Weisung gegeben.'

G. 2664. 'Englische Recruten Transports (aus dem oberen Theil Schwabens) sind von diesseitigens Militari angehalten worden.'

1782

G. 974. 'Recruten sind in Reichs landen für fremde Mächte angeworben, und dahin transportirt worden, welches angezeigt, und das weitere darüber veranlasst worden.' *Nr. 238.* 'Zu Anspach aufgebrachte Jäger über Hanau und Bremerleh für Cron Engelland nach America abgegangen.'

1783

G. 4. *164.* 'Werbungen sind für dortige Engelländische Truppen in Reichs Landen aufgestellet worden, und wird wegen deren Abschaffung, dann Verhinderung der Auswanderung der Reichs Unterthanen dahin die Vorsicht getroffen.'

G. 1608. 'Handlungsschiffe diesseitige sind auf der Rückreise von America zu Grund gegangen.'

G. 2181, 2278. 'Hessische Truppen in englishem Sold gestandene (und zurück erwartete) werden zu diesseitigen Diensten angebothen, und hierauf der Entschluss ertheilt.'

B. 892. 'Commerzienrath Kayserl. (Freyherr von Beelen) ist zur Beförderung der Wechselseitigen Handlung zwischen diesund jenseitigen Unterthanen dahin abgesendet und solches kundgemacht worden.'

MEMOIREN (Faust, 246)

Mem. 28/104. 'Kapitulationen zwishen dem amerikanischen General Washington und dem französischen General Rochambeau, dann dem englischen General Lord Cornwallis . . .' 2 documents of 1781.

Wiener Haus-, Hof- und Staatsarchiv

The Wiener Haus-, Hof- und Staatsarchiv contains the central records of the Hapsburg Empire. L. Thomas and D. Case, *Guide to the Diplomatic Archives of Europe* (Philadelphia, University of Pennsylvania Press, 1959)., 3–20, cover the history, organization and bibliography of this archive. The standard printed guide is Ludwig Bittner, *Gesamtinventar des Wiener Haus-, Hof- und Staatsarchiv* (Vienna 1936–40, 5 vols.), which also contains information on the history of the various sections of the archive and the administrative backgrounds which produced each record group. A survey of the America-related material can be found in Faust, 185–237.

HABSBURG-LOTHRINGISCHE FAMILIENARCHIV

Sammelbände (*Gesamtinventar* II, 28)

Papers of Fürst Wenzel Kaunitz, 1765–92, *Bd. 12, 14, 59.*

Papers of Florimund Graf Mercy d'Argenteau, 1769–92, *Bd. 32, 75.*

KABINETTSARCHIV

Nachlass Kaunitz (*Gesamtinventar* II, 196)

One carton of papers of Wenzel Kaunitz, State Chancellor, 1753–92, but none are later than 1769. (For other papers of Kaunitz: *Hababurg-Lothringische Familienarchiv,* above; *Sonstige Sammlungen, Grossen Korrespondenz, below; Staatsrat, Gesamtinventar* II, 228, below)

Staatsrat (*Gesamtinventar* II, 223 ff. Faust, 188)

The records of the *Staatsrat* contain a few acts concerning emigration and America as follow:

1771. **Nr. 1864.** 'Auswandern, ist den gemeinen Handwerken einzuschranken.'

1773. **Nr. 340.** 'Auswandern, oder Reisen ausser Landes, das desfalls bestehende Gesetz ist auch in den Militär-Gränzen einzuführen.'

1774. **Nr. 2927.** 'Auswanderungen an den Gränzen sind nicht allegein, sondern nur in gewissen Fällen zu gestatten.'

1777. **Nr. 1955.** 'America wird in einem Buch beschrieben, so zwahr von der Censur in Anstand gesogen, dannoch aber passiret wird' [the book was *Erdbeschreibung von ganz Amerika*].

1782. **Nr. 4095.** 'Amerikanische colonien. Dahin wird eine Schiffahrt von dem Consul zu Cadiz eingeleitet' (concerns mainly the Spanish-American colonies).

1783. **Nr. 1467.** 'Amerikanischer Handel: In Absicht auf denselben wird eine Consignation der Hung. und Siebenbürgischen Naturprodukten und Manufakturen, und deren Preys überreicht' (deals with North America).

ÖSTERREICHISCHE AKTEN

The section *Länderabteilungen* contains a group of miscellaneous material on foreign countries which is not otherwise classified (*Gesamtinventar* IV, 3 ff.; Faust, 217 ff.). The earliest document of interest concerns German emigrants to America in transit through Holland, 1768. In 1774, a number of interesting documents appear, including one concerning relations between Parliament and the colonies and another dealing with the Dutch munitions trade to the colonies. From 1775 to 1783 there a number of documents listed for each year which concern the Revolution in one way or another. Most are reports concerning events in America and British policies, some fewer concerning Dutch-American relations, American privateers, Franco-American relations, and the peace negotiations.

REICHSARCHIV

Instruktionen (*Gesamtinventar* I, 327–8)

Instruktionen A–Z, Fasz. 1–18. 3 fascicles are titled: *Instructionen für die kaiserlichen Gesandten an verschiedenen Hofen*, 1624–1784; while 8 other fascicles are: Instructionen von der Reichskanzlei an die verschiedenen Gesandten im Reich, 1568–1805.

Vorträge (*Gesamtinventar* I, 328–9)

Reports, 1636–1805, 8 fascicles.

Ministerialkorrespondenz (*Gesamtinventar* I, 353–5)

Correspondence of the following statesmen: Christian Graf Seilern, 1763–1880; Leopold Graf Neipperg, 1763–1800; Franz Josef Graf Wurmband, 1769–89; Adam Franz Graf Hartig, 1769–89; J. P. Marx, 1775–94; Ludwig Freih. v. Lehrbach, 1775–94; Egidius Freih. v. Borié, 1775–94; Ludwig Graf Lehrbach, 1779–1801; Franz Graf Sickingen, 1768–96.

STAATSKANZLEI (MINISTERIUM DES ÁUSSERN)

Vorträge an den Kaiser (*Gesamtinventar* I, 421–3)

Reports of the Ministry of Foreign Affairs, the Privy Conference, the Privy Council, and synopses of other sessions related to foreign affairs. Chronologically ordered, 1558–1860.

Friedensakten (*Gesamtinventar* I, 435–8)

Comprises peace treaties, preliminaries, armistices, congresses, conferences, secret missions, negotiations, etc. Chronologically ordered from the Treaty of Westphalia to 1860.

Carton 96. Österreicher-russische Mediation 1780–1782'.

Verträge betreffende Akten (*Gesamtinventar* I, 438–40) Comprises negotiations, ratifications, declarations, settlements, etc.

Faz. 4 (alt 9). 'Russlands System der bewaffneten Neutralität 1780–1781, Handelsvertrag mit den Vereinigten Staten 1784, Allianz mit Russland 1781–1789, . . .'

STAATENABTEILUNGEN (VEREINIGTE DIPLOMATISCHE
AKTEN)
AUSSERDEUTSCHE STAATEN

Frankreich (*Gesamtinventar* I, 530–2)

The series are *Hofkorrespondenz*, 1480–1832; *Berichte*, 1500–1871; *Weisangen*, 1504–1863; *Varia*, 1416–1865; *Noten*, 1526–1871; *Druckshriften*, 1500–1844.

Grossbritannien (*Gesamtinventar* I, 534–5)

The series are *Hofkorrespondenz*, 1518–1845; *Berichte*, 1515–1867; *Weisungen*, 1516–1861; *Varia*, 1292–1861; *Drucksachen*, 1514–1848.

Holland (*Gesamtinventar* I, 535–6)

The series are *Berichte*, 1705–1805; *Weisungen*, 1705–1806; *Instruktionen*, 1707–1802; *Hofkorrespondenz*, 1706–1806; *Notenwechsel*, 1710–1806; *Interiora*, 1759–87; *Varia*, 1709–1808.

Portugal (*Gesamtinventar* I, 569–70)

The series are *Reichshofkanzlei* (*Lusitana*), 1513–1792; *Staats(Hof)kanzlei* (alte Reihe, erste Folge), 1704–1800; *Staatskanzlei (neue Reihe)*, 1780–1837.

Russland (*Gesamtinventar* I, 571–3)

The series are
I. *Alter Bestand* (*Russica der Reichshofkanzlei*), 1481–1805: *Berichte, Weisungen, Varia*.

II. *Neuere Akten* (*Provenienz meist Staats(Hof)kanzlei* 1726–1806: *Berichte, Weisungen, Varia, Instruktionen*—1721–1806; *Memoires*, 1738–1803; *Hofkorrespondenz* to 1806, including correspondence with members of the Russian royal family, 1781–1805.

Carton 138. Correspondence of Joseph II with Count Cobenzl, 1780–90.
Carton 139. Correspondence of Prince Kaunitz with Russian statesmen, 1758–90.

Cartons 144–5. Notes of the Russian embassy to the Chancery, 1733–1806.
Carton 146–7. Exchange of notes between the Austrian embassy in St Petersburg and the Russian Ministry, 1750–1806.

Spanien (*Gesamtinventar* I, 577–80)

The series are *Hofkorrespondenz*, 1527–1841; *Korrespondenz* (*Berichte, Weisungen, Varia*), 1535–1848; *Varia*, 1396–1815; *Druckschriften*, 1763–78.

SONSTIGE SAMMLUNGEN VON ARCHIVALIEN VERSCHIEDENER HERKUNFT GROSSEN KORRESPONDENZ
(*Gesamtinventar* I, 587–94)

In addition to a fascicle titled *Korrespondenz Verschiedener*, 1742–95, there is correspondence of Fürst Wenzel Kaunitz, 1740–92; Graf Philipp Cobenzl, 1770–1810; Graf Franz Colloredo, 1757–1803; Baron Franz Thugut, 1775–1818.

Wiener Hofkammerarchiv

Formerly the *K. u. K. Gemeinsames Finanzarchiv*, the published guide to the *Hofkammerarchiv is Inventare Österreichischer Archive, VII: Inventar des Wiener Hofkammerarchivs* (Vienna, 1951). A few items relating to trade with the United States are listed in Faust, 252–3, in the series *Kommerz, Litorale*, which is described in the *Inventar*, 97–100.

29. *Kommerzhofstelle mit Sonderbeständen*, 1749–1830

4. *Litorale*, 1749–1813.

1776–7. 17 August 1776. 'America, Project ein Commerce dahin einzuleiten. Christoph Beller, Hauptmann des Fabrischen Regiments, machet den Vorschlag, hin nach America zu schicken, um alldort bei denen zwischen den Engländern und Colonisten obwaltenden Zwistigkeiten das Commerce zum Vortheil der k. k. Erblande einzuleiten.'

1780–1. 29 July 1780. 'America, wegen Verproviantirung der dortigen französischen Besitzungen von Seite der diesseitigen Handelsleuten.'

1782–3. 7 August 1783. 'Die Dahinsendung des Freiherrn von Beelen zur Beförderung des diesseitegen Handels.'

Österreichische Nationalbibliotek
Wien I, Josefsplatz

Formerly the Hofbibliotek, or Imperial Library, this institution is said by both Faust, 256, and David M. Matteson, *List of Manuscripts concerning*

American History preserved in European Libraries and noted in their Published Catalogues and similar Printed Lists (Washington, D.C., Carnegie Institution, 1925), 170, to contain a *Codex* which includes the following item: **12613.** (Suppl. 602), Ch. XVIII. 77f. 'Discours sur la grandeur et importance de la dernière révolution de l'Amérique septentrionale; sur les causes principales qui l'ont déterminée et sur son influence vraisemblable sur l'état politique et sur le commerce des puissances européenes . . .'

GERMANY

INTRODUCTION

At the time of the American Revolution Germany consisted of a number of states, the largest and most important of which were Prussia and Bavaria. Prussia remained neutral during the American war but some of the other German states provided much needed troops to the British for service in America. The historical sources in Germany for the American Revolution thus fall into two broad categories: that material relating to the British use of German mercenaries and that concerning the diplomatic role of Prussia.

Always low on manpower for military purposes, Britain had been contracting for German troops at least since 1752. The system had been well developed in the Seven Years War so that when the need for larger forces in the American colonies appeared in 1775, negotiations were both smooth and speedy. Contracts were made with the states of Hesse, Brunswick-Lüneburg, Hesse-Hanau, Anhalt-Zerbst and Anspach-Bayreuth. Hence there is a large body of records pertaining to the negotiations for these troops, their recruitment, organization, transport to and from America, and their reports, journals and orders in America. Apart from Prussia, the other German states had little contact with the colonies until their independence was an established fact in 1783, after which diplomatic and commercial negotiations were opened.

As Prussia had come close to disaster in the Seven Years War, Frederick II had no desire to antagonize his recent enemies, but was still eager to wring as much advantage as possible from Britain's difficulties. As had Maria Theresa of Austria, he forbade Prussian subjects from entering mercenary service, thus denying British recruiters access to the largest source of potential recruits in Germany. The outbreak of the war also interrupted the growing Prussian trade with America which Frederick had been carefully building through commercial treaties with Spain, France and Britain. Fully aware of this Prussian commercial interest, American agents early approached the Prussian Minister in Paris with commercial proposals, hoping in return to secure some sort of diplomatic recognition. There is a large body of material recording the negotiations between various American agents and the Prussian Minister of State, Schulenberg, showing how Frederick shrewdly tried to benefit Prussian trade without provoking his neighbours. In the end, however, Prussia maintained its neutral stance, participating in the Armed Neutrality of 1780, and giving diplomatic recognition to the United States only in 1783.

As a result of the damage and dislocations of World War II, the archives and libraries of both the German Federal Republic and the German Democratic Republic have been reconstituted and reorganized. There is no central archival administration in the German Federal Republic and no published general description of the archives, but for each archive of any significance there is usually a printed guide or inventory of post-war vintage. In the German Democratic Republic the Staatliche Archivverwaltung is responsible for the archives but there are far fewer published guides as yet.

Material for American history in Germany was first surveyed in Marion D. Learned, *Guide to the Manuscript Materials Relating to American History in the German State Archives* (Washington, D.C., Carnegie Institution, 1912). David M. Matteson, *List of Manuscripts concerning American History preserved in European Libraries and noted in their Published Catalogues and similar Printed Lists* (Washington, D.C., Carnegie Institution, 1925), surveyed the catalogues of a number of German libraries, while in 1929–30 Paul Weidman made another survey for the Library of Congress as a guide for the micro-filming of material. This last survey was never published and the present editors have not had access to a manuscript copy of it. These early works were followed in the post-war period by *Americana in Deutschen Sammlungen: Ein Verzeichnis von Materialen zur Geschichte der Vereinigten Staaten von Amerika in Archiven und Bibliotheken der Bundesrepublik Deutschland und West-Berlins.* (Deutschen Gesellschaft für Amerikastudien, 1967, 10 vols.). Hereafter cited as 'ADS', this work completely supercedes Matteson and almost completely supercedes Learned, whose main value now is that he gives on occasion a more detailed description of individual volumes or items than does ADS. As ADS covers only the German Federal Republic, Learned also retains some value as a guide to those archives now in the German Democratic Republic, although as will be discussed below, in only one case does there appear to be any significant material for the American Revolution in East Germany. It should also be noted that Learned's survey ignores Prussian participation in the Armed Neutrality.

Other useful reference works are Ludwig Denecke, *Die Nachlässe in den Bibliotheken des Bundesrepublik Deutschland* (Boppard am Rhein, Harald Boldt Verlag, 1969), and Wolfgang A. Mommsen, *Die Nächlasse in den deutschen Archiven* (Boppard am Rhein, Harald Boldt Verlag, 1971). A short discussion of the history and organization of archives in Bavaria can be found in L. Thomas and D. Case, *Guide to the Diplomatic Archives of Europe* (Philadelphia, University of Pennsylvania Press, 1959), 311–20.

The central records of Prussia were in pre-war days located in the Preussischen Geheimes Staatsarchiv in Berlin. Therein were contained the papers relating to diplomatic relations between the colonies and Prussia, Prussian policy, and participation in the Armed Neutrality. The standard guide to this archive was Archivverwaltung, *Übersicht über die Bestände des geheimen*

Staatsarchivs zu Berlin-Dahlem (Leipzig, 1934–9, 3 vols.). The material concerning the intercourse between Prussia and the American agents in Europe is described in Learned, 17–39, who also records that he made copies of many of these papers for the University of Pennsylvania. It is probable that the Library of Congress microfilming project of 1929–30 copied these documents as well.

During the war most of the archive was evacuated to salt and potash mines in central Germany, then fell into Soviet hands, and ultimately was turned over to the Deutsches Zentralarchiv (Deutsches Demokratisches Republik), Berlinerstr. 98–100, Potsdam. The Prussian records are now located in the Zentralarchiv, Abteilung II, Merseburg, Weisse Mauer, 48. There is as yet no published inventory of the Merseburg section. Some series were lost during the war, hence it cannot be certain that the papers pertaining to the American Revolution have survived. The part of the archive which was not evacuated from Berlin is now in the Berlin Hauptarchiv, Berlin 33, Archivstr. 12–14. ADS V, 1–16, records no material of any pertinence to the American Revolution in this archive.

The following survey is based on ADS with indications where Learned gives a more usefully detailed description. Printed works pertaining to the American Revolution listed in ADS have not been included nor have the extensive listings of material solely concerning emigration matters.

BADEN-WÜRTEMBERG

Badisches Generallandesarchiv, Nördliche Hildapromenade 2
Karlsruhe

(Rep.) Abt. 48 Haus- und Staatsarchiv. III. *Staatssachen, Diplomatische Correspondenz* (ADS X, 6)

Consulatsberichte. Anhang: Zeitungen aus London, 1748–69, 1774–7, 1782.

Hauptstaatsarchiv, Konrad-Adenauer-Str. 4
Stuttgart

(Rep. 202) *Geheimer Rat* (73. Gesandtschaften) (ADS X, 51)

37. Correspondence of William Romer in London, 1779–88.

BAYERN (BAVARIA)

Historischer Verein für Mittelfranken Regierung von Mittelfranken, Regierungsbibliothek
Ansbach

MS. Hist. **485–7.** Papers relating to the Anspach troops in America, 1777–95. (ADS IX, 140)

Bayr. Staatsarchiv, Hainstr. 39
Bamberg

(Rep.) A. 160. 3. Lade 596/3716 (ADS IX, 5. Learned, 204–5)

Original contract and one copy thereof for the hire of two Anspach regiments and one company. Anspach, 13 August 1778.

Amtsbibliothek des Staatsarchivs (ADS IX, 5)

73⁸, 75⁸, 77⁸, 78⁸, 531⁴. All miscellaneous items relating to troops in America, 1777–83.

(Rep.) C.5. *Geheime Landesregierung Bayreuth* (ADS IX, 6)

13. Journals of the two regiments in America, 1777.

Historische Verein für Oberfranken
Bayreuth

85, 85a, 100, 113. Daybooks and other papers of Bavarian troops in America, 1777–83. (ADS IX, 144)

Bayr. Hauptstaatsarchiv, Geheimes Staatsarchiv, Ludwigstr. 14
München

(Rep.) *Kasten Schwarz* (ADS IX, 38–9. Learned, 175 ff.)

4147. Documents relating to British-Bavarian relations, 1756–98.

4148. Petition of Munich merchants Mayer and Schwab concerning goods confiscated by Admirals Rodney and Vaugham.

7601–2. British affairs in 1776–7 during the ambassadorship of Count Seinsheim.

13879. French affairs, 1778–85.

13887. British affairs, Count Haslang, 1778–86.

15373. Correspondence of Lehrbach with Baron Reichlin in Vienna, 1776–86, with discussion of British recruiting in Germany.

15379. Letters concerning military operations in America.

15380–4. Reports and correspondence of Count Haslang, 1778–82.

15385. Haslang and Lerchenfeld from London, 1783.

15438–43. Reports of von Posch, Bavarian *chargé d'affaires* in Berlin, mentioning *inter alia* the reception of news from America.

16096. Correspondence of Hermant from Paris, 1777–9, including reports on Franco-British relations and the American war.

16137. Affairs in London by Count Haslang, 1782–3.

(Rep.) *Kasten blau* (ADS IX, 43)

354/7, 10, 12. Letters from the Bavarian ambassadors in Paris, London, Vienna, etc., 1760–83.

(Rep.) *Bayerische Gesandtschaft London* (ADS IX, 45–6)

241–60. Political correspondence, 1763–83.

434. Correspondence of Count Haslang with Count Seinsheim in Munich, 1778–83.

669. Return of confiscated goods to Bavarian merchants, 1781.

(Rep.) *Bayerische und Pfälzische Gesandtschaft Paris* (ADS IX, 48)

36. Political correspondence, 1777, reporting *inter alia* the arrival of Franklin and military operations in America.

Bayr. Hauptstaatsarchiv, Kriegsarchiv, Leonrodstr. 52/I
München

HS IV. 1. Daybook, 7 March 1777 to 3 June 1780, of Lt. von Feilitzsch of the Jäger Corps.

HS IV. **2.** Description of the North American campaign, 7 March 1777 to 9 December 1783, by Johann Ernst Prechtel.

HS V. **62.** History of the American service of the Eyb Regiment, including orders, reports, accounts, 1777–83.

(ADS IX, 109)

Bayr. Hauptstaatsarchiv, Staatsarchiv für Oberbayern, Himbelstr. 1
München

(Rep.) *H.R. Hofamts-Registratur* (ADS IX, 110)

Fasz. **299. 157.** Embassy in Britain, 1742–78.

Bayr. Staatsarchiv, Archivstr. 17
Nürnberg

(Rep. 105) *Verträge mit benachbartigen Reichsständen* (ADS IX, 126)

Verträge mit England. **1–3.** Contracts and related papers concerning the hire of Brandenburg troops, 1777.

(Rep. 165a) *Ansbacher Oberamtsakten* (ADS IX, 127)

1551. Documents concerning the quartering in Ketteldorf of Anspach –Bayreuth troops in British service.

(Rep. 212–18) *Bezirksämten, Bezirksamt Uffenheim* (ADS IX, 130)

125. Baggage transport, 1777.

(Rep. 233) *Akten den Kriegsregierung in Ansbach, insbesondere Ritterschaft-liche Akten* ADS IX, 131)

593. Documents relating to the supply of the Anspach forces, 1777–81.

Stadtarchiv
Ochsenfurt

The Ratsprotokollbuch for the 18th century contains several pieces on the embarkation of troops for America, 1777. (ADS IX, 169)

Archiv der Freiherrn von Rotenhan
Rentweinsdorf

This archive contains 'Die Berufreise der Generalin von Riedesel', a diary of her residence in America. (ADS IX, 175)

Stadtarchiv
Wunsiedl

Journal of Johann Conrad Döhla 'Marschroute und Beschreibung der Merkwürdigsten Begebenheiten in und aus Amerika 1777–1783.' (Published in *Archiv für Geschicte und Altertumskunde von Oberfranken*, 1912, and *Deutsch-Amerikanisches Magazin*, 1886. ADS IX, 182.)

Bayr. Staatsarchiv, Residenzplatz 2
Würzburg

(Rep. 77) *Aschaffenburger Archivreste* (ADS IX, 137)

MRA Hessen—KK **359**/966, 969, 970, 972; MRA Kasten **267**/13. All items relating to recruiting of troops and service in America.

(Rep.) *Gebrechen Amt* (ADS IX, 138)

VII. H. **39**/171, 174. Recruiting by Count Wertheim, 1781–2.

Anhang (ADS IX, 138. Learned, 217–18)

Miltärsachen. **95–8.** Papers concerning the Anspach troops in British service, 1777–9.

BREMEN
Archiv der Handelskammer, Haus Schütting
Bremen

B. 45 a, C. 48 d, e. Hannoversche Werbung; nach Amerika treibende Häuser in Bremen; eingekommene Schiffe, 1781–1824.

C. 76 b. Erste Expedition nach Amerika, 1782.

(ADS III, 117)

Staatsarchiv, 28 Bremen I, Präsident-Kennedy-Platz 2
Bremen

B.13.c.l.a. Verträge und Traktate mit den U.S.A. (ADS III, 37)
1. Discussion of the proposal made by Dr Johann Ulrich Pauli to conclude a commercial agreement with the US.

R.5. Militär-Sachen vor der französischen Zeit (ADS III, 54)
e. Werbungen. *B.1*—Braunscweig; *E.1*—English; *H.1*—Hessian; *W.1*—Waldeck; *W.2*—Wolfenbüttel; *D.19.e.*—Deserters.
n. Durchzüge fremder Truppen. Includes Hessians to America, 1776–83; newspaper clippings on the hiring of German troops for the American war, 1776–84; papers from the Registratur der Kgl. Hannoverschen Landdrostei zu Stade concerning the transit and quartering of foreign troops in the Hanover district, 1756–1802.

Ss.2. Handlung (ADS III, 70).
a.4. Tabellen über den Bremischen Warenhandel.
i.2.b. Angabebücher der auf der Weser ankommenden Schiffe und Ladungen, 1769–99.

HAMBURG
Staatsarchiv, Rathaus
Hamburg

Bestand. *Senat*

C1. VI., 16p. Vereinigte Staaten von Nordamerika (ADS II, 21. Learned, 279)
Vol. I. Generalia. Handelsverträge . . . Fasc. la. Pieces relating to the promotion of commercial relations with the US and compliments of the *Senat* to the US on its independence, 1783.

C1. VII. Lit. G⁸. Werbungen, Deserteure und fremde Soldaten (ADS II, 66–7)
Pars 1, **7.** Englische Werbungen hierselbst. *Vols. 4–5.* British recruiting, 1775–8.
Pars 1, **9a.** Hessische Werbung. *Vol. 1.* 1778, refusals of service in America.
Pars 2, **7a.** Hessische Deserteures. *Vol. 1. 1776,* arresting of deserters on the way to America.

Cl. VII. Lit. G^h. Einquartierungen und Durchmärsche.

12, *Vol. 2b.* Im hamburgischen Amte Ritzebüttel. Papers concerning the quartering and transport of Braunschweig and Hesse-Cassel troops, and the return of invalids during the war and the troops after the war, 1776–83.

Cl. VII. Lit. K^d. Neutralitas et Libertas Commercii (ADS II, 76–9. Learned, 272)

3. Hamburgs Neutralität während des amerikanischen Unabhängigkeitskriegen. *Vols. 1–9.* 1778–83, comprising regulations, certificates, correspondence with agents abroad, reports of privateers, and papers relating to neutrality as Spain and Holland enter the war.

Cl. VIII. 1. Protokolle der Admiralität (ADS II, 94. Learned, 273).

108–10. Specification aller in Hamburg angelangten Seeschiffe nebst deren Ladungen, 1778–80.

Cl. VIII. X. Protokolle des Senats (ADS II, 98–102)

Many reports on British recruiting, contraband, return of Hessian invalids, privateers, activities of the British resident Mathias, neutrality regulations, etc.

Bestand. *Amt Ritzebüttel I.* (ADS II, 464)

VII, Fach 7. *Vol. B.* Embarkation of Hanover and Braunschweig troops in British service, 1775–6.

Vol. C. Debarkation and transit of Hessian and Braunschweig troops, 1782–3.

Bestand. *Landschaft Ritzebüttel und Kitchspiele in Ritzebüttel* (ADS II, 466)

A.I. 4. Presence of foreign (Hanover and Hessian) troops in Ritzebüttel, 1775–6.

HESSEN
Archiv der Stadt, Schlossplatz 2
Hanau

IX. 1. *Militaria* (ADS VII, 241)

Allgemeine Verordnungen . . . Hanauisches Regiment in Amerika. Includes a printed ordnance of Crown Prince William of Hessia, 23 September 1776, concerning the reduction of taxes of relatives of soldiers serving in America.

Murhard'sche Bibliothek der Stadt Kassel und Landesbibliothek
Brüder Grimm-Platz 4A
Kassel

This library contains a rich collection of material concerning the Hessian forces in America, including many regimental journals, some regimental correspondence, some diaries and letters of officers and enlisted men, day books, field orders, etc. (ADS VII, 244–7)

Archiv der Stadt
Korbach

A I b 45. Verordnungen der Waldeckischen Regierung, 1709–1898.

A IV 1. Akten betr. Militär und Kriegslasten, 1666–1830.

A IV 29. Bekamtmachung betr. Pardon für Deserteure, 1784.

A IV 46. Werbung für das Bataillon Waldeck für Holland oder England, 1776, 1785.

The Nachlass Hanxleden/Huyn. Probably contains papers of General Huyn who served in one of the regiments in the American war.

(ADS VII, 248)

Bücherei des Hohhausmuseums
Lauterbach

This repository contains letters of Baroness von Riedesel from America, 1776–83. (ADS VII, 250)

Hessisches Staatsarchiv, Friedrichsplatz 15
Marburg

(Learned, 112 ff., has a good description of the material in this archive)

Bestand 4. *Politische Akten nach Landgraf Philipp*

a. Fürstliche Personalia. Landgraf Friedrich II (ADS VII, 28). Occasional pieces relate to the Hessian troops in the American war.

f. Staatenabteilung. England.

(a) Gesandtschaftsberichte (ADS VII, 30–2). **279** (1764–5) to **344** (1770–). Many reports and letters concerning Anglo-American relations.

(b) Akten (ADS VII, 32–3). Contains a few pieces on Hessian troops in America and on Col. Fawcett, British agent in Germany, 1776–81.

f. Staatenabteilung. Frankreich.

(a) & (b) Gesandtschaftsberichte und Akten (ADS VII, 33–4). **1711** (1776–7) onwards. Reports of the Ambassador to Paris, von Bode, on France and the American war, with related papers.

h. Kriegssachen (ADS VII, 34–8). This series contains the records of the Hessian forces in America, including regimental journals, order books, muster lists, reports, correspondence, accounts of the attack at Trenton, papers relating to recruiting and transport.

Bestand 5. *Hessischer Geheimer Rat* (ADS VII, 38–9)

This series contains a few items concerning orders and discipline for the Hessian troops in America., 1775–84.

Bestand 10. *Kriegsbehörden vor 1821* (ADS VII, 46–7)

a. Kriegskollegium und Vorbehorden:

Verz. 1. acc. 1906/I, **55**; and II, **6.** Cases of desertion.

Verz. 2. Subsidientraktate. **35–7, 39, 41,** 45a. Deals with the hiring of German troops by the British.

Bestand 11. *Militärkabinett mit General- und Flugeladjutantur* (ADS VII, 47–8)

Verz. 1. F 1. Feldzüge:

(b) Concerning recruiting, 1777–81.

(d) Concerning recruiting and military dependents, 1776–83.

Verz. 2. Mass- und Rangierbücher, Offiziers-Ranglisten, Grundbücher (ADS VII, 48–50). This sub-series contains muster books of 25 different regiments as well as officer lists.

Bestand 12b. *Kriegsministerium* (ADS VII, 50–7)

This series mostly concerns the payment of money by Britain for German troops, with some items on recruiting and desertion. There are also monthly reports on the state of the German regiments in America.

Verz. 11. Contains the day books and regimental journals of the German field command in America.

Verz. 13. Contains some miscellaneous material of similar nature.

Bestand 13. *Generalstab.* (ADS VII, 57–62)

This series consists of:

A. Kriegsakten, 6. Nordamerikanische Freiheitskriege, 1775–83. Contracts with the British and related papers; marching orders; recruiting lists; instructions to commanding officers; lists, reports, and journals; much correspondence with British ambassadors and ministers; etc.

D. Akten von einzelnen Regimentern, Korps und Truppenteilen, 1776–93. Documents pertaining to specific regiments.

F. Lebensbeschreibungen, Personalien, Ranglisten, Journale. Army lists of the Hessian army, 1732–96.

Bestand 81. *Regierung Hanau*

Repertorium E. (ADS VII, 80–3).
1. Generalia III. **4, 8, 9, 11, 13–17, 19, 22.** All items concerning recruiting.
2. Alstadt Hanau III. **3.** Papers concerning confiscation of property of deserters in America, 1784.
3. Neustadt Hanau XVIII. **2.** Concerns recruiting.
43. Amt Altenhaslau IX. **2.** Concerns transit of invalided troops from America, 1783.
55. Amt Bieber X. **3.** Recruiting, 1781; **7.** Confiscation of the belongings of a deserter, 1786.
129. Amt Steinau und Schlüchtern XI. **10.** Transit of troops returning from America, 1783.

Bestand 86. *Hanauer Nachträge*

Militaria. Amerkan. Feldzug (ADS VII, 89–90). **5393, 5395, 9671–4, 9701.** Various documents on the payment of troops, transit, embarkation, and debarkation in Bremen, 1776–86.

Bestand 118. *Waldeck. Kabinett* (ADS VII, 98–106)

a. Kabinett. This sub-series contains many items relating to the various aspects of the service of the Waldeck regiment in America, including muster rolls, annual reports of the state of the regiments, correspondence of agents in London, recruiting, personal dossiers of officers, etc.

Bestand 300. *Hessen-Rumpenheim* (Philippsruhe)

Verz. 2. Abteilung 11. Geheimes Kabinet. (ADS VII, 124). E 11. **6.** Correspondenz mit dem Ministerresidenten Capitän von Kutzleben in London, 13 vols., 1775–89. These reports are valuable for the British viewpoint on the war. Karten.

Verz. 6. Wilhelmshöher Kriegskarten (ADS VII, 125).
Band I. **62.** Plans of St Lucia, with positions of the French and British forces, December 1778.
Band 28. Plans of the North American war of 1775–82, containing over 100 items.

Westdeutsche Bibliothek, Universitätsstrasse 25
Marburg

F2e. 1752. Letter of Franklin, 9 September 1777, encouraging Prussia to trade in arms and clothing directly with America. Letter of Franklin and Deane, 10 September 1777, to Cornie et Fils, merchants of Morlaix.

2L2. 1789. Letter of Thomas Jefferson, 21 March 1780, recommending Edmund Clark as ensign in the 6th Virginia Regiment.

(ADS VII, 286–90)

Hessisches Hauptstaatsarchiv, Mainzer Strasse 80
Wiesbaden

Abt. 150 *Herrschaft Weilburg* (ADS VII, 127)
2664–5. British recruiting, 1776–97.

Abt. 350 *Nassau, Dreiherrisch* (ADS VII, 139)
Gen. VII a9. Departure of recruits and prohibition of foreign military service and recruiting in Nassau and Miehlen, 1771–83. Contains 'recruits for America with the Hessian troops'.

NIEDERSACHSEN (LOWER SAXONY)
Staatsarchiv, von Ihring-Strasse 17
Aurich

Rep. 28. *Landratsamt Emden*, 24a. *Schiffahrt; Generalia*, 158 (ADS IV, 12)

Verfugungen für die neutrale Schiffahrt, 1781–3.

Depositum I. *Ostfriesische Landschaft* (ADS IV, 15)

LVII. Militär- und Kriegssachen. **75, 166, 170, 171–3, 176.** All deal with recruitment and desertion, 1756–91.

Depositum IV. *Archiv der Fürsten zu Inn- und Knyphausen* (ADS IV, 15)

III. Akten einzelner Familienmitglieder. (m) Freiherr Wilhem zu Inn- und Knyphausen, landgräfl. Hessischer Generalleutnant. 2. News of the death of Knyphausen's wife in America, 1778.

Stadtarchiv
Buxtehude

B.V.A. **13.** Transit and quartering of Braunschweig troops en route to America, 1776–80.
14. Return transit of these troops, 1783. (ADS IV, 241)

Niedersächsishe Landesbibliothek, Am Archive 1
Hannover

Calenberger Brief-Archiv Des. 15. *Privatakten Band I* (ADS IV, 55)

F. **34.** Gift from His Royal Majesty to Col. Fawcett, 1776.

Han. Des. 41. *Akten des General-Commandos mit den Militär-Akten der Londoner Kanzlei* (ADS IV, 57–61)

V. Durchmärsche fremdherrlicher Truppen durch hannoversches Gebiet, 1776–80.

Vols. 1–5, 10. All contain material on the transport and recruitment of troops for the American war. Bodies of troops specifically mentioned are Anhalt-Zerbst, Anspach, Hanau, Hessian, Kurhessian, and Waldeck.

Han Des. 47. *Akten der Kriegskanzlei, 17.–19. Jahrhundert* (ADS IV, 61–2)

Abt. II, **113–16.** Reports of recruiting agents, quartering and transport, embarkation, and gift to Col. Fawcett.

Han. Des. 74.

Amt Bleckade (ADS IV, 63). Militaria I. Loc. 19, **4, 18.** Transport of Wolfenbüttel and Braunschweig troops, 1776.

Amt Blumenthal (ADS IV, 64). IX Polizeisachen, (A) Gewerbepolizei, *Fach. 233*, **6.** Release of some Hanover subjects seized aboard Dutch ships during the American war, 1781–99.

Amt Bremervörde (ADS IV, 64–5). H, *Fach 8*, **11–16.** Transit and maintenance of Hessian troops, 1776; return transit and maintenance of Hessian and Braunschweig troops, 1783–4.

Amt Grohnde (ADS IV, 69). V. Ab, **3.** Transit of Hessian troops in British service, 1776.

Amt Hagen (ADS IV, 70).

   Fach 1. Generalia, **25.** Orders concerning foreign recruiting, 1721–1881.
   Fach 44. Verpflegung fremder Truppen, **5–10.** Concern the transit and return of Hessian, Hanau, Hanover, Waldeck, Anspach and Braunschweig recruits and invalids, 1776–84.

Amt Osten (ADS IV, 74). I.M., **1.** Transit of Hessian troops, 1776.

Amt Otterndorf (ADS IV, 74). C. Loc. 4, **4.** Embarkation at Ritzebüttel of Hessian troops in British service, 1776.

Amt Rotenburg (ADS IV, 77). I.L. 7.d., *Fach 426*, **8.** Papers concerning the transit and return of Braunschweig, Hessian, and Anhalt troops, 1776–83.

Han. Des. 92. *Akten der Deutschen Kanzlei in London* (ADS IV, 94–5).

XXX, III, 10. Probable need for war *matériel* for the American rebellion in Hanover and neighbouring districts, 1775–7;
   11. Arrest of two American ships at Hamburg, n.d.

LXXV, **19d.** Peace preliminaries and treaties, 1783.

Archiv der Familie von der Wense
Holdenstedt

25. Quartering of Braunschweig troops in Holdenstedt, 1776. (ADS IV, 285)

Museumsverein für das Fürstentum Lüneburg
Lüneburg

Handwritten diary, 22 February 1776 to 20 June 1776, of an unnamed officer in Burgoyne's command. This officer was probably a Braunschweiger in the regiment of Prince Friedrich Dürchlaucht. (ADS IV, 289)

Staatsarchiv, Damm 43
Oldenburg

Aa. Herrschaft Jever. Abt. A., Tit. XXXIII.
17a, b. Passage of Anhalt troops to England, 1778–89.
18. Passage of troops returning from America, 1783–5.

Staatsarchiv, Schlossstrasse 29
Osnabrück

Rep. 100. Abschnittsarchiv. Abschn. 240, **19.** Transit of Hanover and Hessian troops, 1776. (ADS IV, 118)

Schulrat a.D. Karl Vogt, Dingelstedtwall 30
Rinteln

Among the manuscripts are 4 muster rolls of the Lossberg Regiment for 1776, on station in New York, 1782, 1783, and 1 for the Grenadier Company. (ADS IV, 330)

Gutsarchiv
Söder

Weihe, V.H. *Militär und Krieg*, **123.** Quartering of Hessian troops, 1776. (ADS IV, 333)

Staatsarchiv, Regierungsgebäude
Stade

Han. Des. 74: *Amt Blumenthal*, II, *Militaria. Fach 58*, **15.** Papers on the transit of Hessian and Waldeck troops, 1776. (ADS IV, 152)

Niedersächsisches Staatsarchiv, Forstweg 2
Wolfenbüttel

Urkunden Abt. 142. *Bündnisse, Verträge, etc.* (ADS IV, 163)

506–9. Contracts and related papers concerning the hiring of Braunschweig troops by George III, 1775–6.

Hs Abt. VI. *Fürstenhaus und Land betreffende geschichtliche, heraldische und juristische Handschriften* (ADS IV, 164–5)

Contains a number of diaries of officers in America and a list of officers in 1776.

Hs Abt. IX. *Urkunden, Darstellungen und Collectanean* . . . (ADS IV, 165)

11, item 3. G.S.A. von Praun's *Krieg zwischen England und Nordamerika 1776–1783.*

L Alt Abt. 7, 1¹¹. *Justizkanzlei II* (ADS IV, 166)

7¹¹. Von Riedesel, Friedrich Adolph, Oberst 1776.

L Alt Abt. 8,

Bd. 1. Amter Achim bis Fürstenberg (ADS IV, 166)
Campen, Gr. 25, **9.** Concerning the return of troops from America, 1783–4.

Bd. 2. Ämter Gandersheim bis Lutter a.B. (ADS IV, 166). Jerxheim, **178;** Lutter, a.B., **129, 503, 506.** All concern return or support of German troops in America, 1775–85.

Bd. 3. Ämter Neubrück bis Seesen (ADS IV, 167). Neubrück, **199.** Support of returned troops, 1783–4.

Bd. 4. Ämter Schöningen bis Warburg (ADS IV, 167). Staufenberg, **20.** Contains reports on soldiers disbanded and remaining in America, 1783–4.

Bd. 5. Ämter Wickensen bis Wolfenbüttel (ADS IV, 167). Wolfenbüttel, **967, 980.** Items pertaining to the support and return of troops, 1776–86.

L Alt Abt. 38B. *Ältere Militärsachen* (ADS IV, 168–71)

231–60. All items concerning recruiting, formation of corps for British service, letters and reports of officers from America (including many of von Riedesel), orders, muster rolls, etc.

N Abt. 7. *Depositum von Münchhausen,* 1 (ADS IV, 193–4)

III.e., 154. Letters and papers of the Hessian minister Moritz Friedrich von Münchhausen, including many letters to his brother Albrecht von Münchhausen in Braunschweig on political and military affairs, 1756–89.

155. Letters and papers of Borries Hilmar von Münchhausen, 1757–94, including news of the Hessian forces in America.

N Abt. 8. *Archiv der Ballei Sachsen und der Landkommande Lucklum des Deutschen Ritterordens* (ADS IV, 194)

Gr. II, **221.** Military service of Captain Freiherr von Wolzogen in America, 1781.

N Abt. **34.** *Vom Stadtmagistrate sowie aus Privatbesitz . . . Akten der Stadt Wolfenbüttel* (ADS IV, 194)

Gr. IV, **3–4.** Papers relating to the disbandment of troops serving in America, 1783.

N Abt. **783.** *Briefschaften und Akten des Generalleutnants von Riedesel, Freiherr zu Eisenbach* (ADS IV, 194–218)

II. Aus der Zeit des Nordamerikanischen Krieges. Papers of von Riedesel, mostly letters but some other documents as well.

Abt. Slg. **40.** *Namenweiser zur Verordnungssamlung,* 1 Ausf. (ADS IV, 218–19)

11–12. Contain numerous documents concerning the recruiting, transport and disbandment of Braunschweig troops in British service.

The library of the archive contains a number of printed works, mostly 19th-century, relating to the German troops in America. (ADS IV, 220 ff.)

NORDRHEIN-WESTFALEN
Landesarchiv, Regierungsgebäude
Detmold

Lippische Regierung. Ältere Registatur, *Fach 231*, **1.** Transit of the Hessian America corps, 1782–3. (ADS VI, 3)

RHEINLAND-PFALZ UND SAAR
Fürstliches Archiv
Neuwied

Schrank 2. Gefach 13.
Fasc. 1. French service of Graf Wilh. v. Schwerin, 1777–8.
Fasc. 2. Correspondence with von Schwerin during the campaign in America, 1779–82.
Fasc. 3. Other papers relating to von Schwerin.

(ADS VIII, 81a)

SCHLESWIG-HOLSTEIN

Konrektor Hans Jessen, Schleswiger Landstrasse 9
Eckernförde

He possesses papers of General Ewald who served in the American war, including memoirs of his America service. (ADS I, 45)

Archiv der Hansestadt Lübeck, St. Annenstrasse 2
Lübeck

Rep. 13 X. *Externa, Generalia und ausserdeutsche Staaten I. Vereinigte Staä-
ten von Amerika; Texas.* (ADS I, 2)

Vol. A. Handels- und Schiffahrtbeziehungen.
   Fasc. 1. Papers relating to the conclusion of a commercial treaty between
the Hanseatic towns and the free states of North America, 1782–4.

Stadtarchiv, Feuerwache, Ecke Jungfernstieg/Holstenstrasse
Rendsburg

IV.8. *Handel und Gewerbe.* (ADS I, 63)

54. Prohibition against sending munitions under Danish flag to the West
Indies, 1775.

56. West Indies commerce, 1777.

57. Tobacco trade, 1778–95.

Schleswig-Holsteinisches Landesarchiv, Schloss Gottorf
Schleswig

Abt. 11. *Regierungskanzlei* (ADS I, 9)

Reg. VI, **47a.** Prohibition of the munitions trade with the West Indies, 1776.
   50. Order concerning commerce with the Danish islands in America, 1777.

Nachlass von Knud Jungbohn Clement (ADS I, 36)

Manuskripte; Der Seeheld Paul Jones im Dienste der Vereinigten Staaten von
America. Nach authentischen Quellen, 31 pp.

ITALY

INTRODUCTION

During the period of the American Revolution, Italy consisted of a number of independent states and kingdoms. The Italian states took no direct part, either militarily or diplomatically, in the American war of independence but were intensely concerned, as were other neutral European states, about the effect of the war on the shape of European politics and power relationships. Italian statesmen thus watched the course of events in America and Europe carefully for its potential influence on their own states. The diplomatic correspondence of the major Italian states is generally quite rich in material concerning the American war as the ambassadors of these states were unsurpassed in the discovery and transmission of news. As Carl Fish has noted, the courts of Britain and France were scarcely better informed of the progress of events than were those of Italy. Italian material for the American Revolution is thus largely diplomatic correspondence which tends to be secondary in nature, often consisting of news culled from newsletters and other printed documents but also including reports of conversations and informed comment on policies as well.

This correspondence is now to be found in the State Archives of Italy and in the Vatican Archives. There are nineteen state archives, most of which correspond to the capital cities of former Italian states and which are administered by the Ministero dell' Interno. There is no national archive or central record office for the period before the unification of Italy. From that point the State Archive of Rome tends to be the national archive. In all public archives an open letter of introduction or document proving serious research intentions will suffice to gain admission.

A general introduction to the Italian State Archive system is L. Thomas and D. Case, *Guide to the Diplomatic Archives of Europe* (Philadelphia, University of Pennsylvania Press, 1959), 125–57, which also has a useful bibliography. A more detailed guide is Jose Gomez Perez, *Guia de los Archivos de Estado Italiano* (Madrid, 1961), which covers the state archives and their local sub-sections and has a thorough bibliography. Summary descriptive lists have been published in *Gli Archivi di Stato Italiani* (Bologna, 1944) and in a series of inventories, *Pubblicazioni degli Archivi di Stato*, in progress. Also of value is Luigi Schiaparelli *et al., Guida storica e bibliographia degli archivi e delle biblioteche d'Italia* (Rome, 1932–40, 6 vols.). The material relating to American history in the State Archives of Florence, Naples, Turin and Venice, and the Vatican Archives and libraries of Rome, has been cursorily surveyed in Carl R. Fish, *Guide to the Materials for American History in Roman and Other Italian Archives* (Washington, D.C., Carnegie Institution, 1911). David M. Matteson, *List of Manuscripts concerning American History preserved in European Libraries and noted in their Published Catalogues and similar Printed Lists* (Washington, D.C., Carnegie Institution, 1925) surveyed the catalogues of a number of Italian libraries for American material, but lists nothing of interest for the American Revolution. The following is a brief survey, based mainly on Fish and covering four State Archives, the Vatican Archives, and several libraries.

FLORENCE

Archivio di Stato, Palazzo degli Uffizi
Firenze

In this state archive the diplomatic material is located in the sub-section *Lorenese* (House of Loraine period, 1765–1800) in the series *Affari Esteri*. Much news and comment is included in the correspondence of the ministers to London, Paris and Madrid during the American war. The French material is richest in interest as the Sardinian minister was well acquainted with Franklin, from whom he received much of his news and in whom he apparently had implicit confidence. (Fish, 249. *Gli Archivi di Stato Italiani*, 67–106)

NAPLES

Archivio di Stato, Via Grand' Archivio
Napoli

This archive contains the diplomatic records of the Kingdom of Naples in its *Fondo Ministero Affari Esteri*. The material bearing on the American war is found in the correspondence and reports of the Neapolitan ministers to London, Paris and Madrid. The letters of Count Michele Pignatelli from London are of the most interest as he followed the war and English politics with great assiduity. (For a general description of this archive: *Gli Archivi di Stato Italiani*, 209–70. The following are listed by Fish, 233–5, as of interest for the American Revolution)

621. Inghilterra, no. 30. Letters of 1772–4, with some from 1783, on the Anglo-American dispute. Serious reporting of American news begins in May 1774, after which it forms most of the material.

623. Inghilterra, nos. 33, 34, 1779–80. Almost every letter pertains to America, including one, 28 March 1780, on the attempt of the King of Naples to mediate between Britain and Spain. When Caramanico succeeds Pignatelli as minister in London in 1780, the letters become less full and interesting but still contain much concerning neutrality and neutral trade.

1805. Spagna, no. 89, 1776–9 and 1809. Spagna, no. 91, 1779–80 contain some news of American ships in Spanish ports, Spanish neutrality before 1779, and privateering. The Neapolitan minister to Madrid confined himself quite closely to strictly Spanish affairs and does not seem to have had access to much confidential information at court, hence his letters are not that valuable.

The correspondence of the Neapolitan legation in France was not examined by Fish, but is known to be richer than either that of England or Spain for the period of the American Revolution, especially since Pignatelli became minister to France in 1780.

ROME

Archivi Vaticani, Città del Vaticano
Roma

The most recent and valuable guides to the Vatican Archives are K. A. Fink, *Das Vatikanische Archiv* . . . (Rome, 1951) and Leonard E. Boyle, *A Survey of the Vatican Archives and of its Medieval Holdings* (Toronto, Pontifical Institute of Medieval Studies, 1972), both of which completely supercede Gisbert Brom, *Guide aux archives du Vatican* (Rome, 1911). Thomas and Case, op. cit., 288–310, contains a general introduction to the archives, with bibliography, as does Gomez Perez, op. cit., 48–55. Material relating to American history in the Vatican Archives is surveyed by Fish, 20–100, but should always be checked against Fink or Boyle. Permission to work in the archives can be obtained on presentation to the Prefect of a letter from a university, library, or other institution of learning.

SEGRETARIA DI STATO

Like its neighbours, the Papal States maintained a highly effective system of diplomatic reporting through the *nunziatura* system. Hence the correspondence between the papal *nuncios* in Spain and France and the papal *Segretaria di Stato* is found in the archives of the Secretary of State, one of the eight main divisions within the Vatican Archives. It should be noted, however, that because of the peculiar organizational structure of the Vatican

Archives, the archives of the Secretary of State do not contain all the diplomatic records, hence the student may also have to refer to other parts of the archives.

The archives of the Secretary of State consist of three chronological sections: the *Fondo Vecchio*, the *Epoca Napoleonica*, and the *Fondo Moderno*. Covering the period to the end of the 18th century, the *Fondo Vecchio* has four main sections; *Nunziature e Legazioni, Lettere, Miscellanea,* and *Fondo Diverse*. The *Nunziature e Legazioni* series contain the correspondence of the papal diplomatic corps with the Secretary of State, with each other, and with individuals at the various European courts. These letters are filled with news of events and plans and constitute a valuable commentary on events in the country to which the respective *nuncios* were posted. The records of the *nuncios* in Spain and France are the most important in this respect for the period of the American Revolution.

Nunziature di Spagna (Fish, 66–8)

271. Letters from the *nuncio* to the Secretary of State, 1778–9. 17 February 1778, forwarding with comments a Spanish decree of 2 February on extending the free commerce to America. 10 July 1779, on the rights of neutrals. 10 July 1779, letters and enclosures concerning privateers. 13 July 1779, Spanish declaration of war on Britain with note from Floridablanca to the *nuncio* enclosed. 13 August 1779, letters and enclosures on the motives of the Spanish King in the war with Britain.

272. Letters from the *nuncio* to the Secretary of State, 1780. 25 January, 7, 28 March, cases and orders concerning neutral trade. 2 May, relations with Russia, enclosing a letter from Catherine II and the Spanish reply. 20 June, proclamation of 1 November 1779 recognizing the power of the French Consul in Morocco to act for the 'Etat de l'Amérique'. 27 June, 29 August, 17 October, 28 November, cases and discussion concerning neutral rights.

273. Letters from the *nuncio* to the Secretary of State, 1782–3. 3 April 1781, case of neutral rights with the discussion in the Spanish court. 5 February 1782, report on the military and political affairs of Spain. 11, 28 November, 23 December 1783, letters and enclosures concerning the peace treaty.

435. Letters of the Secretary of State to the *nuncio*, 1776–80. 5 August 1779, on Spanish regulations for privateers in the war with Britain. 6 January, 23 March. 25 June, 13, 27 July 1780, on maritime cases affecting the Papal States, including Dutch vessels. For replies to these cases, see **271–3** above. 21 September 1780, on the new rules of neutrality.

248–50, 251–84. Letters, registers of letters, and minutes of letters of the *nuncio*, 1743–97, which probably also contain some pertinent material.

Nunziature di Francia (Fish, 73–7)

462. 22 September 1779. To the *nuncio*, 'le notizie ch' Ella prosegue a darmi di quanto va' accadendo non meno in Europa che in America tra le armate navale delle Potenze Belligerenti, si sono veduto con piacere, come con gradimento'.

555. Letters from the *nuncio*, 1782. Almost all letters contain news of the war, with source indicated, and many enclosures of maps, public papers, etc.

556. Letters of the *nuncio*, 1783. Similar to **555.**

562. Ciphers from the *nuncio*, 10 July, 11 December 1775, concerning the war.

563. *idem*, 13 May 1776, reporting the British abandonment of Boston and retreat to Halifax.

564. *idem*, 30 September, 14, 21 October, 12, 18 November, 2, 16 December 1776, all contain war news. 25 November 1776, on the neutrality of France. 16 December 1776, on the arrival of Franklin.

565. *idem*, 1777. 27 January, enclosure of the Declaration of Independence. 3 March, on Stormont and the insurgents and the capture of General Lee. 7, 14 April, 19 May, departure of Lafayette.

566. *idem*, 1777. 10 November, defeat of Washington on 11 September. 24 November, capture of Burgoyne.

567–9. *idem*, 1778. Much diplomatic and war news.

570. *idem*, 1780–1. Same.

The following may also contain enclosures and reports concerning the American war:

    448–9, 454, 454A, 456, 460, 462. An irregular series of letters to the *nuncio*, 1758–84.

    449A, 450A, 453, 455, 455A, 461, 461A. An irregular series of ciphers to the *nuncio*, 1758–79.

    451, 463A. Notes to the French Ambassador, 1758–94.

DE PROPAGANDA FIDE

One of the twelve sacred congregations of the Papacy, the *Propaganda Fide*, was responsible for the areas of the world considered to be missionary territory, of which the American colonies were one. Its archives are kept in the Palazzo della Propaganda, Piazza di Spagna, Roma. Permission of the Congregation must be obtained to examine the archives. (Fink omits this congregation but see Boyle, 84 ff. The following American items are listed by Fish, 170.)

Scritture Referite Nei Congressi

America Centrale, dal Canada al 'Istmo di Panama, dal 1776 al 1790. II.
ff. 186–7. 10 February 1783, from the *nuncio* at Paris on his efforts to guarantee religion in the peace negotiations and on his conversations with Franklin.
ff. 193–8. 1 July, 27 September 1783, from the *nuncio* in Paris on the same subject.
ff. 206–11. 1 September 1783, from the *nuncio* in Paris on the same subject.
f. 213. Note of the *nuncio* in Paris to Franklin.

(With the exception of *ff. 193–8*, these have all been printed in *American Historical Review* XV, 4, July 1910, 805–7)

Istruzioni

1. *ff. 41–4.* 15 January 1783, to the *nuncio* at Paris concerning the peace negotiations. (Printed in *American Historical Review*, op. cit., 801)

GARAMPI COLLECTION

6. Unbound papers in paste-board covers. N. 'Nota Ministeriale della Cose d'Inghilterra, e di Parigi, e notizie risguardante la Guerra dell' America, delle Provincia Unite', by Sig. Abb. de la Seria to Mons. Caleppi in Florence. 3 January 1778, News from Paris, 3 pp. 'Franklin nous promet dans la dixaine de grandes Nouvelles, il faut avouer que jusques ici il a tenu parole.'(Fish, 97)

Biblioteca Nazionale Centrale Vittorio Emanuele di Roma, Via del Collegio Romano
Roma

The *Fondo Gesuitico* of this library, **269.** or **2398.**, *ff. 275–308*, contain a letter, 15 June 1778, relating to the Anglo-Spanish controversy over the seizure of British ships in America. (Fish, 218)

Biblioteca Vaticana, Città del Vaticano
Roma

The Vatican Library is a separate entity from the Vatican Archives. The original nucleus of the Vatican Library is also designated *Biblioteca Vaticana* and is a continuous numerical series to which new acquisitions are still added. Fish, 118, notes the following item:

Vat. Lat. **10364**. 'Differenza fra l'Inghilterra e le Colonie dell'America,' 436 pp. Extracts and summaries of such news and documents relating to America as the collector, Mgr Lazzarini, was able to gather, but nothing of unique interest.

TURIN

Archivio di Stato Sezione Prima, Piazza di Castello 205
Torino

This archive contains the records of the Kingdom of Sardinia and Piedmont whose ministers were quick to note the importance of the American Revolution. Nearly every letter of the Sardinian Minister to London, Cordon, contains news and informed discussion of events. (For a general description, see *Gli Archivi di Stato Italiani*, 406–48; for some comment on the American material, see Fish, 247–8)

VENICE

Archivio di Stato, Campo dei Frari
Venezia

The records of the Republic of Venice are housed in this archive. (There is a printed guide by A. da Mosto, *L'Archivio di Stato di Venezia*, Rome, 1937–40, 2 vols. but it is cursory and not always to be relied on. There is a general description in *Gli Archivi di Stato Italiani*, 486–542, while the America-related material is dealt with in very summary fashion by Fish, 238–44)

CORTE

This series contains official copies of letters and dispatches addressed to ambassadors and other officials.

160. 1783, *f. 160*. Letter of 30 August to the Ambassador in France, approving his conduct regarding the call of Franklin.

DISPACCI AL SENATO

This series contains the well-known dispatches of the Venetian ambassadors to the senate. (*Archivi di Stato di Venezia: Dispacci degli Ambasciatori al Senato*, Roma, Pubblicazioni degli Archivi di Stato, 1959, XXX).

Francia

250. 1764–6. Dispatch, 16 September 1765, reports agitation in America over the failure of England to prevent exclusion of English goods from the French West Indies.

257. 1776–8. The largest amount of material is news concerning all aspects of the war, with copies of many documents. Some items relate to Franklin and American diplomacy in Europe.

259. 1780–2, **260.** 1782–4. Apart from much war news, there are some reports on the manoeuvres surrounding the peace negotiations and a few on the revival of trade.

Inghilterra

126. 1773–5. is the only volume listed by Fish and contains some reports concerning America in British politics and the character of American resistance.

Spagna

179. 1776–9. The reports contain much concerning the war at sea and on Spanish relations with France and Britain. Many Spanish documents concerning the war are enclosed.

180. 1779–81. There is much material on neutral rights, the Armed Neutrality, naval engagements, the Cumberland mission, Jay in Madrid, and the recognition of American independence by Spain.

RUSSIA

INTRODUCTION

The Soviet Union maintains a highly centralized system of state archives but most of these repositories now lack adequate published guides. Earlier guides, including such pre-revolutionary guides as existed, have never been brought up to date despite considerable archival reorganization, transfers of documents, and acquisitions. There are, however, a number of reference works in both English and Russian to which the researcher can turn. The most important of these is Patricia K. Grimsted, *Archives and Manuscript Repositories in the USSR: Moscow and Leningrad* (Princeton, Princeton University Press, 1972). This up-to-date and authoritative work contains a wealth of information on the development and organization of archives, access to records, research conditions, finding aids, an extensive annotated bibliography on archives and research aids, and description of major archives and repositories. Paul L. Horecky, *Libraries and Bibliographic Centers in the Soviet Union* (Indiana University Publications, Slavic and East European Series 16, 1959), provides more detailed information on some of the major libraries, such as the Lenin State Library in Moscow and the Saltykov-Shchedrin State Library in Leningrad. Frank A. Golder, *Guide to Materials for American History in Russian Archives* (Washington, D.C., Carnegie Institution, 1917), is useful only for description of material in various individual fonds since the archives which he surveyed no longer exist.

The only general handbook of archives ever published in the Soviet Union is G. A. Belov, A. I. Loginova, S. V. Nefedova, and I. N. Firsov, eds., *Gosudarstvennye arkhivy Soiuza SSR. Kratkii spravochnik* (Moscow, Glavnoe arkhivnoe upravlenie pri Sovete ministrov SSR, 1956). Although somewhat dated now as a result of subsequent reorganizations, this work covers the nine central state archives as well as state archives on the *krai*, *oblast*, and republic levels. L. E. Shepelov, *Arkhivnye razyskaniia i issedovaniia* (Moscow, Izd-vo 'Vysshaia shkola', 1971), is especially useful for researchers working in the 18th century because in addition to describing archival organization, classification methods, and reference publications, this work also describes Russian administrative organization with reference to pre-revolutionary state documentation, its current locations and classification schemes. A last Soviet reference work worth noting here is E. V. Kolosova *et al.*, comps., and Iu. I. Gerasimova *et al.*, eds., *Lichnye arkhivnye fondy v gosudarstvennykh khranilischakh SSR. Ukazatel'* (Moscow, Soviet Academy of Sciences, Lenin State Library, and Main Archival Administration, 1962–3, 2 vols.). This is a direc-

309

tory of personal and family papers in state repositories which covers the holdings of many archives and libraries.

The question of access is always uncertain for foreign researchers in the Soviet Union. The authorities have traditionally viewed archival research, especially by foreigners, not as an unrestricted public right but as a special privilege. The facilitating of scholarly research is a function definitely subordinate to the primary archival function of protecting and preserving documents. Policies concerning access were ostensibly liberalized in the late 1950s and early 1960s but are still qualified by limiting access to documents which are deemed to affect the interests of the state or of individual citizens. Generally, material up to and including the 18th century is open, but the date of documents is usually not the governing factor controlling access to them. The nature of the topic, who the researcher is, and the interest of the state are all reasons bearing on refusal. Diplomatic, political, economic, and military matters are considered sensitive even in the 18th century. It should also be noted that in Soviet state archives, the archival officials have the right and obligation to choose which documents individual foreign readers should be shown for their topics. The Foreign Ministry, military and naval records are well guarded from foreigners and their pre-revolutionary records have been open for only a few carefully selected topics.

Application to do research must be made through appropriate bureaucratic procedures. Normally archival research is limited to scholars participating in one of the educational exchange programmes of the Soviet Union. In such cases, formal arrangements for research are made by the appropriate office of the scholar's host institution in consultation with his Soviet adviser. It is next to impossible for a person not part of an official exchange programme to carry out archival research. In the United States, arrangements for scholarly exchange are handled by the International Research and Exchanges Board, 110 East 59th Street, New York, N.Y. 10022, from which further information on academic exchanges can be obtained. In Britain, information on postgraduate student exchange can be obtained from the Universities Department, British Council, State House, High Holborn, London WC1. Exchange arrangements for university staff members are administered by the Committee of Vice-Chancellors, 29 Tavistock Square, London WC1.

The Russian role in the American Revolution was almost entirely diplomatic, involving first the efforts of the British to hire Russian troops for service in America, then Russian attempts to mediate, and the Armed Neutrality of 1780. The relevant material thus lies in the records of the 18th-century College of Foreign Affairs. The Armed Neutrality theoretically involved naval patrols, hence the records of the Russian navy may also contain marginally relevant material. For these reasons, only the archives of the Foreign Ministry and of the Navy are here discussed.

LENINGRAD

Tsentral'nyi Gosudarstvennyi Arkhiv Voenno-Morskogo
Flota SSR, ulitsa Khalturina, 36
Leningrad

This archive contains the records of the College of the Admiralty from 1718 to 1827. These comprise material concerning the activities of the Russian fleet and the chancellery papers of many important naval leaders of this period. (There is no published guide. The most recent Soviet description is in G. A. Belov *et al.*, op. cit.; see also Grimsted, op. cit., 138–42). The archive is officially closed to foreign readers, but documents from some of the earlier historical *fonds* are occasionally made available to them in the reading room of the *Tsentral'nyi gosudarstvennyi istorecheskii arkhiv SSSR*.

MOSCOW

Arkhiv Vneshnei Politiki Rossii
Bol'shaia serpukhovskaia ulitsa, 15
Moscow

All the official diplomatic records back to the reign of Peter the Great are under the control of the Foreign Ministry and hence outside the governance of the Main Archival Administration. The archives of the Foreign Ministry are divided into two sections: the *Arkhiv vneshnei politiki SSSR*, comprising the post-revolutionary diplomatic records; and the *Arkhiv vneshnei politiki Rossii* (AVPR), consisting of the diplomatic records of the Russian Empire from 1721 to 1917. The 18th-century division of AVPR contains the records of the College of Foreign Affairs which were formerly in the pre-revolutionary *Moskovskii glavnyi arkhiv Ministerstva inostrannykh del.* (Golder, op. cit., 149–50, briefly mentions the diplomatic records for the years 1776–83, which pertain to the Anglo–Russian negotiations over troops, Russian mediation, and the Armed Neutrality. Golder's article 'Catherine the Great and the American Revolution', *American Historical Review* XXI, 1915, 92–6, gives a further indication of the nature of these records).

There is no general guide or published description of AVPR but a survey of the 18th-century *fonds* of the pre-revolutionary *Moskovskii glavnyi arkhiv Ministerstsva inostrannykh del*, now in AVPR, can be found in Part I, V.N.

Shumilov *et al.*, comps., and S. K. Bogoiavlenskii, ed., *Tsentral'nyi gosudarstvennyi arkhiv drevnikh aktov. Putevoditel'* (Moscow, Glavnoe arkhivnoe upravlenie pri Sovete ministrov SSR, 1946). This work also lists publications and other descriptive literature about these fonds.

Few western scholars have been given access to this archive, although access for the 18th century has been somewhat easier than for later periods. Card catalogues, shelf lists and inventories are not available to researchers for consultation. The documents which a researcher may consult are ordinarily chosen by the archival staff. For a general discussion of the archives of the Foreign Ministry, see Grimsted, op. cit., 248–55.

SWEDEN

INTRODUCTION

The involvement of Sweden with the American Revolution revolves partly round the attitude and diplomacy of Gustav III and partly round the officers and men who served with the various armies engaged. Gustav was initially quite interested in the American Revolution which aroused considerable public discussion in Sweden. Later Gustav appears to have developed a strong aversion to the Americans, coincident with the growth of his personal conservatism. The tendency of the political opposition in Sweden to idealize the American Revolution can only have added to his personal animus.

At the same time Gustav was interested in obtaining such advantage as he could from the European political situation, specifically defined as retrieving the lost territories of Bremen and Verden. He considered French intervention in the American war a mistake when the War of Bavarian Succession offered more concrete possibilities for France and her ally-client Sweden. This line of diplomacy was ended by the Treaty of Teschen of 1779, but by this time Gustav was already playing an active role in the diplomacy leading to the Armed Neutrality of 1780, of which Sweden was a member. In 1782 Gustav advanced a plan for mediation between France and Britain and at the same time was negotiating a treaty of commerce and friendship with Congress. There was a Swedish consul in New York from 1780. Swedish trade with America during this period has yet to be studied but was not negligible.

At least fifty Swedish officers served with the British navy and a number more with the French fleet, while a few found their way to the Continental forces. The motivation for such service was practical rather than ideological because the Swedish aristocracy was essentially a service nobility and, after a prolonged period of peace, it was in straightened circumstances. Thus, for example, Baron von Stedingk was forced by financial exigencies into service with d'Estaing, while Count von Fersen is known to have deemed a change of venue prudent after being linked romantically with Marie Antoinette and hence joined Rochambeau's staff. Perhaps the largest group of officers and men, however, served with the Dutch navy from 1780 where opportunities were better and discrimination less than with the British or French.

To the records of Swedish diplomacy and Swedish mercenaries must be added those of the Swedish mission in America. In the revolutionary period these records consist largely of letters and journals of ministers commenting on the effect of the war on the Swedish communities and the life of the church.

313

For an introduction to Swedish libraries and archives the student can turn to Gösta Ottervik *et al., Libraries and Archives in Sweden* (Stockholm, The Swedish Institute, 1954). L. Thomas and D. Case, *Guide to the Diplomatic Archives of Europe* (Philadelphia, University of Pennsylvania Press, 1959), 263–78, also have a useful discussion. For the memoirs and letters of Swedish soldiers and missionaries, Esther E. Larson, *Swedish Commentators on America, 1639–1865. An Annotated List of Selected Manuscript and Printed Materials* (New York, The New York Public Library and Chicago, The Swedish Pioneer Historical Society, 1963) is a valuable introduction. Old but also still important is Samuel E. Bring, *Bibliografisk handbok till Sveriges historia* (Stockholm, 1934), which has a good account of the contents of various archives, a bibliography of published diplomatic correspondence, and lists of guides to archival material.

STOCKHOLM

Kungl. Biblioteket, Box 5039
102 41 Stockholm 5

The Royal Library is the national library of Sweden and contains the following materials according to Larson, op. cit.

3 letters, jointly composed by the Revs. Collin, Girelius and Hultgren, 1780–4, to Archbishop Mennander, on the impossibility of continuing the mission because of war conditions and the assimilation of the Swedish population.

Untitled manuscript of Carl Olof Cronstedt (1756–1820), who served as a midshipman on a British frigate and later became admiral and Marshal of Sweden. Summary of his service in America from 13 October 1776 to 8 September 1778. Captured 1776, describes condition of Continental Army as he saw it, exchanged, subsequent actions in West Indies, New York, Harbour and Delaware Bay; fete in honour of Gen. Howe's departure. (Published in Wilhelm Odelberg, *Vice Admiral Carl Olof Cronstedt's Levnadsteckning och Tideskildring*, Helsingfors, 1954. Partially translated and published in Amandus Johnson, *Swedish Contributions to American Freedom, 1776–1783*, Philadelphia, 1953.)

Letter of the Rev. Anders Goransson, 14 March 1776, from Philadelphia on the relation of the colonies to England, the Continental Congress, the post office under Franklin, the Whig Party, the desire of the colonies for independence, the *Common Sense* pamphlet, etc.

Manuscript of the Rev. Matthias Hultgren, 'Anteckningar om America', 1000 pp., 7 vols. *I.* The colonization of North America; *II.* Notes about politics in North America, natural resources, topography, Indians, and finances; *III.* Climate and natural history; *IV.* Religious affairs; *V.* Literature, industry, commerce; *VI.* Federal and state governments; *VII.* Revolutionary war.

Manuscript of Otto Henrik Nordenskjöld (1747–1832), an officer serving with the fleets of de Vaudreuil and de Grasse. 'Berättelse on Kriget, 1778, 1779, 1780', 92 pp. Describes action on the *Fendant* under de Vaudreuil; the storming of Savannah; care of the sick and hospitable Americans at Yorktown; military engagements and naval manoeuvres in the Chesapeake Bay area.

Manuscript of Johan Herman Schützercrantz (1762–1821), an officer in British service, 1778–9, and in French service, 1780–1. 'Lefvernesbeskrifning Johan Herman Schützercrantz, Kontre-amiral, 1762–1821.' Brief autobiography describing the spring of 1781 with de Grasse at Chesapeake, news of Cornwallis, and the siege of Yorktown.

Manuscript of Frid. Crist. Sternlow (1729–?), a seaman in British service, 1777–9, and in American service, 1779. 'Utkast till en Beskrifning om Mina Sjö–resor Upsat of Mig Sjelf. Frid. Crist. Sternlow pa Fogelvik, ar 1794', 56 pp. and notes. Describes his experience on the British *Annapolis*, his capture and imprisonment at Boston, his service aboard the American ship *General Washington*, and comments on America.

Copy of a printed book *Grefve Grasses Siö-batailler, och Krigs-operationerna uti Vest Indien, ifran Början af år 1781 till Krigets Slut;* . . . , Stockholm, 1781, 107 pp. Covering the period January 1781 to April 1783, the book describes the landing near Hampton, Va.; the siege of Yorktown; has diagrams of naval battles; personal records of Swedish officers serving with the French fleet. (Translated by Amandus Johnson, *The Naval Campaigns of Count de Grasse during the American Revolution, 1781–1783*, Philadelphia, 1942.)

Manuscript of Hans F. Wachtmeister (1752–1807), a naval officer in service with the British fleet, 1775–7, later Rear Admiral of the Swedish navy. 'Utdrag af en Journal, Kallen 1775–1778 pa Engelska Fregatten, Phoenix, under en Resa fran England till New York i Norra Amerika samt under Kriget därstädes, med Anmärkningar', in collaboration with Herman F. von Walden, another Swedish officer serving with the British. Extracts from a journal, 4 August 1775 to 13 December 1776: the summer expedition up the Hudson River; battle at New York, 22 August 1775; Cape Cod, November 1775; naval manoeuvres near New York, December 1775; first-hand accounts of battles and unflattering remarks on the conduct of Americans. (Translated as Wilhelm Odellberg, Nils W. Olsson, and Paul Varg, 'Two Swedes under the Union Jack, A Manuscript Journal from the American War of Independence', *Swedish Pioneer Historical Quarterly* VII, July 1956, 83–120)

Kungl. Vetenskapsakademien
S–104 05 Stockholm 50

Papers of the Rev. Nils Collin. Consists of 4 letters, 1773–5, from Philadelphia and Raccoon, to P. J. Bergius, botanist, with some comment on democratic trends in America; 5 letters, 1774–1826, from Philadelphia and Raccoon to Prof. J. J. Berzelius, discussing *inter alia* the blockade of 1775, and why war would be fatal for both America and Britain; manuscript 'Relation om Norra Amerika, 1775', 48 pp. This document sets out the reasons for the conflict between the colonies and Britain; discusses the colonies in terms of climate, customs, commerce, religion, government; gives the prospects for the colonies in terms of army, defence, religious conflicts, and general unrest; asks if Britain can govern the colonies later if she subdues them now.

Riksarkivet, Fyrverkarbacken 13–17, Fack
100 26 Stockholm 34

The Riksarkivet is the central depository for government records in Sweden. For the study of Swedish diplomacy during the American Revolution, the Registers of Foreign Affairs, archives of the Cabinet of Foreign Affairs, and archives of the Chancery Council provide the main material. The Registers are a chronological record and copy of all correspondence expedited by the foreign secretaries of the Chancery. The archives of the Chancery Council contain special dossiers on the international problems of the time, filed according to subject matter. There are also diaries, consisting of chronologically arranged summaries of in- and out-letters. In addition, the papers of most ministers and many diplomats have been deposited, as have those of members of the Royal family, with the exception of Gustav III (for which see *Uppsala University Library*).

The Riksarkivet is covered by a card catalogue kept in the reading room, while such inventories as are published appear in *Meddelanden fran Riksarkivet*. There is no general handbook or guide.

The following material is contained in the Riksarkivet, according to Larson, op. cit.

Manuscript of the Rev. Anders Goransson. 'Joint testimony with John Stille, "Prices of Eatables after the arrival of English troops in Philadelphia. Price of Eatables and Clothing in Congress Time".'

Manuscript of Samuel G. Hermelin (1744–1820), sent by Gustav III in 1782–4 to study American industry and the commercial and diplomatic possibilities for Sweden. 'Berättelse om Handeln och Bergwärcken i Amerika, 1783', 56 pp., dated Philadelphia, 15 October 1783. Descriptions of iron ore fields, mountain ranges, forests; statistics on imports and exports; notes on varying standards of currency in the colonies; wages and prices. (Published as Amandus Johnson, 'Report about the Mines in the United States of America, 1783', *Swedish–American Historical Bulletin* IV, February, 1931, 7–54)

Manuscript of Samuel G. Hermelin, 'Berättelse om Nord-amerikas Förenade Stater, 1784', 74 pp. 4 letters addressed to the Chancellor, giving descriptions of the thirteen colonies, the division of the western lands into states, Indian problems, boundary disputes, tax problems, treatment of loyalists, and maintenance of the army and diplomatic corps. (There is a printed edition of 1894 held by the Riksarkivet, the Library of Congress, and the New York Public Library)

Correspondence of Curt B. L. von Stedingk (1746–1837), a naval officer serving with d'Estaing, 1778–9, and later Field-Marshal and Minister.

Letter, 2 November 1780, from Forbach, France, to his family concerning the storming of Savannah and his return to Europe after being wounded.

3 letters from Paris to Carl Sparre: 2 letters, 1780, in which he is pessimistic about the war, fearing that the American cause will collapse and that they will make peace; 1 letter, 1783, in which he considers the peace terms a triumph for Franklin.

(These letters have been printed in Hans von Dardel, *Fältmarskalken von Stedingks tidigare Levnadsöden. Skildrade efter Brev till Överstathallare Carl Sparre,* Örebro, 1922)

UPPSALA
Landsarkivet i Uppsala
Uppsala

Papers of the Rev. Nils Collin. 4 letters jointly composed by Collin and his associates Girelius and Hultgren, 1781–4, from Wilmington, Philadelphia and Raccoon to the Uppsala Consistory, setting forth the effect of the war on the mission and asking for recall because of war hazards, lack of food and clothing, etc. Manuscript 'Dagbok av Nils Collin, 1770–1782', 272 pp. A diary of sorts dealing mainly with the effect of the war on the church, his imprisonment by the militia, the behaviour of the English and American soldiers, etc. (Published as Amandus Johnson, *The Journal and Biography of Nicholas Collin, 1746–1831*, Philadelphia, 1936)

Manuscript of the Rev. Matthias Hultgren. 'Dagbok av Prosten Hultgren, 1779–1786', 14 pp. Mainly day-to-day items, some description of the condition of the church in 1779.

Letter of the Rev. Johan Wiksell, 6 March 1775, from Stockholm to the Uppsala Consistory, in which he foresees possible independence for the colonies, trade possibilities for Sweden, and discusses the relation of the mission to proprietors. A long letter of general interest on the times.

Uppsala Universitetsbiblioteket
Uppsala

This library contains all the papers and correspondence of Gustav III and the following items drawn from Larson, op. cit.

3 letters of Pehr U. Lilliehorn (1752–1806), who was probably an adjutant to Rochambeau, 1781–3. All are to Gustav III: 26 September 1782, from Philadelphia, describing a naval engagement where he served on a ship commanded by de Vaudreuil; 12 October 1782, from New York, describing the devastation of New York state and paying tribute to Washington after being presented to him; 20 December 1782, from Boston, lauding Rochambeau. (Extracts published in Johnson, *Swedish Contributions to American Freedom*, op. cit.)

Manuscript of Adolf F. Rosensvard (né Pettersén) (1753–99), a naval officer in the fleet of d'Estaing. 'Utdrag av Journal Hallen under Belägringen av Pensacola, 1781', 11 pp. Journal dated Pensacola, 25 May 1781, describing operations of the French and Spanish forces against the British and Indians. (Johnson, *Swedish Contributions to American Freedom*, op. cit., contains his report to the Admiralty on the same subject)

Letters of Curt von Stedingk to Gustav III, 1780, describing the expedition against Savannah, battle plans, weakness and warweariness of the Americans and their need for help. (These letters plus much additional material have been published in Général Comte de Björnstjerna, *Mémoires posthumes du feld maréchal, comte de Stedingk, rédigés sur des lettres, dépêches et autre pièces authentiques laisées à sa famille*, Paris, 1844–7.)

PRIVATELY-HELD MANUSCRIPTS

Although no inventory of privately held manuscripts has yet been undertaken in Sweden, there are other relevant papers in private hands. For example, the papers of General M. F. F. Björnstjerna, Swedish Ambassador to Britain, 1772–99, are at the Almare-Staket estate in Uppland; while the papers of Count Hans Axel von Fersen, adjutant to Rochambeau, 1780–2, and later Marshal of Sweden, are at Löfstad, Östergötland. There are a number of published collections of Fersen's letters, including those from America (see Larson, op. cit., 58–61, for a critical listing).

GENERAL INDEX

Abercairny Collection, 129
Aberdeen Town Council, 121
Abergavenny, Marquess of, 18
Adam, Captain C. K., 126
Addington, Dr. Anthony, 40
Additional Manuscripts, British
  Museum, 25 et seq.
Admiralty, 65
  High Court of, 67
Aix-en-Provence, 170
Albemarle Papers, 111
Algemeen Rijksarchief, The Hague, 152
Allen & Hanburys Ltd, 23
Allen, Ethan, 71
All Souls College Library, Oxford, 104
Alman, M., xxii, xxiii, 4
Amcotts Deposit, 23
American Museum in Britain, The,
  Bath, 108
Amiens, 171
Amity and Commerce, Treaty of, 221
Amsterdam, 150
André, Brigadier J. R. C., 112
André, Major John, 112
Andrews, Charles M., 4, 64
Angers, 171
Angus, 122
Anhalt-Zerbst, 282
Ansbach, 285
Anspach-Bayreuth, 282
Antrim, 139
Archiv der Handelskammer, Bremen, 288
Archiv der Familie von der Wense,
  Holdenstedt, 296
Archiv der Freiherrn von Rotenhan,
  Rentweinsdorf, 288
Archiv der Hansestadt Lübeck, 300
Archiv der Stadt, Hanau, 290
Archiv der Stadt, Korbach, 291
Archives administratives, Val de Marne,
  245
Archives and History of North Carolina,
  Office of, 5
Archives de la Bastille, 233
Archives de la Ministère de la Guerre,
  Vincennes, 239
Archives du Ministère des Affaires
  Etrangères, Paris, 178
Archives départementales de la Côte
  d'Or, Dijon, 174
Archives départementales de la Gironde,
  Bordeaux, 174

Archives départementales d'Ille-et-
  Vilaine, Rennes, 174
Archives Nationales, Paris, 211
Archives Office, Kent, 18
Archivio di Stato, Florence, 302
Archivio di Stato, Naples, 302
Archivio di Stato Sezione Prima, Turin,
  307
Archivio di Stato, Venice, 307
Archivi Vaticani, Rome, 303
Archivo General de Indias, Seville, 253
Archivo General de Simancas, Valladolid,
  262
Archivo Histórico Nacional, Madrid, 248
Arkhiv Vneshnei Politiki Rosii, Moscow,
  311
Armed Neutrality of 1780, xxii, xxiii,
  310, 313
Arras, 171
Aswarby Muniments, 23
Athenaeum Library, Liverpool, 19
Atholl Papers, 121
Atkinson, William, 46
Auckland Papers, 32, 43
Audley End Papers, 14
Aurich, 294
Austria, French correspondence, 191
Avignon, 172
Ayrshire, 122

Badisches Generallandesarchiv,
  Karlsruhe, 284
Bagshawe Collection, 117
Bamberg, 285
Banffshire, 123
Barbados, 26
Barcelona, 27
Barham Papers, 107
Barnes, Colonel A. C., 112
Bastille, Archives de la, 233
Bath, Marquess of, 114
Bathurst, Earl, 17
Bayly Papers, 142
Bayreuth, 285
Bayr. Hauptstaatsarchiv, München, 285-7
Bayr. Staatsarchiv, Bamberg, 285
Bayr. Staatsarchiv, Nürnberg, 287
Bayr. Staatsarchiv, Würzburg, 288
Bedford, Duke of, 8, 40
Bedfordshire Record Office, 7
Bell-Macdonald, A. M., 125
Berkshire Record Office, 8

320

Southesk, Earl of, 122
Southwell Papers, 16
Spain, 30
Dutch relations, 156
French correspondence, 191, 206, 209
Sparling and Bolden, 20
Staatliche Archivverwaltung, 283
Staatsarchiv,
Aurich, 294
Bremen, 289
Hamburg, 289
Oldenburg, 297
Osnabrück, 297
Stade, 297
Stade, 297
Stadtarchiv,
Buxtehude, 295
Ochsenfurt, 287
Rendsburg, 300
Wunsiedl, 288
Staffordshire Record Office, 109
Stamp Act, opposition and unrest, 33, 40
State Paper Offijce, 88
State Paper Office, Dublin, 144
States-General (Dutch), resolutions of, 152
Steijn, Raadpensionaris, Papers, 162
Steuart Papers, 128
Stevens, Benjamin Franklin, 41
Stevenson, Stuart, Papers, 129
St Germans, Earl of, 11
St Lucia, 26
Stockholm, 314
Stowe Manuscripts, 48
Strachey Papers, 108
Strachie, Lord, 108
Stuart of Torrance Papers, 128
Stuart Papers, 7
Stuttgart, 284
Suffolk, 110
Surrey, 112
Sussex, 112
Sweden, Dutch relations, 156

Tarleton Papers, 20
Teschen, Treaty of, 313
Tipperary, 144
Tods, Murray, and Jamison, W. S., 131
Toulon, 238
Townshend duties, 38
Townshend, George, 45
Trade, Board of, 90
Treasury, 90
Treasury Solicitor, 92
Treaty of Paris, xxii, 3, 168, 169
Tropenmuseum, Amsterdam, 152
Tryon, Governor, 39

Tsentral'nyi Gosudarstvennyi Arkhiv, Leningrad, 311
Turin, 307
Twigg, J. B. and R. H., 141
Twisden Family Papers, 18
Tyrone, 141

USA, French correspondence, 197, 206, 207, 209
Underwood, W. Weston, 15
United Society for the Propagation of the Gospel, 98
Universitetsbiblioteket, Uppsala, 318
University Library, Cambridge, 10
University of Durham, 14
University of London Library, 99
Uppsala, 317

VOC (Dutch East India Company), 150
Val de Marne, 239
Valladolid, 262
Van der Capellen, J. Derk, Papers, 161
Van de Spiegel, Laurens, Papers, 162
Van Hogendorp Papers, 162
Vassall, William, 118
Vendome, 246
Venice, 307
Vermont and Colonial Office, 79
Verulam, Earl of, 17
Verulam Papers, 17
Vienna, 274
Virginia, and Colonial Office, 79
Colonial Records Project, 5

Wales, National Library of, 119
Walt, W. E., 16
War Office, 92
Warwickshire, 113
Washington, George, xxii, 34
Watson, Henry, case book, 110
Wedgewood Museum, Stoke-on-Trent, 110
Westdeutsche Bibliothek, Marburg, 294
Westminster, Archbishop of, 100
Westminster Papers, 10
Westminster, 2nd Duke of, 10
Weston Papers, 15
Whately, Thomas, 41
Whitaker family, 13
Whitefoord, Caleb, 36
Whitehaven, 12
Wiesbaden, 295
Wiener Haus-, Hof- und Staatsarchiv, Vienna, 276
Wigan, Rodney Street Public Library, 22
Wilkes, John, 32